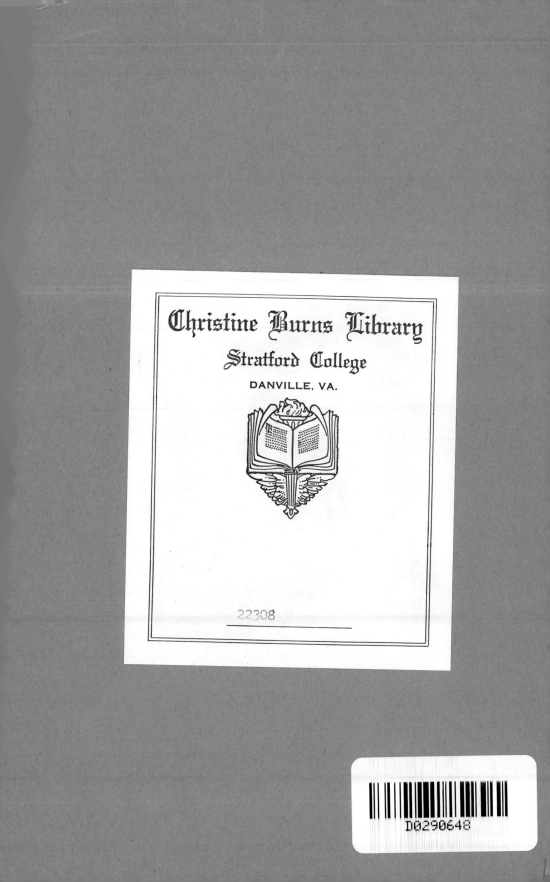

Bandeirantes and Pioneers

BANDEIRANTES

AND

PIONEERS

by Vianna Moog

TRANSLATED FROM THE PORTUGUESE BY

L. L. BARRETT

GEORGE BRAZILLER
NEW YORK

Translator's Note

Since the term *bandeirantes* lacks an English equivalent, it has been retained throughout this translation, and therefore ought to be explained at once.

At the end of the sixteenth century, or at the very beginning of the seventeenth, expeditions were organized to explore the hinterland of Brazil in search of valuable minerals or other natural wealth. The officially organized groups were known as *entradas*, but these government expeditions always stopped at the line of demarcation set by the Treaty of Tordesillas, about 50° W. longitude. The great majority of expeditionary groups, however, were unofficial, a form of private enterprise: often, a wealthy man would organize and equip the group and pay all its expenses, reserving the profits for himself. The caravan usually included the variety of professional functionaries required for carrying on civil life in the interior—priests, legal authorities, chroniclers, soldiers, and workers. As it set out, such a group was headed by a flag, a *bandeira*, and so, by a kind of antonomasia, the group became known as a *bandeira* and its members *bandeirantes*. The Northeast of Brazil was the rich section; it was only natural that the *bandeiras* generally originated in the then poor region of São Paulo.

The *bandeirantes'* search for gold or other quickly won wealth was long unproductive, so they turned to a different source of easily acquired gain. "Wherever they found Indians grouped together around one of the Jesuit missions they carried them away to be sold into slavery. When there were battles to be fought, or dangers to be encountered, the *bandeirantes* were willing and eager. Their expeditions . . . constituted a way of living for a restless people in a land which, for them, contained few resources they could turn into wealth."* They stopped in their wanderings to plant crops and harvest them; they grazed their cattle on the plains as they moved along; they intermarried with Indian women, producing the half-breed known in Brazil as *mameluco* and in Spanish and Anglo-American countries as mestizo (*mestiço* in Brazilian Portuguese means "mulatto"). Despite their nomadic existence, the *bandeirantes'* pauses occasionally resulted in permanent settlements that grew into towns and cities, and thus, gradually, sporadically, they pushed back the frontier, westward and southward, extending and consolidating the territories that comprise present-day Brazil.

L. L. BARRETT

* James, Preston E., *Brazil*. New York, 1946. Pp. 131-32.

3

Preface

For a long time this question has been in the air, awaiting a comprehensive answer: How was it possible for the United States, a country younger than Brazil and smaller in its continuous continental area, to achieve the almost miraculous progress that it has, and come down to our own time in the forefront of nations, an amazing present-day reality —in many ways the most amazing and stupendous reality of all times— whereas Brazil, whose history antedates that of the United States by more than a century, still appears, even in the light of the most optimistic interpretations and prophecies, only as the uncertain land of the future?

How has all this been possible? What happened to bring it about? What facts can have so determined the course of the two histories as to produce so great a contrast?

There is no evading these questions or formulating them differently. They will arise repeatedly, at every moment and at every step, prompted by the most varied pretexts, apropos of everything and sometimes of nothing at all, with the persistence of leitmotivs, compulsive and inescapable.

What is involved, accordingly, is an inquiry that has already begun. And, as relations develop between the United States and Brazil, broadening the possibilities of comparison between the two civilizations, the subject is fixing itself more and more firmly in our national consciousness. This makes it really imperative to seek, if not a definitive answer, at least an explanation on a level with the question's importance.

Bandeirantes and Pioneers, the product of direct observation of the two countries rather than of bookish research—although it may at times give a different impression—is nothing more than an honest effort in that direction. It was initially inspired by the wish to study the United States, whose culture derived in great part from the work of the pioneer, as compared with Brazil, whose culture is in the same measure the work of the *bandeirante*. Our hope was thus to gain a critical understanding of the United States as a global phenomenon, the better to unravel and explain the unknown quantities in Brazil's civilization and her destiny.

Has this book attained, or will it perhaps come to attain, its objective? I hold no great illusions on that score. The theme, dynamic in its very essence, presenting a nearly unlimited number of unknown quantities, all of them varying in their relation to one another, is not exactly the sort that permits definitive pronouncements or judgments free from errors of observation, of emotion, and of interpretation. That does not

5

matter. What does matter is that *Bandeirantes and Pioneers* (a book to which the title of *Conquistadors and Colonizers* could equally well be given, since this parallel between Brazil and the United States is applicable to the contrasts between the United States and the other countries of Latin America), with all its possible contradictions, errors, and mistakes, probably contains some new ideas and perhaps some good ones. But if somebody contends, with Leibnitz, that the good ones are not new and the new ones are not good, I certainly have no right to resent it. Anyone who deals with such inflammable materials as some of the themes upon which this essentially polemical book turns, even though he does so with the best intentions and solely for purposes of study and research, should be prepared for much more than that.

The above note was written in 1954 as a foreword to the original Brazilian edition. Since then, of course, many things have happened, both in the United States and Brazil, affecting each country not only internally but in its relationship with the other. Yet I do not think these changes have materially altered in any way the main outlines of my book. It is true, for instance, that the whole immense problem of the Negro in the United States, even within the past year, has taken on new and drastic significance. On the other hand, having written in the early 1950's that "the Negroes will not always agree with" the then prevailing conditions, I can see no reason to change my text. If my book is to withstand the test of time to any degree, the best way to prove this is to let the English edition remain faithful to the Portuguese original, written a decade ago, without attempting to "update" the text.

VIANNA MOOG

Contents

Introduction

Adolf A. Berle

In its lovely jewel-like building, the Brazilian Academy of Letters held a meeting late in 1945. One of its purposes was to install a new member, Vianna Moog.

The circumstances were dramatic. The Vargas dictatorship had recently fallen. One victim of its politics had been this young writer. His hero was Abraham Lincoln, his convictions were democratic, and his writing had been disturbing to the dictatorship. Exiled to the wilderness of the upper Amazon, he had used the restricted liberty of movement conceded him to observe and study the outermost parts of Brazil. Now, democracy having been restored to Brazil, he had returned to Rio de Janeiro, and the Academy rose to salute its new member. His installation speech traced the psychology of a freedom-loving people, struggling against repression. As Ambassador of the United States—perhaps more accurately as a friend of Vianna Moog—I attended the meeting. Coming out of the session into the luminous blue tropic night of Rio de Janeiro, it was clear to me that a new genius was rising on the hemispheric literary scene.

It was, therefore, no surprise when his next book, *Bandeirantes e Pioneiros*, was acclaimed in Paris and Lisbon as well as in Brazil, or that today its author is one of the best-known writers in Brazil.

Originally Vianna Moog had proposed to write a book about the United States, which he had come to know well. Working on it, he discovered that "to explain the United States, I must also explain Brazil." The result, *Bandeirantes e Pioneiros*, published eight years ago in Brazil, is a fascinating analysis of two countries whose great likenesses and equally great differences command attention.

"Bandeirantes" ("flag-bearers") were the explorers and settlers of the interior of Brazil, as "pioneers" were the conquerors and colonizers of the great unoccupied heartland of the United States. The difference lies in their motives and ideals. The Brazilian bandeirantes were perhaps the last wave of colonial conquistadores. The American pioneers, though of all kinds, were predominantly Reformation settlers. The resulting civilizations set up by the two groups of wilderness-conquerors were therefore quite different, despite many elements common to both.

The United States and Brazil are the two largest geo-political components of the Western hemisphere. What each thinks of the other may well determine the course of New World history. It is thus important

9

that Americans should understand Brazil, and that Brazilians understand the United States. Brazilians know this; their scholars indeed have already contributed greatly to this end. Their great sociologist, Gilberto Freyre, for example, has studied the Southern Negro problem here, as he has also analyzed in a brilliant volume, *Masters and Slaves*, the sociology of the former slave-civilization forming the base of the Brazilian Northeast.

The best books about the United States have regularly been written by foreigners. One thinks of De Tocqueville's *America*, Lord Bryce's *American Commonwealth* and, more recently, Andre Siegfried's, *America's Coming of Age*. These were analyses of America seen through West-European eyes. The unique quality of the volume here offered is that America is presented through the eyes of a friendly, clear-sighted Brazilian. So much of Moog's life has been passed in missions outside his own country that he writes of Brazil with much of the detachment he applies to the United States.

Appearing in Portuguese, *Bandeirantes e Pioneiros* immediately took rank as one of the classic studies of Brazilian as well as of American development. It has long been acclaimed in its own country, where it is now in its seventh edition. Already well known to American scholars, it is now presented in English translation and is entitled to be esteemed here, as it has been in Latin America, as a work of first importance in inter-cultural understanding.

Columbia University

September 1963

1

Race and Geography

1

THE OLDEST AND PROBABLY THE MOST FREQUENTLY OFFERED EXPLANATION for the fact that the United States has prospered incomparably more than Brazil, in almost all sectors of human activity, is based on the idea of racial superiority.

Has the United States, then, prospered more than Brazil? The reason is simple, extremely simple: The United States, despite its time handicap of more than a century—for that is the sum of the years between the discovery of Brazil and the arrival of the *Mayflower* in the New World —and the disadvantage, in space, of a smaller territory, was peopled by the superior Anglo-Saxon race while Brazil was peopled and conquered by the backward Portuguese, a people that on the score of ethnic purity cannot be compared, even remotely, with the former. Moreover, the Anglo-Saxon preserved his racial purity, crossing with the Indian and the Negro only uncommonly, while the Portuguese carried such inter-marriage to extremes never known previously.

And so the problem was quickly resolved, definitively settled, and no more was thought of the matter. It was as if the problem did not exist, or was not really a problem, seeing that the question had an almost uni-versally hallowed and accepted solution. In case of doubt, there was the immense authority of the Comte de Gobineau or that of Houston Stew-art Chamberlain to appeal to.[1] And in the absence of either of these, Gustave Le Bon could serve just as well. The doctrine that races are born unequal and remain unequal in intelligence, worth, and capacity for creating and absorbing culture, independent of the conditions of climate, physical environment, social background, and historical period,

11

solved everything. It solved not only the problem of the contrasts between Brazil and the United States but also that of the differences between the latter and Argentina or Mexico. All the complex differences between Anglo-Saxon America and Latin America, with the enormous number of unknown quantities—geographic, political, social and economic—that engendered or conditioned them, were summarily resolved by the racial doctrine. Not even the theories of Alexis de Tocqueville,[2] which had such wide acceptance in the past century and contributed so much to transforming the Latin American constitutions into veritable paraphrases of the American Constitution—not even de Tocqueville's theories, attributing the preeminence of the North American civilization over the others of the hemisphere primarily to political and institutional causes, enjoyed equal prestige.

At that time both the Anglo-Saxon and the Latin world were indeed not lacking in disciples of Gobineau. If they were especially numerous in the United States, in Latin America they were more notable for their quality. The fact that in Argentina racism was one of the principal sources of inspiration of the sociological and political work of a Sarmiento or even of a Juan Bautista Alberdi, and that in Chile, in Bolivia, and in Mexico it had apologists like Nicolás Palacios, Alcides Arguedas, and José Vasconcelos, gives a measure of the prevailing trend.

There was resistance, here and there, to accepting the democratic refined features of the American Constitution as the principal and almost exclusive cause of the prosperity of the United States. But to believe in the doctrine, or rather, in the myth, of racial superiorty and inferiority, no proof was required, whether biological, sociological, anthropological, or historical. Everything was taken for granted.

Accordingly, there was nothing to do but draw the inevitable conclusions from Gobineau: Brazil's backwardness in comparison with the United States was inherent in her people's Portuguese descent, and also, and principally, to the debasing mixture of the Portuguese with the two other races, Indian and Negro, that entered into the formation of the nation. In this way everything was explained, everything perfectly solved. Since the white race alone could create progress, the sole hope for the inferior races was to continue intermarrying with the superior whites. If in that process the latter would lose their former noble attributes, the inferior races would gain, provided always that the qualities of the nobler and stronger predominated in the results of the racial cross.

The most curious thing in all this was not that the thesis should gain currency in Germany, England, the United States, Canada, or even in Argentina and Chile. The shocking thing was that it should gain ascendancy and wide acceptance in Brazil. For as far as reaction against racial doctrines in Brazil is concerned, properly speaking there was none. And when there was any, it was not to question the pseudoscientific bases on which those doctrines were founded, but to oppose emotionally the superiority of the aborigine to the superiority of the white and European, in the dogmatic and demagogic manner of the various nationalisms that Protestant liberalism has managed to provoke and foment in Hispanic America, at a time when, on the pretext of hastening her emancipation, it in fact precipitated her splitting up into small republics incapable of resisting its dictates. So, in one way or another, some more, some less, all ended by succumbing to the witchcraft of racial myths.

It was only recently—and this is due in great part to the studies which Nina Rodrigues has been carrying out in the field of anthropology —that Brazilians have begun to suspect the validity of the racial explanation for social phenomena and for disparities in the cultural levels of different countries. However, some more modern essayists, with Gilberto Freyre, Roquette Pinto, Artur Ramos, and Gilberto Amado at their head, must be credited with having rebelled against the ethnocentric doctrines, in transferring social studies from the exclusively racial plane to the cultural, as had been done for a long time, for that matter, in the most advanced centers of scientific research.

Before that, though, the ruling theory was that of the inequality of races and of the congenital superiority of the blond, blue-eyed dolichocephalic type over the rest of humanity. This was almost the official doctrine, since even ministers of state embraced it.

For example, in 1897 Joaquim Murtinho, in his famous report to the Ministry of Industry that earned him the portfolio of the Treasury, cautioned the government against any excess of optimism in regard to the industrial possibilities of Brazil: "We cannot, as many aspire to do, take the United States of North America as a model for our industrial development, because we do not possess the superior aptitudes of that race, the force whch plays the principal rôle in the industrial progress of that great people."[3] To attempt more, in the view of the great minister of Campos Sales, was to aim too high. How could the tortoise keep up with the flight of the eagle? Nevertheless, Joaquim Murtinho was not an isolated exception. And, not to go so far back, there is the contemporary work of Oliveira Viana to testify that the thesis of Brazil's difficult ethnic situation has always found a good hearing there. It is enough to say that the message of hope that he offers is wholly based on the expectation that the peoples of Brazil will gradually become Aryanized, an expectation that implies tacit recognition of the validity and legitimacy of Gobineau's and Chamberlain's doctrines, recently reanimated by National Socialism. For him the Indian has no value whatever; yet the happy crossing of a superior type of Indian with a eugenically well-endowed white may produce a superior *mameluco*, if, perchance, in the interplay of hereditary influences, the eugenic qualities of the white type predominate. That is to say: If the white's eugenic qualities do not predominate in the crossing, there will be no felicitous combination, because the ambition for wealth and the desire to rise in the world, dominant in the white, disappear in the half-breed, destroyed by the regressive action of barbarian atavism.[4]

2

Authors whose works orthodox Aryanists can cite in their support will apparently never be lacking. A scant six years after the last war, when it seemed that the doctrines of ethnic superiority were forever liquidated and the world had forever recovered from the catastrophe, lo and behold! those doctrines sprang up again in *Teutonic Unity*, a book that is nothing more than a tardy sprouting of Gobineau's old theory.

Has it, by any chance, come back changed, ready to make concessions? Not at all! In handsome, brand-new format, wrapped in cellophane, it looks more attractive than ever, but without any change in tactics or objectives. At bottom, *Teutonic Unity*, by Earnest Sevier Cox of Richmond, Virginia—one of the strongest redoubts of racial discrimination against the Negro and, secondarily, against the Jew—is confessedly and intrepidly rascist, Aryanist, and anti-Christian. With regard to its anti-Christian aspect, the book does not make it clear whether we are confronted with a convinced atheist or an anachronistic pagan, a little matter of some two thousand years late, still intent on restoring to the Teutonic peoples the Germanic gods of the time of Tacitus. Probably the author is a pagan. In any case, it is certain that this new prophet's concern for the preservation of Teutonic racial purity is stronger than his religious preoccupations. The white race is the object of devotion, his religion, the predominant if not the exclusive motive for his cogitations. It suffices to say that he is also the author of *White America*, that he frequently cites Houston Stewart Chamberlain, and that he dedicates his latest work, *Teutonic Unity*, to Theodoric the Great (493–526), "Gothic king of Italy who sought to form a league of Teutonic peoples in order to put an end to the wars which they waged on each other, diminishing and weakening themselves before other peoples and races less well endowed than they."[5]

Only one thing Earnest Sevier Cox cannot forgive the white race: the fact that it has adopted a religion borrowed from the Semites. This seems to him all the more inexplicable in that he considers it certain that all that is obviously best in the world was brought about by the white race under the leadership of the Teutons. Culture and the capacity for creating superior civilizations are possessed by the whites alone. The capacity for invention is to be found only in the white race, more particularly in the Nordic whites, the Teutonic whites.

And what of the great maritime discoveries of the Portuguese and Spaniards in the fifteenth and sixteenth centuries? Reply: This was possible only because Portugal and Spain were ruled by elites that were probably Teutonic. And the Italian Renaissance? Ah, that is traceable to the blond Lombards, a tribe of Germanic origin. And Camoens, and Dante, Vasco da Gama and Magellan, Christopher Columbus and Amerigo Vespucci? Some were Lombards, others Goths, nearly all probably of Germanic origin. And the geographic situation of Portugal, squeezed between Spain and the Atlantic Ocean—could not that have had something to do with her vocation for maritime voyages? No question of geographic factors, only race. As long as the Nordics kept themselves intact, all went well. Decadence got its start when miscegenation began.

Racial miscegenation! There is another point on which Mr. Cox—like Aryanists in general—permits no evasions. For him the crossing of different races, besides degrading the individuals who participate in it, degrades the product, a person unsuitable for civilization and culture. And he explains the spectacular progress of the United States as compared with the more or less general backwardness of Latin American countries—among them Brazil, of course—by the absolute preponderance of the white race in the United States in a proportion of 90 per cent of the total population, in contrast with the spread of mixed breeding in South and Central America. What counts with him is race. Geophysical conditions—orography, hydrography, geology, botany, and climatology —not to mention social and historical conditions or the motives and purposes that governed the two migrations, Nordic and Iberian—none of all this has any importance.

Is our author anti-Jewish, anti-Negro, anti-Slavic? Strictly speaking, one cannot say that he is any one of these. If he is not anti-Christian— it might be better to say, anti-Catholic—he is not anti-anything. He is, indeed, for the Teutonic race, he is all for the purification of the white race, for the return of the Negroes from America to their original habitat, for the broadening of the lebensraum allotted for the emigration of whites from overpopulated Europe. It is therefore likely that he is anti-Slavic, anti-Negro, or anti-Semitic only insofar as Africanism, Slavism,

and Judaism put in check the race to which he belongs, or at least thinks
he belongs.

And now what? Why, now we should be facing a really alarming fact
if the theories of *Teutonic Unity*, with its suggestion of sending back to
the African jungles and to their primitive habitats all those who show a
touch of Negro blood, were taken seriously by the whole of the American
people. In point of fact, however, this is not what is happening. Moreover, the fact that *Teutonic Unity* was published by its own author in a
modest edition of a thousand copies, none of them intended for sale, to
be distributed among government officials in Washington and a select
group of individuals, particularly historians, in the nations located in the
Teutonic area and in the different nations formed during the Teutonic
migrations, constitutes an excellent indication that there is no longer
the audience there used to be for the lucubrations of racism. Indeed,
American racism is losing ground daily. If it is true that the emotional
reaction of thousands, perhaps millions of Americans, still shows itself
as a stubborn determination to maintain segregation and discrimination,
while others are for the absurdity of segregation without discrimination
(according to the extravagant doctrine of "equal but separate"), it is no
less true that segregation is no longer maintained on the doctrinal basis
of the racial superiority of the white, but on the pretext of defending the
prerogative of the states to enact substantive laws within the limits of
their own jurisdiction. It is on the pretext of defending the autonomy
of states against the interventionism, whether spontaneous or solicited, of
the federal government, that the Southerners, fighting a rearguard action,
have succeeded in delaying the inevitable integration of the Negroes
and other racial minorities into the American culture, while the best in
science and thought in the United States, in the domains of politics,
anthropology, and literature, continues implacably in favor of the racial
democratization of the country.[6] While books advocating discrimination
find no publisher and become rarer and rarer, the bibliography on the
other side is torrential. The truth is that American racism has lost the
doctrinal battle and knows it has. The rest is a question of time.

Nevertheless, until the final capitulation comes and as long as matters
go on in terms of law, custom, and immigration regulations, as if the
doctrine of the ethnic superiority of Anglo-Saxons over other human
groups were in full sway, perhaps it is not entirely inapt to appeal from
its judgment to the other interpretations which the comparison between
the American and the Brazilian civilizations permits.

After all, in drawing a parallel between the progress achieved by the
North American civilization in contrast to the Brazilian, it may not be
heretical to give some credit to such factors as orography, hydrography,
botany, geology, and climate, that have been invoked in the interpretation

of social factors elsewhere. For that matter, the difficult thing is not to take those factors into account, but to ignore them, since, in a comparison between Brazil and the United States, at every step they keep forcing themselves on the attention of even the most inattentive observer.

3

To start with, take the example of the orographic factor. It is the first to attract the observer's attention. Immediately on his arrival in the United States, on the Atlantic coast, the visitor who travels by train from Miami to New York, or from New York to Philadelphia, Washington, or Chicago, is surprised by the plains stretching as far as the eye can see. No mountains to blacken or erase the horizons. An occasional gentle elevation at great intervals, and then the train once more comes out on the flat plain. No granite parapets, no tunnels or viaducts to make one catch his breath. At most, some engineering construction or other in the variations of level, as may be necessary for the rail and highway crossings.

What a contrast to the routes from Rio to Belo Horizonte, from Rio to São Paulo, from Paranaguá to Curitiba, or from São Paulo to Santos! On them the plain is the exception; the rule is mountains, cliffs, tunnels, viaducts, curves molded by the precipices of inhospitable mountain ranges.

And yet these contrasts are simply the exact translation of the geographic reliefs of Brazil and the United States. One consults the map and confirms the fact that in the United States the whole Atlantic coast from Florida to the state of New York is an uninterrupted plain, and that the chains of the Alleghenies and Appalachians are many miles from the coast. And once past the Alleghenies, new chains of mountains, the Rockies, will only begin to appear far beyond the Mississippi, well toward the Pacific.

Now look at the map of Brazil. From the point of view of rail and highway construction in the temperate zone, a rather difficult geographic relief obtains from the center to the south, and only fair from the center westward. From Rio de Janeiro toward the south, the Maciço Atlântico, consisting of three more or less distinct systems—the Serra do Mar, the Serra Geral, and the Serra da Mantiqueira—along the whole coast, always in sight, accompanying the sea at an average distance of perhaps twenty miles and never drawing farther away than thirty. And always rising vertically, at times advancing to the ocean itself, making man's penetration difficult.

Fernão Cardim, who made the trip in four days from São Vicente to São Paulo in 1585 under the best conditions possible for those times (for he was accompanying the Visitor of the Company of Jesus, Father Cristóvão de Gouveia), refers thus to the route traversed: "The road is so steep that at times we were clinging by our hands." "The whole road is full of muddy stretches, the worst I ever saw, and we were always climbing up and down very high ranges and crossing rivers and torrents of extremely cold water."[7]

According to the chronicler Simão de Vasconcelos, the mountain ranges of Brazil inspired fear in the first settlers: "Those rustic folk even came to suspect that those mountains were fortified in self-defense."[8]

How many difficulties had to be overcome in the construction of Brazilian railways and highways! What prodigies of engineering were necessary for the construction of railroads from São Paulo to Santos or from Paranaguá to Curitiba! When the problem is not mountains it is erosion, or else a morass; where it is not a morass or quagmire, it is excessive heat or humidity. The Madeira-Mamoré, undertaken by English engineers with Barbados labor and completed by men from Ceará under the direction of Brazilian engineers, is a symbol. If we believe the legend, every crosstie of the Madeira-Mamoré railroad represents a man's life.

Nothing like this occurred in the United States on the Atlantic side, which was the side first penetrated. It is true that Americans had to confront the problems of the Rocky Mountains on the Pacific side, not small problems, nor few. As it happens, however, when they did so they had already conquered the rest of the country and were already technically prepared for the task. They did not have to stay scratching away at the littoral, held back by the mountains on the very threshold of conquest.

Under these conditions it is not necessarily rash to conclude that the conquest of the land in the United States, as far as the possibilities of penetration are concerned, must have been much smoother than in Brazil. Stagecoaches and covered wagons were already crossing and recrossing the United States, articulated into a unified system of communications, at a time when the Indian, the Negro, the burro, and the ass were still the only means of transport in Brazil. And cannot orographic factors be partly responsible for the startling difference between the systems of transportation in the United States and in Brazil: nearly 228,000 miles of railways and 3,125,000 of highways in the United States, all of the first quality, and a scant 22,000 miles of rail and barely 150,000 of highways in Brazil?

And as regards hydrography, is Brazil's situation any better?

Here is another aspect to which the traveler's attention is attracted independently of maps. Everywhere in the United States, along railroads or highways, he will constantly encounter among the cities of the interior magnificent navigable rivers and excellent ports, some even with warships and freighters in the roadstead or moored to the warehouse docks. Between Miami and New York he will find the Indian River, the St. Johns, the Altamaha, the Savannah, the Santee, the Cape Fear, the Roanoke, the James, the Potomac, the Susquehanna, the Delaware, and the Hudson, some of which are still freely navigable despite the fact that river transportation is being relegated to second place in some cases. And between New York and Chicago, again the Delaware and the Susquehanna, the Schuylkill, the Ohio, the Scioto, the Miami, the Maumee, the St. Joseph, the Kankakee, the Wabash, the Muskingum, and the Monongahela.

No doubt is possible: the United States possesses the best hydrographic network in the world. Thousands of rivers, thousands of lakes. The American can travel along his rivers and lakes and canals to the farthest points of the country: from New York to Chicago or to Canada; from St. Paul, Minnesota, to New Orleans in Louisiana. As a matter of fact, that is what the pioneers of colonial times did, as the river dwellers of today still do. The two celebrated journeys of Abraham Lincoln, drifting with the current on rafts built with his own hands, first down the Sangamon, then the Ohio, and finally down the Mississippi, to go and sell, besides Illinois products, the very wood of the rafts, are no more than repetitions of the innumerable journeys of the same kind made during the whole colonial period, on the Hudson, the St. Lawrence, the Ohio, the Mississippi.

The Mississippi! As if two lateral oceans, the Atlantic and the Pacific, were not enough for the Americans, they have been further endowed with that prodigious inland sea, the Mississippi, which is indeed the true river of a national unity.

Consider now the case of Brazil. Poverty of rivers, almost a total lack of lakes. Where are the freely navigable rivers? And the lakes? And where the possibility of controlling them for the purposes of irrigation and benefit to agriculture? Properly speaking, there are none in the temperate zone; there were none in the strip occupied in the earliest period of the formation of Brazil, for in that time Rio Grande do Sul, with its magnificent system of rivers and mountains, its splendid valleys, its four well-defined seasons, its plains extending as far as the eye can reach, a paradisal semi-opening deep in the continent, was scarcely known. The rivers are full of rapids and falls, with a regular, maddening round of flood stages and droughts. In contrast to the American rivers, they were of no use to the conquistadors and the *bandeirantes* other than as points of reference in their marches toward the backlands.

True, there was the São Francisco. But that stream, too, interrupted at about 150 miles from the Atlantic by the Paulo Afonso Falls, was far from being a river of national unity. The same may be said of the Paraná, in which the Sete Quedas (the Seven Falls) irremediably block its navigability. Today, with means available for exploiting hydroelectric power, the waterfalls constitute one of our richest patrimonies. But during the colonization period they were rather a hindrance than an instrument of progress.

And what of the Amazon? The greatest river in the world. But only in volume of water. Economically it is not worth as much as the Mississippi, it is not as good as the Nile. It runs erratically along the equator through lands where, in the succinct phrase of Euclides da Cunha, "the last chapter of Genesis" is being enacted. A monstrous and untamed river, and one very poorly prepared for the advent of a stable culture. Angered, it swallows up land, leagues and leagues of land; it leaps from its bed, sweeping all before it. Moreover, it is an unpatriotic river, since, if experts are to be believed, the land it swallows up only to disgorge later in the Atlantic is carried along by the Gulf Stream to add new territories to Mexico and the United States, in the alluvial formations of Yucatán and Florida.

Everything, then, adds up in favor of the United States. Besides their orographic and hydrographic systems, the Americans also have in their favor the considerable advantage of a climate more or less identical to the European, with four definite seasons to facilitate the acclimatization of the human avalanches that Europe has poured into the New World.

The climate of the United States! All the temperatures imaginable for the purposes of the most varied human, zoological, or vegetable transplantations. Is it the cold of Siberia that is wanted? One need not go to Alaska to find it. In New York State itself, in New England and throughout the Middle West, when there are great blizzards a Siberian cold will furnish a sample of its attractions. Do you want the heat of Hindustan? You will find it right there in Washington or Chicago, in the still sultriness of summer, in June or July, without its being necessary to go down to New Orleans or Miami. Do you want neither of those, but rather the mildness of spring or autumn? In that case you have only to wait.

Springtime in Maine, in New Hampshire, in Vermont, or in the vicinity of New York or Washington, beside the Potomac, in the magic week of the cherry blossoms! One who has never undergone the experience of a prolonged winter of heavy snows, and seen the springtime budding forth again, can hardly have any idea of what it is. Day by day the scene is transformed. Yonder where some remnants of snow still lie in sheltered nooks and among the roots of the leafless trees in the parks, and where everything seems condemned to death, life bursts forth in sudden bloom. The evening before, all was gray, ashen. Now there is no more rationing of colors and tints and shadings. All is life, all is color, as if legions of impressionist painters had been abroad during the night, bedecking the parks.

But if spring in the Center and the North of the United States is like that, the American autumn is in no way inferior in its effects. The difference is merely one of shades and tones of color. In spring the colors are violently affirmative, while in autumn the indecisiveness of half-tones and shades is predominant.

In the United States it is almost certain that the European, be he Nordic or Mediterranean, from the mountains or from the plains, will find a climate corresponding to that of his native region, if not an improved version of the natural conditions of his land of origin.

Given these circumstances, it is not surprising that people have so often extolled the conditions that the immigrant finds in his new environment.

Can the same be said, by any chance, of Brazil's climate, or that the new environment has bettered the immigrant's biological conditions thanks to climatic conditions?

For a long time precisely the opposite has been believed. The propaganda spread in Europe was that the climate of Brazil was a menace to health and to life. While in cold countries disease was regarded as a fatality independent of climate, in the tropics the climate had to answer for everything. To it was attributed the responsibility for yellow fever, malaria, and those tropical diseases against which the policy followed until recently was that of quarantine and the *cordon sanitaire*. Today, happily, it is well known that the climate has nothing to do with what are wrongly called tropical diseases and that it all boils down to a question of hygiene. More: it is known that the climate of Brazil—especially that of the tropical regions, where the average temperature, by virtue of a providential combination of geographic situation and cycle of wind and rain, does not rise above 72° Fahrenheit, with maximum temperatures of no alarming figure—has been truly a maligned climate. But to conclude from this that it is excellent from North to South, or that it can stand favorable comparison with the climate of the United States—especially if the comparison is made from the point of view of the relations between climate and ecology, or between climate and productive capacity—is possible only by greatly stretching the truth.

On this score it is of course necessary to note that in more than two-thirds of the national territory there is no winter, spring, or fall. In other words, there is no incentive for the production of heat, the incentive that constitutes perhaps the first step in all industrial development. What does exist there is perennial summer. Springlike summer, autumnal summer, summer with rain, summer without rain, but always summer.

This in two-thirds of Brazil. In the other third, it is true, things change a good deal. Not so much, however, that it can be said that the Brazilian winter, from the Center to the South, constitutes an inescapable stimulus to thinking in terms of heating and of coal. On the contrary, even in Rio Grande do Sul, where the cold is most severe, they think only in terms of personal endurance and woolen covering, and even in wealthy homes they still consider that a fireplace or central heating is a luxury.

Consequence: When the month of August arrives, mortality rates rise, just as happens, for that matter, in winter in Portugal and all along the Mediterranean, where the cold is not sufficiently severe even to caution man against the insidiousness of pneumonia and tuberculosis, or to stimulate him more decisively to produce heat and power, as does the cold weather in northern Europe and the United States.

And here we have another advantage—the cold—to add economically to the score of the United States in its better preparation for the advent of the industrial era. And this not to mention the effects of cold and heat upon the productivity of individuals.

In countries of hot or temperate climate it may still be possible to ignore the tremendous importance of the climatic factor; not so in those of cold climate, like the United States. There, in midwinter, with snow falling, the temperature dropping, a strike of coal miners is enough to banish all doubt. The coal miners on strike? Alarm is general, there is panic. The American bears up well under other strikes, but when the strike is in the coal industry he is on the verge of losing his self-control. That steel can no longer be manufactured, or that the factories whose power depends on coal may be paralyzed, he can bear perfectly. But that he should lack heat in his home, when he retires at night chilled to the bone, is no pleasant prospect. At such moments there can be no American who has any doubt about including cold and geophysical considerations among the factors that accelerate or retard the march of civilizations.

Not one? No, naturally there will be many, especially in the South, capable of contesting the importance of climate. One of these will be Mr. Earnest Sevier Cox of Richmond, Virginia, the author of *Teutonic Unity*. A good racist, Mr. Cox, like Gobineau, does not tolerate geography much and detests mesological and geophysical explanations. For him culture and progress are completely independent of environment, and therefore of climate and geography. And to prove that this is so, he cites the case of Iceland compared with that of Sicily.

"Sicily," he says, "rather than Iceland ought to have been the locale propitious to the advance of civilized culture, if we accept the hypothesis of those who attribute cultural progress to environment instead of to race. Applying the criterion of the proponents of environment, we find that the climate of Sicily is ideal for cultural progress, but that of Iceland is not. We find that Sicily is on the crossroads of ethnic migration and is exposed to racial contacts. But we also find that for a thousand years illiteracy has been practically unknown in Iceland, while during the same thousand years illiteracy has with few exceptions been the universal heritage of Sicily."[9]

There it is: the climate of Sicily is ideal for the development of culture! But where is the proof that Sicily possesses these ideal conditions and Iceland does not? Where is the proof that hot and temperate climates are more conducive to concentration of thought and the activities of the imagination than are cold climates? Is it not, rather, the reverse, at least as far as scientific thought is concerned? And can it be different with respect to industrial development?

Looking at things from this point of view, should we not rather say that Iceland, not Sicily, is the country that has ideal conditions for the development of a culture of its own? The fact is that Sicily, neighbor of two continents (as is the case with the Corsica of the Bonapartes, an example which, to cite one case, *Teutonic Unity* does not deign to contemplate), is merely a stopover, a way station, for migrations from Africa to Europe and vice versa. The same is not true of Iceland. For centuries isolation there has been almost absolute, condemning the inhabitants to create their own culture instead of assimilating already corrupted alien cultures, or going abroad to seek them.

And as to the climate of Sicily in relation to industrial development: Hot or temperate climates, which by their very nature do not compel thinking in terms of fire and heat, surely must not accelerate the advent of industry in the same measure as cold climates where man is periodically obliged to think in terms of heat and fuel. In other words, that which from the angle of physical well-being seems an evil, from the point of view of progress ends by proving to be a great blessing.

From the viewpoint of orography, hydrography, or climate, the advantages of the United States are obvious. When in 1607 John Smith, the famous founder of the colony of Virginia, said of that land that "Heaven and earth never combined so well to create a habitation for man," he knew what he was talking about, and the future was to confirm his impressions.

Unhappily, this is not so in the case of the celebrated statement of Pero Vaz de Caminha, official chronicler of the discovery of Brazil, when he writes that there the land is so good that, "if it is cultivated, it will grow everything." Vaz de Caminha was evidently prone to exaggeration. As the official chronicler on board, his great preoccupation, as appears from his famous letter to Dom Manuel, was to please his king, his lord and master. How? The best way, probably the only way, would be to tell him of gold mines, precious stones, glittering riches, such opulence as that of India or New Spain.

Since that was not possible, for, as the letter says, "in [this land] until now we have not been able to find that there is gold or silver or any thing of metal or iron,"[10] and the disappointment of the king, of whom he wished to ask a boon, must be soothed, it was essential to announce some excellence of the recently discovered land. Hence, probably, that hasty "if it is cultivated, it will grow everything," destined to have such a vogue even in our day.

Now, Caminha offers no concrete basis for his attractive statement. Did he perhaps see tilled fields, planted by the Indians? Did he know anything of agriculture, or was he assisted by someone familiar with the secrets of tropical soils? Did he stay in Brazil long enough to see the country in all its aspects, as would be only right for the author of a statement that was to come down through the centuries and against which the centuries could not prevail? Nothing of the sort.

The letter is dated from Pôrto Seguro, on the island of Vera Cruz, May 1, 1500. Brazil had been sighted on April 21. From April 21 to May 1 is only ten days. And those days Caminha decidedly did not utilize for research in the field of agriculture or even for excursions into the interior. Nor was there time for any such thing.

On the twenty-first of April the first signs of land had been seen; on the twenty-second the coast was finally raised. First the mariners saw a great mountain, very high and rounded, and to the south of it other, lower ranges. "The high mountain the captain named Monte Pascoal and the land, the Land of Vera Cruz."[11] On that day, however, Cabral's fleet merely anchored in the roadstead. No one disembarked. And it was only on the twenty-third that they proceeded directly to land, dropping anchor before the mouth of a river. But even that day and the next our chronicler did not debark. He remained at the rail watching what was going on along the beach.

Even on the twenty-fourth Caminha does not leave the ship. He spends the day observing the moving of the fleet to a more sheltered port, Pôrto Seguro, and the incidents of the commander's meeting with the Indians. He is charmed by the natives and never wearies of describing them: "Their appearance is of a brown, somewhat reddish color, with good faces and well-cut noses. They go naked with no covering at all. They pay not the slightest heed to covering their privates; and in this they are as innocent as in displaying their faces."[12]

On the twenty-fifth, Saturday, the same thing: "In the afternoon the commander went out in his boat with all of us and with the other ship captains in their boats to take our pleasure in the bay opposite the beach. But no one landed because the commander would not allow it, although there was no one on the beach."[13]

Caminha landed only on the 26th of April, Easter Sunday, to hear Mass, the famous first Mass celebrated by Frei Henrique of Coimbra. And from the twenty-sixth of April to May 1, the date of the letter, nothing indicates that he was particularly interested in agricultural matters. He seemed, rather, impressed by the look of the Indian women, who, to quote him, seemed "very good-looking and elegant, with very long black hair down their backs and their breasts so high, firm and pointed and unconcealed by their hair that we stared at them openly."[14]

What, then, is the justification for his, "if it is cultivated, the land will grow everything"? Caminha explains: Everything will grow in it "by virtue of the waters which it possesses."

Obviously, pure impressionism, probably the same quality of impressionism that led Alexander von Humboldt to declare, when confronted with the luxuriant vegetation of Amazonia, that the great valley would be the "granary of the world." With this difference: in Pero Vaz de Caminha, chronicler of the expedition, the impressionism is perfectly forgivable and understandable; not so in Humboldt, a man dedicated to science and objectivity.

Modern science, if it had to take an official stand on the matter, would certainly not speak with the same optimism, because what has been proved experimentally is that tropical soils (laterite soils) are extremely poor. The great rains wash away the earth and its chemical components, impoverishing the soil, in strong contrast to the chemically rich soils of the cold and temperate Euro-Asiatic plains of the Danube and the Ukraine, and the plains of the Middle West in the United States.

Humboldt, nevertheless, was probably not the first, nor was he to be the last, to let himself be deceived by appearances in the tropics and in Amazonia. Let us have the testimony of the Ford Motor Company's technicians, they who until recently were engaged in realizing the prophecies of Humboldt and Pero Vaz de Caminha.

It is an episode worth mentioning because of its significance.

4

Around 1928 Henry Ford was in the grip of a fixed idea. He wanted to find a solution to the vexing problem of supplying rubber for his enterprises. He was tired of putting up with the prices imposed on him by the English in Ceylon and the Dutch in Java. And he had decided that the rubber empire in the hands of the English was immoral, and that the way to purify and redeem that empire was to transfer it from the backward guardianship of English capitalism to the progressive tutelage of young, healthy American capitalism. How? By planting rubber in Amazonia. Hadn't the English subject Henry Wickham smuggled the shoots of the Amazonian rubber tree to England? And hadn't those shoots, after being acclimatized in the hothouses of Kew Gardens—the London botanical gardens—flourished in the Orient, becoming the greatest rubber plantations in the world?

If the slips of *Hevea brasiliensis* flourished so under conditions of transplantation, transferring the hub of the fabulous rubber business from Belém in Pará to Ceylon, what prodigies might not take place once the same kind of shoots were planted symmetrically in their original soil? It was all a matter of organizing homogeneous groves of rubber trees in suitable lands.

So, on to Brazil, on to Amazonia. The ideal spot would have been the Everglades in Florida; but Henry Ford, who knew of his friend Thomas Edison's failure in experimenting with the planting of rubber on American soil, was too pragmatic to insist. The thing had to be in Amazonia. And in Amazonia, in Pará. And in Pará, on the banks of the Tapajós. And on the banks of the Tapajós, precisely on the spot where Henry Wickham in 1892 had collected, along with his rubber shoots, his future title of nobility. It was lamentable, but unfortunately those trees, so coveted by American industry—perhaps because they, like the gods, had white blood and therefore, on the vegetable plane, must have corresponded to the Aryan on the anthropological plane—those trees, by some mistake of Nature, would flourish only in the tropics.

In short, since it could not be in the United States, let it at least be in America. So it was decided: Henry Ford was going to plant rubber in Amazonia. The days of the English rubber monopoly were numbered. Divine punishment, by the sword of the avenging angel Henry Ford, was going to descend upon a monopoly whose origin lay in theft, trickery, and contraband.

Since, when Henry Ford got ideas they immediately took form and issued forth to be converted into action and be the object of ecstasy and applause on the part of the American press and people, the world immediately got news of the new plan of the demiurge of Dearborn. England trembled. Brazil exulted. And then the government of the state of Pará, with the acquiescence of the federal government, welcomed the emissaries of Ford as it habitually welcomes Americans in general—with open arms.

So Mr. Ford wanted to plant rubber in Pará? Splendid, an excellent idea. And where did Mr. Ford want to set out his plantations? On the banks of the Tapajós? Perfect. And what was the amount of land he desired for the undertaking? Two million, four hundred and seventy thousand acres? Why, of course. But, converted into square kilometers, how many would that be, more or less? And, more or less, to what could such an extent of land be compared, just to get an idea? Exactly five-sixths of Connecticut. Ah, then everything was fine . . . five-sixths of Connecticut. . . .

And then the decree of concession was executed, and thereafter the business began to move forward.

Is everybody happy? Obviously, not everybody was happy. The English in Java and Ceylon and on the stock exchange in London knitted their brows. And along with them, naturally, the colonels of the Amazonian river borders, owners of lands as extensive as whole countries. And with good cause. At the rumor that Henry Ford was going to pay from two to five dollars a day to his laborers in Tapajós, equivalent at that time to forty to a hundred *cruzeiros* in Brazilian currency, they, who were not accustomed to paying more than five *cruzeiros*, realized that they would have to tighten their vigilance over rivers, lakes, tributaries, and canals so that the "volunteers" in the old battle of rubber would not run away. Otherwise they would not get a kilo of raw gum.

Meanwhile in Dearborn, on Lake Michigan, activity is feverish. Ships are being outfitted for the conquest of Amazonia. They are to carry a whole city, disassembled, "knocked down," but ready, as if it were a question of automobiles emerging from the Ford Motor Company assembly lines: houses, hospitals, cafeterias, drugstores, cement, sand for the tennis courts, sanitary apparatus, bulldozers, sawmill—a complete city to be set up. Not since the departure from Amsterdam of the fleet with which the Dutch conquered Pernambuco and the Northeast in 1624 had such a well-fitted-out civilizing expedition set sail for Brazil.

Now Henry Ford's ships are sailing the waters of the Great Lakes; now they have entered the St. Lawrence Canal; now their prows are dipping to the waves' onrush as they cleave the waters of the open sea. Now they evade the hurricanes of the Caribbean, now they raise the muddy fringe of the Amazon delta; now, bearing to starboard, they gallantly stem the current of the river-sea's delta; now they leave Belém and Santarém behind and, veering to port, between great walls of verdure, they emerge from the muddy waters of the Amazon to plunge into the "liquid emerald" of the Tapajós.

Once arrived at Fordlândia, they tie up to the river bank. All this time, the world press is shouting. The battle between Mr. Ford and the Amazon jungle has begun.

In North America newspapers report the struggle in minute detail.

The jungle growth resists, but retreats. And with it the jaguars, monkeys, parrots, and snakes, as the bulldozers go knocking over trees for the clearing where the city is to be erected. Ceiba trees, butterfly trees, mimosas, cedars, figs, rubber trees, the giants of the forest together with the vegetal varieties that Bates classified in Amazonia and that served as a basis for Darwin's theories about the survival of the fittest— all fall back, are cut down almost by the roots, roots for that matter too shallow to support such ostentation.

Now the houses have begun to take shape, and the hospital, and the hygienic facilities and the tennis courts, and the directors' mansions, and the workers' dwellings, and the cafeteria, and the drugstore, just as in New England or the Midwest. In the Amazonian jungle the Yankee had caused a new city to spring up.

And everything was going according to plan. Three thousand half-breeds were working in Fordlândia, receiving fifty to one hundred and fifty cruzeiros a day. A million rubber seedlings were planted in the fields that had to be continually wrested from the jungle. The rain forest breathed hard, but it yielded. From afar, by telegraph, Henry Ford directed the battle against the jungle. Everything was wonderful.

And when, after barely two years, the rubber trees begin to blossom in platoons, in companies, in battalions, in regiments, no one has any remaining doubts about the outcome of the struggle.

On the London Exchange the price of rubber starts a dizzy plunge. From a dollar and a half per pound, the price of rubber goes to one dollar, then to eighty cents and then to seventy, to twenty-five. The planters in Java are utterly ruined.

In 1936 Edward Tomlinson, in the December 12 issue of Collier's, proclaimed, full of enthusiasm: "In the very heart of the region where inquisitive archeologists and self-styled scientists, bitten by the adventure bug, go out in search of the walls of mythical cities and peoples descended from Phoenician nomads and other ancient peoples, deep in the jungle, Henry Ford is laying the foundations of a civilization."

Fordlândia was indeed resplendent. It was, on a smaller scale, an industrial city as complete for the ends to which it was destined as Dearborn itself. It had a refrigerating plant that could store food for more han two thousand persons for six months. It had a hospital that was the last word in efficiency and comfort. The Amazonian half-breed, who had never before known anything better than his one-room *mocambo*, now enjoyed a house with as many as three rooms, and running water.

Is everybody happy? The families of the managerial force could not have been happier. Many times happier on the Tapajós than in Detroit. In Detroit there were always labor troubles, the ferment of agitation, refusal to conform to Mr. Ford's paternalism and generous ideas. Not in Fordlândia. The Amazonian half-breed, how gentle! What simple, grateful, humble, lovable folk! And what prodigious tales they could tell about the mysteries of the jungle: the great snake, the dolphin that could turn into a man, the *uirapurú* songbird. What beauty there is in the story of the *uirapurú!* The whole forest would stop to listen to the *uirapurú* sing; the trees would not bend or rustle, the jaguar would not howl, the parrots shut their beaks. And yet the *uirapurú* was the ugliest and sorriest bird in the jungle.

Suddenly, in the midst of this idyll, the first unexpected trouble. The *caboclos*, those meek, humble half-breeds, turn into wild beasts. They start by smashing up the whole cafeteria, they tear everything down. A riot. The officials of the Ford Motor Company run with their families, all terrified, for the freighters anchored in the port. The *caboclos*, armed with clubs like the French in the taking of the Bastille, march on the strongholds of the directorate and management, roaring something unintelligible to the listeners aboard ship. What can they be howling about so angrily? Can it be "Down with Mr. Ford!"? Can it be "Down with the Ford Motor Company!"? Nothing of the sort. It appeared that it was a personal disagreement with Popeye the Sailor. What the half-breeds were yelling was, "Down with spinach! No more spinach!"

The breaking and smashing during the night helped to calm them down. Only next day, when the military detachment from Belém arrived, did the managers learn what the affair was all about. The *caboclos* were full of boiled spinach and well-vitaminized foods; they could not even look at spinach any more. As for corn flakes, better not even mention them. They wanted dried meat, and a *feijoada*[15] now and then. Hasn't a man got a right to a good *feijoada* and a shot of rum once in a while? And hasn't he got a right to get a little drunk on *cachaça* occasionally? Enough is enough.

And in one night the officials of the Ford Motor Company learned more sociology than in years at a university. They learned that those mild half-breeds could turn into brutes for motives that completely escaped the comprehension of Mr. Ford; they learned that the *caboclos* detested, simply detested, the tiled houses in which they lived and the Puritan way of life the officials wished to impose upon them. Built in

the American fashion, directly on the ground, and not in the style o
the *caboclo's* hut, on stilts, those houses were veritable ovens, as is easily
imaginable when one considers how hot the majority of American
houses are in summer, when air conditioning is not used to solve the
heat problem, as the cold problem was solved with central heating.

In Dearborn, Henry Ford thought about spinach and despaired of
human nature. As if his troubles with the workmen in his own industry
were not enough, on top of that here came those half-breeds of Amazonia
—men whom he had rescued from the most wretched conditions and on
whom he had bestowed the supreme good fortune of the American way
of life, with vitaminized food and the same rules of work-efficiency as
obtained in Dearborn—to increase his doubts about the essential goodness of human nature. Mr. Ford understood assembly lines and the
designs of Divine Providence. He did not, absolutely could not, understand the psychology of the *caboclo*.

At that time, moreover, there were other people who were embittering
Henry Ford's life. The English, the Jews, and the negativists. The river-
land colonels of the Amazon and Pará, who did not like the raise in
workers' wages, who longed for the good old days when they had theaters built for their mistresses, lighted their cigars with 200-*milreis* and
500-*milreis* banknotes, sent their sons to study in Europe, and never
entertained any notion of rational planting and even less any idea of
raising the rubber-gatherer's pay—Ford paid no attention to those men.
But the Jews, the English, and the negativists, those were the ones who
were ruining his sleep.

And to think that even in the United States there were negativists, real
Cassandras joining in chorus with the Jews and the English about the
future of Fordlândia! They were not exactly denying Mr. Ford's high
qualities. They recognized in him the pioneer, the Yankee, the industrialist, whose new kind of capitalism had made communism obsolete at
the very moment of its birth, since everything that Russia was promising
workers for the distant future—high wages, low prices, civil equality,
economic brotherhood—through the sacrifice of present generations and
of liberties already won, Henry Ford, with the new blood he had trans-
fused into capitalism, was already bestowing on the present generations
with no sacrifice of freedom. Only such as were irremediably lacking in
any capacity for admiring and applauding could have any doubts or
reservations about Ford's contribution to the general betterment of
humanity.

Nevertheless, the fact was that even his admirers did not exactly think
that Henry Ford was an emissary of the gods, but merely a lucky
mechanic who, contrary to his own system of manufacturing cars, in
which specialization was carried to its ultimate extreme, liked to meddle

in what was none of his business and to pontificate upon what he did not understand. They did not think that the orange tree, just because it yielded good oranges, should produce quinces or guavas, in the way that Henry Ford, at the same time that he produced automobiles, produced formulas for the world's salvation.

Anyway, Ford's failure in the case of another expedition, organized by him in 1917 to save the world in the midst of war, was too vivid in the memory of those stubborn negativists for them to be moved by and surrender to the news of Fordlândia's early successes.

Meanwhile, Henry Ford was receiving and reading reports. And these told rather different stories from those that figured on the front pages of newspapers. Besides the *caboclos'* riot there were some technical difficulties. For example, the sawmill intended for cutting all the trees of the heterogeneous tropical forest had proved ineffectual. The trees whose wood was of interest to the American market, such as the *acapú*, broke all the saws and burned out the motors, and no matter how their power and speed were redoubled, there was no way to overcome the resistance of the wood. This is equivalent to saying that saw machinery adequate to the varied timber of Amazonia was yet to be invented. From this point of view a forest of Alaskan pine was worth the whole Amazon jungle. But the worst of all was yet to come. The worst thing was that the million rubber seedlings were dying from the excessive sun and lack of humidity and humus. After flourishing exuberantly for a time, they were withering in the local sun just as coffee does in Amazonia if it is not planted in the shade of bushes to protect it. For lack of the protection of tropical forest shade, Mr. Ford's army of rubber trees was going to die in the sun. It was tragedy in the vegetable world in all its horror. According to Darwin, life is a struggle, and in the struggle the strongest triumphs. In Amazonia the disorderliness of the jungle was triumphing over the discipline of the rubber grove.

Thenceforth the story of Fordlândia moves more swiftly. In 1938 Ford asks for a new concession of lands from the Brazilian government—the cultivable land of Belterra—getting rid of the former land at bottom prices. The Brazilian government immediately accedes. The Brazilian government did everything he wanted, as though Ford had already received extreme unction. Afterwards, silence, Fordlândia yielding first place, and the first page of newspapers, to inventors and producers of synthetic rubber, with which the United States would, from 1944 on, solve the rubber problem.

To cut the story short: In January of 1946 the melancholy news goes round the world: *Ford Withdraws from Brazil.* It was the end. The whole outcome of the story is summed up in that headline. For that matter the whole history of Fordlândia can be concentrated in the telegraphic style of the newspaper and magazine headlines. And, to re construct it, it suffices to gather up these headlines at random, as they were catalogued in its own book by the New York Public Library from 1928 to 1946 under the subject "Rubber." They constitute the summary of a fascinating story.

In the first phase they reflect the euphoria of great expectations: *Reply of America to British Monopoly of Rubber. End of British Control of Rubber. Freeing the Rubber Market.*

In the second phase expectation becomes certainty: *Rubber for America: Factory in United States, Plantations in Brazil. Taming the Jungle in the Amazon Basin. Jungle Gold: Fordlandia, where Brazil's Rubber Returned to Life. Ford in Brazil. Ford on the Tapajoz. Rubber Plantations in Fordlandia. Miracle-City of the Amazon.*

Finally, the first unexpected news of failure and the abrupt retreat: *More News About Rubber. Golden Leaves of Rubber Tree Affected by Sunlight. Synthetic Rubber. Ford Withdraws from Brazil.*

The rest is silence.

5

Ought we to conclude from this that in Amazonia it is impossible to establish homogeneous groves of rubber trees, or that the great valley is unsuitable for the flowering of a great civilization? Not yet. For the present the conclusion to draw is a different one, and that is that until now the Amazonian environment has implacably defeated everyone, and that Humboldt's prophecy, at least in the current stage of techniques, is in the same class as Pero Vaz de Caminha's "the land will grow anything." Pure impressionism.

In truth, what was done on the Tapajós is what has been hastily done everywhere—the transplantation to the tropics of techniques, methods, and processes tried and tested only in temperate or cold climates. Because the science and the technique of soil cultivation in the tropics is still in an empirical and elementary phase of development.

In Amazonia, and for that matter in nearly the whole country, the soil does yield crops, but with difficulty. In the extreme North it is excess of water; in the Northeast it is lack of water; the Center is too mountainous and plagued by erosion.

That is the truth about the famous fertility of Brazilian soil, as opposed to the hyperbolical praise it has received. It is true that, if we
leave aside the drought-scorched Northeast, the Amazonia of Humboldt's
dreams, the mountainous regions, land subject to erosion, and land that
is unsuitable for mechanized farming—all of which taken together add
up to nearly half of the national territory—happily there is still much
to praise and to use in the other half, especially if we compare its poten-
tialities with those of the rest of the Latin American countries, in which,
as William Vogt puts it, "Geography is one of the severest limiting
factors in achieving progress."[16]

Brazil is still in no condition, then, to bear comparison with the
United States in this particular, in spite of the superb fitness of her
"purple soil" for coffee and in spite of the abundant fertility of her Central highland and the southern part of the Matto Grosso. Would that
she could! Why, the United States possesses, between the Rocky Mountains and the Alleghenies, the largest continuous surface of cultivatable
lands in the world, lands already cleared of undergrowth and forest, and
irrigated by the Mississippi and its tributaries, among them the Missouri,
the Ohio, the Arkansas, and the Red rivers.

Apparently only a veritable miracle, or exceptional historical circumstances, such as the discovery of gold and a sudden rise in the price of
the products of Brazilian extractive industry, or of the products of
monoculture, like brazilwood, sugar, coffee, and rubber, could help
Brazil achieve the pace of the United States in progress and civilization.

There is no question, then, of attributing to the Anglo-Saxons as a
race the triumphs of North American civilization, and still less of
attributing to the Portuguese, or to the Negroes, or to the Indians and
half-breeds, the responsibility for Brazil's failures. Actually, having
achieved as much civilization as she has—perhaps the only tropical civilization worth mentioning—by overcoming, reducing, or getting around
obstacles of climate, orography, hydrography, and poverty of the soil and
to a certain extent of the subsoil also, Brazil warrants not only our faith in
her but the willing acceptance of our origins.

In any case, we can be sure of one thing: the absence of racial discrimination in Brazil has not been physiologically an evil. Paradoxically,
it may have been a good thing, and may in time come to be, if it is not
already, one of the best legacies of Portuguese-Brazilian culture, despite
the high price Brazilians have been paying and may still have to pay
for it.

6

In fact, if Brazilians were asked what the highest, most edifying and significant aspect of Brazilian civilization is, they would have not the slightest hesitation in pointing to the almost complete absence of insoluble racial problems. Not that these are entirely nonexistent or that the institution of slavery has not also bequeathed, in terms of discrimination and segregation, the heavy burden of its odious heritage, or that the psychological passivity resulting from it has already been fully overcome or is even on the way to being fully overcome. That odious passivity has ramified emotionally through all sectors of our national life and will probably take centuries to extirpate. But at least its most aggressive and menacing branch—pure race conflict—is tending to disappear. And when at times it attempts to revive, it no longer appears under the open and prickly form of the racial issue, properly speaking, but as a function of class conflict, contrary to what occurs in the United States, where race conflicts exceed those of class, the latter tending to disappear.

So in a general way the racial problem in Brazil, dissolved into the social, can be considered as being, if not solved, at any rate on the road to solution. On this score Brazil's position and the attitude of the great majority of Brazilians admits of no doubt whatever. As a whole they are against racial prejudice, not only because they do not believe in ethnic purity in absolute terms, but also because they refuse to accept racial superiority or inferiority as the exclusive or even preponderant explanation of the differences between civilizations.

Are they right? Are they wrong?

To convince them at this stage of the twentieth century that they are wrong, it would first be necessary to persuade them of the existence of an ethnically homogeneous nation in the West. Portugal, from whence came the Brazilians' ancestors—a mixture of Celts, Phoenicians, Greeks, Carthaginians, Romans, Goths, and Swabians—after eight centuries of Moorish occupation, and in a position squarely on the crossroads of two continents, obviously cannot and does not claim for herself any title to homogeneity or to purity of origin. Can Spain or France do so? Can Germany, perchance, be the nation so privileged? But is it possible to speak of pure race in Germany, when it is well known that her territory has been the point of passage for all the invasions from East to West, the turbulent crucible in which Bretons, Germans, Chinese, Russians,

Slavs, Tartars, and Mongols have been melted? And what of Italy, nest
of Umbrians, Venetians, Arabs, North African peoples, Turks, and Jews?
To talk of pure race in any of these countries is nearly as nonsensical as
to speak of pure ethnic homogeneity in the United States or in Russia.

In the opinion of Julian Huxley and A. C. Haddon the notion of a
Britannic, French, German, or Italian race is a political fiction, and certainly a very dangerous one. Another fiction is that of the Jewish race:
"The Jews are not a 'race' any more clearly marked than the Germans
and the English. They are originally of mixed ancestry. During their
dispersion they mingled with the peoples surrounding them, and the
Jewish communities came to resemble the local populations in many
respects. Thus the Jews of Africa, of Eastern Europe, of Spain, of Portugal, and of other regions, came to differ a great deal among themselves
in physical type. What they have preserved and transmitted are not
'racial qualities' but religious and social traditions. The Jews do not constitute a definite race, but a society that forms a pseudo-national group
with a strong religious base and peculiar historic traditions. Biologically,
it is almost as erroneous to speak of 'Jewish race' as it is of 'Aryan race'."[17]

The same biologists, after examining more closely the differences that
form the commonly accepted distinctions between racial lineages and
nationalities, and dismissing them as having no intimate relation with
the physical traits by which a race may be distinguished in the biological
sense, make this further important revelation: that the famous passage
in which Tacitus, in his *Germania,* shows himself in agreement with
those who maintain that the Germanic peoples had not been contaminated by crossing with other peoples—a passage which gave rise to the
Nordic legend of Teutonic superiority—has not the slightest scientific
foundation.

"A glance at the map that depicts the known movements of the
European peoples during the first seven or eight centuries of the Christian era ought to banish from our minds any notion of tribal fixity or
racial purity. Europe was a crucible on the boil, and what emerged from
that crucible had to be very different from what went in."[18]

Clearly, the time has passed when one could accept uncritically the
myth of congenital virtues in certain races, and when—without taking
into account historical, cultural, ecological, and geophysical factors
(climate, latitude, and orographic, geological, and fluvial systems), and
especially the economic resources that make possible or impossible the
advent of advanced cultures—we classified peoples solely and exclusively
by the degree of progress they had momentarily attained. Today it appears that we are becoming more reasonable. Instead of being impressed
by statements unaccompanied by proofs, to the effect that all our ills
derive from our ethnic origins, more or less balanced by racial advantages,

we are beginning to understand that there are no superior or inferior races but only ethnic types with differing inclinations, cultures, and tendencies, equally capable of success or failure according to the type of culture predominating at the time they are called to fulfill their destiny.

Are we to consider the Latin peoples inferior to the Anglo-Saxons because, lacking coal or better sources of energy, they did not adapt themselves as well as the Nordics did to the industrial civilizations of our time? That would be the same as concluding that the Aztecs, the Incas, and the Mayans were inferior because, lacking gunpowder, they allowed the Spaniards to destroy the magnificent pre-Columbian civilizations that they had created in Mexico and Peru.

Are we to consider the Portuguese an inferior race because they did not do in Brazil what the English did with their colonies in America? To do so it would be necessary to lose sight of the plane of world history and to forget that, when the Portuguese and the Spaniards were out discovering "worlds for the world," the Nordic peoples, apprentices to the former in geography and cartography, were taking their first painful steps by comparison with the new exploits that the Sagres school of navigation was making possible. Why then should we attribute to the so-called Aryans any superiority over other racial groups, or waste time over dogmatic statements, unsupported by proofs, that all Brazilian ills are traceable to Portuguese ancestry and the later mixture with Indian and Negro stock? Would Brazil's destiny have been better if it had been discovered and peopled by Anglo-Saxons or the Dutch?

The experience of the Dutch conquest and colonization of the Northeast of Brazil was of too little duration for definitive conclusions to be drawn from it. As for the Anglo-Saxons, or rather, the North Americans, they left no better impression of themselves as colonizers in South America.

7

What has become of the Southerners from the United States, for example, who came to Brazil after the Civil War in their country because they would not live on a footing of equality with their former slaves?

Here is a still incompletely clarified chapter of the history of the two

Americas. One might say a blank chapter, so great is the scarcity of positive data about this strange episode, so great the silence about it.

Indeed, what at once catches the attention of the person interested in getting a general picture of that important migratory movement is the poverty of documents dealing with the subject. In the New York Public Library, or even in the Library of Congress, which overlooks nothing in the way of publications of interest to the United States, not more than a handful of articles can be found buried among the contents of state historical magazines such as the *Alabama Historical Quarterly*, or of the *Hispanic American Historical Review*. On the Brazilian side, except for an occasional retrospective glance at the subject in technical magazines like the *Boletim de Imigração*, the same sparsity of references is to be found.[19]

But, poor as this documentation is, it permits us to partially reconstruct the great adventure.

It all began about 1865. The Civil War hardly over, in the South of the United States the movement for a great migration to Brazil took shape. Some Southerners had already established residence below the equator, and the South had some time before entered into contact with Brazil through the coffee trade. These Southerners started writing to friends and acquaintances, assuring them of a warm welcome on the part of Brazil, as well as fertile land, a great deal of land, a pleasant climate, and crops that were familiar to them. Besides, they gave information about the low cost of labor and—what was still more alluring—declared that in Brazil cotton-growing would prove successful.

Nothing more was needed. People who had lost everything in the Civil War, people weary of battles and humiliations, suddenly saw in Brazil the Promised Land, with living space sufficient for new farming communities that might be organized along the lines of those they were going to leave behind.

Thenceforward, from New Orleans, Charleston, and Mobile, little ships with small groups of men, women, and children, set sail toward the south, bound for Brazilian ports.

That, however, was only the beginning. Soon afterwards a more grandiose plan was afoot. This plan was to settle in Brazil, leaving to the hated Yankees, who at the time were committing horrors in the South, the former States of the Confederacy, now ruined and depopulated.

Nevertheless, there was no hasty action. On the contrary, everything was done in the good American fashion, as was fitting, with study, organization, and planning. First, the Southern Colonization Society was founded. Immediately three authorized members of the Society, two from Georgia and one from North Carolina, were sent to Brazil to study the situation meticulously. Only after the arrival of their report approving the move would the bulk of the emigration get under way.

On Brazil's part—so it was believed in both countries—never was an immigration so welcomed and desired. The Imperial Government made concessions in the form of payment of one-third of the cost of passages and distribution of lands on a scale perhaps never equalled by the United States in her best days. And there were no complaints against the Imperial Government on this score. On the contrary, Brazilian hospitality was acclaimed and praised by all voices. Enthusiasm was general, euphoria attacked one and all.

A certain Reverend Dunn, ex-Confederate Army, after obtaining free 1,500,000 square meters of coastal lands suitable for rice- and sugar-growing, "in a beautiful location two days' steamer trip from Rio," brought back to New Orleans a volume written about Brazil. Brazil, Dunn declared, was the ideal land for the Southerners. A land of moving lyricism. And he clamored for the organization of at least three new navigation companies by 1867 at latest, to assist in the great crusade for populating Brazil with the former Confederates.

One Captain W. Frank Shippy, late of the Confederate Navy, proclaimed, "We, the advance guard of the Confederate Legion, believe that the children and grandchildren of those who join us will rise up to call us blessed."

The traveler John Codman, writing in 1867, told his public in the United States, "Years hence it will be concluded that one of the results of the Civil War will have been the repopulation of this land."

As a rule, those who are making history are not fully aware of the fact. With the Confederates who participated in the propaganda of the great exodus it was different. They felt as if they were in actual contact with the history of their time.

And so, during the years '66 and '67, the great exodus continued, as though inspired by that other one of the Old Testament: "Leave thy land and thy people, and the house of thy father, and come to the land which I shall shew unto thee."

So intense was this migratory movement that it alarmed the American authorities. Newspapers went so far as to boycott all news concerning the undertaking. But, as the outrages and dangers and uncertainties persisted in the South, an ever increasing number of families continued to embark in groups bound for Brazil.

How many went, all told? Any estimate is difficult. Between two and three thousand, perhaps. It is known, furthermore, that of those two or three thousand, two hundred settled in Santarém on the banks of the Trapajós, in the state of Pará. The remainder set out for São Paulo and Espírito Santo. And beyond that, on the American side, apart from a sporadic reference here and there, there is an almost complete absence of information.

However, in 1940, the *Saturday Evening Post*, seventy-five years after the arrival of the first Confederates in Brazil, resolved to conduct an inquiry into the fate of its fellow-countrymen who embarked for Brazil. It assigned the task and furnished credentials to one of its ablest writers, James E. Edmonds. This writer had no racial thesis to prove or to defend. His sole mission was to discover what had become of the former Confederates and their descendants. His objective was to answer the extremely American question: "Well, what about those Secessionists who settled in Brazil?"[20]

Mr. Edmonds began his investigation in São Paulo.

"Through the years the capital of São Paulo from an interior city came to be the third largest city in South America. A republic took the place of the Empire. Forests were cut down, deserts were peopled, railroads constructed. Light and power penetrated the interior. Factories brought prosperity. Tall buildings outlined new silhouettes against the sky. New states were created. Fortunes were made, lost and made again. Reputations were made.

"And not one of these conquests, or very few, bear the mark of those self-exiled men of the lost Confederacy. In the official list of the important business firms not a single name now seems to be American."[21]

The land was indeed repopulated, just as the traveler Codman foresaw, but by Europeans and not by North Americans.

"Among all the newcomers, never did the ex-Confederates, and rarely their descendants, come to be really of the land. Rarely did they master it. Nor have their numbers increased in that prolific region."

The valuable thing is that this testimony does not come from Brazilians but from a man belonging to a cultural group opposed to recognizing defeats or worrying about them.

In judging the same case the Brazilian chroniclers are not so pessimistic. For them the North American colonization in São Paulo is far from being the failure depicted by Mr. Edmonds. It can be failure only if measured by American standards, where everything is done on a large scale. By Brazilian standards, however, the success of the Americans in São Paulo, if not exactly spectacular, is not far behind that of other immigrants. According to Sérgio Buarque de Holanda, the mechanization of Brazilian agriculture was not brought about by the Americans, nevertheless it was they who made it more effective. "Campos Sales tells us," comments Buarque de Holanda, "that, unaccustomed to the use of machines, farmers sometimes utilized a whole team of oxen to operate a single machine, often with poor results. Only the example of the North American families immigrating from 1866 on finally demonstrated that each machine requires no more than one man and one animal to perform all the operations for which it is designed."[22]

Another who testifies in favor of the North Americans is José Artur Rios, in his excellent monograph, "A Imigração de Confederados Norte-Americanos no Brasil." It cannot be said that the Southerners contributed nothing to Brazil, although their contribution was necessarily restricted to small portions of the country on account of its immensity and the small number of the colonists. The plow factory that Mark Jefferson saw in Santa Bárbara, the typically Southern wagons loaded with watermelons (one of the products of the region), the corn bread that a visitor enjoyed in one of those houses with glass windows and brick chimneys—all these were typical things that they brought and incorporated into the local patrimony."[23] The Southern contribution, in his view, was not confined to the material domain: "Something of their spirit also passed into the local patrimony. They enriched our society with their progressive mind, their capacity for action, their technical competence. And perhaps into the hearts of their Paulist descendants has filtered a little of that love of freedom that is an American tradition and that pride of the old planter that is a Southern tradition."[24]

Evidently the *Saturday Evening Post's* journalist, accustomed to seeing North Americans triumph spectacularly everywhere and beat all records, expected something better; but in proportion to the number of immigrants that came, these gave no poor account of themselves. And there, to prove it, is the prosperous city of Vila Americana, which in no way lags behind its São Paulo sisters in spirit of initiative and accomplishment.[25] Perhaps more ought not to be expected. If it were a case of Italian colonists, whose average influx into Brazil was between 50,000 and 200,000 a year up to 1940, some surprise might be justified. Not so, however, in the case of the North Americans.

8

And what of the fate of the group that settled on the right bank of the Tapajós under the sponsorship of the Baron de Santarém and of the Emperor himself?

Here, as is easy to divine, the story which Mr. Edmonds has to relate is a moving one, at times heart-rending.

Since there was vague news that even in 1878 a certain number of Confederate families were holding on and prospering, reverting to the way of life of their ancestors, he went in search of the mark which those tamers of the forest must have stamped on Amazonia in the form of buildings on the order of those of the Old South.

Little did the journalist know what the Amazon jungle does to marks of civilization. If he had seen formerly-flourishing places like Borba, Barcelos, or Humaitá, which preserve hardly any trace, any vestige, any sign of their past opulence or even of the presence of human communities, certainly he would not ask for signs of the old Confederate South or seek out the cemeteries where his compatriots had been buried. There on the crest of the ravines through which he wandered not even a Schliemann, he who excavated the ruins of Troy, could have located the houses or the tombs of the departed, for in those wastelands where man is buried the tentacled forest ends by entirely recapturing its former domain. The jungle respects nothing. Of the old churches and dwellings not one stone is left upon another, for the ant, that great collaborator with the jungle, takes it upon herself to pulverize all ruins.

What has become, for example, of Barcelos, the old capital of the upper Rio Negro, built by the Portuguese plenipotentiary João Pereira Caldas, sent in 1780 to the Amazon with a glittering retinue of astronomers and geographers? Already by the time the naturalist Alexandre Rodrigues Ferreira visited it, it was reduced to a dilapidated group of houses in a state of decomposition. The imposing ex-Palace of Demarcations, with its indigenous thatching of cogon grass and palm leaf, was a living definition of architectural absurdity and incongruity. The famous cotton cloth factory had disappeared. The fate of the Carmelite convent and of the governor's country house was identical. And Borba, and Humaitá, and that vast number of Amazonian towns which still flaunt the name of cities?

In spite of all that, the envoy of the *Saturday Evening Post* was happy. Strolling along the river bank at Santarém, he saw on the wall of a wooden house, with no bars over its windows, the American eagle roughly painted in blue and red.

It was the home of one of the last survivors of the exodus of '67. He had come as a child with the Confederates, and now there he was, gray-haired, married to a woman from Ceará, a landowner and father of eleven *caboclos*. On learning the visitor's mission his eyes cloud with sadness. He prefers to talk about his sons and daughters and grandchildren; he evades any return to the past. The visitor persists. But it is only in bits, a sentence here, another there, that he succeeds in drawing out the history of the group.

Of the Rikers of Charleston, of the Pitts and the Vaughans of Silver

Springs, Tennessee, no one is left. And of the Wallaces, Emmetts, Steels, Troups, and Robbinses of Alabama? And the Mendenhalls, Henningtons, and Rhomes of Mississippi? And the Jenningses, all of pure Anglo-Saxon or Teutonic stock? All gone. Except for himself and his brother, who was still a bachelor and had property down the Amazon, and spent his days on his veranda, waited on by his half-breed servants, with his pipe, reading his Bible and watching the river roll along below, no one was left. "One by one, the ex-Confederates and their wives had died."

Finally, after nightfall, while a little *caboclo* flourished a Confederate sword that had flashed at Fort Sumter, came the farewell and an answer to forestall a question long foreseen:

"I'm glad I stayed on. God has been good to me. My sons are good sons, my daughters are good daughters. My wife is good and true. We lack for nothing we ought to have. How many can say the same?"

A profoundly native attitude; a profoundly American explanation. Because if there is no one like the American for being optimistic about everything, for not cursing the struggle against droughts and floods and the job of confronting problems of life and death, while having every reason to do so, there is no one like the *caboclo* of the lowlands, both the indigenes and the Northeasterners who have emigrated there. They never utter a curse to unburden themselves of contained despair. On the contrary, they seem to have made a tacit agreement to keep silent about their own frustrations. In this, perhaps, is the pride of men who came to conquer and feel the shame of recognizing failure and admitting defeat.

9

Are the partisans, open or covert, of Teutonic racial purity going to surrender, with that example, to the predominance of geophysical over ethnic factors? One would have to ignore the emotional founts from which the preconceptions of ethnic superiority and racial discrimination flow, to suppose that such a thing could happen. The racial purists will not surrender to the examples of the Confederates or to the failure of the Ford Motor Company in Amazonia. Indeed, they are already circulating their explanations for both cases. As to Ford, one of the versions carried by the American press is that he did not withdraw from Amazonia in defeat, but only because, with the discovery and manufacture of synthetic rubber, the project of standardized planting of rubber trees, when it ceased to have any economic justification, had no reason for continuing. And as for the defeat of the Confederates, they declare that if these failed in São Paulo where the most varied types of immigration have succeeded, it is because they were either not of the best Anglo-Saxon stock or else weakened by prolonged contact with the Negro and with the corrupting sensuality of the feudal system. Had they been immigrants from the North, genuine Yankees, acting not as the managing elite over an amorphous mass of mixed breeds, like the English and the Dutch in the Far East and in Central America, but as colonists perfectly integrated in the same ethnic group, like the Germans in southern Brazil, the situation would have been different. They would be dominating the country by now, and Amazonia would be bent to the will of the pure Aryan, as the soft muddy lands of the Everglades and the Mississippi Delta had been in the southern United States.

What can be said in reply to that is that everything is possible and nothing is definitely proved. That the Confederates were not really ideal colonists is a perfectly acceptable statement.

There was, in fact, a great mistake on both sides in the general expectations about the Southerners' prospects in Brazil.

While the Emperor, foreseeing that slavery was bound to end—he himself, as is so often proclaimed, had perhaps been the first abolitionist —was expecting colonists like the Germans who were creating the prosperity of southern Brazil, the Confederates emigrated with the intention of reestablishing their cotton plantations, and slave labor, in the new land. The Southerners came to Brazil, as José Artur Rios notes, supposing that they would find cheap labor there, whereas there was already difficulty in getting slaves or wage-laborers. "They imagined they would find in Brazil, a slave-holding country, the same segregation between whites and blacks. The fact is that even in that day, within the Second Empire's society of landed estates and slaves, factors were at work which were to contribute to the peaceful solution of slavery and to the nonexistence of segregation in Brazil. For a long time, for example, the social rise of Negroes and mulattoes had been going on, and the Southerners found themselves, to their stupefaction, in a society in which the color criterion was not the dominant one for social classification. With consternation they saw mulattoes and Negroes in the bosom of society, occupying important positions, and, through that fact, ceasing to be regarded as Negroes."[26]

With their attitudes based on mistakes of this kind, it was really difficult for things to turn out well in the end. And indeed they did not turn out well. Along this line, then, proceeds the objection. But as for accepting the notion that Amazonia would bow to the omnipotent will of the Teuton—that would have to be proved, seeing that up to now the proofs, all proofs, direct as well as inductive, militate against it.

10

Are there, indeed, other experimental proofs beside that of the Confederates and that of Fordlândia to clarify the matter? There are, to be sure. And one extremely important one, because in the way of material for contradicting racial theses Amazonia produces enough for everything.

Nevertheless, this case occurs not in Brazilian but in Peruvian Amazonia. It is the case of the Germans who in 1857, with the aid and on the initiative of President Lleguía, made the rash attempt to colonize the lands watered by the River Posuso, in the region of Ucayali. This episode is told by Euclides da Cunha in his À Margem da História:

"Halfway from Iquitos, near the navigable tributaries of the Ucayali and in a region of fertile soil, the nucleus established was, militarily and administratively, the firmest strategic point of that combat with the desert, justifying the efforts and the extraordinary expenditures made for rapid development, which the best natural conditions favored.

"But the plan did not succeed. As had happened in Loreto, the new colonists, although more persistent, wore themselves out in futility. The colony became paralyzed, stagnant, among the splendors of the forest. It was reduced to rudimentary crops which hardly sufficed for their consumption. And the processes of heredity almost imperceptibly resulted in a lymphatic progeny in whom the stiff Prussian frame shrank into the withered, bowed figure of the Quichua. When the prefect of Huánuco, Colonel Vizcarra, visited the colony in 1870, he was astounded and deeply moved; the colonists came to him ragged and famished, begging him for bread and for clothing to cover their nakedness. The romantic D. Manuel Pinzás, who described the journey, paints for us in lengthy, lachrymose sentences the details of that 'heart-rending picture!!', punctuating it with two rigid exclamation points.

"Dr. Santiago Tavarra, in describing the first journey of Admiral Tucker, still saw it in the same somber colors five years later.

"Finally, thirty years afterwards, Colonel P. Portillo, on his way to Ucayali, had definite news of the colonizing nucleus: it was a horrifying

Thebaid. Deep in the wilds the primitive colonists and their degenerate progeny writhed, victims of a hopeless fanaticism, in the dolorous sloth-fulness of penances, praying, telling their rosaries, and intoning inter-minable prayers to the Virgin, in a scandalous competition with the monkeys of the jungle!"[27]

What to conclude from all this? An indigenous medicine man or a half-breed of the region, following literally the racist method of inter-preting history by results without taking into account orography, hy-drography, climate, geographic relief, historical antecedents, and ecologi-cal conditions, would be well within his rights in drawing the conclusion that the Teutonic race is irremediably inferior. If, with all the aid of the Peruvian government, good land, and official protection, the Teutonic race did not succeed in doing better, it is because it simply had no apti-tude; it was a question of an inferior race.

And that is what the interpreting of peoples and nations, cultures and civilizations solely by the criterion of results in a given historical moment can lead to. To conclusions like this, however, it may be more sensible to oppose the thesis that if there is no great civilization in Amazonia it is not because of the fault or the racial inferiority of the Indian, the half-breed, the Portuguese, the German, or the Anglo-Saxon, but is due in great part to the difficulties inherent in the environment. In Amazonia, Nature has implacably routed everyone, up to the present. The only difference to point out is that in time all others flee; the *mestiço* remains. His lack of ambition, his resignation, has made of him a man adapted to the land. And in the last analysis it is that despised, calumniated half-breed who assures Brazil its hold on the wilderness. Perhaps it is for this reason that, in the opinion of Ratzel, father of anthropogeography, with-out the *mestiço*—that is, without the miscegenation that made him possible—Brazil today would be one of those many tropical or subtropical countries in which, due to discrimination, a dominant foreign class has to renew itself constantly by recruitment from abroad, in order not to become degraded in the eyes of the permanent population of natives engaged in agricultural labor, more or less fatal to the Aryan under the tropical sun. Pursuing Ratzel's thought further, if Brazil is what she is, she owes it to the fact that on her soil the white race mixed with other races. Had the Portuguese and Spaniards of tropical America not done so, the white race, conqueror of the temperate zone, would by now be completely excluded from the productive tropics by the adverse climatic conditions.[28]

It is possible that Ratzel, in this case, as happens in many others, exaggerates his beliefs. And yet it is certain that Brazil's expansion was accomplished by her *mestiço* population, since, as Afonso d'E. Taunay reminds us in his monumental history of the *bandeiras*, the Portuguese, more addicted to long voyages than to journeys by land, preferred to keep to the coast. "The amalgamation of their qualities with those of the sons of Brazil was necessary in order for the real work of *bandeirismo* to be initiated."[29]

On the score of race all goes well when and as long as there is some coincidence between the traditional culture and the habitat. As soon as this equilibrium is upset, however, the race comes to an end, its civilizing vocation ends. Such, at any rate, is the rule that has prevailed until now with regard to all the types of immigration experienced in Brazil— whether Portuguese, German, North American, Swiss, Italian, Russian, Polish, or Japanese.

Were the ecological conditions favorable, exceptionally favorable, that the German immigrants encountered in Rio Grande do Sul, Santa Catarina, Paraná, and São Paulo? In São Paulo, Paraná, Santa Catarina, and Rio Grande do Sul, the German colonists have been working prodigies from the date of the arrival of the first settlers in 1824 at the Feitoria Velha, in the municipal jurisdiction of São Leopoldo, up to the present day. But weren't the ecological conditions that the Germans found in the state of Espírito Santo just as favorable? Despite the fact that it is a question of the same race, or rather, of a social group with the same cultural antecedents, they have not been able to do as much. Besides, even in Rio Grande do Sul the settlers have not been uniformly successful. The immigrants who, instead of settling along the valley of the Jacuí where now flourish, near Pôrto Alegre, the privileged municipalities of São Leopoldo, Santa Cruz, Novo Hamburgo, Taquara, Cachoeira, Lajeado, Estrêla, Montenegro, São Sebastião do Caí—to mention only a few—were sent on to Tôrres, where for lack of communications they were left marooned on terra firma together with a Portuguese-Brazilian colony long in decadence, would furnish material for a story, if one not so horrifying as that of the Germans in Ucayali, in any case a very sorry one.

And it is for these and other reasons that, just as we do not accept or recognize the inferiority of the Portuguese, we cannot accept the inferiority of this or that race without biological and anthropological proofs in hand.

Can such proofs be possible? Professor Wilton Marion Krogman, of the Department of Anthropology of the University of Pennsylvania, says no, and sums up the problem thus:

"There are no pure races; there are no superior or inferior races. We know through history that all peoples, on coming into contact with each other, cross their physical features on a genetic basis. We know from human anatomy that in fundamental structure all peoples are identical.

"As regards man as a biological being, what he is is connected with is his cultural environment rather than with any innate or inherited ability or aptitude. There is no Germanic race, but only a Germanic nationality; there is no Jewish race, but only a socio-religious community; there is no Aryan race, but only an Aryan tongue; there is no master race, but only a bombastic political tirade."[30]

In different terms the same thesis is maintained by Huxley and Haddon, for whom the distinctive qualities accentuated among the different nationalities "are far more cultural than physical," and "when physical, they are frequently influenced by climatic and cultural conditions."[31] On the other hand, in the present state of biological knowledge, it seems to them that, as far as the existence of correlation between psychological characters and races is concerned, there is no scientific proof whatever that such relations exist. It is the conclusion reached also by Otto Klineberg, professor of psychology in Columbia University: "Scientists do not recognize any relation between race and psychology."[32]

After all this testimony, are we still going to acknowledge that Brazilian customs of ethnic coexistence are biologically and socially wrong, and that the progress of the United States compared to the relative backwardness of Brazil and Latin America is the consequence of the Anglo-Saxon's having preserved his racial purity in America? Evidently, we no longer have to yield on this point. More than refusing to believe in dogmas of racial purity, we refuse to accept the interpretation of differences in civilization in the various countries on the unilateral basis of ethnic differences.

And it is because we think thus that today we are constituting an original civilization, or if not absolutely original, the first great effective experiment carried out in the West of fraternal, cordial, and Christian coexistence of all races.

In any case, one thing is certain: In explaining the differences between the United States and Brazil, or between the United States and Mexico, or the United States and Argentina, anthropogeography is much more useful than ethnography.

II

Ethics and Economics

1

HOWEVER IMPRESSIVE THE GEOPHYSICAL FACTORS MAY BE IN CLEARING up the problem or problems deriving from the differences between the North American and the Brazilian civilizations, such factors—orography, hydrography, geology, climate—for all their importance, are far from totally determining those differences. Nor could it be otherwise. And to admit the contrary would mean accepting man and his creations—progress, sicence, art, religion, philosophy, culture—as mere products or by-products of geography.

No, this is clearly not the position to take in facing the problem. Just as one should not accept any explanation of differences among civilizations and cultures that is based on racial inequality, so there is no reason to accept the physical interpretations of the same differences purely and simply on the basis of natural environment. Nor is man a subproduct of geography—if he were, he would always and invariably be a sculptor in regions rich in marble, and necessarily a mechanic and capable of developing an industrial civilization if located among coal mines or petroleum deposits, both of which propositions are yet to be demonstrated—nor is the history of civilizations and cultures, in short, world history, a mere prolongation of nature. Between *nature* and *history*, between *facts that repeat themselves* and *facts that succeed each other*, the difference is profound.

But if history is not merely a consequence of the behavior of the white race in defense of its own purity, as described by Gobineau, for whom the fatal approach of the end of civilization could be seen in the crossing of the pure races with degenerate human stock, if history is not merely a consequence of geography, as Ratzel suggested, what then can it be?

Can it be indefinite progress, as Spencer said? Or a simple march of peoples from the theological to the positive stage, by way of the metaphysical, as Auguste Comte declared? Or thesis, antithesis, and synthesis, as Hegel maintained? Or the product of the economic factor, as the Marxists swear with their hands upon Karl Marx's *Das Kapital?*

There was a time when positivism was the great fashion among us. Everything in history had to be viewed in terms of Comte's supposed Law of the Three Stages.

In the theological stage, societies are dominated by the clergy and the military. In the metaphysical stage, societies enter into conflict with the conservatives: this is the phase of libertarian struggles, the phase that culminates in the victory of the reformers. Finally, in the positive phase, society is no longer based upon the divine will, nor on that of the military leaders, nor on metaphysical disorder, but on a definite rhythm that has "order as its base and progress as its end."

In spite of the enthusiasm that positivism aroused in Brazil and in all Latin America, it did not take long to discover that humanity does not always obey that unilinear law of history. There were tribes and peoples that moved from the metaphysical to the positive stage without ever having gone through the theological stage, as there were others that leaped from the theological to the positive without passing through the metaphysical. And of the famous Comtean edifice, the laws of postivism, and the attempt to equate social phenomena with the phenomena of nature, not one stone was left upon another.

Not even Auguste Comte's famous classification of sciences, that had seemed to establish a definitive order and hierarchy in the processes of knowledge—in accord with the interdependence of phenomena, the more complex depending on the more simple—managed to endure. So long as it was a question of the physical sciences, from the simple to the complex—first, mathematics, then astronomy, then physics, then chemistry—things still went well. Where they became complicated was in the fatal leap from chemistry to biology, and from biology to sociology. As if the difference between biology and chemistry, or between biology and sociology, were the same in degree as that between physics and astronomy, or between astronomy and mathematics! As if it were possible to equate the forms of psychic and moral life to phenomena of nature and to study society, religion, or art as vegetable and animal organisms, and with methods borrowed from biology!

Thenceforth, obviously, adherence to the Comtean classification was no longer possible. Just as in biology there enters a new element called *life*, that has never entirely fitted into the laws of physics and chemistry, into sociology and history there enter elements that have never entered into mathematics and into nature: passions, will, intelligence, morality. And, as José Honório Rodrigues notes, interpreting the thought of Ernst Troeltsch, "exactness, clarity, logic, and calculability are properties of natural knowledge." "Mutability, creation, plenitude, and responsibility, drama, and personality belong to history."[1]

And away went the majestic conception of Auguste Comte!

Do the systematicians, the statisticians, the physicists, the mechanists, the causalists desist from trying to submit life to the mathematical and physical laws of cause and effect, or at least from attempting to capture integrally the rhythm of man's march over the face of the earth, in order to formulate the law capable of being adjusted to the old scientific aspiration of recognizing, in order to foresee, in order to forestall? They are not capable of it. Despite the warning of Aristotle that in certain domains of knowledge one should not seek greater certitude than those domains admit, it seem that there will never be an end to discoverers of laws that are mathematical in their precision, applicable to social and historical facts. The hour of Auguste Comte once past, next comes that of Karl Marx.

2

The fashion now, the great vogue, is Karl Marx, and the structure and superstructure based on the economic factor.

It is no longer ethnology or geography that governs social facts and explains the differences between civilizations and between cultures. Nowadays what directs, omnipotently, the rhythm of sociology is economics, the technique of production. Since history, according to Karl Marx, is chiefly the product of economic factors, it is around economics that social facts gravitate, and everything depends on the productive system prevailing in a given epoch. Political and social transformations, laws, religions, philosophies, institutions, the collective and individual consciousness, differences in culture and civilization—everything is born of reactions produced by the processes to which man is obliged to resort in exploiting nature.

Now everything is to be credited to the economic factor.

So the United States has progressed and prospered more than Brazil, in spite of being under a handicap of more than a century in time and with the disadvantage of a smaller continental territory? What a piece of news! The economic possibilities of her soil and subsoil have always been more solid. And, to simplify the problem, she had coal. The proof that the great difference, in its simplest expression, was coal and not race, lay in this: During the first two or three centuries, or rather, during the seventeenth, eighteenth, and nineteenth centuries, Brazil and the United States (disregarding the secondary aspects of the comparison) went forward almost in parallel lines, as far as civilization and progress were concerned. Were there cotton plantations in the English colonies of America? There were sugar mills in Brazil. There was an intense slave trade in the Anglo-Saxon colonies of America; the same thing occurred in the ports of Brazil. Was there opulent and elegant living on the plantations of the southern United States? On the sugar plantations of the Brazilian Northeast, of the fertile regions of Bahia and of the Rio de Janeiro plain, the way of life was in no way inferior. If differences existed, they were often favorable to Brazil. And when they were in favor of the United States they did not leap to the eye, they did not startle. This, despite the race, the climate, the mountain system, and the river system.

Suddenly, at a certain point in the nineteenth century, the United States enters upon a bewildering geometric progression of development, while Brazil drags along in a simple arithmetic progression. What happened? Did the Portuguese race become decadent through crossing with Indians and Negroes, while the Anglo-Saxons began to perfect their atavistic qualities thanks to their having resisted the darker races? Not at all.

According to the Marxists, there was just one explanation for the fact, the economic one. And the quintessence of this explanation was *Coal*.

It was still possible to counterbalance differences of soil and surface one way or another. In the subsoil, granted the near nonexistence of coal and the poor quality of what did exist, Brazil would be utterly beaten. What race, orography, hydrography, climate, and the other geophysical factors had been unable to do in two or even three centuries, coal would achieve in less than fifty years.

Before the steam engine, which unfortunately does not run on molasses from Brazil's sugar mills but principally on rich combustibles like coal, with a little good will one might say that Brazil in some degree kept up with the progress of the United States, or, dropping the good will, that the United States was advancing proportionately faster, but that the two progressions revealed, in their rhythm, at most a slight difference in arithmetic, never in geometric, ratio.

After the steam engine what happened is history: England, thanks to coal and iron, consolidated and expanded her empire in the nineteenth century; Germany ceased to be the field of passage for invading armies and became the most strongly important nation in continental Europe; the former American colonies (despite Thomas Jefferson and Benjamin Franklin, who wanted a rural, Rousseauan democracy), because coal was available in abundance and iron in addition to coal, the deposits of the one lying close to those of the other, rose almost instantaneously to the peak in international importance, becoming the center of attraction and the hope of the greatest human migrations in history.

During all this, Brazil has been outdoing herself ever since D. João VI in efforts to establish her heavy industry, her iron and steel production, her blast furnaces. Efforts useless from the start, considering her poverty of coal. Iron, Brazil has in abundance—she has the greatest iron reserves in the world—but, besides the fact that the iron is not near the coal, the coal is not very suitable for heavy industry. Moreover, this is the situation that obtains today. As the majority of Brazil's carboniferous lands are located at great distances from the present industrial centers, and the quality of the coal is inferior (yielding not more than 5000 calories per kilo while that of Cardiff or Pennsylvania develops 7000 to 8000), wood still represents 80 per cent of Brazil's sources of energy.

At the beginning of the industrial era, which was totally dependent on coal, since petroleum and waterpower were to come later, no nation poor in coal reserves could think of progressing in the same measure as countries like the United States, where coal was almost on the surface of the ground and within easy access to iron.

But—incredible coincidence—it is not only Brazil that struggles against the lack or the scarcity of coal in the industrial era. That is the fate of the majority, nay, the totality of the Latin countries: Portugal, Spain, Italy, and, to a certain degree, France.

The rule is this: Where there is no coal in abundance, civilizations, if they have not remained anchored to the past and to the feudal spirit— Italy, Portugal, Spain—have not been able to develop and prosper in the same tempo as the others. Poverty of coal in France, offset by proximity to and common borders with countries rich in coal, results in equilibrium between the feudal spirit and the industrial.

But where coal appears, and later petroleum, alongside iron, as a rule there appears an industrial civilization, an industrial mentality, with the consequent perfecting of science and the scientific mind: England, Germany, the United States, and more recently the Union of Soviet Socialist Republics.

In sum, for the Marxists, the differences between the American and the Brazilian civilizations depend not on race, nor solely on geography, but on the economic factors. Economic factors—principally coal[2]—are the real reasons for the growth of the United States in geometric progression and of Brazil in arithmetical. Race, religion, education, cultural quality of the migrations explain the differences only superficially. The essential differences were the predominant if not the exclusive function of the means of production; they varied according to His Majesty King Coal or His Majesty King Iron. Had coal mines or oil wells emerged at the proper instant in Brazil, on the surface of the ground and at random, in the implacable determinism which rules the phenomena of the universe there would be no backward racial or cultural spirit capable of holding her back.

In history what counts are the structures and superstructures based on the economic factor, but everything is an economic factor. The only concession to make on this score would be that already made by Karl Marx when he magnanimously consented to substitute, in the slogan "history evolves exclusively around economic factors," the word "predominantly" for "exclusively."

And now? Any doubt left after Karl Marx's rectification? To be sure, after Karl Marx no one will any longer think of interpreting social facts without bearing in mind his method of historical interpretation, one of the greatest contributions ever made to historiography and to sociology. As Troeltsch says,[3] in the same way that racial, political, religious, aesthetic, and geographic causalities were formerly recognized as belonging in the context out of which history rose, this new causality—the economic—is to be taken into account and accepted in its full significance, as much as the causality deriving from the class struggle, another discovery of Karl Marx the merit of which nobody will dream of contesting. From that, however, to concluding that the fundamental Marxist principle, giving preference always and invariably to the economic factor and to the class struggle over other factors, does not leave room for doubts, is quite another matter. Of course doubts always arise. And with doubts, impertinent questions. These, for example:

Was it entirely indifferent to the evolution of the two histories that Brazil had been peopled by Portuguese and the United States by Anglo-Saxons?

Was the march of the two civilizations not influenced by the circumstance that the first settlers in the United States had been Calvinist Protestants and the first settlers of Brazil Renaissance Catholics?

Have the economic factors had as much psychological importance in Latin America as they have in Anglo-Saxon America?

Are the categories of the capitalist society of the nineteenth century applicable to the historical processes of all times?

Did economic factors prevail in the Middle Ages in the same measure as they prevail in the present day?

3

The Middle Ages and economic factors! In the Middle Ages, as Max Weber[4] and R. H. Tawney[5] among others point out, to base a science of society upon the presumption that economic factors—the profit motive, property, usury, money-lending and the collection of interest—constitute a constant and measurable force to be accepted among other natural forces as an inevitable and self-evident datum would seem to the medieval thinker something irremediably immoral and irrational.[5] That is understandable. In the Middle Ages economic factors were completely subordinate to ethics, and to admit that one day economics would come to constitute an autonomous science, completely detached from and unconcerned with the moral aspects of life, was an enormity that would not occur to the most reckless pontiffs of progress. As everything was created to the greater glory of God, *ad maiorem Dei gloriam,* there was no great room for the cult of material values, except in the degree that these values contributed to that glory. "It is lawful," said St. Antoninus, "to desire temporal blessings, not putting them in the first place, as though setting up our rest in them, but regarding them as aids to blessedness, inasmuch as they support our corporal life and serve as the instruments for acts of virtue."[6] Religion at that time, says E. R. Adair,[7] was a living force, and its precepts guided man in all the steps of his life. "If one wishes to know the economic theories of the time, it is to the moralists, to the theologians, to the scholastic writers that he must turn." Architecture, painting, sculpture, philosophy, science, literature, family organization—all were oriented in one direction: *ad maiorem Dei gloriam.*

In architecture the maximum achievement of the Middle Ages was the Gothic cathedral, "the Bible in stone." In painting and sculpture the material and sensory values counted for absolutely nothing, or counted for very little. Their only themes of inspiration were God, the angels, the saints—and, for contrast, the sinners—the soul, and the mysteries of Creation, the Incarnation, the Redemption, the Passion, and Salvation. It was an art that admitted no compromise with the world of the senses and sensory reality. In it there was no place for the landscape, or for the portrait, or for individuals or things. No portraits, therefore, or interpretations of Nature through the imagination. Their end was not to entertain but to edify, to lead believers to prayer and to God.

To paint or carve, just as to contemplate medieval sculptures and paint-
ings, was the same as to pray.[8]

In literature likewise all inspiration came from the Bible. Motifs of
a secular nature were hardly tolerated. What was sought for reading was
the *Imitation of Christ* by Thomas à Kempis and the lives of the saints.
The medieval drama and theater were entirely at the service of the
Church's ideals; as in sculpture and painting, the sensory world was
simply ignored. In music, no compromise with the melodies that turn
the mind toward things of the earth and of the senses; but chanting, the
Ambrosian chants, the Gregorian chants, the *Kyrie Eleison*, the *Alleluia*,
the *Agnus Dei*, the *Gloria Pater*, the *Requiem*.[9]

As in art, so in everything. In philosophy, rather than the provisional
truths of reason, the eternal truths of revelation were sought. Today
revealed truth is admitted only to the degree that it finds support in the
arguments of reason. In the Middle Ages the truths of reason (which was
quite rightly considered a very precarious source of truths) were admitted
only to the degree that they did not clash with revealed truths.

And property, money, usury, accumulation of wealth, commerce, industry, money-lending and interest, and the other divinities of modern
capitalism—how were they regarded? With distrust and alarm.

Oh, the contrast between the Middle Ages and the contemporary
world in the manipulation of these values! The scruples with which the
scholastics, St. Thomas Aquinas at their head, approached each one of
these subjects!

As regards property, for example, the doctrine generally accepted was
that it was a necessary evil. Private property, they said, is an institution
which must be tolerated: men work harder and dispute less when goods
are private than when they are owned in common. But it should be tolerated only as a concession to human frailty. The ideal, if human nature
could rise so high, would be communism: *Communis enim usus omnium,
quae sunt in hoc mundo, omnibus hominibus esse debuit*. In any event,
private property must be legitimately acquired and distributed among the
greatest possible number of persons. It must also provide for the maintenance of the poor and, whenever possible, be held in common.[10]

How far we still are from Locke's doctrine, according to which "the
great and principal aim of men who unite themselves into a republic and
place themselves under a government is the preservation of property"!
And how distant we still are from the time when the slightest attempt to
establish cordial relations between economics and ethics will be regarded
as an intolerable provocation!

Was the Middle Ages perhaps less severe toward capital, commerce,
and profit, economic factors all-powerful in these days? In principle,
trade was considered to be the most perilous of activities: *Summe peri-*

culosa est venditionis et emptionis negotiatio. To St. Thomas Aquinas the state which most nearly approximated the ideal one would be that which had least need of merchants and which could satisfy its needs with the product of its own soil. It is obvious that commerce, then as now, constituted an unavoidable necessity. Never, however, did it succeed in winning public esteem nor in being regarded as a commendable occupation. On the contrary, trade was considered the most suspect of all activities: *Homo mercator, vix aut nunquam potest Deo placere.* The general desire was to suppress the intermediary between the producer and the consumer.[11]

The scholastics understood and applauded the work of the artisan and respected him even when he had to acquire things for a fixed price and sell them at a profit after transforming them. But the purely acquisitive appetite of the merchant, the stimulus of profit, a stimulus which in the view of modern thinkers is the mainspring of all human progress, was barely tolerated.

The artisan works for his own support; he seeks what is necessary and sufficient to sustain him and no more, while the merchant goes after *turpe lucrum.* Gratian makes the distinction between the two in this way: "Whoever buys a thing, not that he may sell it whole and unchanged, but that it may be a material for fashioning something, he is no merchant. But the man who buys it in order that he may gain by selling it again unchanged and as he bought it, that man is of the buyers and sellers who are cast forth from God's temple." The fact is, in accord with all scholastic definitions, that man who "buys in order that he may sell more dear," that is, the merchant, is being impelled by an inhuman preoccupation with his own pecuniary interest, a self-interest unmitigated by any tinge of public spirit or private charity. He converts what ought to be a means into an end, and his occupation, consequently, "is justly condemned, since, regarded in itself, it serves the lust of gain."[12]

Of course, in the eternal conflict between the ideal and the reality, commerce was maintained as a necessity. After all, how supply the deficiencies of a region by means of the available products of another without the collaboration of the middleman? But how many precautions, how many cares were necessary so that, from an essential activity deserving of a profit equivalent to the sum of work expended, and ultimately sufficient for the respectable maintenance of the merchant and his family, as well as the support of those on whose labor he depended, it should not turn into a sinful and abominable activity!

And how reconcile the conflict between commerce as an activity necessary to the subsistence of society and commerce as an activity perilous to the soul? Why, in the Marxist fashion. Profit was treated as a particular case of wage on condition that the merchant should seek gain, not as an end, but as the remuneration for his work. The medieval theorist condemned as a sin precisely that which modern society applauds most vehemently: the effort to obtain a continual and unlimited increase in material wealth. "He who has enough to satisfy his wants and nevertheless ceaselessly labors to acquire riches," comments a Schoolman of the fourteenth century, "either in order to obtain a higher social position or that subsequently he may have enough to live without labor, or that his sons may become men of wealth and importance—all such are incited by a damnable avarice, sensuality, or pride."[13]

And to think that when this doctrine was preached and universally accepted, the Western world was hardly two steps away from the doctrines of Calvin, according to whom the best way to be pleasing to God is to accumulate wealth!

The essence of medieval thought, in which Karl Marx found inspiration for the elaboration of his theory of the *just value,* was the just price, in which payment could properly be charged by the artisan who makes things, or by the merchant who transports them, since both work according to their capacity and serve common needs. The unforgivable sin is that of speculating or that of the middleman who takes advantage of public needs to augment his private gain. "He who buys corn, meat and wine in order to raise their price," Tritemius declaims, as if he were presenting a general denunciation to the Central Committee on Prices, "and to accumulate money at the expense of others, is, according to the law of the Church, no better than a common criminal. In a well governed community every arbitrary rise in prices of foodstuffs or of articles of clothing is peremptorily prohibited; in times of scarcity the merchants who hold stocks of such articles can be compelled to sell them at a just price, since it should be the care of every community that all its members be looked after, and not that a small number be permitted to grow rich and waste wealth on luxury, to the detriment and prejudice of the majority."[14]

Ugly as was the sin of "filthy lucre," there was another still more censurable: It was the impious sin of usury, that is, the sin of charging interest for the formation and accumulation of capital. Here the theorists of the Middle Ages were implacable. They put usury in the same rank as adultery and fornication. Monsters of iniquity—that is how moneylenders for interest were regarded before Calvin appeared on the plane of history.

According to St. Thomas Aquinas, to receive usury is contrary to Scripture, contrary to Aristotle, contrary to nature, because it means to receive without work; it is selling *time,* which belongs to God, for the advantage of evil; it is robbing those who use the money loaned and on whom the benefits should devolve, since it is they who make the money beneficial. "The word comes from *usus;* usury sets a price on the loan of money and sells the use of the money which is loaned."[15] It is unjust in itself, because the benefit of the money to the borrower cannot exceed the value of the principal sum lent to him; it is a defiance of juridical principles, since, when a loan is made, the ownership of the thing lent passes to the borrower, and what right has the creditor to charge payment to a man who is now simply using that which is his? "To lend money upon usury is a grave sin, not because it is prohibited; rather it is prohibited because it is against natural justice."[16] *Pecunia pecuniam non parit.*

It is not entirely impertinent to the judging of the medieval attitude toward economic factors that this doctrine comes precisely from the Dominican Thomas Aquinas and not from some Augustinian thinker. Coming from the Augustinians, the condemnation would not have the same force, since they have always been against *matter*, against the *senses*. Platonic and not Aristotelian, their historical tendency was to deny Nature. With Thomas Aquinas it was different. Not opposing transcendentalism, he claimed for reason the right to nourish itself on the testimony of the senses in the world of matter. For him Nature was no illusion but a reality, and a reality of which reason took cognizance only through the senses.

It is the Angelic Doctor, then, the philosopher who resets Christianity in its point of origin, and who preaches the possibility of attaining to God by the earthly paths of the senses and of well-informed reason, who shows himself most unyielding on the necessity of controlling the economic factors!

Vehemence against usury is not peculiar to Thomas Aquinas. The Schoolmen in general, in Italy as in Germany, in France as in England, manifested their opinions in like fashion. Innocent IV, who cannot be termed an ideologist, since in truth he was a hardened realist, was against usury because he feared that "men would not give thought to the cultivation of their land except when they could do nought else, and so there would be so great a famine that all the poor would die of hunger; for even if they could get land to cultivate, they would not be able to get the beasts and the implements for cultivating it, since the poor themselves would not have them, and the rich, for the sake both of profit and of security, would put their money into usury rather than into minor and more risky investments."[17]

After that, are we still going to admit in any absolute way that historic events—all historic events without any exception at all—have always and invariably been determined by economic factors, and that it is not man's conscience that conditions his way of being, but rather his social way of being—his conditioning to the means of production—that determines his individual conscience?

After that, are we still going to talk about "predominance" of the economic factors in the Middle Ages with the same nonchalance with which we speak of "predominance" of the economic factors in the present day, or accept the idea that history evolves "predominantly" about these factors? Why "predominantly"? Can it be possible to subject the so-called forces of social physics to dosages or to a system of weights and measures? Can there be any possibility of reducing them to a common denominator in order to compare them with one another? No. In this case one cannot speak of "exclusiveness" or of "predominance," for the science of exact classification of social factors is yet to appear.

Impossible, therefore, to endorse the mechanistic, or the geophysical, or the economic interpretations of history. History is life, and life has, rather than causes, an origin, a past. Past, present, and future. The error of materialistic and physical interpretations of history lies in ignoring the distinctions between origin and cause, and in transferring, by simple analogy or association of ideas or images, the mechanistic language of *cause and effect*, valid in the physical and inorganic world, to the world into which enters the new, unpredictable, and uncontrollable element that is called *life*, without taking into account the distinctions between the various kinds of cause. And where there is life there is no exhausting knowledge and its causes.

Where there is life—it is well to repeat—there is no unilateral causality, but concomitant causes and a past. That is why social facts, actions, and human reactions will never be sufficiently understood without having recourse to their historical antecedents, as the thinkers of the Middle Ages did, by the way; to explain any fact they would always go back to the first days of the Creation. "In the beginning was the Word." It is in history, in the background of ages and not on the surface of current appearances, that the secrets of their origin and structure are hidden. And the more one delves into their antecedents the better, for just as facts which repeat themselves belong to Nature, facts which succeed each other belong to history.[18]

4

This being well established, let us take up once more, by way of example, the facts that are already thoroughly known to us: social wealth in the United States and social poverty in Brazil; racial discrimination and racial segregation in the United States and absence of discrimination in Brazil.

Can it be granted that the religious past of the two countries—the religious factor—has had nothing to do with either of them? In other words, can it be assumed that Protestantism has nothing to do with the advent of capitalism and racial discrimination? Can the simultaneous appearance of Protestantism, of capitalism, and of racial discrimination have been sheer coincidence?

The conclusion derived from history seems to be another and very different one. From history one concludes without exaggeration that without Protestantism—or better, without Calvinism—there would be neither racial discrimination nor capitalism. Or could the medieval and Greco-Roman civilizations from which ours proceeds have been racist and capitalistic? Not at all. The contrary seems to be true. If it is certain that the Greeks, on the one hand, considered as barbarians all foreigners in general and the peoples whose customs, language, habits, and traditions they did not succeed in penetrating, it is no less sure that they never erected a barrier to the incorporation of social groups of other origins on a footing of equality with them. From the moment these barbarians assimilated Greek culture, they ceased to be barbarians and were considered Greeks.

The Romans did nothing more than follow the Greek tradition.

As for the Middle Ages, it is evident that, instead of tending toward racial discrimination, the period contributed rather, through Christianity, to real brotherhood and to perfect racial tolerance. In the Middle Ages there was, properly speaking, no dividing line between Latin and Teutonic peoples. It was an epoch in which discrimination on racial grounds simply did not exist.

Such discrimination came about, just as capitalism and nationalism did, doctrinally at least, with the Reformation. If it was not the Reformation that instituted them, everything seems to indicate that it was Protestantism, and particularly Calvinism, that gave them theoretical stratification. As though to confirm the assertion, there are two quite expressive facts: the majority, the great majority, the near-unanimity, of the theorists of racism—Chamberlain, Woltmann, Wagner, Gunther, Wilhelm II, Madison, Stoddart, Grant, Rosenberg, Spengler, Cox—like the great majority of economists—Locke, Malthus, Adam Smith, Ricardo, Karl Marx, Keynes—when they are not Protestants, arise in cultures impregnated with Protestantism.[19] The theorists of the principles of nationalities and of capitalism—these are invariably Protestants. Protestants or Jews. They are the ones who, by opposing nationalism to universalism, also establish the divide between medieval economics and modern economics.

ETHICS AND ECONOMICS   61

Does this mean that Catholicism is absolutely incompatible with capitalism and the principle of nationalities or even racial discrimination? Doctrinally, yes. To declare, however, that it was incompatible in actual practice also, it would be necessary on the one hand to ignore the fact that it was under Richelieu and Catholic France that the principle of nationalities received its great impetus, and to forget the high commercial importance of Antwerp and Florence and Venice on the threshold of modern times, the wealth of the Catholic bankers of Germany and Italy—the Fuggers, the Welsers, the Marchionnis—and many of the capitalistic practices of the Church, among them the sale of indulgences, and the loans on security in the form of real estate, and the collection of interest practiced by certain orders; and, on the other hand, to ignore deliberately the slave trade carried on by Portuguese Catholics long before the Reformation. Although the principle of nationality, and that of the consolidation of the State under its aegis, never turned out well in countries uncontaminated by Protestantism, the generalization would be excessive. And, although the Church's practices in the economic domain lacked the spirit of capitalism while assuming capitalistic forms, since in spirit capitalism is absolutely incompatible with chapellany and corporations of mortmain type and other institutions which govern ecclesiastic properties, the conclusion will have to be more modest. It is summed up in recognizing that there is more doctrinal compatibility between Protestantism and nationalism, or between Protestantism and capitalism, than between capitalism and Catholicism, or between Catholicism and nationalism.[20]

In fact, Catholicism and capitalism are mutually repellent, *ils hurlent de se trouver ensemble.* And yet between Protestantism and capitalism the affinity is perfect, as is also the affinity between Protestantism and nationalism.

In the Catholic countries, strictly speaking, there is no racist nationalism.[21] At most there may be provincialism, as is the case with Spain and Italy, and to some extent with Portugal, where superior minds like Oliveira Martins and Antero de Quental, in spite of strong Portuguese nationalism, adopted the cause of unification of the Peninsular peoples. At most there may be an appearance of racism when social groups, isolated among Protestant countries, retreat into themselves, as in the typical example of French Canada, which repeats in the New World the no less typical examples of Ireland and Poland. In Poland, Ireland, and French Canada, so-called nationalism has nothing to do with defense of race, for it results from the defense of religion and tradition.

For that matter, the continued association of nationalism with the other forces of attack on feudalism, on the old order of the Church and State, and with the forces aiding the rise of the bourgeoisie, constantly indicates where the most genuine sources from which it springs may be found. Another indication of the origins of nationalism is the origin of the word *race*. This passed from the Hebrew into the Western tongues only in the sixteenth century, the first century of Protestantism, precisely the one which was to mark the separation between the Catholic and the Calvinist concepts.

Ah, the differences between the Catholic and the Calvinist concepts!

Was the Church against profit, and did it consider as reprehensible all economic interest that exceeded what was necessary for subsistence, stigmatizing the middleman and the usurer as parasites? The Reformation would rehabilitate trade and *turpe lucrum* by placing them on the same level of respectability as the worker's wage and the landed proprietor's income. "What reason is there," asks Calvin, "why the income from business should not be larger than that from land-owning? Whence do the merchant's profits come, except from his own diligence and industry?"

Did the Schoolmen regard the profit motive as suspect and distrust the capitalist and the usurer as someone who necessarily grew rich at the expense of his fellow man's misfortunes? Calvin applauds the profit motive and sees in economic virtues the true virtues. He is not against the accumulation of wealth but against its evil use for ostentation; against relaxation and the distribution of alms. His ideal is the man who seeks wealth with the sober gravity of one who is disciplining his character and performing a service pleasing to God.

For him interest is perfectly legitimate: From the loan the lender ought to derive as much profit as the borrower, for one should not gain to the detriment of the other. There is only one case in which the loan should be free: when made to the poor.

In truth, though, this loan to the poor without interest is a dead letter in Calvinism, in view of the vehemence with which Calvin excoriates charity and poverty. In this Calvin is a perfect banker: he only lends to him who really does not need it.

The horror he has of the poor! Poverty to him is a sign of damnation.

Woe to St. Francis of Assisi if he tried to make poverty the keystone of his order in a society governed by the reformer of Geneva! Calvin, the supreme pontiff of the "uprising of the rich against the poor," of the strong against the weak, of the pure against the sinners, is furiously against the poor man. Few things so exacerbate this constantly exacerbated man, this man in a permanent state of moral indignation where poverty is concerned. He sees in poverty something intrinsically unhealthy, an invariable sign of idleness. And how he inveighs against almsgiving! He condemns it vehemently in nearly all circumstances. The idleness of the mendicant was at once a sin against God and a social evil, and should be repressed as violently as gambling, blasphemy, and excesses in eating and drinking. Houses should be searched by censors of the community so that they might not give shelter to vagabonds and travelers. In his war on the poor he does not distinguish between moral and economic reasons.

The Schoolmen see in the contemplatives the real men of action, because while the so-called men of action think of building their houses, the contemplatives, that is, the prophets, seek to construct better worlds. Calvin distrusts the men of pure thought and considers all work not requiring great physical effort as something possibly influenced by the devil. Only the man who labors is agreeable to him. For him, only labor "makes the body hale and strong and cures the sicknesses induced by idleness. . . . In the things of this life the laborer is most like to God."[22]

God is to be glorified not only through prayer but above all through labor, through action. Because Calvinism, in spite of repudiating merit— since salvation comes to man, paradoxically, not because he contributes to it, but by an objective determination of the Supreme Power—is all for the sanctification of work and initiative. Work and good deeds, not being the way to attain salvation, are indispensable as a basis and proof that salvation has been attained, and in this lies the secret of all the success of Calvin's fatalism in opposition to Oriental fatalism. In Oriental fatalism ataraxia, immobility, is the supreme good. In the Calvinist predestination God signifies divine election with the rewards that He grants to work, whether in terms of success or in terms of wealth. Now, as no one likes to admit that he is damned, the quest for the proof of election becomes general in an acceleration of work and pursuit of riches such as the world has never known before.

In Catholicism does one need a good moral basis for doing something in the business world? On the contrary, it is in Calvinism, in order not to be bound to the world of business and action that leads to wealth, that the good moral basis becomes necessary. In Calvinism it is the practical action that is blessed, not contemplation. Among Calvinists, to be unoccupied is equivalent to provoking sanctions and states of guilt.

And what of the philosopher, the artist, the thinker? Calvin suspects everything that is not practical and productive of more or less immediate results and that does not require great physical effort. Philosophic and artistic elaboration demands too many periods of pure contemplation and therefore of physical inaction, not to be suspect to him. As in the case of poverty, the moral motives and reasons for such a state of spiritual receptivity do not interst him. What does interest him is whatever leads to the accumulation of wealth or to tangible results.

According to the Church, each man is free to choose between good and evil, to be judged at the last according to his works, since, as Don

Quixote said—that Catholic knight-errant—"Every man is the son of hi
own works." According to Calvin there is no such thing. God choose
His own preferred ones completely without regard to their works and
their human merits. Some men come predestined to salvation. They are
the elect. The rest are consigned to eternal damnation "by a just and
irreproachable, though incomprehensible, judgment." In Calvin's view,
"if we are not really ashamed of the Gospel, we have necessarily to
recognize what is plainly stated therein: that God, through His eternal
good will (for which there is no other cause than His own intention),
has named those who please Him for salvation, rejecting all the rest."[23]
In other words, universal brotherhood is impossible. "Those who believe
in the Kingdom of God as something to be realized fully in a coming
period of social justice and intellectual truth," comments Paul Tillich,
"may never leave the Protestant Church, but they are not Protestants in
the true meaning of the term."[24] For the Calvinist Protestant, brotherhood is unrealizable because the world has always been divided between
the *elect* and the *damned*, between the *pure* and the *sinners*, the elect
and pure being the ones charged with discovering the signs of damnation
and segregating or eliminating the damned.

From that to justification and acceptance, as natural facts, of economic
inequality, of the doctrine of the inequality of races, and later, to the
acceptance of dark forces more powerful than will and reason (Freudian-
ism), and to the concept of class struggle in which the strongest triumphs (Hobbes, Darwin, Nietzsche, Marx), in contrast to the Catholic
and precapitalistic belief in the possibility of universal brotherhood and
social justice under the aegis of the Church, the passage will be rapid.
And there will never more be any lack of historians, sociologists, and
poets to look at wars and the killing of Indians not only as inevitable
fatalities but as mandates of Divine Providence, or of the determinism
that traces "manifest destinies" for peoples, in the sense that the
strongest and fittest triumph. And there to prove it are Rudyard Kipling's
The White Man's Burden, evidently inspired by the forty-ninth chapter
of the Book of Isaiah, or Madison Grant's *The Passing of the Great
Race*. Both acclaim the race chosen to govern the world.

What is going to be lacking thenceforth, and greatly lacking, is belief
in the magical virtues of the *agape* of the Greeks, in the *caritas* of the
Latins, and in the evangelical virtues of Christian love. And it was inevitable that it should be so, and the explanation therefor we are going
to find not only in the structure of capitalism but in the very structure of
Protestantism itself. "It is a shortcoming of Protestantism," says Paul
Tillich, without doubt one of the foremost spokesmen of Protestant
thought today, "that it never has sufficiently described the place of love
in the whole of Christianity. This is due to the genesis and history of

Protestantism. The Reformation had to fight against the partly magical, partly moralistic, partly relativistic distortion of the idea of love in later Catholicism. But this fight was only a consequence of Luther's fight against the Catholic doctrine of faith. And so faith and not love occupied the center of Protestant thought. While Zwingli and Calvin, by their humanistic-Biblical stress on the function of the law, were prevented from developing a doctrine of love, Luther's doctrine of love and wrath of God and the government) prevented him from connecting love with law and justice. The result was puritanism without love in the Calvinist countries and romanticism without justice in the Lutheran countries."[25]

And, obviously, racial discrimination, nationalism, and capitalism, both in the Calvinist countries and the Lutheran.

5

In the face of this, can it be that we still have the right to affirm that religious factors do not really enter into the concomitant causes which stimulated two different historical rhythms for Brazil and the United States? Or that the advent of Protestantism, as previously that of Christianity, is a mere superstructure built upon economic factors? Or is it rather that it is not economic but religious factors that govern history, since it was Protestantism and above all Calvinism that, by modifying the scholastic concepts of property, money, labor, and usury, made possible the advent of capitalism?

Neither the one nor the other. And no conceding of morganatic rights to either group of causes. As Troeltsch says, "causality knows no hierarchies." If on the one hand the Marxist method of interpreting social facts, no matter how much it heightened the understanding of history, cannot be accepted in its totality, for the same reason that biological or geographical, political, and anthropological causation cannot be accepted unilaterally, on the other there is no reason to have recourse only to religious causation, for this would mean, as Max Weber—the true systematizer of the connections between the spirit of capitalism and that of Protestantism—declares, to substitute one unilaterality for another.

It is as wrong to say that capitalism is a predominant or exclusive gift of coal as it is to affirm that it is a predominant gift of Protestantism, or even of both. With all the taste for wealth and all the acquisitive appe-

tite which Puritanism may have infused into the settlers of North Amer
ica, if the latter had not found coal they could never have promoted the
progress of the United States in the way they did. With all the coal of
the earth at their disposal, they would never have developed the indus
trial-capitalist civilization they did, if religion and cultural factors had
not prepared them for it or if the spirit of Protestantism had not joined
with the spirit of capitalism. And with all the coal of the earth added
to Protestantism and to the acquisitive appetite, they would never have
achieved the civilization they did if geography, biology, ecology, and
hydrography, in one way or another, had not cooperated for that result.

The same can be said with respect to racial discrimination. It is beyond
doubt that religion will do much to explain—never exhaustively, however—the attitudes of Portuguese and Anglo-Saxons toward the problem
of the native populations and other racial matters.

By definition, social facts are inexhaustible. Even if the geographer
empties a vital fact of its geographic content, the anthropologist of its
ethnic content, the biologist of its life content, the economist of its economic content, the psychologist of its emotional content, the theologian
of its charismatic content, the philosopher of its metaphysical or theological content—before this fact, impregnated with life, will, and passion,
we shall continue to be throughout all time in the presence of a mystery
never entirely solvable, or rather, to use here the language of St. Thomas
Aquinas, in the presence of an indefinitely perfectible truth. This fact,
starting from a certain point, will belong more to history than to geography, anthropology, or economics. And outside of history there will be no
understanding it either totally or partially.

Just as to understand the evolution of capitalism it has been necessary
to go back at least to the sixteenth century, when the maritime discoveries and Protestantism made its advent possible, so to understand the
exact origin of the position of Brazilians and North Americans—principally that of the Brazilians—in the face of the racial problem we shall
have to go back a little further.

The origin of the discrimination practiced by the Anglo-Saxons could
still be localized in the social frame of the sixteenth century, when the
colonial expansion of the Protestant peoples began. But the origin of the
behavior of the Portuguese in their contact with other races is more
ancient. It goes back, at the least, to the eighth century.

6

Indeed, the history of Brazil's present position in regard to the racial problem began perhaps when the Moors invaded the Iberian Peninsula to establish themselves there as masters for nearly eight centuries. Eight centuries! That is to say: Portuguese civilization matured, not in the presumption of the superiority of the white over the other races, but in the actual, present knowledge of a superior civilization created by a race of darker pigmentation. For eight centuries the lords and masters were the Moslems and not the Christians, the dark and not the blonds, the Moors and not the Celts.

On this basis, clearly, the Lusitanians could not nourish preconceptions of racial superiority in relation to the Moor. They probably felt hatred for him, a tribal, political, and religious hatred; they must have fought him without truce, as always, earlier, they had fought the Romans and would later fight the Spaniards; nevertheless, nothing of that was to prevent them from ending by recognizing, and even accepting in the course of time, the facts of his culture. Furthermore, the great number of words of Arabic origin in the Portuguese language still bears witness to the incorporation of the Moorish culture into the Portuguese, just as do some of the most persistent Portuguese motifs brought to Brazil, among which that of the Moorish princess is certainly not the least significant. This, not to mention the polygamous ideal and reality, so common in patriarchal Brazil and so in conflict with the Christian concept of monogamy.[26]

Now, it is well to note that a people thus psychologically prepared in the cult of Moorish beauty, if not in that of relative tolerance toward polygamy in fact, would not be at all adversely impressed with the Amerindian woman, nor would it have the same scruples as the Anglo-Saxon had about entering into contact with her. On the contrary, to judge by the colonial chroniclers, the impression produced in the first two centuries by the Indian women was excellent. From Pero Vaz de Caminha to Father João Daniel in the eighteenth century, who found the native women of "most lovely features" and "so gracefully nimble and lively" that "they could rival the choicest white women," there is no lack of travelers enthusiastic about the beauty and the exciting innocence of the Amerindian women.

Add to this the fact that the navigators and the first white settlers came alone, unaccompanied by women of their own race, leaving behind their fatherland, their families, and, therefore, their inhibitions of a tribal order, and it will be immediately understood that in the presence of the native and, later, of the African women they would not comport themselves exactly in the fashion of the Puritans of the *Mayflower*. Nor in the manner of the Jesuits, who appalled the Indians by repulsing the offer of their women and of the most beauteous damsels of the tribes to nestle in their hammocks.

They would comport themselves, rather, in the manner described by Camoens in Canto IX of *The Lusiads* which, together with the other romanticizations of a supposed happy and perfect life, free of all guilt, among the savages of Brazil, probably contributed in no small measure to the Utopian idea that, through Montaigne and Raynal, aided Rousseau in composing his *Social Contract*.[27]

All in all, historical circumstances favored the natural process of racial mixture in Brazil.

"On the part of the Indian women, hybridization is explained by their ambition to have children belonging to the white race, for according to the ideas current among them, relationship counted only on the paternal side." "On the part of the foreigners, the scarcity if not the absence of women of their own blood must have influenced them above all else."[28]

The same did not occur in the historical development of the United States. There, on the contrary, historical circumstances, if they did not encourage discrimination, offered no positive incentive to racial tolerance and to the fusing of races.

On one hand, Great Britain never experienced, as did the Iberian Peninsula, conquest and occupation by peoples of darker skins. The Normans were white, as were other invaders as far back as the Romans of Caesar's legions who conquered and subjected her to the dominion of Rome.

On the other hand, the Anglo-Saxons had no contact with more advanced civilizations developed by darker peoples. The first time that the Anglo-Saxon came into contact with such peoples was on his arrival in the New World. Besides not finding on this side of the Atlantic a civilization superior to his own, but only nomadic tribes in a most backward stage of culture, many of them still in the Stone Age, the Anglo-Saxon came accompanied by his wife and children and community, which was to reduce greatly the Dionysian impulse that might impel him toward the Indian woman and later the African slave woman.

Given these circumstances, and even without taking into account that the first settlers of North America were fervently Puritan, and when not Puritan, Protestant, it will be understood that historically the attitude of the American people in relation to the problem of the white's crossing with the Indian, and subsequently with the black, could not be identical with that of the Portuguese. Both were to react to the presence of other races according to the peculiarities of their historical and cultural heritages.

For the colonizer of Brazil, a man of the pre-Counter Reformation Renaissance, life had ceased to be a succession of duties to fulfil; now it was a right, and almost only a right. For the colonizer of the United States, a man of the Reformation, life was duty and almost only duty. The former separated himself from his people, from his community, to live by the law of the strongest and the luckiest. The latter transported himself with his people to live in community fashion. And woe to him or them if they do not do so: the sanctions will be terrible. In 1645 the Puritan Hugh Peters gave some idea, in a sermon delivered before Parliament in London, at a gathering of theologians, of what New England was on the score of virtue: "I have been living in a land where in seven years I have never met a beggar, nor heard a blasphemy, nor seen a single drunkard." Dealings between men and women were permitted, but when this happened the Talmud must be respected: "Have you business with women? Try to see that you are not left alone with them."

For the colonizer of Brazil, a man of the Renaissance, woman is an object of prey. For the Puritan, a man of the Reformation, woman is his companion in work, welded like himself to the duty of earning her bread by the sweat of her brow. In the struggle against the Indians, in the clearing of the forest, in the building of the cabin, in the march toward the West, in the battle of the soil and the field, you will always find her beside him.

Consequently, it was not to be expected that Captain John Smith, that famous John Smith who appears on the threshold of United States history, should react in the same way as Diogo Álvares, the celebrated "Caramuru," when confronted with the native princesses of the Amerindian forests.

Nothing is more appropriate, then, to illustrate the behavior of the Portuguese and that of the Ango-Saxon when the Amerindian is concerned than the legendary stories of Diogo Álvares and John Smith, the former coming from a tradition that included the Moorish occupation and the latter from a purely Aryan tradition.

7

As is well known and fitting to recall, Diogo Álvares was shipwrecked on the coast of Bahia in 1510; his companions either perished by drowning or were barbarously slaughtered by the Tupinambás; he succeeded in saving himself thanks to the musket and keg of powder that he had taken with him on his raft; and he came to inspire a great love in the princess Paraguassú. The opportunity presenting itself, he made good use of the powder and the musket by bringing down a bird with one shot. Thenceforth to the tribe he was to be Caramuru ("the man of fire" or "the dragon from the sea"), a name with which he would live on through time and the ages.

From a prisoner he was to become a great personage; he would lead the Tupinambás in war against the Tapuia tribe, whom he would conquer without bloodshed because of the fame of his musket, and he would then marry Paraguassú.

Years later a French ship enters the port of Bahia. Diogo Álvares decides to see his native land once more, and takes with him, besides a great cargo of wood, his inseparable Paraguassú. Arrived in France, Paraguassú, the first Indian woman ever seen on French soil, makes a tremendous success. And it is in France that she is baptized with the Catholic name of Catarina, whether in homage to Catherine of Navarre, Queen of France, or to Catherine of Aragon, Queen of Portugal, is not definitely known.

Later, then, Diogo Álvares and Catarina, or rather, Caramurú and Paraguassú, return to Bahia, settling down patriarchally for the remainder of their long and worthy lives in the place called Vila Velha, the seat and origin of the most ancient and certainly one of the most noble Brazilian families.

This, in summary, is the story of Diogo Álvares and Paraguassú.

The legend of Captain John Smith and the princess Pocahontas is more elaborate.

In 1607 three ships from England entered Chesapeake Bay. They were bringing people to establish the colony of Jamestown. In one of these ships was the famous Captain John Smith. As leader of a squad of soldiers in search of food, he was later captured by Indians in an ambuscade, while he was exploring the Chickahominy River.

Smith, availing himself of the knowledge he had gained of the forest-dwellers' language, attempts to bedazzle the chief in order to gain time. He shows him a compass, refers to the North Pole and the rotation of the earth, the eclipses of the sun and the moon. All in vain.

The crucial moment having come, after having listened at length to the prisoner, the chief gives the orders to begin the ritual of execution.

Smith's head is already lying on the stone block; the executioners are making ready their war clubs to be brandished over the prisoner's dolichocephalic skull; the warriors are already tasting in anticipation the feast that is to follow the white warrior's death; when behold, Pocahontas, the chief's young and beautiful daughter, leaps into the middle of the clearing, embraces the condemned man and saves his life, since among the redskins the princesses had the right to claim for themselves the lives of prisoners.

Thereafter one cannot count the times that Pocahontas intervenes in behalf of the bold John Smith. For his sake she would do anything, even become a Christian.

When the colonists in Jamestown are on the verge of starvation, Pocahontas emerges from the depths of the forest leading a file of warriors carrying great baskets of corn, venison, and wild turkeys. And week after week the scene is repeated, Pocahontas going each time to prostrate herself at the feet of her white god.

Is a confederation of tribes formed to drive out the whites? Pocahontas runs several miles in the dark of night to denounce the plot to John Smith.

Does Smith marry Pocahontas? By no means. The romance between the two is abruptly cut short by Smith's return to England, where he goes to be treated for burns suffered in the explosion of a powder magazine.

The substantial difference between the two stories: The Brazilian case ends in marriage between the white man and the Indian woman; in the American case the marriage is made impossible by the departure of the white man for England.

There is another difference. The adventure of Diogo Álvares and Paraguassú has never been seriously contested, while that of John Smith and Pocahontas, according to the *Encyclopedia Britannica*, under the entry "Pocahontas," seems to have been nothing more than a myth. ". . . It is to be feared that the temptation to bring her on the stage as heroine in a new character in connection with Smith, ever the hero of his own chronicles, was more than he or the publishers of the *Generall Historie* could withstand."

Whichever it may have been, fable or truth, inspired or not by the tale told by Juan Ortiz to the Knight of Elvas, as Marjorie Stoneman Douglas thinks,[29] the John Smith-Pocahontas legend has one undeniable merit. It translates symbolically the racial attitude, or rather the Anglo-Saxon cultural attitude, toward the problem of the relations between whites and Indians.

Just as Diogo Álvares is very Catholic and Portuguese in marrying Paraguassú, John Smith, by not marrying Pocahontas, is very Anglo-Saxon and Protestant, perhaps more Protestant than Anglo-Saxon. While the latter has not yet freed himself from the preconception of the Western destiny of man and history, the former has already matured to the concept of the universal destiny of both.

That Pocahontas should fall madly in love with John Smith was right and romantic. That she should aid him in all circumstances and be devoted and faithful to him was very right. This is exactly what the racists expect of native princesses and of the so-called inferior races in their relations with the Anglo-Saxons. But they would never have forgiven John Smith's union or marriage with Pocahontas. They would not have forgiven him then; perhaps they would not pardon him now. Although the position of the North American with regard to having Indian blood in his veins may have evolved in seven-league strides—look at the number of American families that claim, with a touch of romanticism, that they descend from Pocahontas through the subsequent marriage of the princess with a less important colonist—the resistance is still quite pronounced.

Marriage of a white man with an Indian woman, or a half-breed or native woman, as it came to be recommended by Portuguese legislation for Brazil? Preposterous! Let Hollywood and Broadway testify to it. At the end of exotic stories, for box-office success, either the native woman sacrifices herself by casting herself into the crater of a volcano, or the white man does not realize the passion he has loosed, as in the case of *Madame Butterfly*. To marry the white man to an Indian or any native woman, failing to follow literally the model bequeathed by John Smith, simply can not be, even in fiction, for everyone fully recognizes what it means in the United States to defy the form established by the community.

8

The community! Here, along with the religious, political, and economic factors, is one of the motives for difference between the behavior of Anglo-Saxons and that of the Portuguese with Indian, half-breed, and Negro women, a factor that must be taken into account.

Had the Portuguese set out from the start with their families in an organized community, it is reasonable to suppose that, in spite of their background of Moorish occupation, in spite of the relative absence of preconceptions of racial superiority where darker pigmentation is concerned, they would have left Indian and Negro women alone, as did happen, for that matter, with the Portuguese from the Azores who immigrated in couples into Rio Grande do Sul, and with the Portuguese emigrants who went to Lourenço Marques under the same conditions. In the latter case their conduct vis-à-vis the Africans is, in certain aspects, as discriminatory as that of the Anglo-Saxon in the British colonies of Africa.

As a matter of fact, it was not every Portuguese who, in the absence of family or community, did not discriminate against the Indian or the Negro. A northern Portuguese—for example, Jerônimo de Albuquerque —for the very reason that the Moorish occupation was less felt in the north of Portugal, resisted marriage with Indian and Negro women. Or if he did sometimes marry an Indian, in any case he never married a Negro woman.

Marriage between white man and Negro woman, legal marriage at church and altar, never took place in the early days of Lusitano-Brazilian civilization.

In Brazil only the Indian woman was idealized as an extension of the Moorish, and the proof of this is the Indianist literature of the eighteenth and nineteenth centuries. Moreover, a reminiscence of that cultural attitude of the Lusitano-Brazilians is to be found in the fact that even today the descendants of white and Negro prefer the classification of *caboclo*, which means a person of white blood crossed with Indian, to that of "mulatto," which is the scientifically correct one for them.

This is easily understood: the idealization of the mulatto woman is a very much later phenomenon, as is also the cultural movement to revaluate and rehabilitate the Afro-Brazilian formation.

Summing up: In the first centuries the Portuguese offers tribal resistance to any crossing of blood; with the Moorish occupation was to come, on the one hand, the idealization of the Moorish woman, and on the other, through the effect of unconscious moral saturation, tolerance toward Arab polygamy and the idea of the slave woman as an instrument of pleasure.

It was written, therefore, that when no more Indian women could be found to prey upon, or even when there was no longer time for it, thanks to the relative social stability of the populated communities, and when immigration to the lands of Santa Cruz continued to be almost exclusively masculine, the turn of the African slave women would come, the chance for transitory unions, for concubinage, for lust, lasciviousness, and shamelessness, with all the devastating repercussions they had upon the emotions and character of the nation.

Apparently, it is not only in the light of religion that racial tolerance in Brazil is to be understood; an exclusively masculine immigration and life away from the community of origin also explains it. It explains it not only in Brazil and in the case of the Portuguese, but even in the case of the French of Canada and of the Anglo-Saxons farthest from their own kind.

While in Quebec, in the bosom of the community, the French Canadians resist crossing with the natives as much as with the English, and no one keeps more aloof from outside contacts than they; when far from Quebec, along the Mississippi, the way they form unions with native women astounds the Americans. Even in 1839, when Abraham Lincoln moved with his parents to the state of Illinois, the fraternization of the French with the Indians was cause for surprise among the Americans. These friendly relations and the frequent intermarriage of Frenchmen with Indian women seemed almost monstrous to the Anglo-Saxons with their ferocious exclusivism. And it is natural that it should be so, for the Anglo-Saxon community would see in the Indian, first of all, the damned, against whom it was necessary to protect oneself with religious zeal, protecting and preserving the community itself and its own culture at the same time. It was a time when even the skeptical Benjamin Franklin considered the possibility that it might be "the design of Providence to extirpate these savages in order to make room for the cultivators of the earth."[30]

Therefore, had the Anglo-Saxons immigrated singly and not in communities, it is reasonable to suppose that despite their religion they would have behaved exactly like the Portuguese. Had their individual conduct not been strongly conditioned by the fear of tribal sanctions also, it would not be comprehensible that the white American of today (and especially the Southerner, who imagines himself incapable of ogling a Negro or a mulatto woman), as soon as he finds himself far from his own kind, can actually be seen in Brazil, in the Caribbean, and everywhere the American forces were stationed during the last war, in open promiscuity with half-breed and native women. Far from noting in them any sexual repulsion toward either kind, one can see, rather, a strong attraction to them. That is, disapproval of racial crossing in the United States is not biological; at most it may be religious and social.

In conclusion: In the historical definition of the racial problem in Brazil and the United States one is always and invariably going to find the community factor alongside the religious factor. This, of course, without prejudice to there being others—particularly the economic factor —and to the greater compatibility between Protestantism and racism than between racial nationalism and Catholicism.

As for that, it is already evident that history has much more to tell us about social facts than have the unilateral explanations of geographic, ethnic, biological, or economic determinism.

It is one thing, therefore, to examine and interpret social facts in terms of cause and effect, of quantity and statistics, or of results, and another and quite different thing to interpret them in terms of life and of history.

In terms of cause and effect, in the unilinear language of the determinists, the Anglo-Saxon will have a biological repulsion to Negro or half-breed women. In terms of history, of coming-to-be, there is nothing of the sort, but only fear of religious and tribal sanctions. Since to marry or to form a union with an Indian or a Negro woman he has to defy the traditions of his clan, which sees in the Indian first of all an enemy to be eliminated, he will naturally try to abstain. Succumbing to temptation, crossing physiologically with the Indian woman and later with the Negro —he will never do so, in any case, with the same nonchalance and freedom and in the same degree as the Portuguese.

In terms of cause and effect, in the unilateral language of the determinists, the progress of the United States in geometric ratio and of Brazil in arithmetical is probably merely the result of geographic and economic factors. In terms of history it can hardly be solely the consequence of these factors but must also be the consequence of ethical and religious factors.

In terms only of cause and effect, and not of *past, present,* and *future,* the Anglo-Saxon, like the Jew, is racially a born merchant, a manipulator of money by vocation and hereditary determination. In terms of history he is not that at all. Historically, while the Jew manipulates money in great part through necessity and through the effect of the successive expulsions which have made him economically ubiquitous, the Anglo-Saxon does it in great part as a result of his Protestantism. If it were a question of an innate and racial quality, it would not be comprehensible that in the heart of the Teutonic and Anglo-Saxon peoples—English,

German, Dutch—where the population is equally divided between Catholics and Protestants, it is always among the Protestants that one finds the greatest accumulation of wealth.

In terms of cause and effect, in the old language of ethnography prior to Sigmund Freud, the Brazilian is an indolent, congenitally melancholy man, the product of three sad races brought together by fate on the soil of America. In terms of history, of psychology, he is nothing of the kind, but simply a great victim—a victim not entirely free of blame and responsibility, obviously—of the environments that shaped his development. For real proof of the congenital sadness of the Indian, the Negro, the Portuguese simply does not exist.

Where, indeed, is there any proof of the congenital sadness of the Indian, the Negro, or the Portuguese?

The Indian is sad? That is not what can be inferred from the chroniclers of the sixteenth century. On the contrary, before coming into more prolonged contact with the white man, there seems to have been no one more joyous and healthy, morally healthy, than the Indian. There is no counting the historians who attest to this.

Now, to expect the Indian to continue to be as joyous through the seventeenth and eighteenth century as he was in the sixteenth, when he still seemed a veritable contemporary of the first day of Creation, is to expect too much. Once the idyllic phase of his first encounters with the white man had passed, from the white man came nothing but calamities: slavery, disease, extermination of his tribes, violence to his nature habituated to open air and nomadism. Preyed upon in the jungles by conscienceless adventurers bent on turning a quick profit, and put to hard work for which he had never served any apprenticeship or undergone any psychological initiation, he would not be long in showing the effects of transplantation and of the violence to which he had been subjected. On this point the Jesuits themselves, in spite of their great wish to bring good to the Indians and to spare them all evil, by falling into inevitable errors in the organization of their communities and by covering the naked bodies accustomed to the sun, caused them (always the fatal language of cause and effect!) great harm. In spite of not exposing them violently to labor—as the colonists did who wanted them only as slaves —the Jesuits did not succeed in protecting them against colds, measles, smallpox, and tuberculosis, diseases that almost put an end to the race.

And where is the anthropological or ethnological proof of the Negro's sadness? Such proof simply does not exist.

On the contrary, what does seem to exist is precisely the proof of the reverse, for of the three races that peopled the New World, none retained as did the Negro the secret of laughter and inward merriment. On this score, what is surprising is not that the Negro knows profound crises of sadness; the startling thing is that, having all the reasons in this world and the next to live in the blackest melancholy, he has been able to preserve so long his capacity for laughter. If it were not for the quite reasonable explanation of this fact, namely, that the Negro had no keen awareness of the injustices he was suffering, considering them normal because slavery in Africa is an ancient institution, one would say that it is a matter of a real miracle.[31] So the assertion has as much validity as those which, taking the Negro as belonging to a branch apart from humanity, with a biological ancestry more or less lost between the white man and the anthropoid, would dismiss the subject by regarding him as destitute of soul and absolutely incapable of progress and utterly unsusceptible of being civilized.

It remains now to find out to what point the Portuguese is congenitally sad, or, if he is not, when it was that the "dim, unworthy sadness," of which Camoens speaks already in the latter part of the sixteenth century, was established in him.

The Portuguese is congenitally sad? This can be said only to the same degree that one may repeat Offenbach's famous song, much sung in Paris even in our own time, to the effect that *Le Portugais est toujours gai*. Nevertheless, leaving aside the operetta's plot, what *is* known of the exact nature of the Portuguese people prior to the Moorish occupation, or at any rate prior to the great discoveries and the creation of its vast colonial empire? Would not that sadness be the consequence of the Moorish occupation and of the more recent psychological modifications that the Indies and the New World imposed on the Portuguese? Can it not be that the riches, the opulence, the Asiatic luxury, the sexual disorders, the abandonment of organic forms of constructive work, have contributed to modifying the character of the Portuguese? Is the Portuguese back from the Indies or Brazil the same Portuguese of the school of Sagres? Is not the Portuguese just prior to Camoens a Portuguese already burdened with sins and remorse and guilt complexes?

9

Let us glance for a moment at the Atlantic adventure of the Portuguese.

See him first in Lisbon, about to depart for Brazil. There he stands on board ship, at the rail, waving toward the shore. Proud and gay, he watches the people who have come to watch the departure of the caravel that is to take him to the New World, the latest model and the last word in the realm of nautical art. He keeps on waving to relatives and friends, among whom he sees his wife, his children, his old father, all either silent or speaking of their apprehensions and fears at seeing him depart.

As in *The Lusiads*, there will never be lacking at the Restêlo anchorage some old man or other, whose knowledge is "of all experience made," to apostrophize and curse adventure with its inevitable abandonment, even though it promises to be temporary, of loved ones:

> My curse on him who first on the dry tree,
> In the waters of this world, set up the sail!
> Worthy of the Deep's eternal pain was he,
> If the just creed I trust in does not fail!
> May no high judgment's wise authority,
> Nor singing lyre, nor genius bright, prevail
> To grant thee either memory or fame,
> But with thee die the glory and the name![32]

If the imprecation to which Camoens gave form does not come from his wife, from his father, his father-in-law, his uncle, or his sister, it must spring from the emigrant's own conscience.

And yet our emigrant will calm his conscience by alleging to himself that the motives taking him to the New World are as noble as were those of his ancestors. He wants nothing but to consolidate the Empire and the Faith and, naturally, to make a fortune to take back to Portugal and add to the wealth of the Kingdom. And to himself he promises that, on arriving in Brazil, he will never temporize with promiscuity and the libertinage of which they have heard in Portugal. And much less with the general lack of scruple in the world of business. To this he will oppose his vigilant Catholic conscience.

Look at him now after some time in Brazil. He still goes to Mass, he still goes to confession, he is still a good Catholic.

All around him, however, immorality is at work. The secular priests themselves are living with mulatto women and *caboclas*, surrounded by half-breed brats to whom they give the name of "foster children," those celebrated foster children of priests of *bandeirante* and patriarchal Brazil. In the struggle between Jesuits and secular priests, at first he regards the Jesuits as in the right, and he holds them in esteem. But the pressure against the Jesuits is great. And suppose the secular priests, living with their concubines, are right, and so, too, those who declare that in the tropics, south of the Equator, there is no sin—*Ultra aequinoctialem non peccavit?* Nowhere, however favorable the circumstances, is it easy to be a good Catholic. In colonial Brazil it was almost impossible. And then the spirit is strong, but the flesh is weak. What to do? Resist?

Our immigrant succumbs to temptation. Life now is full of delights for him, half-breed women seek him out, everything comes easy. And so, from one capitulation to the next, in a short time he is living like a veritable pagan, in the full euphoria of the last flickerings of the Renaissance.

And his conscience? His conscience is relegated to the background. He will resume it on his return, when he goes back rich to Portugal. Meantime, what he must do is give false measure, add sand to sugar for export to Europe, smuggle, grow rich, and enjoy life. For such practices there is nobody like the strayed Catholic.

Ah, but the euphoria of the senses like that of the Renaissance cannot last forever. Besides, it is not with more or less deceptive rationalizations that one's conscience is set aside. It will not be long before conscience— it all depends, of course, on its greater or less elasticity—comes knocking at the door, whether one is wide awake or sound asleep, with its legions of gnomes, goblins, gargoyles, monsters, pursuers, and wild beasts, that make the substance of nightmares.[33]

The Renaissance has passed; the Baroque period, which is the remorse of the Renaissance, has arrived.

With the nightmares and the remorse comes the desire to return, the longing—*saudade*, the loveliest, but also at times the most morbid, of words in the Portuguese language—the impotent urge to be reconciled with one's conscience.

At best, he returns in accordance with the plans long made. Is his conscience pacified? No, because in Brazil he has left half-breed children and the concubine who devoted the best part of her life to him, if not all the fruits of her work. New nightmares, new yearnings, new guilts, new irritations, new remorse, new exasperations, more hobgoblins, and more of the Baroque.

Behold him now at the Restêlo, gazing at the sea, humming Brazilian *lundus*, forcing himself to be unhappy, masochistically unhappy with the help of the *fado*, which, as has been pointed out, is nothing but a musical development, Portuguese and Lisbonian, of the very Brazilian *lundu*.[34]

To sum up: The strong, exuberant Portuguese of the Middle Ages and of the Age of Discovery was succeeded by another, womanizing, avaricious, gluttonous, miserly, inventor of recipes for desserts, Baroque, a prey to anguish and to that "dim, unworthy sadness" in which Camoens caught him at the close of the sixteenth century.

From his crossing with the two other races—not for biological reasons, as we have seen, but for psychological ones—the consequence could only be that which Paulo Prado has traced in masterly fashion: "In the struggle between those appetites—with no other ideal, either religious or aesthetic, with no political, intellectual, or artistic interest—a melancholy race was created in the course of the centuries. The melancholy of sexual abuse and the melancholy of those who live in the fixed idea of becoming rich—in their aimless absorption in those insatiable passions —are the deep birthmarks of our racial psyche."[35]

Substitute cutural psyche for racial psyche, or delete the adjective, and the definition will be perfect.

10

Decidedly, the Portuguese conquistadors, and naturally also the Spanish, did not lack reasons for conflict capable of generating profound transformations and of explaining the Brazilian sadness, in that epoch of transition from the medieval world and from the canonical cult of poverty, sanctity, heroism, chivalry, and the social function of money, to the capitalist world that they would help to create with their maritime discoveries and particularly with the exploitation of mines, and in which the bourgeoisie, property, usury, and money were to have predominance over the moral precepts in which they were raised.

Let it not be said that those dramas of conscience have been of minor importance.[36] They may have more to do with the decadence of Spain and Portugal, and in consequence with the semi-capitalistic, semifeudal regime which was set up in Brazil and in all the countries of Latin America, in which the national economy is still far from being perfectly defined, than the causes commonly invoked to explain them and upon which historians never seem to agree. For, while for Antero de Quental[37] that decadence is a result principally of the transformation of Catholicism by the Council of Trent, of absolutism through the ruin of local liberties, and of the development of the far-off colonies, for Werner Sombart[38] it was a direct and inevitable consequence of the expulsion of the Jews, who were, in his view—a view in which culture and historical necessities imposed by the successive expulsions are confused with race—the real molders of modern capitalism.

Today, well or ill, modern man can calm his disturbed conscience about what he does in the business world by telling himself that religion has nothing to do with trade. But, as Max Weber suggests and Tawney[39] notes, completing Weber's thought in masterly fashion, what today is a truism because for a long time religion and economic interests have been forming two separate worlds—as if it were a question of watertight compartments in which neither could lay down rules for the other—in the Middle Ages was regarded as abominable heresy. It was the time in which priests were sent to Paris to study with the theologians the limits of compatibility between profit-motivated commerce and canonical law, which no one wished to infringe. It was the time when Bellarmine, not without reason, complained of the intolerable complexity of the problems of economic casuistry that pious merchants brought to the confessional. Everything that today apparently occasions no loss of sleep for those who pile up extraordinary profits at the expense of the poor man's nourishment, profoundly disturbed the merchants, contractors, and moneylenders of the Middle Ages. And not only those of the Middle Ages. Even in the sixteenth, seventeenth and eighteenth centuries, there were tremendous spasms of conscience because of the practice of usury, sharp dealing, extortionate prices, and the unlimited, unrestrained use of property.[40] In truth, the struggle in the recesses of men's souls for the complete triumph of the principle of separation between economics and ethics, with the subsequent imposition of the law of supply and demand, a struggle without which the advent of capitalism would have been impossible, was to drag on in the heart of Catholic countries until our day, to the detriment of both religion and capitalism. That is understandable: The capitalist, as such, can be a Catholic only by halves. A Catholic capitalist will always be a clumsy capitalist. In both cases we face a schism of the soul, a schism that, besides providing opportunity for the triumph of capitalism in Protestant countries, will be mainly responsible for the decadence of the Peninsular peoples. Paradoxically— and this is a paradox that historical materialism does not explain—this decadence is going to commence at the exact moment when Portuguese and Spaniards lay hands upon the most fabulous fortunes that the West had ever seen.

The rest is well known. While the Protestants, especially the Calvinists, with the collaboration of the Jews expelled from the Peninsula, in England, Germany, the Low Countries, Switzerland and, on a lesser scale, France and Belgium, were to establish the law of supply and demand and of free competition, invent the bill of exchange and bearer bonds, rehabilitate interest, found stock companies—in short, while Protestants were to shape the economic conditions of the modern world, the Catholic soul of the Portuguese and Spaniards, prepared for heroism and the Faith, is going to be torn between ambition for wealth (the handling of which it had earlier turned over to the Jews so as not to imperil its own salvation) and canonical law, in a vacillation which was to last four centuries and which would end—if indeed it has quite ended —only when, by the internationalization of capital, the Protestant countries forced Spain and Portugal to accept their rules.

11

However, before these rules were fully accepted, the resistance of Spain and Portugal, when examined from the Protestant and capitalist point of view—which gives the password to modern historians—was to border upon madness, so great was its senselessness. It was, as Tawney would say, "an incapacity for economic matters which seemed almost inspired."[41] Really, it is incredible, simply incredible, in the light of that criterion, what takes place in the Iberian Peninsula in the period of transition from the precapitalist feudal society with a directed economy to the definitively capitalistic society of free economy, under the principle of the "savage law of supply and demand." One would say that Portugal and Spain had made a wager on which of the two would act with the greater madness.

After promoting the "price revolution" in all Europe by means of the gold and silver from their colonies—this revolution being quite accurately singled out as one of the material causes of capitalism, and in a time when credit, through the charging of interest, was being beautifully organized in Protestant countries—as if it were not enough for Spain and Portugal to have expelled the Jews, that is, the only people in both empires trained in the handling of wealth, they not only did not benefit from the economic consequences of the wealth that fell into their hands but took pleasure in combating those consequences à outrance. It was as though Carlos I and Felipe II in Spain, as D. Manuel and later D. João III in Portugal, hated their own prosperity.

More royalist than the king himself, or rather, more Catholic than the Church itself (rather softened, then, on the question of interest), in proportion as the capitalism which they had helped to create consolidated itself, they did nothing but combat usury.

Recognize autonomy in economic factors, organize credit with the golden product of the mines, liberate individual initiative—the great propulsor of the Protestant peoples' mercantile capitalism—yield to the idea of free competition in opposition to the centuries-old tenets of Christian cooperation? No, it could not be. On the contrary, the fitting thing at that juncture was to enforce the Council's recommendation that the usurer not be admitted to the communion table or allowed Christian burial. His offerings were not to be accepted by the clergy; no individual or group, on pain of excommunication or interdiction, might rent him a house, and in case this had already been done, he must be evicted within three months; he must be refused confession and his will invalidated until he made restitution of his ill-gotten gains; and any person who stubbornly declared that usury was no sin must be punished as a heretic. In a word, the usurer was to be equated with the criminal.

To this end there were the Afonsine, the Manueline, and the Philippine Ordinances in Portugal, and in Spain the Laws of the Indies and the Edicts of Charles V to the Low Countries. As the Afonsine Ordinances provided "that no Christian or Jew profit by usury," opinion on the usurer could be summed up in these words of Diogo do Couto: "Because the Jews were degraded for making false money, and they merited being burned and gave their lives for persisting in it, and it was wrongdoing not to burn them, because they were usurers."[42]

As for the gold from the mines, what better use of it could be made than to apply it to the building and ornamentation of churches, monasteries, and convents? To use that gold and silver as the means of usury was precisely what could not, must not, be.

Of course, persecution of the usurer and, consequently, of the accumulation of capital funds, was not confined to Spain and Portugal. It was extended to the colonies. And doubtless one of the reasons for sending the Holy Office to Brazil was to curb the usury of the merchants, who no longer wanted to sell for cash but on credit and charging interest. Hence the various denunciations against New Christians caught in the practice of the awful sin. Indeed, usury would reign unchecked in Brazil only after Pernambuco fell under the dominion of Holland and of Calvinism.

But as soon as this dominion was eliminated, after a rapid phase of mercantilism and pure capitalism, Brazil fell back into thoroughgoing feudalism; the country once more predominated over the city, consciences again became disturbed about economic questions, the most important social unit was no longer the shop but the sugar mill, with aspirations to typically medieval self-sufficiency. The Middle Ages, superseded in Europe, prolonged itself in a thousand ways in Latin America: in architecture, sculpture, painting, legislation, customs. But as time does not retrace its steps, the consequence was to be a great wavering between the past and the future; an undefined economy, neither entirely feudal nor entirely capitalistic, but a mixture of medievalism, modernism, feudalism, and mercantilism; a feudalism minus the medieval spirit and a mercantilism lacking in the real spirit of capitalism.

In the field of economics, exactly the same indecisiveness was to characterize the policy of the Kingdom of Portugal with respect to the treatment of the natives. Between the Christian principles advocated by the Jesuits and the exploitative ones highly recommended by the colonists, Portugal never took a clear and definite position.

12

In the Protestant camp, the case was quite different. Among the Calvinists who ruled over the United States there were no noteworthy dramas of conscience for economic motives. They had to face conflicts neither between their religious ethics and their sexual conduct, nor between their ethics and their conduct toward the natives. Between the capitalism that was in the making and the ethics of Calvinism there would be no conflicts. The reformers, especially Calvin, had prepared the way equally for the heedless slaughter of the Indians and the accumulation of wealth with a minimum of conscience pangs. Between Reformation and economic factors, Reformation and capitalism, capitalism and racial discrimination, Calvin had established a perfect accord, an accord that was to last three centuries. In this Calvin went much further than Luther. Indeed, to understand doctrinally the connection between Reformation, racial discrimination, and economic factors, it is necessary to go directly to Calvin.

Doctrinally Luther is of no use. Luther, as far as economic factors are concerned, does not divorce himself sufficiently from canon law to permit us to attribute the advent of capitalism to him. His contribution was to be great, but indirect. In this particular, Luther was not, properly speaking, a reformer: he was a Protestant. Equally a Protestant was Zwingli, who, in insisting on the thesis that private property originated in sin at the same time that he was inveighing against mortgaging land and putting up harvests as security, was warning the rich that they could not enter into the Kingdom of Heaven.

The reformer was Calvin. Luther in economic matters was a perfect scholastic. So scholastic that his protest was motivated by the abuse of indulgence-selling by the Church.

In the struggle between economics and ethics, a struggle which was to be prolonged to our time, Luther was merely the first moment. The great divide was Calvin. It is with Calvin that the doctrinal history of capitalism takes on body and breath, it is with Calvin that camels begin to pass through the eye of the needle.

Thenceforth it is with his famous *Christianae Religionis Institutio* and his famous letters[43]—which are to Catholicism and the medieval order what Karl Marx's *Das Kapital* is to capitalism and the Western world— that the line of Christianity bifurcates in two completely opposed concepts, the Catholic and the Calvinist.

To begin with, from the Calvinist theory of predestination, opposed to the doctrine of free will, determinism would arise. And hard on its heels all the other theories for which determinism serves as a basis.

From then on, no theory or philosophy would fail to bear the mark of Calvinist concepts. These would be visible in Darwin as in Hobbes, in Locke as in Rousseau, in Ricardo as in Adam Smith, in de Tocqueville as in Chamberlain, in Freud as in Karl Marx, in Montesquieu as in Ratzel. In Freud the mark of Calvin, as Hilaire Belloc points out, lies in the "sense of Fate."[44] In Karl Marx it lies in the concept of the class struggle, with the final triumph of the strongest. In the anthropogeography of Ratzel and of Montesquieu, the sign is always determinism, the concept that man, like the universe, is governed by laws just as Nature is, and that all one needs to do is single out those laws and successively study their consequences.

If God is omniscient and foresees everything, the determinists would of course say that He knows beforehand what is going to happen and therefore the thing will have to happen because He foresees it. Now, if the thing has to happen, the individual is not free; or, if he is free and master of his destiny, God cannot be omniscient.

In answer the scholastics explain that the argument holds for human beings who reason in terms of past, present, and future, and not in terms of eternity, in which there are no past and future but everything has been, and will be *now*. Under these conditions God foresees, or rather, sees both the things that have happened and that are yet to happen, because in point of fact they *are happening*, and not because He has determined that they shall happen. To say that things happen because God sees or foresees would be the same, in human terms, as to say that a wall painted white is white because man sees it so, when the truth is that man sees it so because it is in fact white. It is the same with human actions: Man, who is free, is not going to perform a certain act because God sees that he is going to do it or wishes him to do it, but God in His omniscience—which is much more than prescience or clairvoyance— sees him doing it because he, in fact and of his own free will, on the plane of eternity is already doing it.

The explanation, nevertheless, did not melt the Calvinist dissidence. Before this could happen, Calvinism, in its rapid expansion, would first have to exhaust its possibilities, among them, naturally, capitalism.

Once the economic factors and the acquisitive appetite had been freed, probably much beyond Calvin's and Luther's own intentions, there was no holding them in check. They spread out through the world in search of raw materials and markets, in the most unbridled competitive spirit. In vain would the Church seek to hold back the avalanche with the Counter Reformation. *The rise of the rich against the poor, of the strong against the weak, of the elect against the damned,* had advanced too far to retreat. The excesses of the secular clergy, simony, luxury, ostentation, cupidity, in the name of no principle, had gone too far to be able to check the appetite for acquisition and for progress which was now carrying the banner of a new doctrine.

Now men have a moral foundation—a very debatable foundation, to be sure, but in any case a moral foundation—for going out after property and with the aim of competing and accumulating wealth. The bourgeois, the merchants, the artisans, whom the end of the Middle Ages had treated harshly through the action of a clergy which as a whole left much to be desired, no longer need hunt for moral motives to accumulate riches, for wealth is pleasing to God and constitutes evidence of diligence and work, and when it is not the result of work and diligence, it is nevertheless a sign of God's pleasure.

The Catholic retreats, retires into convents the better to communicate with God. The Calvinist communicates with God in the city, in the office, at the loom, in the factory, and especially in the bank, mystically struggling with values that symbolize wealth: stocks, warrants, debentures. According to St. Antoninus, wealth was created for man and not man for wealth. For the Calvinist, granted the charismatic value he gives to wealth, one would say that man is created for wealth and not the reverse. To the Catholic the great virtues are the theological virtues. To the Puritan the supreme virtues are the economic ones—thrift, hard work, utilization of time. Since time is an element of great importance in interest accounting and therefore in the accumulation of wealth—*time is money*—the Calvinist, perfecter of the precision of watches, winds up as a slave to time. Hence the proverbial punctuality of the Protestant peoples, in contrast to the chronic unpunctuality of the Catholic ones. While the Catholic is ashamed to show any preoccupation with filthy lucre, as if material interest always had a pact with the devil, to think of and talk about money is to the Calvinist a condition that may well be termed existential. He is the *homo economicus* par excellence. To the Catholic, as a Catholic, even in the handling of economic values, human values will be accounted higher than things. Hence his incapacity for forming organizations on a major scale in which things matter more than persons, as for example in stock companies or corporations, which in Latin countries, especially in Brazil, are only nominally "anonymous societies" (to translate literally the term current in Latin languages), because in fact there is always a capitalist who holds half the shares plus one. With the Calvinist it is different. The thing, the merchandise, the consumer goods, production, the shares, dividends, and prices and profits —those are what matter, and everything must be subordinated to the exigencies of investment, production, profit, and the accumulation of wealth. Hence his Semitic capacity for organizing trusts, corporations, stock companies. In this no one excels him, not even the Jew. The Jew, in the ubiquity forced on him by historical circumstances, is at times obliged to incur risk. The Calvinist keeps safe. He does not expose himself to risks, he does not venture. Nor is it for any other reason that he, by inspiring much more confidence as a banker than the Jew, is gradually banishing the latter. There is still another difference between the Jew and the Calvinist. The Jew, once he has attained wealth, loves display and luxury. Not so the Calvinist. The good Calvinist, theoretically at least, does not enjoy wealth, makes no display of it, takes no pleasure in the delights of the table; he eats only because it keeps him well, which permits him to redouble his work. The Calvinist is an ascetic, an ascetic *sui generis*, but an ascetic. An ascetic who produces wealth so as to be pleasing to God. The Jew likes adventure, luxury, and gambling. The good Calvinist will not compromise with gambling or drinking or luxury. In life he has only one direction, to pile up riches and power. The Catholic is prepared to associate the state of grace with poverty. For the Protestant the rich will have preference in the Kingdom of Heaven. "Grace in a poor man is grace and is beautiful," a Puritan writer tells us, "but grace in a rich man is more conspicuous, more useful." "If man is affable and religious," says another, "that is, great and rich, he will make a sweeter and more melodious harmony in the ear of God than if he were poor and of low estate." "The moneyed and prudent man is raised above his neighbors with the blessing of God."[45] The Catholic conducts himself with dignity in poverty; in wealth he frequently loses his head. The Calvinist has great dignity in wealth; in poverty he is close to suicide, for only in the world of things and matter does he succeed in realizing himself. This subordination of self was to be carried to such an extreme, things and economic factors would have so much importance for him, that when Protestantism reached its culminating point in capitalism, Karl Marx from his observation post in London would not hesitate to announce the disappearance of heroes in the near future, because men, as capitalism and scientific determinism became perfected, would become nothing but the playthings of economic factors.

13

In the face of what historical research reveals to us, must we still insist on explaining the differences between Brazil and the United States, and the corresponding social phenomena, merely in terms of cause and effect, in terms of purely ethnic or purely geographic or merely economic factors? Are we to ignore the cultural and religious heritages of the two countries, the ethical factors, the philosophical, the psychological, the symbological, and the aesthetic—all of which have constituted the ferment and the past of the two cultures—or are we to consider all that mass of contrasts, plus the circumstance of Brazil's having been conquered by a Mediterranean, Catholic, Baroque, and Latin people, and the United States by a Nordic, Anglo-Saxon, and Protestant people, as things absolutely indifferent to the process of accumulating wealth in geometric progression in the United States and barely in arithmetic progression in Brazil.

Certainly the geophysical factors, like the economic and even the ethnic and political, when confined to their proper field, explain much, and we must never lose sight of them. They are, however, far from explaining everything. If, as in the case of the achievements of the United States compared with those of Brazil, it is impossible to pass over in silence, in the geographic field, the hydrography, climate, and soil and subsoil; in the field of economics, the importance of coal; in politics, the importance of constitutional institutions and the dynamics of parties— these factors are far from exhausting the problem. Accordingly, there is nothing for it but to have recourse to history, to the distant past of the two civilizations, and from them to single out those differences that, distinguishing the two cultures on the religious, moral, and psychological plane, may have contributed through their repercussions on the material and economic plane toward framing the problem that interests us most: civilization in geometric ratio of progression in the United States, civilization in arithmetic progression in Brazil.

Just as very little or nothing is learned about the character of individuals without investigating their childhood, adolescence, and maturity, especially their childhood, very little will be learned about those other equally living and organic entities called cultures unless we investigate the secret of their origins.

Therefore, let us turn to the history of Brazil and to the history of the

United States. Not, it is well to remark, to the whole of each of them, which would be impossible, but to their first moments, the impact of which imprints upon everything that is created the indelible mark of a *meaning*, of a *character*, of a *direction*.

These first moments will have more, much more, to tell us about the Brazilian and North American cultures than will the conjectures clothed in the so-called scientific truths both of the past century's ethnography and anthropology and of the present day's *economism*, *factualism*, and *statisticalism*.

III

Conquest and Colonization

1

ON THE VERY THRESHOLD OF THE HISTORIES OF BRAZIL AND THE UNITED States, even before getting into their content and substance, we are going to run into a fact which must not be entirely unconnected with the process of differentiation between the two countries. That fact is the contrast between the profusion of documents covering North American history and the relative scarcity of documents on which Brazilian history is based.

Is this a sign that there was more cultural and artistic curiosity among the early settlers of the United States than in Brazil? Not necessarily. For the moment we can conclude only that the level of education and literacy was very much higher in the United States.

The early settlers of the English colonies of America, as Protestants, were almost by definition literate. Literate only for the practical, pragmatic purpose of reading the Bible, but literate. How raise the individual to be the supreme interpreter of revealed truths, or the supreme arbiter of competing interpretations, if he cannot read? Impossible.

That one may not know how to read in order to interpret human laws or to delve into the secrets of poetry, Calvinism will accept perfectly, because in Calvinism anything other than the reading of the Bible for ethical ends is suspect of being the work of the devil. But that a man should not know how to read for the purpose of interpreting the word of the New and Old Testaments is a thing that cannot be.

When human laws are in question, the Magna Carta or the Constitution, for example, the Calvinist recognizes the need of judges and of a Supreme Court. But in dealing with divine laws or revealed truths, which are at least somewhat superior to human laws and infinitely more complicated, there is no need of a Supreme Court or of a council of cardinals; the individual's conscience, aided by reason, will resolve any doubt.

To Protestantism in general and to Calvinism in particular can be credited benefits or disservices to humanity according to each man's creed and philosophic point of view: the rupture of the spiritual equilibrium of the West; the breakup of Christianity into innumerable small sects; racial prejudice, nationalism, and the exacerbation of nationalism; usury and the legitimization of usury; capitalism and the exacerbation of capitalism; rationalism and pride of reason; and even communism, which in many ways is not only the last stage of capitalism and of the Protestant break with the order established in the Middle Ages, but also the first step in the movement of return to the predominance of ethics over economics. Nevertheless, as everything has its opposite extreme, the merit of contributing to the general education of the countries in which it has spread, better preparing individuals to assimilate, incorporate, and create progress and civilization later—that merit no one can take away from Protestantism.

And it is not necessary to be a slavish adulator of the printed letter and the alphabet and their use for practical ends, ready to affirm that all the differences between Brazil and the United States are the exclusive consequence of the higher degree of literacy in the latter country—another of those causal interpretations that crop up occasionally to explain unilaterally the contrasts between the two countries.

In the particular case of the histories of the United States and Brazil, the former offering an abundance and the latter a scarcity of documents on the early colonial periods, such advantages are evident and irrefutable. While there are no doubts or substantial points to be cleared up about the beginnings of North American history, Brazilian history opens with the problem of finding out whether that land was discovered by chance or on purpose.

It is true, however incredible it may seem, that the problem of whether Brazil was discovered by chance or deliberately—one of the most important of Brazilian historical problems because it involves the question of intention—is yet to be definitively settled.

All that we know is, not the intention or lack of intention with which Brazil was discovered, but the motives that subsequently determined her settlement.

From the outset, between the history of Brazil and that of the United States, everything or nearly everything is contrast; and the initial contrasts, through their repercussions on the religious, economic, social, moral, political, psychological, and cultural planes, were to end by conditioning all the others.

2

There is of course a fundamental difference of motives in the settlement of the two countries: an initially spiritual, practical, and constructive spirit in the development of North America, and a predatory, extractive and almost only secondarily religious spirit in the development of Brazil.

The first settlers of the English colonies of America, principally the Puritans of the *Mayflower*, did not come to the New World only or predominantly in search of gold and silver mines and easy riches. They came, instead, driven by persecution in their country of origin, in search of lands where they could worship their God, read and interpret their Bible, work, help one another, and celebrate the ritual of their cult in their own way. As they embarked, bringing with them all their possessions, their wives and children, they turned their backs on Europe to found on this side of the Atlantic a new fatherland, the theocratic fatherland of the Calvinists. They did not think of returning; for them there was only one way of being pleasing to God: to read the Bible and to labor, to labor and prosper, to prosper and to accumulate wealth. They were colonizers, not conquerors. Later, it is true, there were those who broke away to the West in search of gold and easy fortune, but when this happened, the *sense*, the *rhythm* of North American history was already established and definitively established—constructive, moral, practical.

In Brazil, unfortunately, precisely the contrary occurred in nearly everything. The Portuguese who came first to take possession of the lands of Santa Cruz were all faithful vassals of the King of Portugal. If, on the one hand, they desired to enlarge the dominion of Christianity, "the Faith and the Empire," their eyes were already over-dilated with greed. They were initially conquistadors, not colonizers, as they would later be *bandeirantes* and not pioneers. Like the King, like the whole Court, after the discovery of the route to the Indies they wanted spoils and riches. And no one took ship with any notion of never more returning to the Lusitanian fatherland. And no one brought with him the purpose of getting rich through constant devotion to work. They were leaving behind their land, their friends, their families, their normal occupations, in the hope of El Dorado. They talked a great deal about honor and glory, about the Faith and the Empire, but they did not fool the old man at the Restêlo, in Camoens' poem:

> What new disasters dost thou now prepare
> Against these kingdoms and against their seed?
> What peril and what death for them to bear,
> Under some mighty name, has thou decreed?
> What mines of gold now dost thou promise fair?
> What kingdoms?—promise lightly made indeed!
> What fame dost thou propose? What legend glorious?
> What palm? What triumph? And what war victorious?[1]

In the Portuguese world they did not fool Camoens; in the Spanish world they did not fool Lope de Vega:

> On pretext of religion
> They go seeking silver and gold
> Of the hidden treasure.[2]

If there were doubts about the purpose or motive of the great sea voyages that followed the opening of the route to the Indies, the letter of Pero Vaz de Caminha was there to dissipate them. The chronicler really leaves no room for doubt about the gold fever, the hunger for gold, that overpowered Portugal hard on the heels of the discoveries and almost simultaneously with them. In no less than four passages in the letter does he dwell at length on the obsession of finding gold.

When, for example, one of the Indians sees some rosary beads and makes signs for them to be given him, gleefully playing with them then, putting them first around his neck, then rolling them round his arm while pointing to the land and then to the beads and to the commander's collar, they all got the impression that the Indian was trying to indicate that he would give gold for the beads. Immediately, however, Caminha goes on to the conclusion with this delightful, precise comment: "We took it so because we wanted it to be so."[3]

See the nature of the interrogations to which the Portuguese subject the natives: "Then the Captain went up along the river which runs down to the beach. There an old man waited, carrying a native canoe paddle in his hand. He talked, while the Captain was with him, in the presence of us all, without anyone's ever understanding him—or he us, all the things we asked about gold, for we wished to find out whether there was any in the land."[4]

And the preoccupation with the Faith, had it disappeared already? Not yet. It was still very much alive, to judge by the description of the first Mass held in Brazil, that famous first Mass celebrated on Easter Sunday by Frei Henrique de Coimbra:

"He had an awning set up in the island, and inside it a very proper altar. And there with all of us he caused Mass to be said, which was said by Frei Henrique in chanting voice and aided in the same voice by the other priests and religious who were there. The Mass, in my opinion, was heard by all with great pleasure and devoutness. . . .

". . . While we were at Mass and at sermon, there were about as many people as we on the beach, more or less the same number as yesterday, with their bows and arrows, taking their ease. And looking at us, they sat down. And, once Mass was over, we sitting at sermon, many of them got up, blew a kind of horn and began to leap and dance a bit."[5]

It was the time in which the land was still called Santa Cruz, or Vera Cruz, as it had been officially christened. In fact, however, the Catholic faith for a long time had been yielding to the mercantilistic spirit of the time, and within a little while the name of Vera Cruz would be "changed for that of the wealth which was then supposed to be the principal one," to the profound displeasure of João de Barros, who in the purity of his Christian faith could not bear that "through diabolic arts" the name of "Santa Cruz, so pious and devout" should be turned into "that of a wood for dyeing cloth."[6]

But before the intensive exploitation of the wood for dyeing cloth began, as no gold, "nor silver, nor any metal or iron" were found in the land, Brazil was a disappointment for the conquerors. No gold? No silver? Then it held no interest.

It was useless for Pero Vax de Caminha to praise the land, pointing to agriculture as a possible recourse. No one wanted to hear about the lands of Santa Cruz. And had it not been for the incursions of the French on the coasts of Brazil, putting the Portuguese conquest in check, the Court would not have thought of initiating the settlement. For a quarter of a century Portugal was to do nothing more, as far as producing a civilization in the recently discovered land was concerned, than send a few caravels, two or three annually, unloading on the littoral the mails and the dregs of society, to take back to Portugal cargoes of brazilwood and enslaved Indians, by way of staple exports, together with parrots and monkeys, under the heading of novelties.

As for the rest, when it could do so without creating political complications with Spain over the Tordesillas Line, the Court would dispatch royal letters and more royal letters, or secret instructions, urging the colonists to press on into the backlands in quest of the coveted metal.

Such expeditions, when not ordered by the government and paid for out of royal funds, were encouraged, protected, and organized by the local authorities. Radiating out from Piratininga, from Bahia, from Recife, they were to become a national phenomenon, not merely regional, often to the detriment of those forms of more or less useful, more or less stable, more or less constructive work which were developing on the coast around the mills for the production of sugar, a merchandise more and more highly valued and in demand in the European markets.

So, while the pioneer conquers the land inch by inch, planting towns and cities, the *bandeiras*, as Capistrano de Abreu emphasizes, "contributed rather to depopulating than to peopling our land, taking Indians away from the places where they lived, causing their deaths in great numbers, either in attacks on villages and settlements or with ill treatment inflicted during the journeys, or, when these were over, by fatal and constant epidemics here and elsewhere as soon as the forest-dwellers come into contact with the civilized men. Moreover, the *bandeirantes* went and returned, they never settled down in the territories they crossed."[7]

While for the Portuguese who came to conquer Brazil—a Renaissance Portuguese, a crusader, more the crusader of the predatory phase of assaults on Moorish castles than a truly Catholic crusader—regular work gradually ceased to be a blessing, for the Puritan Anglo-Saxon, there was only one way to be pleasing to God: to labor and to pile up riches; always to work, never to stop.[8]

While the Portuguese immigrant, in his thirst for gold, comes utterly unprovided with economic virtues, public spirit, and the will to political self-determination, the Anglo-Saxon colonists in their famous *Mayflower Compact*—having sworn before God to constitute themselves into a civil and political body for their own preservation, promising each other to devise and decree laws, acts, and ordinances that would best promote the common good, and to revise those laws from time to time when deemed suitable to the interest of the Colony, to which all owed submission and obedience—already presage the future American independence, both political and economic, in the form in which it was put into effect.[9] More than this: they already presage, with their Puritanism, the advent of capitalism.

3

It will be said that not all the settlers of Brazil were conquistadors and adventurers; nor were all the settlers of the Anglo-Saxon colonies of America victims of religious persecution or born handlers of money, ready to profit by opportunity.

Indeed, that is true, and to attribute to the Portuguese, as to the Spaniards, only greed for gold, forgetting the eagerness for glory and for evangelism that they sometimes possessed, and to attribute to the English only noble religious motives underlying the desire for profit, would be to oversimplify the problem. Not only to oversimplify the problem but to omit, on the one hand, the thousands of farmers, artisans, merchants, and artists who in time established themselves on the Brazilian littoral, while the adventurers plunged into the backlands in search of wealth, and on the other hand, to forget that the colonies of Virginia, New York, and the Carolinas were established principally by men who, going there in quest of riches, shared the official religion of England.

In spite of the tendency to polarization, there was no exclusive and single historical process at work on either side. As the American historian Charles C. Griffin has observed in a notable study undertaken for the Pan-American Institute of Geography and History, not even in New England itself, the main goal of the Calvinists' Puritan immigration, do we find a society founded exclusively for religious ends, for even the Pilgrim Fathers of Plymouth, who bulk so large in the national history of the United States as saintly men imbued only with the desire for freedom of worship, were also seekers after easy profit, and English colonists blinded by eagerness for gold were never lacking. Many died in the first years of the Virginia colony, obsessed with the golden dream, and did not cease hunting for mines until the tobacco cultivated by Negroes began to offer them a surer road to fortune. "The difference which has been stressed so much is due, more than to anything else," concludes Griffin, "to the fact that in Mexico, Peru, and New Granada precious metals existed, while in Virginia and New England such metals were not to be found.[10]

All this is certainly irrefutable. It happens, nevertheless, that in the history of Anglo-Saxon America, whether for geographic or for psychological motives, or for a combination of the two, the spirit of colonization prevailed over that of conquest, while in Latin America precisely the reverse occurred: it was not the pioneer who prevailed over the bandeirante, but the bandeirante over the pioneer. It is true that the English also were greatly deluded by dreams of riches and power, for the myth of the Seven Cities of Cibola or of other great sources of gold and precious stones in the center of the continent must have lasted long. But, as the historian James Truslow Adams observes, the Anglo-Saxon adventurers, after some frustrated attempts at predatory exploration, turned to fishing, to cultivating tobacco, and to hard daily toil to get their sustenance from the land or from the sea. "Empire builders though they were, they seemed to think and move in inches, tilling their farms or plantations in serried rows as they advanced. No mines of Potosí, disappointingly but fortunately, turned their minds from the steady work of daily toil, nor did it occur to them to go on wild expeditions merely to trace the course of rivers a thousand miles from where their shops needed tending or their fields tilling."[11]

It is certain also that not all the settlers of the Anglo-Saxon colonies of America were Calvinists. After the Calvinists, and almost simultaneously with them, came Lutherans, Wesleyans, Zwinglians, Quakers, Jews, Catholics—the Quakers of Pennsylvania, the Dutch and Portuguese Jews of New York from Amsterdam and from Recife when Dutch rule ended in northeastern Brazil, the Lutherans of the Midwest, the Catholics of Maryland, all with conceptions of the universe differing from the Calvinist one. It happens, however, that the tonic accent of North American life in the realm of economics was to be furnished not by the Quakers, nor by the Catholic, nor by the Lutheran, but by the Calvinist. By the Calvinist and, to a certain extent, by the Jew. For that matter, the accord between Puritanism and Judaism in economic matters is very nearly complete, which is perfectly understandable when one notes that the economic doctrines of Calvin in their relation to ethics were inspired by the Old Testament, not the New, and that as regards questions of property, interest, trade, and accumulation of capital, the positions of both are nearly identical. The differences are of degree, not of substance.

Not to go too far afield, where usury is concerned the Jew has only one limitation: he may not charge interest of another Jew. Exodus says, "If thou lend money to any of my people that is poor by thee, thou shalt not be to him as an usurer, neither shalt thou lay upon him usury."[12] And Deuteronomy: "Thou shalt not lend upon usury to thy brother; usury of money, usury of victuals, usury of any thing that is lent upon usury: unto a stranger thou mayest lend upon usury; but unto thy brother thou shalt not lend upon usury: that the Lord thy God may bless thee in all that thou settest thine hand to in the land whither thou goest to possess it."[13] Deuteronomy makes this other very important recommendation: "The Lord shall open unto thee his good treasure, the heaven to give the rain unto thy land in his season, and to bless all the work of thine hand: and thou shalt lend unto many nations, and thou shalt not borrow."[14]

Between Jews and Calvinists there are many similarities. It is not merely a question here of that Hebraizing influence that is to be noted in all the heretical movements of the Middle Ages, and in the religious movements of the Reformation in general. In Calvinism there is more than influence. There is imitation, there is identification.

The Puritans of New England were convinced that they had come to found a new Israel. They felt that they were the chosen people. For them England was the Egypt from which they had fled, as James I was Pharaoh. The Atlantic Ocean figured as the Red Sea and the New World was Canaan, the Promised Land. Imitation of the style of the Old Testament is evident in everything, in the early settlers' profound knowledge of Hebrew, as in the way they identified the most outstanding members of the colony. John Cotton, for example, was "the high priest of the Theocracy," Roger Williams, a "Joshua." Massachusetts legislation was impregnated with Mosaic influence; Scripture took precedence over civil law. Then, as regards the preservation of blood ties and the condemnation of worship of images, the similarity is very clear.

Other similarities: The manner in which the colony was summoned for war against the "pagans," that is, the Indians; the names they gave their children: men were named Jacob, Abraham, Mordecai, Joshua; the women, Abigail, Eve, Rachel, Sarah—all names inspired by the Old Testament.

4

It may be objected that if the number of names taken from the most remote Hebraic antiquity was great, one of the commonest names in the colony was Martha, a name taken from the Gospels.

The objection proves too much. Martha, while in fact a figure from the New Testament, is one of those in the Gospel that most retain the spirit of the Old. Indeed, it is precisely Martha, the sister of Mary, who seems least in accord with the new message of Christianity.

So true is this that when the Messiah visits their home, seeing Mary seated at the feet of the Lord, she who is all activity and toil cannot refrain from asking, "Lord, dost thou not care that my sister hath left me to serve alone? bid her therefore that she help me." To which the Lord replies: "Martha, Martha, thou art careful and troubled about many things: but one thing is needful: and Mary hath chosen that good part, which shall not be taken away from her" (Luke 10:40-42).

It is in Martha, the one who could not comprehend why Mary should be prostrate at Jesus' feet while she, Martha, worked, as probably she did not understand Jesus' tenderness toward Mary, that the Puritans found inspiration for naming their daughters. Which is to say that the idealization of life à la Martha, and not à la Mary, with the dominant note on work and not on mysticism, was much more in accord with the concept they harbored.

And what of Mary and Maryland? Maryland was initially a Catholic colony, and if they had to choose between the two idealizations of woman—that of the mystic Mary, who leaves everything to anoint the feet of the Lord, and to listen to His words, and that of the active Martha, more zealous in the care of the house than in edifying contemplation—the Americans of colonial times, like those of today, never hesitated: they chose Martha. The woman who works and who, besides working, is always full of moral indignation at idleness and vice, and always quick to promote a crusade against them both, is the kind that appeals most to the country's imagination; she is, without any doubt, the one the American prefers in all circumstances.

Indeed, in spite of Marys and Maryland, the United States was not to be a country consecrated to the cult of Mary; it would be, rather, a country that, on the march toward matriarchy, moves by preference in the direction of Martha.

For that matter, that is the secret of the prestige and strength of the moralistic and prohibitionist campaigns promoted throughout the country by women's clubs on the order of the famous Daughters of the American Revolution.

The feminine symbols of Mary the Mother of God, or of Mary the sister of Martha, are symbols that Calvinism and Puritanism do not accept. And much less, of course, that of the Magdalene or the repentant adultress, predecessors of those sinful women who, in the good old days when witches were being burned in Massachusetts, were ducked and stoned by the populace as were the whores of Jerusalem. The women adopted by Calvinism will be those who, besides their capacity for moral indignation, in the continuous exercise of Protestant righteousness have no doubt about the superiority of those values that, while owing much to Judaism and the Old Testament, also constitute the keystones of Calvinism and Puritanism.

As one can see, Judaism and Calvinism are in almost complete accord.[15]

But where the identification would be perfect would be in the taste for rationalization and accountancy in life. On this point, as Werner Sombart says, there is no distinguishing Calvinists from Jews. "In both will be found the preponderance of religious interests, the idea of divine rewards and punishments, *asceticism* in the world, the intimate relationship between religion and business, an arithmetical conception of sin, and, above all, the rationalization of life."[16]

Now, this being so, and if it is true, as Ratzel says, that he who dominates the mouth dominates the whole river, Calvinists and Jews in New

York at the mouth of the Hudson—from the start the outlet for American goods bound for Europe—would strategically control American
commerce by imposing their laws, leaving the other sects no alternative
but to supplement the economic deficiencies of Calvinism and Judaism.
And, in fact, that is exactly what happened.

The mouths of the rivers along which production flowed being con-
trolled by Calvinists and Jews, the Lutherans, closer to canon law than
any other branch of Protestantism with regard to economics, would
settle in the West as agriculturists, giving new values to agricultural life
and creating for the nation the ideal image of the pioneer. Meanwhile
the Methodists, more compatible with poverty than with riches, with
humility than with pride, would first become independent artisans, and
later supply their great laboring masses to the great Calvinist and Jewish
enterprises. Thus all branches of Protestantism, already founded or yet
to be founded, each in its own way contributed to the victory of
capitalism. To alter the situation, the Catholics remained, but their
opportunities, given the spirit of the time, were less than nil, no other
alternative being left to them than to adapt themselves to certain uses
and customs of Protestantism, as they also adapted themselves to the conventions of capitalism. They carried the adaptation so far that in many
Catholic churches of the South this sign may still be read: "For Whites
Only." "The differences between Calvinism, Lutheranism, Presbyterian-
ism, Anabaptism, Episcopalianism, Quakerism," as James Burnham
states, "were not trivial in the sixteenth and seventeenth centuries and
on many occasions led from philosophical debate to bloodshed. But
these were all, at least as against medieval Catholicism, capitalist religious ideologies, all contributing in variant ways to the development of
attitudes favorable to capitalist society as against feudal society."[17]
Paradoxically, in the same fashion that it began clamoring violently
against the clergy's lack of chastity only to end by permitting the marriage of its ministers, Protestantism, after inveighing against the sale of
indulgences and other mercantile practices of the Church, would see
only one corrective for this: Open wide the doors to capitalism.

It may be objected: Were not the Protestants of the southern United
States contributing, with their great cotton landholdings and their introduction of slavery, to the return to the style of medieval economy? By no
means. To reply affirmatively it would be necessary, on the one hand, to
ignore the predominantly mercantilist nature of those landholdings, and
on the other hand to forget the capitalistic origin of the use of slave
labor. Nor because it has been deliberately promoted and encouraged by
the theorists of capitalism can the confusion stand any examination.
Slavery is not a feudal but a capitalist institution, as is indentured service,
current in the United States until the middle of the eighteenth century.

To confuse the indentured servant and the slave of the cotton fields in the South of the United States and of the sugar mills of the Center and North of Brazil with the serf bound to the glebe, is equivalent to confusing the spirit of self-sufficiency of the medieval latifundium with the monocultural and mercantilist spirit of the modern latifundium, which revived slavery in America to accelerate capitalist development. "The predominance of slavery and of wages, together with the scant importance of serfdom—in the historico-economic sense—confirms us in the belief that the colonial work regime resembles that of capitalism much more than it does that of feudalism," says Sergio Bagú.[18] For this writer, slavery, dormant as an institution during the Middle Ages, must have revived principally because of the discovery of the American continent as a prodigious depository of raw materials.[19] Slave labor was employed to create a flow of merchandise that would be consumed in the European markets. Thereafter, America, enriched in her turn by slave labor, would create her own domestic market, becoming herself an important consumer of European products. Now, this is a typically capitalistic, not a feudal process. The slave not only works within an unquestionably capitalistic mechanism, but the sale of slaves to colonial enterprises, to provide labor for the vast machinery of colonial capitalist production, is in the hands of societies and individuals organized according to capitalistic canons and seeking commercial profit. "The bases of the slave trade, in its economic aspect," says Bagú, "are the same as those of the capitalistic enterprise: shareholding companies or individual impresarios— according to the importance of the business—dividends, accumulation of benefits, international competition."[20]

Thus, the Protestant farmers of the South likewise do not escape the rule of contributing to the consolidation of capitalistic society against feudal society.

With the passage of time, it is true, in the whole South and especially in Virginia, the birthplace of future statesmen, pure Calvinism will be superseded by Lutheran, Wesleyan, and Quaker ideologies; and, when the American Constitution is written, Calvinist pessimism, according to which man was irremediably steeped in original sin, will be supplanted by the theory of innocence preached by Rousseau and Jefferson. Within a short time, even in Boston, the stronghold of Calvinism, only the reactionaries will defend it; the rest will be liberals and Unitarians who, despite Calvinist predestination, are going to raise the vigorous belief in human perfectibility to heights never before known.

Soon the Germans, Scots, and Irish whom Europe will spill forth in avalanches at the United States ports of entry—Protestants, Anabaptists, Methodists, Jews, and even Catholics—will almost all be liberals contaminated by the creed of Rousseau, and very little of Calvin's doctrine of predestination will be left. The Germans, with their Lutheran taste for noisy gaiety, are going to contribute heavily to de-Anglicizing the country and, in a certain way, Germanizing it. The Jews will communicate to the American civilization the disquietudes of their "century-laden humor." The Irish, on their part, will gradually introduce into the American culture—to use here a felicitous expression of André Siegfried—"that nameless something, diabolical and fascinating, which is the spirit of the Celts, that taste for fantasy, for jesting, for disorder, without which the Puritan atmosphere would become unbreathable."[21] All these transformations, however, were to take place without substantially modifying the Calvinistic structure of American capitalism. This would not only maintain itself within the United States, the only country that was born Calvinist, but would spread, irresistible and dominating, through Protestant countries in general and even through the Catholic ones.

With some differences:

Where the Anglo-Saxon, with the amalgamation of these several influences, is going to construct a practical capitalism with evangelistic and political preoccupations about collective well-being in general, the capitalism free of social duties and too careless of the moral aspects of its mission, where the Puritan is going to overestimate the concept of the essential dignity of labor, the ex-crusader is going to debase it by handing over all labor to the slave alone. Where American capitalism is going to benefit from the Anglo-Saxon immigrant's intention of staying in the country—an immigrant who became spiritually Americanized immediately—Brazilian economy will have to wait two centuries for the Portuguese and his descendants to become organically Brazilian.

5

Indeed, until the middle of the seventeenth century, and even the beginnings of the eighteenth, the term *brasileiro*, "Brazilian," as an expression and affirmation of nationality, was practically nonexistent. "Brazilian" at that time had various meanings. On this side of the Atlantic it served to designate those who exploited brazilwood; on the other, it was the nickname applied to the Portuguese who, after making their fortunes in Brazil, returned rich and proud and bedecked with honors to their native land, already marked by the moral and psychological changes that the New World had produced in them.[22]

In those days, the sons of Portuguese born in Brazil were *mazombos*, a social category apart, and to which no one wanted to belong. So much so, that to avoid the epithet, which sounded like the essence of ono-matopoeic ridicule, the son of a native of Portugal did not hesitate to claim birth in the Kingdom and to adduce noble ancestry to prove it. He even made voyages to Portugal with the sole object of deleting the epithet, since that was the only recourse accepted as legitimate for the purpose of obliterating the unpleasant circumstance of having been born in the colony.[23]

In the United States there was nothing like that. The immigrant brought to the shores of the New World refused from the first to be anything but an American. Turning his back on Europe, first for religious reasons, later for economic and political reasons, bringing with him his wife and children and possessions, as soon as the ship rigged the gangplank he promptly severed the umbilical cord that bound him to his country of origin. From that moment on, psychologically if not culturally, he was no longer English but American, and only American. He was American by choice, as his children and the generations that followed him would be American.

Latin Americans in general resent the North Americans' calling themselves "Americans," *tout court,* not bothering to identify themselves in any other way. They consider it usurpation. In point of fact it is not. Because while the children born in America of Portuguese and Spaniards are *mazombos* in Brazil and *criollos* [Creoles] in New Spain, the sons born to Englishmen in the American colonies are the first to adopt the title of "American" and to take pride in that status.

That is not what happened in New Spain and in Brazil. No one embarked for Brazil with the *animus permanendi* of the American, but with the intention of getting rich quickly and returning even more quickly—if that were possible. The Portuguese who embarked for the New World, unlike the Puritans of New England, had no intention of establishing a new religion and founding a new country. He was satisfied with and proud of his old Portugal, which was still glittering then, before the defeat of D. Sebastian on the sands of Alcazarquivir, in the full splendor of its glory. The emigrant came to Brazil without his wife, without his children, without his possessions, in search of wealth and adventure.

Stay there? No, almost no one wanted to do so of his own free will. Permanent residence in Brazil was something for the convicted criminal, who had no alternative.

A symptomatic fact: Among the first four white settlers of the land of Santa Cruz, two were exiled criminals.

And it is under this fateful sign that European settlement of the newly discovered land begins. During the first thirty years, that land attracted only ruined noblemen and would-be gentry, or adventurers, deserters, and Jews in flight from the Tribunal of the Inquisition.

As to the Jews, evidently, with the memory of the expulsion and persecutions still quite vivid in their minds after centuries of nearly complete integration into the cultures of Portugal and Spain, to which they felt deeply bound, no kind of stable activity could appeal to them at all. And if it is true, as Corneille's personage says, that the dearer the offender, the graver the offense (*Plus l'offenseur est cher et plus grave est l'offense*), the Jews probably had reason rather to wish the ruin of the Peninsular peoples than to encourage the economic development of the Spanish and Portuguese possessions in America. In any case, they certainly had no reason for desiring the economic consolidation of the Catholic countries, in which they continued to feel themselves menaced. On the contrary, because of the treatment accorded them by Spain and Portugal, they would become from the first, in the economic, ethical, and scientific fields, the natural allies of Protestantism, and particularly of Calvinism. Consider the contribution of the Portuguese Jews to planning and administration in the Dutch regime in Brazil, and also the difference between their modes of economic conduct in the Catholic colonies of Latin America and in the Protestant colonies of English America.[24] In the latter, allied to the Puritans, they devoted themselves to useful types of activity; in the former, disguised as New Christians, burning with resentment, their activity as a general rule was predominantly mercantilistic and predatory. The time had passed, evidently, when the Jew, by monopolizing the handling of money and the banker's functions, in which he was protected by the princes of both Church and State, performed a task considered useful. Now he had to hide, to make himself out to be what most often he was not, to avoid the synagogue, to avail himself, in short, of every means of survival. He was no longer interested in the consolidation of the Catholic states; he was, indeed, deeply interested in their growing weakness. And, when the period of mining came, he would smuggle gold from the mines of Brazil to the United States, where his blood brothers, at the same time they could openly frequent their synagogues, were frankly dedicating themselves to increasing their fortunes and to developing the economic and financial system of the Anglo-Saxon world in which they already occupied a place apart.

In Brazil, meanwhile, everything that might imply an obligation to remain permanently would be shunned. As long as it was a question of making a quick fortune, fine. To remain, to devote oneself definitively to stable activities or to other permanent forms of work was an ideal which did not enter into the cogitations of the Jew. Neither of the Jew nor of anyone else.

Coming to Brazil with the intention of staying would be a much later phenomenon. What happened to a great number of hereditary *capitanias*,[25] the same kind of *capitanias* which later were to be so successful in the American colonies, is illustrative. Donated by the King in order to encourage the development of the colony, six of them never saw their owners. This despite the powers and advantages attached to the grants, which would perhaps yield more than enough to repay the difficulty of the undertaking.

Save for the occasional exception, the European and the descendant of the European, the New Christian and the descendant of the New Christian wanted only two things from Brazil: a land to exploit and a refuge in time of trouble. But whether land for exploitation or refuge of deserters and fugitives, Brazil was no more than an intermezzo of adventure. It was an intermezzo for the recipients of royal grants as it was to be for the governors-general and for the Court of D. João VI, driven out of Portugal by the troops of Junot.

It is true that no one conquers a land or takes refuge in it without ending by being to a certain extent conquered by it. In time, some because they cannot return, others because they no longer want to return, nearly all end by adjusting themselves to the new land, no longer wishing to exchange it for any other. João Ramalho and Diogo Álvares are in this category. The same would be true of Anchieta, Manuel da Nóbrega, Antônio Vieira, and the Jesuits in general.

If, in the classic definition of Crèvecoeur, "He is an American who, leaving behind him all his ancient prejudices and manners, receives new ones from the new mode of life he has embraced, the new government he obeys, and the new rank he holds,"[26] he who brings with him his European traditions only to absorb later a South American experience capable of reducing in him the ancestral desire for a definitive return to Europe, that man is a Brazilian. It is very nearly what happens with Prince Maurice of Nassau. In a certain way, this is also the case of D. João VI. Everything leads one to believe that, if left to his own wish, he would have remained in Brazil among the palms he planted there, never more to return to his old Portugal. With thousands of New Christians an identical phenomenon was to take place. So complete would be their acculturation that today their descendants, having lost the memory, or the very notion, of their Semitic origin, their economic virtues replaced in them by canonical virtues and by Brazilian qualities and defects, now absolutely indistinguishable from Portuguese-Brazilians of the purest Lusitanian or Lusitanian-Indian strain, constitute an utter contradiction of the theory that attributes innate, permanent, and inevitable psychical qualities to races.

This was the process of incorpation that took place on a large scale in Brazil. There was another, however, which yielded nothing to it in importance: It was nationalization on a more reduced scale, but highly selective, that took place far from Brazil among those who, paradoxically, struggled hardest to assimilate Lusitanian nationality, the *mazombos*.

They went as adolescents to study at Coimbra in order to become Portuguese, in the same way that the *criollos*, the Creole youth of Spanish America, set sail for Madrid and Salamanca to make themselves Spaniards, and when they became conscious of themselves they no longer wanted to be, no longer could be, anything but Americans and Brazilians. Different from the Portuguese, different from the European, marked by those special and unmistakable peculiarities that geography and history had been impressing upon them in the process of regional differentiation, it was in foreign parts and particularly in Portugal that they finally discovered Brazil. On the banks of the Mondego they were to receive the real revelation of their new fatherland. In Europe, Portugal, and in Portugal, Coimbra, is where they were to be possessed of that sentiment of nostalgia that characterizes the Brazilian songs of exile and for which Gonçalves Dias found its highest and definitive expression in his immortal

> My land has palm trees,
> Where sings the *sabiá*;[27]
> The birds that warble here
> Sing not as those do there.

From the moment they became conscious of the new mental and emotional character instilled in them by the world from which they had departed, they could no longer belong integrally to Portugal, and from among them were to emerge the principal precursors and molders of the new nationality. From Basílio da Gama to Cláudio Manuel da Costa, from da Costa to José Bonifácio, from the *Inconfidência*[28] to Independence, perhaps none of the precursors and leaders of political, economic, and cultural emancipation failed to undergo this process, which was, moreover, the process of integration undergone, from Miranda to Bolívar, by the great liberators of Hispanic America.

To be sure, these young Americans of Brazil retain much in common with the Portuguese. They have the same Catholic emotionalism, the same attachment to family, they live much more in terms of family than of community, they still speak the same language. Nevertheless, the language they speak is no longer strictly the same. In their manner of speech as in their way of looking at the world and at life they not only differ from the Portuguese, they also differ among themselves. But, different as they are among themselves, those of the North shaken by the terrors of nature, those of the extreme South relieved of such fears, those of the littoral loquacious, those of the highlands, discreet, those of the mountains reticent and taciturn—they all have that indefinable something that was already permitting foreign travelers in the eighteenth and nineteenth centuries to identify them as Brazilians.

6

And what of the *mazombas* who stayed in Brazil? The title of *mazombo* died out and disappeared. Not so the type that originated it. Even at the beginning of the present century Brazil was swarming with *mazombos*. In spite of four centuries of civilization, in spite of already having, in a certain way, solved the racial problem, in spite of the victorious struggles against the French and Dutch invaders, in spite of the revolutions of nationalist aspiration, in spite of the First Kingdom and the Second and the Republic, in spite of the extinction of yellow fever, and in spite of the country's growing importance in the international markets and councils, Brazil still continued to be infested with *mazombos*. Conscious *mazombos*, unconscious *mazombos*, but always *mazombos*. Until the beginning of this century the expression still circulated. "I am a Brazilian, *mazombo* or mulatto," said João Ribeiro in a notable page of criticism, as though to synthesize the ethnic and social constitution of Brazil.[29]

And in what does this Brazilian "mazombism" consist? Just as in the earliest colonial times, it consists essentially in this: the absence of determination to be, of satisfaction in being, a Brazilian, the absence of a taste for any kind of useful activity, the lack of initiative and inventiveness, the lack of belief in the moral perfectibility of man, the scorn for everything other than quickly won fortune, and above all the lack of any collective ideal, the nearly total absence of any feeling of the individual's belonging to the place and community in which he lives. The American's "sense of belonging" does not exist in the *mazombo*.

At heart the *mazombo*, without knowing it, was still a European astray in Brazil. Of Brazil and America, of their history, their needs, their problems, he knew little or nothing because he lived on the coast with his back turned mentally to the interior. Did things go badly in Brazil? Ah, that had nothing to do with him. Besides, what could he do, since he stood alone against all the others? In public or private life it was never through his fault or negligence that such things happened. The blame always attached to others. Abstaining, rationalizing, contradicting himself, not participating, reducing to the minimum his physical, spiritual, and moral efforts toward elevating and making more wholesome the environment in which he lived, paying not to be bothered when it was a matter of the collective interest, flattering, compromising, corrupting,

moving heaven and earth when it was a question of his own interest—
there was none like him for contaminating the atmosphere with sadness,
immorality, indifference, and defeatism. Inexhaustible as were his reserves of ill will toward all that had to do with Brazil, he insistently gave
his sympathies to all that was European.

At the beginning of the past century the *mazombo* was spiritually
Portuguese, and was constantly irritated with Brazil because Brazil was
not an exact copy of Portugal. At the end of the century, as the sympathies of Portugal had turned toward France, he was irritated with Brazil
because Brazilian culture was not an exact projection of French culture.

Detached from what was going on about him and living in his imagination on the other side of the Atlantic, if he were told that the South
American peoples in general and the Brazilians in particular were among
the worst-nourished in the world, or that they were suffering from chronic
hunger, or that the infant mortality rates in Brazil could be compared
only with those of India, it would not trouble him in the least. Something more would be required if he were to show himself moved. It
would be necessary to talk, in the early decades of the present century,
of the hunger being suffered by European children in the First World
War. The poor Belgian babies! The poor French babies! And *Vive Paris!*
And *Vive la France! Oh, la France, la France éternelle!*

Culture? Only France had that, and wisdom, and learning, and patriotism, and finesse, and savoir faire. In the world, Europe; in Europe,
France; in France, Paris; and in Paris, Montmartre. Decidedly, without
a trip to Paris no cultural education worthy of the name could be
complete.

And let someone timidly venture to say that in North America, also,
there were inventors, that among every ten inventors at least five were
Americans, that America was already producing a quite reasonably good
literature, sometimes even a stirring one, perhaps the most exciting of
our time; that she had a superb theater, superior even to the French;
that she was gathering up all that was best in the world in all branches
of knowledge and comfort. The *mazombo*, European to the marrow,
would take the statement as a personal slight.

Culture in the United States? That's ridiculous! And also he was
informed on good authority that there was "more civilization in a back
alley of Paris than in the whole vast city of New York."[30]

By all logic, with this passion of his for everything French, the
mazombo ought to have been politically a liberal spirit, a lover of
the trio, "liberty, equality, and fraternity." But the truth is that the
mazombo, like other living beings, was not logical. On the contrary, he
was a bundle of contradictions. Politically, in Brazil, with few exceptions,
he favored authoritarian regimes more than democratic ones. Liberalism

to his mind was all very well—and note this!—for France or for other nations of a high cultural level. But in Brazil, given the crass ignorance of the majority of the populace, a people of mixed blood, that was not possible. Political equality? Utter nonsense! Wherever have you seen your vote worth only as much as that of your lackey or your washerwoman?

No, the *mazombo* did not favor political equality, and much less social equality. He was, rather, frankly and openly on the side of privilege, provided, naturally, that the privilege was for him. Yes, everything was different for the *mazombo*. With what unconcern he sued for and accepted privileges and favors! That others not be granted what he wanted, that laws and regulations be invoked against others, was right and proper. But that he, son of a great sugar planter or the grandson of *bandeirantes*, should be entangled among the commas of legal documents—that could only mean premeditated injury, pharisaical provocation. Why, didn't they know that everything they might give or grant him would always be less than what he deserved in exchange for the favor he was doing them by living among half-breeds and savages? Life for him, the son of somebody, ought to be a sum of rights and privileges, never a sum of work, responsibilities, and duties.

And woe to him who denied him what he demanded! He was consumed with hatred and resentment, a resentment that was the more destructive to his emotional balance in that it redounded against himself. And because he had lost his sense of proportion he suffered intensely, for great and small motives too, and at times more for the small than for the great. Taking little pleasure in what was given him, suffering intensely because of what was refused him, the *mazombo* was incapable of only one thing—being happily at work.

Work? Well, that is . . . It depends. If it were a question of a simple sinecure, with money to be had at the end of each month, on the order of a life pension, very well. In the absence of a gold mine, a chief or providential protector, a government concession to sublet to a third person, an administrative legal post thanks to friendship with some minister of state, one should not turn up his nose at the sinecure. Nothing, however, that might mean having to work regularly and creatively, or, what is worse, having to confess to his acquaintances that it required any effort, for hard work was made for the Negro. Besides, what advantage was there in earning one's living by honest work? Where was the stroke of fortune in that, where the gold mine? These lay in adventure, in gambling.

To win at gambling—here was one of the great joys of the *mazombo*. Indeed, among all his pleasures in life these two stood out: to gamble and win, to gamble and lose. Just so long as he was gambling. To gamble was for him, without his knowing it, another way of symbolically seeking the vein of gold, of fighting destiny, once more the fight of one against all, of all against one, as in the search for the gold mine. Because earning a salary regularly, in routine fashion, in industry or commerce, had no savor to it and was not for him. After all, trade was the monopoly of the Portuguese. There was even a real monopoly in fact from which *mazombos* were excluded by the incessant hostility of the established merchants. "Up to Independence and even in the heyday of Empire . . . Brazilian trade is exclusively foreign, and from it nationals are systematically excluded."[31]

The Puritan saw the mark of the Lord on the man who prospered. The *mazomba* saw the mark of destiny, of fate, on the man who "hit it just right." In adventure, in life, in gambling, in the lottery, at roulette, the essential thing was to hit it right.

Another passion of the *mazombo* was the indiscriminate chase after women. Just as in the world of intelligence no one had wit but himself and his friends—*Nul n'aura d'esprit hors nous et nos amis*—in the world of morals no woman had honor, virtue, and decency except those of his own family and, sometimes in cases of special deference, those of the families of his few friends. If he had to draw up a code of morality, he would shut his family up inside the home and accept willingly that all the rest be governed by the law of free love. As for other women, married, maiden, or widow, white or dark, they would almost invariably be regarded as the object of the chase or of conquest. The prospect of an elopement, an adventure without involvement, would always find him ready; more than that: a man capable of real effort, he generally disdained every honest form of activity.

The impudent air with which he would stare at a woman in the street! Certainly staring at women and taking pleasure in their beauty has always been a universal pleasure, "a feast for the eyes," but for stripping women with one's gaze there was none like the *mazombo*. In this both Europe and the United States had to bow to Brazil.

As for the rest, neither good nor bad. Merely reticent, uncommunicative, taciturn. Nothing but a disgruntled man with an impatient and historical desire for self-assertion, awaiting a culture in which he might realize himself normally.

7

Faced with one of these human specimens in which, unfortunately, Brazil's fauna was fertile, the Anglo-Saxon tourist used to conclude that there were structural defects in the character of the Brazilian. But he came to a hasty conclusion, because truly there is nothing structural or hereditary or immutable about character. In essence the *mazombo*, as to a certain extent the *criollo* about whom similar conclusions were drawn, was only the unconscious victim of his cultural heritage, of the falsity of the idealized images that contributed to his development, as the descendant of the pioneer in many respects would also be, in part, the reflection, the unconscious beneficiary, of the authenticity and adaptability in historic time of the idealized images that he inherited from his elders.

From the amalgamation of contradictory images entering into the training of the *mazombo*, it was evident that no healthy, happy, cordial, constructive entity would emerge. Rather, a gloomy, peevish, quarrelsome being, just as the dictionaries define him, would come forth. For, besides the meaning assigned to the term by the dictionaries, to designate "an individual born in Brazil of foreign, especially Portuguese, parents," *mazombo* further served as an adjective to signify "somber, gloomy, taciturn; ill-tempered."

Why gloomy, taciturn, ill-tempered? Merely a question of resentment. Resentful yesterday against the Portuguese for not allowing him to rise to their social level, resentful later toward foreigners because he had neither the conditions nor the qualifications to allow him to compete with them and make his mark upon the environment in which he lived. With these feelings the *mazombo* could not contribute in any way to elevating, exalting, bettering the civilization or the social well-being of the environment in which he moved; instead, with his jeremiads, his quarrels, and his calumnies, he helped saturate it with discouragement and defeatism.

Where, for that matter, could the *mazombo* turn to seek inspiration and guidance for higher moral conduct? To the example of his father or his grandfather? To the suggestions of the "big house" and the slave quarters, of the mansions and the jungle huts of the rural and urban patriarchate? To the more remote inspirations of the *bandeira*?

Now, there was no world less moral than that of the *bandeira*. To start with, its principal, if not its only, mainspring was greed. Greed and lust, the hunting of the Indian and the hunting of his woman in constant South American reiterations of the rape of the Sabine women—this, on the ethical plane, is the synthesis of the history of the *bandeiras*. In them what ruled was not moral law but the law of the strongest, incarnate in the figure of the leader holding the royal charter. Everything must stem from him—the initiative, good or evil, reward and punishment. All favors and benefits were to come from him. He alone distributed the spoils—the gold taken in or the product of the sale of enslaved Indians.

Virtue? Belief in the natural goodness or the moral perfectibility of man and humanity? These were problems that never occurred to the members of the *bandeira*. Virtue was not what the priest preached as virtue, but rather what was the use and custom of the chief or what he approved of. If on the coast he pursued women with the same dash and abandon with which he took the Indian woman in the backlands, then virtue would be polygamy and not monogamy or chastity. If courage, fidelity, and gratitude were the qualities that most merited his approbation, the first as an existential condition of the *bandeira* and the last two as the condition of his permanent authority as leader, then in the moral code of the *bandeirante* there would be no room for virtues other than gratitude, loyalty, and courage.

As for principles, only one would have any importance and must be guarded by every means and at all costs—the principle of authority.

And woe to those who infringed it! And woe to those who considered they had a right to more than what the chief's generosity accorded them! Woe to the ingrate, woe to the insubordinate, woe to the unfaithful! Then the chief would be implacable, because he would be lost as soon as his authority suffered the slightest scratch. Not even with his closest friend, in the event that he could permit himself to have friends, could he temporize. Fernão Dias Pais, ordering his half-breed son killed for insubordination, furnishes an example of what the *bandeirante* leader was capable of doing when the principle of authority was at stake.

Cruel? Neither cruel nor mild. His procedure in this case was not guided by personal feelings or by ethical concepts, but solely by the greater or less resistance that society offered to the imposition of his authority. If the social group were plastic, docile, and willing, why would he be choleric and violent?

In the presence of these two worlds, that of the father and that of the Jesuit educator, what could the *mazombo* do? Follow the teachings of the Jesuit or the examples of the father? Align himself with the priest, who assured him that the supreme virtue was chastity and the supreme manliness the mastering of his own passions, or with the father, who, as the son reached fourteen or fifteen years of age, was already taking alarm at his son's not yet knowing a woman, at the same time that he seemed to prove by example that the strongest man was not the one who mastered himself but the one who dominated others and had the capacity to possess the greatest number of women and to beget, along with his legitimate children, the greatest number of bastards about the world? Side with the father, who had an animalistic concept of life and family, or with the Jesuit, who understood them humanistically as projections of a moral and theological idea?

In a world in which polygamists and adulterers were toasted as heroes, where could the *mazombo* find the strength of mind to react and alter the idealized image that the father offered him? There were only two alternatives. He either revolted against the father, setting up for himself a new mode of conduct, facing reproof, raillery, and reprisals, or, despite the initial revolt, followed the paternal example, even seeking to surpass him, preparing body and soul to succumb to the physical and moral infirmities that his anti-Christian conduct and his unchivalrous chasing of women would generate in him.

And yet, as in life facts do not repeat themselves but only succeed each other, between the *bandeirante* and the *mazombo*, in spite of the proverb "Like father, like son," there will be a profound difference. The *bandeirante* father, though intrepid and preying upon Indian women, succumbed in the beginning to what was almost biological necessity, while the *mazombo*, who was in a position to marry and live decently as befits a man in organized and established society, succumbed to pure imitation. The *bandeirante* was natural, and when occasion required, brave; while the *mazombo*, forcing himself to appear valiant, lived inwardly in a state of panic, in fear of death, fear of mystery, fear of disease, fear of decisions, fear of change, fear of the future.

Another thing. The father sinned without boasting of the sin. The son, a prey to narcissicism, would have an irrational need to be admired because he had sinned. Between the sin of the one and the sin of the other there is the same difference as there is between the sinners of the Middle Ages and those of the modern world. In the Middle Ages, not even through much sinning did the sinners lose respect for virtue and sanctity; in the modern world, with the advent of the Renaissance and, on another plane, of Protestantism, and the abolition of confession, sinners and dissidents, instead of doing penance, went so far as to demand admiration for their errors, nothing causing them more uneasiness than the existence, in the absence of saints, of simple honorable men.

Such was the case with the colonist and especially with the *mazombo* in the sixteenth, seventeenth, and eighteenth centuries in the presence of the Jesuit. Such was the case with the anticlerical, heretical *mazombo* of the late nineteenth century who, incapable of healthy admiration, could see in the most generous purposes only trickery, fraud, and rascality. Honor was to be found nowhere. Dignity, patriotism, propriety, respectability, clean living, honesty, great purposes, high and noble intentions—he would not allow talk of those beyond the limits of his corrosive, fulminating, final, definitive judgment. The idea that such things might be the subject of serious thought would be insupportable to him.

Absolutely incapable of respect and tenderness? That would be an overstatement. Toward his father, toward all that represented the social projection of his father—the priest, the most immediate authority, society—perhaps. With his mother and the projections of the maternal image it was different. Under his emotional rigidity, in the innermost recesses of his sensibility, he retained infinite reserves of love and affection for his mother, or for the idealized image he created of her as the compensation for the deformations and disfigurations to which he would subject the paternal image. In his eyes, his mother would always be a saint and on her all his affection would be concentrated, for on this point his drama or his neurosis is connected with the drama of the half-breed, of which, indeed, it shows strange reflections.

Just as the half-breed has a maternal fixation, the *mazombo*, from early childhood stricken, deeply stricken, in his affections either by the long absences of his *bandeirante* father or by the sufferings the latter inflicts upon the mother with his wildness and irregularities, also takes refuge unilaterally in the maternal love, from which he detaches himself only to turn to the narcissistic love of self or to the idealized image he gradually forms of himself, in proportion as he finds himself incompatible with external models and as his social environment rejects him. So that, outside himself, whether as a baby or as an adolescent or as an adult, the maternal love will be the only one in which he will feel secure and to which he will be capable of responding. Hence the Brazilian glorification of the maternal image.

In all civilizations, in all religions, the mother and the projections of the maternal image are loved and venerated symbols. In none, however, not even in the North American civilization, where the tendency toward matriarchy is accentuated day by day, could public worship rendered to the mother be as exalted as it was in Brazil. Exalted and exacerbated. So much so that the *mazombo* resented much more the insult addressed to him obliquely through his mother than the impact of a direct insult.

In this his reactions were really identical with those of the mulattoes.

Dangerous to take in vain the name of mothers of mulattoes and of *mazombos*, for in no country was the cult of the maternal image so intense and alert as in *bandeirante* and patriarchal Brazil.

Furthermore, discounting whatever there was incestuous, neurotically incestuous, in the worship of her, the colonial mother, *bandeirante* and patriarchal, did much to merit the admiration and respect of the civilization and culture that she helped to shape. Resigned, faded, and dim, suppressing her resentments, suffering silently, it is around her and thanks to her that Brazil was to be formed. Around her and around the family feeling inherited from the Portuguese. If Brazilians constitute a people today, a more or less homogeneous civilization, with the various races on the way to a perfect social understanding, in spite of the harm done by the males of early times, that is due in great part to those exemplary Christian figures of *bandeirante* and patriarchal Brazil.

Those women were truly notable in the unconscious collaboration they gave to the constructive in the century-long struggles of the constructive and humanistic against the animalistic and predatory! Admirable as mothers, admirable as coadjutors of the clergy, admirable as foster mothers. Sheltering under the same roof together with their own children the half-breed children of the errant loves of their husbands—nests of vipers in their homes—there was nothing they would not do to palliate the condition of the foster children and make them forget they were bastards.

One thing, nevertheless, they rarely gave their foster children: gaiety. No one gives what he does not have, and for them marrying was only "childbearing, trusting, and weeping."

With the advent of the patriarchal, slaveholding, latifundian Brazil of the sugar cane plantations, this changed in part. Not so much, however, that the position of children and foster children was fundamentally altered in regard to customs and moral conduct. If, on the one hand, for the wives of the sugar lords marriage was not only "bearing children, trusting, and weeping," as it was for the wives of the *bandeirantes*—and there were also exemplary patriarchs to serve as exceptions to the rule of the colonial family of "saturnine fathers, intimidated mothers, and terrified children" of *bandeirante* Brazil—there was, on the other hand, the corrupting influence of the slave quarters to retard the winning back of the *mazombo* for the Christian concept of life and for work, especially for work.

8

While this was going on in Brazil, in the United States the colonist, and later the pioneer, the son and the grandson of the pioneer, turning their backs definitively on Europe and the past, with instincts whetted by a new capacity—the capacity to adapt themselves, proper to those who emigrate with the intention of remaining—are working and inventing, adapting and perfecting, creating with the existing good the good that never existed. While the heroes of the *mazombo,* on the cultural plane, are the scholars, the erudite, the dilettantes, the depositaries of culture with no immediate practical end, the heroes of the descendant of the pioneers are the mechanics, the engineers, the organizers, the accountants, the managers, the inventors; and where the measure of the *mazombo's* values is static culture, that of the pioneer is dynamic culture, capable of *accomplishment,* a word significantly untranslatable into the Brazilian tongue.

While the *mazombo* does not believe at first sight, and almost as a matter of principle, in anyone's virtue, the pioneer's descendant is a believer in the possibility of the moral perfecting of man through the perfecting of things; while the *mazombo* lives with eyes turned toward Europe and his European past, the American has turned his back on Europe and the past; while the *mazombo* is a non-practicing Catholic, the descendant of the pioneer, an assiduous reader of the Bible, Protestant or Catholic, is profoundly religious; while the *mazombo* has an aversion to laboring with his hands, the American enjoys only activities in which the use of the hands is highly important, since even in his favorite sport, baseball, that is imperative; while the elegant thing for the *mazombo* is to display scorn for money, the American attributes a mystical value to money, making of his banks veritable cathedrals of the dollar; while the *mazombo's* hobby is gambling or woman-chasing, or both, the American's is gardening, the workshop, or the research-laboratory.

Artisan's workshops and research laboratories! There is another immense contrast between the civilization created by the pioneer and that created by the *bandeirante.* Rarely to be found in Brazilian homes, they are the rule in American homes. An American's house without its workshop or its lab, or something that resembles laboratory or workshop, is the exception.

Hence the thousands of inventions and gadgets[32] with which America annually contributes to the progress of humanity. Startling, the swiftness with which these inventions follow one upon the other! In 1783 Benjamin Franklin invents the lightning rod; in 1787 John Fitch makes his first demonstration of the steam engine on the Delaware River; in 1793 Eli Whitney unveils his cotton gin; in 1798 David Wilkinson invents a machine to make machines; by 1802 Oliver Evans completes his high pressure steam engine, still more powerful than James Watt's; in 1807 Robert Fulton makes his steam vessel, the *Clermont*, go up the Hudson from New York to Albany; in 1833 Obed Hussey and Cyrus McCormick patent their mechanical harvesters; in 1834 Samuel Morse inaugurates his telegraph line between Washington and Baltimore; in 1847 Richard Hoe prints eight thousand copies per hour of a newspaper in Philadelphia; in 1851 William Kelly begins to develop his process for making steel, anticipating Bessemer's discoveries; in 1862 Gatling patents a machine gun; in 1868 C. L. Schole puts out his writing machine; in 1875 G. F. Swift finishes and puts into use his refrigerator car; in 1876 Alexander Graham Bell sends his first telephone message; in 1877 Thomas Edison invents the phonograph; then comes Goodyear with the vulcanization of rubber, and Howe with the sewing machine, and Waterman with the fountain pen, and Merganthaler with the linotype. And the list does not end here. But it is not just the specialists, the professionals, who devote themselves to the business of inventing. The men of pure thought, the patriarchs, the humanists, themselves do not lose sight of the practical view of things. Thomas Jefferson, favored son of a patriarchal and slaveholding civilization, also invents. George Washington Carver, the educator born in Missouri in 1864, professor of botany in the Tuskegee Institute from 1896 and anticipator of plastics, discovers more than three hundred products into which the peanut can be converted.

Result: Counting both inventions and "gadgets" up to 1952, more than 2,600,000 patents registered in the Patent Office.

In the face of this startling figure, a racist would say that only the Anglo-Saxons or the Teutons have a capacity for invention. He would be wrong. George Washington Carver was a Negro, a black, the son of slaves, without a tinge of the "Aryan." Should we conclude from this that the black race sometimes, by way of exception, has some capacity for invention and research? The conclusion is obviously different. The prodigious Negro George Washington Carver, winner of the Spingarn Medal in 1923 and the Theodore Roosevelt Medal in 1939, became a researcher and inventor because the environment and culture in which he received his education was saturated with inventiveness and research and with respect for inventors and the enterprise of research. In Brazil, as in the other countries of Latin America, a George Washington Carver would be almost inconceivable. He would hear stories of Pedro Malasarte[33] tricking inventors and researchers, instead of the morally edifying stories about inventors and scientists that are, along with the tale of Robinson Crusoe—which is at once a great lesson in political economy and in inventiveness—the delight of American childhood. And woe to him if his mates come to find out that in the basement of his house he is studying the problem of the use of the peanut, or of coffee, or of the babassú nut, or of rubber, with the purpose of raising the standard of living of his region! He would certainly be taken for a madman. The parents, moreover, to put a stop to the lad's idiocies, would no longer allow either laboratory or workshop in the house.

Even if that thing they call "vocation" existed—and it does not—how to find inspiration and a taste for constructive work and initiative in the slave quarters? Where to get inspiration? In the example of the *bandeirantes*? In the stimuli of the sugar mill? In the lessons of Latin ancestors, lessons lent force by the Renaissance?

9

Here too, as in the case of racial prejudice, perhaps it is fitting to go back a little beyond the immediate origins of the Lusitanian-Brazilian civilization and recall that the distant ancestors of the *mazombo* stemmed from the Greco-Roman civilization in which handicrafts, as well as everything that would later come to make possible the industrial development of the modern world, were entrusted to slaves. A patrician had more to occupy him than devoting himself to the inferior trade of artisan. For him there was public life, the administration of property, war, the making of rules of law indispensable to the preservation and protection of his property and his privileges.

Could the ineptness of the *mazombo* in manual skills and subsequently in industrial technique come from that? It positively did not come from Christianity. On the contrary, if there is a great social accomplishment performed by Christianity, it is certainly that of having raised the dignity of labor. Recognizing a sacred function in labor, the whole Christian economy is based upon it. "The laborer is worthy of his hire," says St. Matthew.

It is true, as J. Lúcio de Azevedo observes,[34] that religious sentiment, "through the defective application of Christian charity," contributed, together with the discouragement produced by the Black Plague, to the increase of idleness to the point of obliging Afonso IV to order that the vagrancy of those who begged alms be punished by flogging; but what there is no doubt about is that, in contrast to the ancient world, which scorned labor, regarding it as proper only to slaves, it was Christianity that promoted respect for work and for the worker.

However that may be, in the middle of the fifteenth century the immediate ancestors of the *mazombo*, the Portuguese prior to the discoveries, as well as the Italians, had surpassed the Roman tradition and were admirably prepared for various forms of practical activity. In agriculture they were insurpassable. Portugal was a land of farmers. Moreover, fusing the Roman tradition with the Nordic and the Moorish, Portugal's craftsmanship and technique, and her science also, were then among the most advanced in Europe. In cartography, in any case, no one excelled the Portuguese. Notable also were her architects, master-builders and artisans, her sculptors and carvers in relief. And there stand Brazil's colonial churches with their altars, their lavaboes, and the beauties of Brazilian baroque, to testify that even in the eighteenth century such admirable technical skill, with its corresponding spirit, had not been completely extinguished.

One thing, however, the Portuguese had not transplanted to Brazil with their architecture, their sculpture, their craftsmanship, and their technique—the inspiring flame of the master artificers of the monasteries of Batalha and of the Hieronymites. This flame was dying there and then, to do no more than flicker in Brazil, together with the spirit that engendered it.

That is understandable. Those who in Portugal had been artisans, master craftsmen, or even farmers, in Brazil turned to such occupations only if they failed at the profession of finding gold mines.[35] In other words, they turned to those occupations as failures and not as conquerors, for the ideal image they first entertained was that of the conquistador, that of the discoverer of mines, a symbol before which all the other idealizations of colonial society—the priest, the educated man, the farmer, and the patriarch—fell to a secondary plane. At bottom, the desire of all was to follow to the letter the oath exacted of them by the Kingdom: "[I swear that] I will perform no manual labor so long as I can get a single slave to work for me [by the grace of God and the King of Portugal]."[36] Why waste time in producing goods of secondary value when there were treasures to win? If they came to Brazil to discover mines and treasures and did not succeed, they considered themselves robbed when they had to earn the equivalent of mine and treasure by the normal processes of arduous labor in their old line of work. They worked, and worked hard, when necessary, but without the good will and devotion of those who take joy in their work, for the Kingdom itself did everything possible to degrade the dignity of manual work and every form of useful labor.

"I did not come here to work like a laborer but to seek gold,"[37] Cortés declared, the Conquistador of Mexico. The statement is Cortés', but it could well serve as the device for the attitude of conquistadors and *bandeirantes* in the early days of Brazil. "The whites and the natives of Portugal, even though they be reared with hoe in hand," says the governor of Rio de Janeiro, Luis Vahia Monteiro, "on setting foot in Brazil not one of them wants to work, and, if God does not provide them with lawful means to get along, they usually support themselves by theft and fraud."[38]

Against this the Jesuit also clamored in vain, seeking to protect the Indian from servile labor. The colonists, in reprisal, waged war without truce on the fathers of the Company of Jesus. "Those fanatics," they used to say, "are delivering us up to the claws of the Indians."

According to Gandavo, slaves were the first thing the colonists tried to secure: "And the first thing they seek to obtain is slaves to work their lands for them; and if a person manages to acquire two pairs or half a dozen of them (even if he has nothing else of his own), he then has a means of honorably supporting his family, since one fishes for him, another hunts for him, the others till and cultivate his fields and this way men have no expense for maintenance, neither for their dependents nor for their own persons."[39]

"It seems incredible," comments Roy Nash, "how enslaved by the ideal of having someone else do all your daily work, originally strong, energetic, able-bodied men could become. Pope Urban VIII in 1639 pronounced the severest censures of the Church against any one who enslaved an Indian, converted or not. When the Bull of Excommunication was read in Rio de Janeiro, the people broke open the gates of the Jesuit college and would have murdered some Paraguayan fathers if the Governor had not intervened; in Santos they pulled down the Vicar General who was publishing the Bull and trampled upon both him and it; in São Paulo they rose and expelled the Jesuits from the city."[40]

Of course, it was not to be expected that the *bandeirante* would restore in Brazil the Portuguese tradition of craftsmanship. Nor could it be expected of the rural patriarchate of the sugar-cane cycle, all based on slave labor. Wherever technique, inventing, creating, and not merely transplanting, might be needed, there the *bandeirante* was not to be found, nor later, the *mazombo*. When the stream-borne gold was exhausted, and sluices were no longer adequate for extracting it, *bandeirantes*, patriarchs, and *mazombos* would see no other recourse than to relinquish the exploitation of the mines to foreigners, in whose hands they still remain.

What else could they do? With the kind of education that had been given them, they could hardly avoid that solution. In the best of cases they came to be learned men and even genuine humanists; never or very rarely, as in the exceptional case of a José Bonifácio or an Alexandre Rodrigues Ferreira, authentic scientists or technicians. To recite in Latin, to compose hemistichs, to cultivate drawing-room skills—that was their forte. But solving practical problems with the help of science— that was not within the scope of *mazombos*.

Applied science was too closely related to the idea of work, and there- fore to the shame of slavery and loss of social standing not to be suspect to them. And then, never would the Jesuit dare to offer any sort of practi- cal apprenticeship to *bandeirantes* or patriarchs or to the sons of patri- archs and *bandeirantes*. For daring far less than that they had already incurred more than enough troubles. It was all right to make stone- masons, carpenters, or blacksmiths of the Indians or Indian half-breeds. To teach them, the Jesuits themselves became masters of all trades. "They made sandals of wild thistle and cactus fibers, which served them for shoes; they learned to be bloodletters, barbers; they learned all the other trades and callings with which they could be of use to all their fellow men in that exile from the world."[41]

But working at mechanical trades was not much esteemed; quite the contrary. Hence the air of justification with which the Jesuits refer to their own activities. "Nor should it seem a new thing," explains Padre Simão de Vasconcelos, "and much less one not respectable, that our religious should busy themselves at such trades; for neither did Saint Joseph think it a thing unworthy of the father of Christ (which he was in the general conception of men); nor did Saint Paul consider it un- worthy of an apostle of the school of Jesus to earn what they were to eat by the labor of his hands and the sweat of his body: rather, he was an example imitated by the most perfect religious of antiquity, accustoming, with this plan, his body to labor and his soul to humility: it came to be a rule sent from Heaven, which the angels dictated to the holy abbot Pacômio."[42]

As the lack of professional craftsmen was great,[43] the Jesuits saw no other solution than that of teaching such trades to the Indians.

With *mazombos*, however, their tack had to be different; they had to form child prodigies, the kind that would be the amazement of patri- archal Brazil and would shine at Court.

To shine at Court! The Jesuits' schools were right at hand to educate those young prides of their families, those precious adolescents, those high talents who then lost their adolescent ways to become grave, learned, well-speaking, omniscient men. There were positively none like the Jesuits to instruct those young prodigies who were the delight and dazzlement of patriarchal Brazil. In everything else, a plague, those Jesuits; but for that purpose—one had to admit it—there was none like them.

And why take up science, which conquers Nature, when there were so many Latin authors to consult? Why worry about real problems when time was so short for cards and the classics, sacred and secular history? The terrible thing was not the not knowing how and the not learning how to extract gold from the depths of the earth, or how to organize the sugar trade on a permanent basis; the awful thing, the inexcusable thing, was to be ignorant of the latest European events, the most obscure passages from Virgil, the subtleties of the grammarians, the minutest rules of rhetoric. To be ignorant of the Portuguese classics in those days —horrible!—was a matter of civil death, so great was the shame that this could mean.

This taste for the show of erudition, for fake humanism and false universalism, this preoccupation with purely ornamental culture, was to affect all the centers of education in the country. And as a result, in part, of the latifundian, slaveholding, and *bandeirante* civilization of Brazil it is so strongly rooted even today that, in spite of abolition, in spite of the fall of the Empire and the advent of the Republic, it could not be completely extirpated. Alberto Tôrres, as late as 1920, declared that "on the general level of society and as regards the higher forms of culture, dilettantism, superficiality, dialectic, empty flights of language, a taste for ornamental phrases and for conceits consecrated by notoriety or by the sole prestige of authority, replaced the ambition to educate the mind for the purpose of guiding conduct. Applause and approbation, the satisfactions of vanity and self-conceit, compose the whole ambition of men's minds. To attain to the truth, to be capable of a solution, to train the mind or character to resolve and to act, are things alien to us."[44]

In other words: We have reached the present century still utterly unequipped for the industrial era that the great scientific discoveries of the past century have established. And were it not for the haloed name of Santos Dumont to save the situation, this revolution would have been consummated without Brazil's, and in general Latin America's, contributing to it with a single invention, the least achievement. Whenever inventions were required, neither *criollos* nor *mazombos* were ever to be found.

10

To the *mazombo* what was good enough for his father, for his grand-father, for his great-grandfather, was good enough for him and for his children, too. To the American, on the other hand, everything is sus-ceptible of improvement, institutions as well as things. Unhampered by prejudice against change and by the experience of his European ances-tors, he is the perfectionist par excellence.

The Brazilian, *mazombo* or half-breed, and also the *criollo*, with their profoundly European mentality, reacted toward the past either in the manner of Auguste Comte, for whom the living must always be more and more governed by the dead, or in that of Karl Marx, for whom the past was such a mountain of opprobrium, ignominy and injustice that everything must be swept away and destroyed until not one stone of the past should be left upon another. Among the former the dominant thought was return to ancient times. They might be called exiles in time, whom unavoidable fate had banished from the golden age in which everything was admirable, beautiful, just, and perfect. Among the second group, in contrast, the fundamental idea is the frenzied and implacable smashing of all traditional values crystallized into an order intolerable to them, an order that would cease to oppress and harm them only on the day that they could reduce it to a heap of rubble.

The American, however, faced with the past, reacts neither in the manner of the Brazilians and Europeans nourished on Auguste Comte nor in the fashion of the Brazilians or Russians nourished on Karl Marx. And much less, of course, like the Germans, Italians, and Spaniards, who until recently were dreaming of restoring Germany to the gods of Germanic paganism, Italy to her past Caesarean and imperial grandeur, and Spain to the times of Philip II. The American's attitude is different. He feels neither obfuscated nor oppressed nor impeded by past ages. The past does not bind him, does not subjugate him, does not annihilate him. He preserves the past when the past seems preservable to him. He destroys it with the greatest nonchalance whenever that appears to be necessary.[45] The Englishman, especially the Englishman of before the last war, the Frenchman, the Portuguese, defend the past for the sake of the past. The American, though, preserves things not merely because they are old but because they once yielded good results. He is practical and pragmatic. What use is there in changing something that once turned out well in the practical world? Has the Constitution turned out well? Then the Constitution is untouchable. Have capitalism and economic liberalism succeeded? One must lay no hand on the structure of liberalism and capitalism. And so the most timeless institutions, which long ago passed beyond the limits of their vital cycle, are preserved because once upon a time they yielded good results. Result, accomplishment, is their measure of values. Once a value is established, whether it be a matter of business custom or of political institutions, only when the world threatens to fall apart does the American feel inclined to reconsider the subject. Has the myth of free competition turned out well, and likewise unlimited production? He would never have altered his system of free enterprise had it not been for the crisis of 1929. Has Monrovian isolationism proved right? He would not have changed his isolationist attitude had it not been for Pearl Harbor.

Nevertheless, where the practical side of the past does not come into question, the American has not the slightest hesitation in destroying it. Hence, in contrast to his pragmatic conservatism, his eagerness to create the new, the unforeseen, and to alter styles consecrated by time, preserving nothing, or nearly nothing, in its primitive purity. Hence, in short, the American civilization, the most recent, the newest, the most disconcerting fact in world history.

Recent, new, and disconcerting not only in the sense of the inventive power of this people, but also in the sense of its power to create, based on perfectibility, an ethic in perfect accord with its technical power.

On this score the position of American civilization is unique on the plane of world history, not resembling that of any other people or civilization.

It is sufficient to compare it, we shall not say with the Oriental civilizations (the Hindu, the Egyptian, and, until very recently, the Chinese, to which their millennia-long past seemed so present that one might call it a chamber-music present—civilizations, one may fairly say, mummified and cold, impermeable to the present and to the future), but with the position of the most advanced European civilizations of the West, to ascertain how far the American civilization has outdistanced them with regard to the meaning of the past.

What a contrast, to be sure, between the American civilization and the Peninsular, from which the Brazilian directly stems!

Ancient, beloved Portugal, for example, lyric and sentimental, profoundly Sebastianist, if she no longer dreams of the return of D. Sebastian from the sands of Alcazarquivir,[46] still lives profoundly divided between the past and the present, between Europe and the colonies. In Europe the Portuguese dreams of far-off lands; in Asia or in Africa he is overwhelmed with longing for Europe. As for changing his way of life, creating new forms of economy, carrying out great changes, that is not for him. Fixed in Renaissance concepts of grandeur, he wishes to keep even the Portuguese language just as it was in the times of João de Barros or Bernardim Ribeiro.[47] And it is with the aim of preventing its enrichment with new instruments of expression that he supports, vigilant and inexorable, his brigade of purists. Moreover, the purist, perpetual member of historical institutes, his fists sticking out of his coat sleeves, his overcoat collar sprinkled with immemorial dandruff, monotonously celebrating the feats of his ancestors and the glories of the language, resentful and touchy about everything and apropos of nothing, was until recently, if we may believe the caricatures of Eça de Queiroz, the very picture of Lusitanian reaction, if not of the very decadence of Portugal.

And can the purist be the only one in Portugal who clings frantically to the past? Let no one be deceived about that. In evoking the past, in wishing to reproduce the forms of the past, there is general agreement.

Take for example the case of Eça de Queiroz himself. He spent his life acrimoniously censuring Portugal because she would not renew herself, would not adjust herself the spirit of the time; Eça could not see a purist or a *saudosista*, that is, a yearner after the past, without trembling with rage. And yet when the time came to present his own message of national salvation, he did nothing more than point to the formulas of the past.

In A Ilustre Casa de Ramires, in which he seeks to build after destroying so much, that is precisely what happens. At first the lord of Tôrre appears, Gonçalo Mendes Ramires, attempting to reproduce the past, his own past. He wastes long hours dreaming about the deeds of his ancestors. Beyond that he does nothing. He becomes déclassé. He sees his only opportunity in politics, in gaining a seat in parliament. He leads a neurotic existence between surrenders and longings for something better. He does not know how to get out of the trap into which he has fallen through his lack of energy. A perfect *mazombo* transplanted to Portugal.

Until one day he is attacked by a man of the people who had been provoking him for a long time. Gonçalo Ramires, in an outburst of shame and nervous energy, rises in his stirrups and lashes the insolent fellow who has seized his horse by the bridle. And in that decisive moment he finds himself again, with his profound ego, his heroic ego, the ego bequeathed to him by his forebears. He is saved. From that moment onwards Gonçalo sees everything clearly and goes on to assert himself. No longer is he interested in the seat in São Bento,[48] obtainable at the cost of basely selling his sister. He sets things in order on his farm. He is now a free man, no longer subject to the emotional dictatorship of his neurosis. He is therefore in a position to transmit his message to Portugal, his rehabilitating message.

In that very moment, when one expects that Gonçalo Mendes Ramires, after his two profound self-confrontations, will at last tell Portugal what course to follow to check her decadence and save herself, what does he do? He takes ship for the Orient, as though to indicate that, for Portugal, outside her colonial empire there is no salvation.

So the freshest mind that Portugal has produced in these last three centuries, that great European who was Eça de Queiroz, either because there was really no other solution or because he could not hit upon the right course, ended like every European by clinging to the past that he had spent his life inveighing against.

Was it for this, then, that he devoted his life to destroying and satirizing? His formulas for national salvation in economics very nearly coincide with those of the Portuguese who, having just emigrated to Brazil, leaving behind them family and community as had been done centuries before, continually protest against the restrictions that the government, through the Bank of Brazil, sets up to prevent the transfer of funds to foreign countries, and remain unconvinced that Portugal should no longer count on what her sons may be able to send from the former colonies.

Nevertheless, in this matter of seeing no other way out for Portugal but overseas adventures, Eça de Queiroz is not the most celebrated example. However incredible it may seem, the most illustrious is Camoens. The most illustrious and perhaps the first. With this peculiarity: No one sensed better or more opportunely than the author of *The Lusiads* Portugal's need to alter her course and return to productive work after the cycle of her geographic expansion. He saw that the thirst for gold and quick riches was debasing and corrupting the Portuguese people, who, once they had allowed themselves to be caught by the infamous vice of greed, were plunged into a "tenacious, indifferent, and abject despondency." If there is a message to extract from his work it is precisely this: the need for a change of course, because it was no longer possible to continue on the old one. In his opinion there was a time for conquest and another for the consolidation and assimilation of what had been conquered. It was fine for Portugal to take great pains to exalt and worship the glories of her forbears—he, Camoens, had set the model for it—but the glory of the new generations toward the end of the sixteenth and in the seventeenth centuries could not be the same as that of the fifteenth and the beginning of the sixteenth. It had to be a different glory, and it had to be won in the battles of peace.

Well, in spite of this clear understanding of the historical moment— and no one had a more sensitive intuition of it than the poet—it is *The Lusiads* that most profoundly influenced D. Sebastian, and with D. Sebastian the whole Portuguese kingdom, to launch forth on the adventure of Alcazarquivir, which was to precipitate the Portuguese national consciousness into the first shadows of her decadence.

Before the appearance of that epic work of genius, D. Sebastian, the fervent proponent of the North African adventure for the conquest of Morocco, was still heeding the voice of reason and the counsel of the men whose wisdom "was all of experience made." But once acquainted with the immortal strophes of *The Lusiads*, and with their effect upon all social classes in Portugal, there was no holding him back. He rushed feverishly into preparations for the journey from which he was never to return.

The meaning of all this is clear: *The Lusiads* aided in creating the ideal climax for the adventure of Alcazarquivir at the very moment when the possibility of risk in the undertaking, which so alarmed the conservatives, seemed to set it aside. And—a still more singular fact—it is Camoens himself who, while at first the partisan of a policy congruent with the Portuguese medieval past, would end his poem foreseeing and in a way advocating the perilous enterprise. That, indeed, is the sense of the exhortation addressed to D. Sebastian at the close of the poem, since in this finale, at the same time that the poet's prefiguring mind sees the king's inclination, he seems to encourage it, telling him that he has at his service an arm made for weapons and a mind consecrated to the Muses to sing his glory. One would say that for the Portuguese there was only this alternative: conquer or perish.

No, decidedly it will not be in Portugal and among the Portuguese that one may hope to find a healthy reaction to past conquests.

And much less, it is perfectly clear, in Spain among the Spaniards. Here the desire to return to or preserve the past is still more intense. Times change, forms of government are amended everywhere, new rhythms are imposed on the West, but feudal, Catholic Spain, even at the beginning of this century, was spiritually still clinging to the past, very ill-resigned to the loss of her vast empire. And it cannot be other than symptomatic that, a few years back Ortega y Gasset, one of the most luminous Spanish minds, frightened by the rhythm of our time, wrote *The Revolt of the Masses*—which, after all, is nothing but an anguished clamoring for a return to hierarchy, to aristocratic government, to the now impossible discipline of the patriarchal world.

The spectacle of France, under her bespangled glitter, was a painful one even before the war. She had constructed her Chinese Wall on the German border and thought herself well protected. She had exhausted herself in the trinomial motto of *Liberté, Égalité, Fraternité*, and neither knew how nor wished to create anything more. She considered that she had reached perfection, and saw no reason to change. Was not Paris the capital of the world? Was not everything already accomplished? Yes,

everything was perfect, nothing should be altered. And today as yesterday, and as always, the living continued to be "ever more and more
governed by the dead."

11

In the United States, however, things change considerably in appearance and significance. For the American as pioneer, the past does not
count. Or, as an American essayist stresses, "the past, in the historical
sense, did not exist for the pioneer."[49]

That is why the reaction of the American people to the past is so
different from that of other peoples. And to see this it is not necessary
to go very far. It is sufficient to go visit the American in his home. There
one can find all the elements needed for understanding his exact position
with regard to the past. In his house is reflected, furthermore, not only
the position of the American toward the past but also his tendency
toward inventiveness in, novelty in, and adaptability to the world in
which he lives.

Isolated in the middle of a park or jammed together with others in
the standardized monotony of housing "developments," the American
house in its structure and planning is nothing but the log cabin ampli-
fied—that is, the pioneer solution of the problem of shelter for the present, without compromises with the remote past and without regard for
the distant future. While in Brazil, as regards architecture, the colonist
limited himself, despite the country's wealth of timber, to transplanting
the "big house" and the two-story house, or to accepting the African
hut and the Indian straw-thatched dwelling, combining or innovating
very little, the pioneer in his westward march left to the eastern coast
the preservation of English architecture in order to improvise upon the
log cabin, progressively revising it to fit new circumstances of space and
time.

Another thing: Eminently extroverted, American houses as a rule, like
the primitive cabins of the pioneers, are not separated from each other
by walls or fences, there being even a pronounced tendency to abolish
entirely any kind of fence or hedge. In any case, high walls of the Spanish
type, walls topped with pieces of bottle glass, so common among Latin
Americans even in the early years of this century before the extinction

of yellow fever, when they served to collect rain water and the stegomyia that carried the disease—such walls do not even exist as a reminiscence of colonial times in the United States. On the whole, American houses from the beginning presented rather a feeling of community than of defense, protection, and individualism.

Let it not be concluded, however, that American houses are better than the Brazilian in solidity of construction. On this score the latter, a transplant of the Mediterranean masonry houses, are much more solid and durable. Of course, great houses and mansions are also constructed in the United States with the European sense of time and posterity. There are, however, the exception. What predominates is the house built of wood, the sense of immediate utility, present, "right now," a nonchalant disregard for its resistance to time and the ages, a circumstance that well sets forth, on the plane of architecture, the American's psychological position before the idea of the past, so different from that of the European and the Brazilian.

Further, it is not only in this aspect that the American house exemplifies the nature, the tendencies, and the conceptions of American culture. Many others also reflect them.

Observe, for instance, their dining rooms. They are the least important rooms in the house. But how well they reflect, in their discreetness, the sobriety, the near-frugality of Americans in the matter of pleasures of the table! While Brazilians put all their luxury and care into the room destined for meals, for their heavy lunches and dinners in the Portuguese manner, the American dining room, puritanically modest, is a secondary part of the house or apartment, even tending in small apartments to being replaced by improvised tables, or else totally abolished. In this detail one may clearly see the scant importance given in Calvinist America to culinary satisfactions. A typically American dining room having been observed, it is not surprising that, if a special cuisine corresponds to each civilization—a French cuisine, a Chinese, a Spanish, even a Brazilian!—there is no real American cuisine, a circumstance of which European and South American sociologists and tourists avail themselves to deny any civilization, or rather, any culture, to the United States.

And yet, what those tourists and sociologists do not point out is the excellence of the American diet from the point of view of health. In the morning, when the stomach has had a long rest and is unburdened, the Brazilians—the well-to-do ones, of course—never get beyond their insubstantial coffee with milk and bread and butter. At noon they stuff themselves with lunch after the Portuguese fashion, in a hot, almost tropical climate, incapacitating themselves for really productive work in the early hours of the afternoon, which are generally devoted to napping, to indolence and heaviness, if not to suffering hangover headaches. Only at night, when they dine early, do they eat with some propriety, order, and discrimination.

But for order and discrimination at meals there is none like the American. In the morning, breakfast: tomato or orange juice, to prepare the stomach and refresh it; then scrambled or fried eggs and ham or bacon, some cereal or other with milk (not to be confused with what Brazilians call milk) or cream. And then comes coffee with cream, and bread and butter. And so the American is ready for the morning's work without waiting for the lunch hour in anticipation of Homeric *feijoadas* or *bacalhoadas*[50] irrigated with wine.

While the Brazilians, in their hot climate, drink wine and beer, eat *feijoada* and *bacalhoada, vatapá* and *caruru*,[51] encouraging heavy somnolence and hangovers that give a stuffed feeling, making them complaining, indolent, and inefficient during the first hours of the afternoon, the American eats his frugal lunch composed of light, scientifically vitaminized foods. As a drink, just milk (not to be confused, it is well to emphasize, with the stuff that Brazilians are obliged to call *leite; milk* is something different), tea or coffee with cream. And no wine, no beer during meals. It is not at table that America gets tipsy. It is positively not in the dining room that America achieves her startling consumption of alcoholic beverages. That takes place in the bar, before or after meals, rarely during them. In the bar and in the living room.

The living room!

Impossible to understand the psychology of the North American without penetrating the significance of the living room. If the middle-class Brazilian contents himself with a vague, crowded little cubicle to receive, sometime or other, the vague and uncertain visits that are going to interrupt him and occasionally upset his eminently private and individualistic nature, the American, much more gregarious, social, and socialized than he admits, in spite of his much proclaimed individualism, makes of the living room the center, the most characteristic and welcoming part of the house. There is where he likes to be; there is where he receives visitors; there is where he discusses the problems of the day; there is where he holds his social gatherings; there he feels himself a pioneer again, like his ancestors. A pioneer, and of the community, whose problems he regards as an extension of his own problems, especially when they are of a technical nature. And he will never refuse to confront a question that directly or indirectly affects him and the country, alleging that he is only one against all others, or that the question ought to be solved by government action. While the Brazilian expects everything of government, the American sees—sees and senses—in governments mere agents of the will of the people. While the Brazilian exempts himself from responsibility and from the duty of watching over the public weal, accustomed as he has been—by written and particularly by oral tradition —to seeing in the government the real owner or master of the country, the American never ceases to regard the country as only an extension of his own home, always, being on the alert, vigilant, demanding of his representatives, of the President, congressmen, and senators an accounting for the administration and use of the goods over which it is their duty to watch. While the Brazilian, in the realm of sociability and social duties, gets beyond the bounds of the family only with difficulty, the American lives permanently within and for the community—and at times considerably more as a member of the community than of his family. The Ibsenian legend that the strongest is he who is most alone positively has nothing to do with him. On the contrary, he is always in meetings for the purpose of solving collectively the problems of his section of town, or the problems of his profession, or those of his city or community. And his prestige will be the greater in proportion to the number of clubs, fraternities, societies, and brotherhoods to which he belongs, or the number of conventions he attends and in the work in which he participates, whether as a consequence of his specialty or as the representative of his county, municipality, or state.

12

The conventions! Startling, the number of conventions held annually in the whole country. Rare is the hotel in large cities where one or more conventions are not being held. In the Waldorf-Astoria alone, in New York, nearly four-hundred a year are held. The same thing, *mutatis mutandis*, is true of the Shoreham in Washington or the Drake in Chicago, and so on.

The uninformed observer, in view of the noise with which the convention members, overflowing with cordiality, scatter at night through the cities like veritable adolescents in search of adventures, may suspect that these conventions are merely Protestant substitutes for the saturnalias of the Middle Ages, a mere social mechanism of compensation for the constraint imposed by the stifling Puritanism of certain towns and cities in the interior. The impression will be false. Not that the descendants of the Puritans are as exemplary in their conduct as their *Mayflower* ancestors, and absolutely never misbehave. Of course they have their peccadilloes! Discreetly, methodically, they do behave badly sometimes. Nor will it be necessary to go to the scabrous data of the famous *Kinsey Report* on the sexual habits of the American male to learn that, in this matter, the American of our time does not keep rigorously to the model of his Puritan ancestors, or that, when he hangs the well-known card DO NOT DISTURB on the knob outside the door of his hotel room, he is probably not always reading St. Paul's Epistle to the Corinthians, as Calvin recommended.

Nevertheless, it is true that, despite the abundance of the DO NOT DISTURB cards in American hotels, there continues to be a great difference, a difference of degree if not of kind, between Americans and *mazombos* on this score. While the *mazombo*, putatively Catholic, sins with ostentation and even makes a hobby of his sin, sinning with sin and sinning with open scandal—which is the most devastating of all sins, for the terrible effects it has on the spirit of new generations—the descendant of the Puritan sins like the medieval sinner, without making a display of the sin (this, naturally, when he does not avail himself of divorce to legitimatize his adulteries). While the former gives himself up wholly and openly to sin, the latter, besides paying lip service to virtue with the maneuvers of his duplicity and hypocrisy, reserves his best energies for his puritanically confessable hobbies. And, of course, for the central theme of the conventions in which he participates. No one can dissuade him from taking the items on his agenda seriously.

An example will illustrate the case.

In 1943, in Chicago, suffering from a heavy cold, a Brazilian newspaperman spent several days in his room at the Drake Hotel, on doctor's orders, protecting himself from the severe, cold, treacherous winds off Lake Michigan. Those were three days of absolute isolation. The only human beings who appeared in his haven of rest were the waiter who brought him his meals, and the maid.

The maid, like certain orators, liked to hear her own voice. As she changed the towels she would flutter from one topic to another. The Brazilian was stuck in the middle of Chicago like a Robinson Crusoe without parrot or monkey, and so he found pleasure in listening to her.

The maid was intrigued by the guest in the next room, a gentleman from Oklahoma who strode up and down, nervous, agitated; he drank whiskey, he ate nothing, he received no friends. He had come to attend a newspaper convention that was to be held soon, and he was interested in nothing. In vain did the maid try to get a word out of him. The man from Oklahoma remained mute and impenetrable. And this fascinated the maid.

To the point that she could not restrain herself and went to report the fact to the management. A little afterwards she came back with the explanation: on the list of Oklahoma men missing in action was the son of the guest in the next room, and what is more, his only son.

The Brazilian, obviously, felt the enormity of that grief almost as his own. He could see it all, the return home, his neighbor's meeting with his wife, the mother of that son who had died because of hate, he who had been engendered by love. And because he had not the strong nature of those who can master themselves, the Brazilian fell prey to an extremely powerful emotion. He was moved as he had not been for a long time, remembering his own sons.

But several days later he heard with surprise the name of his Oklahoma neighbor mentioned by one of his colleagues as the most capable, active, and hard-working in the whole convention. No one had worked so hard, no one had presented so many projects, no one had taken his task so seriously (connected with the war bond drive), the project that constituted one of the principal objects of the convention.

At first, the Brazilian journalist deplored the emotional expense he had been put to, he who did not know the Oklahoman and had not known the son.

Later, however, he understood everything. The Oklahoman had stifled his grief, his father's feelings, because the death of his son had taught him that it was necessary to work, to do something useful and definitive, so that other fathers, millions of fathers, might not have to go through what he was undergoing. Yes, it was necessary to win the war, but it was necessary above all to win the peace. It got one nowhere to look back when time does not turn back. Great was his grief, but beyond the grief of a father was the social duty of preserving others from new reasons for distress, and, above all, the human duty of finding the means of sparing other American youths from being slaughtered. His way of overcoming grief was to work with human objectives, not to stop, not to look back. The Oklahoman, his nerves stiffened, mastering his emotions, was the very image of Puritan America.

And now one may comprehend the reason for the respect inspired and commanded by these conventions held in America.

Extending their ramifications throughout the country, bringing the North closer to the South, the East to the West, functioning as channelizers of collective experience and knowledge on every specialty, as channelizers of public opinion, these conventions constitute the real government of the country. It is enough to say that it is from them that presidential candidates emerge. The political conventions are not, indeed, the ones of major importance. The scientific ones, those that bring together the commercial and the industrial worlds, are as important, or more important, since it is by them that the life of the American man and woman is conditioned.

Is there, for example, a problem of education or of production or distribution or health disturbing the life of the community? Or a problem of a technical nature that, once solved, would save the industry in question millions of dollars? Already a group of Americans is gathered in the living room discussing the matter and stating the problem. If the living room is too small, the problem is taken to the community house. And if the community house or town hall is insufficient, being very limited and local, the problem ends as the object of a round-table discussion or of a convention.

There a great number of technical experts, specialists, or ordinary amateurs inform themselves about the subject, and the convention, with all the weight of its authority, makes the problem the target of nation-wide concern.

From that moment they will not let the matter rest. Throughout the country there will be thousands of individuals in search of a solution. Only in university laboratories or in the offices of the great industries and foundations? No. In his own home there will be many an American who has turned the collective problem into a hobby and transformed the basement of his dwelling into a workshop or laboratory.

13

And here we come to the most consistent, most revealing part of the North American civilization and culture: the basement. The living room and the dining room and the bathroom itself—into which the Puritan does not admit the *bidet* and where the pioneer taste for the bathtub sometimes dispenses with the shower—explain a great deal, of course. But ever since the workshop that the pioneer maintained in his cabin was detached from the living room, from the point of view of American civilization the most important part of the American home has definitely been the basement.

In Portuguese dictionaries, basement is *porão*, the part of the house between the ground and the floor. But only with great disrespect can one confuse one thing with the other. Brazilian *porões* lack what the basement rarely or never lacks, the workshop or the laboratory. Along with the washing machine and a whole array of apparatus connected with the heating of the house and with other comforts, in a room apart;

the American will not do without any of them. One would say that he could live without music, without drink, easily without literature, and with some difficulty he could live without a show or entertainment, or without the Bible, but he will not live without his workshop or lab where he can give himself full scope and opportunity to use his hands and indulge his taste for research.

When Francis Bacon, in his *New Atlantis*, after condemning the "degenerate learning" of the metaphysicians, recommended experimentation, cooperative investigation of Nature, empiricism and rationalism, tireless observation, the recording of new observations and investigations, as a principle of conduct leading to full mastery of the subject in the most utilitarian sense possible, making efficiency and utility the touchstone of all conclusions, he could wish for no more faithful disciple than the American in his basement. Perhaps he might be alarmed and even a little horrified at the loss of human substance that the complete subordination to fact and to the objective world would require of the disciple, but that was to be the price of the world he dreamed of. Perhaps, too, he might become impatient with the intuitive slowness that this constant subordination to objectivity involves, to the point of its being said in our own day that the continual practice of exact measurements ends by dulling the mind; but as regards combining, coordinating, integrating, and applying the abstractions of those who have the capacity for sensing intuitively, for abstract thinking and generalizing, Bacon could want no better. The technical man he foresaw, enemy of metaphysics and philosophy, adapted to the world of experimentation in which qualities superior to the average are not necessary and in which sometimes even qualities inferior to the average are a good thing, the twentieth-century North American was to exemplify fully. When it was a question of great boldness of intuition, of discovering unknown worlds, of advancing like the discoverers through "never before navigated seas," of believing without seeing—with that blind faith that Don Quixote demanded of the Toledo merchants when he proclaimed the beauty of his peerless Dulcinea del Toboso—Bacon's disciples would leave much to be desired. But no one can beat them in following in the footsteps of the true discoverers, in establishing their hold on the territories poetically and magically foreseen, in making useful the theories and hypotheses they at first disdained, until they have carried out in practice, with their insuperable know-how, all that might be proclaimed possible in theory. In this not the English nor the French nor even the Germans are superior. Germans, French, and English, however imbued with Protestantism, are still too deeply impregnated with Catholic and humanistic qualities to be able to compete on this point with the North Americans, who have emerged uncontaminated from the bosom of the Reformation. Just as Calvinism prepared the American for the economic revolution of the seventeenth century and the final advent of capitalism in the nineteenth, rationalism, pragmatism, materialism, and utilitarianism, stemming from that same revolution and from the final flowering of Protestantism, were to prepare him, more than anyone else, for the industrial revolution of our time. He would be a technocrat par excellence, as the United States would be the paradise of technocracy. In theology, in philosophy, in metaphysics, in pure mathematics, in poetry, in culture without immediate utility, he would consent to be excelled. But that he should be excelled in mechanical ability, in know-how, in capacity for organizing, combining, and mastering the world of matter, he would permit only against his will. His passion would not be for philosophical systems; his passion would be for gadgets. And just as he swells with pride when someone mentions his ability as a mechanic, cabinetmaker, lathe operator, or research worker, so he resents being called an intellectual. "I am not an intellectual" is a reaction frequently heard in the United States, even among philosophers.

In this the difference between Brazilians and North Americans is abysmal. So different are the former that, if there were no danger of oversimplification, one might say it suffices to invert the terms of the North American problem to say that, while the American's passion is practical knowledge, which leads to the gadget, the Brazilian's is for general ideas, which leads to nothing. At bottom the Brazilian admires uncommitted culture much more than science in action, in the same way that he covets both fortune and learning obtained through strokes of luck and boldness far more than learning and fortune gained through constancy in study or in work.

Is there, for instance, a professor who does not work, who spends months without bothering about his university chair, and another who is pure devotion to work and approaches all the points of his program with practical sense? Between the two, Brazilians frequently do not hesitate in preferring the one who does no work. The general assumption is that the one who does no work is cultured, and not the other. Learning, fame, and fortune won at the cost of practical efforts do not as a rule inspire great respect in Brazilians. What they really admire is not culture in action, but culture and knowledge in the pure state. From the moment that culture enters into action and is to be put to the proof, ceasing to be a mere idling about in the disembodied void of the imagination to descend to the world of action, which time and experience and circumstances must demarcate, the deterioration of its respectability begins, because what is really wanted is that culture be static, not dynamic and practical.

This is why, were it not for a few famous names such as those of

Santos Dumont, Osvaldo Cruz, Carlos Chagas, Vital Brasil and, more recently, those of Manuel de Abreu and César Lattes, Brazil would have nothing to offer to humanity in the way of inventions, or even technical refinements and improvements.

Can anything more be needed in order for us to understand and explain the rhythm of Brazil's backwardness compared to the speed with which the North American civilization has advanced since the Industrial Revolution of the nineteenth century? Can it be necessary to go still further through the histories of Brazil and the United States to understand what it is that, together with coal and petroleum, makes the American civilization go forward in a geometric progression and the Brazilian in an arithmetical?

No, not that much is needed. The *bandeirante* and the pioneer—the former, symbol of Brazilian civilization, and the latter, symbol of American civilization—if they do not exhaust the subject, nevertheless tear away the veil that used to conceal Brazilian mysteries.

There are no longer any mysteries.

Add to North American geography the pioneer's attitude toward the fundamental concepts of the past, moral perfectibility, and the dignity of labor, the first two creating the ideal climate of psychological saturation for the fulfillment of the last, and one will grasp, with the exception of the imponderables that escape science and human comprehension, the essence of North American development. Add to the unfavorable Brazilian geography the *bandeirante's* limitations concerning the status of labor, the possibilities of rectifying the past, and the question of the moral perfectibility of man and humanity, and one will have, once again discounting the mystery of the imponderables, the essence of Brazilian development.

And now?

Well, now, unless a fundamental change of course happens in the development of the two histories, and new symbols and new images replace the old, or unless the main lines that have presided over the formation of Brazil's culture are rectified, this rhythm—geometric progression in the United States, arithmetic progression in Brazil—will tend, instead of toward reducing, to accentuate the differences more and more.

Is such a change capable of being realized, such a rectification feasible and desirable?

IV

Image and Symbol

1

FROM THE RESISTANCE OF THE INDIVIDUAL TO MODIFYING HIS MENTAL categories in mid-life and to replacing the symbols dear to him, even when he recognizes the advisability of the change, it can be concluded that the task of renewing collectively idealized images cannot be one of the simplest. It is indeed a most difficult task, granted the persistence through the ages of the idealized images fundamental in the process of the elaboration of cultures.

Impressive, this persistence! Times change, cultures broaden their radius of action, branch out into subcultures, cultural continents break up into archipelagoes with autonomous and differentiated islands of subculture—this is the case of Brazil; cultural archipelagoes fuse into continents at the same time that they broaden their sphere of influence —this is the case of the United States; new ideas are substituted for the old, new techniques and new ways of life are adopted, but the images first idealized and magnified as symbols in the heart of cultures—as, for example, that of the *bandeirante* in Brazil and of the pioneer in the United States—these might be said to be irremovable and indestructible.

Not that there have not emerged, in the course of the histories of Brazil and the United States, social movements tending toward replacing those images with others more in conformity with the new times. These movements have never been lacking. But the truth is that, in spite of them and the new images that seek to destroy the old, the romanticized images of the pioneer and the *bandeirante* still continue strong throughout their respective areas of influence.

138

2

Observe, to begin with, what has happened in the United States to the image of the pioneer.

No sooner was it sketched in more or less definite outline in the early days of the eighteenth century than, with the appearance of urban concentrations and intense maritime activity, this image, as a symbol, came to be seriously threatened in New England, the seat of its first triumphs. The great men were now no longer only those who cleared the forest, built their cabins, plowed the soil, provided their own sustenance, read their Bible, and maintained in their gatherings the spirit of the evangelical community. The great men suddenly turned into city men, outfitters of ships, lawyers, merchants—principally merchants. In Massachusetts, in Maine, in Connecticut, in all New England, with the land divided and parceled out, and many areas exhausted, no longer able to bear the clearing away as in early times, anyone who wished to pursue the pioneer way of life had to make ready his wagons, his belongings, and head for the West.

If the first really creative influence in the development of America stemmed from the pioneer spirit, the second would come from the broadening of the mercantile spirit through the effect not only of Calvinism but also of the sterility of the Massachusetts soil. Both these influences encouraged the bolder men to seek wealth in more lucrative activities than could result from the tilling of poor land. And from this group was to emerge a new social class, the famous New England merchants who were to have so great an influence and importance in the whole country. They would be the Yankees, a strange combination of regional conditions, Puritanism, and economic pragmatism, or, as Vernon Parrington says, "a product of native conditions, created by a practical economics."[1]

On the Atlantic littoral the zenith of the pioneer was evidently passing. Now the one who lorded it there was the shipyard owner, or the banker, the business agent, the pastor, the preacher, the moneylender, the Yankee. The small artisan, ally of the pioneer, would shortly have to emigrate in order to remain independent, since he could offer no resistance to the competition of the mills that were already rising.

At this juncture it was the West that saved the situation. The great trek westward was beginning, and it would end only at the Pacific.

But hardly does he set up camp on the new frontier when the pioneer feels a new threat. And one perhaps more dangerous than the first. The enemy this time is not the Yankee but the aristocrat with lace at his wrists from the cotton plantations of the South: the farmer, the planter. Patriarch, owner of slaves, autocrat in the fastnesses of his plantations, gentleman in his relations with the neighboring planters, extending the empire of cotton to the North and to the West the Southern planter is the type that began to speak to the national imagination; it is he who was to govern the country. Washington, Jefferson, Madison—three of the first four presidents, would all come from the South.

The consequence was that while the North, or rather New England, prospered and grew rich, and the South grew rich and governed, the pioneer came to be squeezed between those two worlds that he, with the habit of individual independence he had acquired, hated equally: the Yankee world of New England and the aristocratic, authoritarian, slave-holding world of the South.

To the Southerner, especially to the Negroes of the cotton plantations that are advancing toward the Northwest, the pioneer is merely the "poor white" who, not owning slaves, has to plow his land himself, build with his own hands the rough cabin in which he lives. To the Yankee, the pioneer is the poor relation who insists on keeping his independence when he could and ought to work in the Yankee's business firms, his shipyards, his shops, his banks, and his factories—for low wages, true, but sure pay and sheltered from the weather.

To simplfy: The Northerner extended his living space toward the West; the Southerner advanced northward and westward. The pioneer, hating them both equally, saw no other recourse for the moment than to advance upon the territory of the Indians and decimate them on both banks of the Mississippi. Not a very pious solution, to be sure, but in perfect consonance with his Calvinist credo, for even though there had been cases of kindliness toward the Indian, the general sentiment was in favor of extermination. And as the historian James Truslow Adams points out, if there was talk now and then of the glory of converting the pagans, most often little or nothing was done to that end. "The Reverend John Eliot, in Massachusetts, did attempt it, and translated the Bible into the Algonquian tongue, but he was almost the only person who ventured to think of the Indian as a soul to be saved."[2] The great majority saw in the Indian the son of the devil, the "devilish man who serves nobody but the devil."

Nevertheless, in the North American cultural triangle—Northerners in New England, patriarchs in the South, pioneers in the West (the Midwest of today)—the pioneers were not the ones who most hated the other two groups. More profound than the feeling of the pioneer toward Northerners and Southerners were the contempt of the South for the North and the hatred tempered with reverence of the North for the South.

Indeed, between Northerners and Southerners the most profound differences arose. Here they were political and social differences that separated them; there, economic, spiritual, and cultural divergences widened the gulf between them. Thus, for example, on the political side the North was frankly pro-Hamilton, while the South was pro-Jefferson. And as Hamilton, in the matter of government of the people, inclined toward a strong executive and greater and greater centralization of power, being notable for his worship of efficiency, order, and organization, while Jefferson fought for a broader and freer democracy in every way, it follows that the North—the North of the Yankees and the captains of industry, of course, not the North of the small rural proprietors—did not much believe in government by the majority but rather in the destiny of the moneyed oligarchies. The North thought that the government, besides being strong and centralized, ought to be ruled by the rich, and that laws, to be good, ought frankly to protect wealth and the merchant class, or at least not interfere with wealth, because, among the several freedoms for which it was fighting, the one that clearly most interested the North was the freedom of trade. This, in the Northern view, was the only freedom that man really lacked. Even if Calvin's doctrine about the intrinsic evil of human nature was no longer accepted, the North was too realistic to get excited about the excellence of human nature, a fundamental of the principle of government by the majority. To the Yankee, man was neither good nor evil, but simply an acquisitive being. Therefore it was proposed to organize a new society and a new political and social philosophy in accord with the needs of a capitalistic order, taking more thought for the exploitation and the rights of trade than for justice and the rights of man: "Its aspirations were expressed in the principle of laissez-faire, and in elaborating this cardinal doctrine it reduced the citizen to the narrow dimensions of the economic man, concerned only with buying in the cheapest market and selling in the dearest."[3]

As for social and humanitarian interests, the State had nothing to do with them; such functions remained outside the sphere of its cares. In this particular the North believed that the economic law—a term by which it designated the free play of the acquisitive instinct—was capable of regulating the life of men in society, and that, if full freedom of trade were attained, all the other little liberties would come in consequence.

And yet, the South of the great planters—not that of the small proprietors, nor that of the slaves, naturally—without disdaining free trade, considered it simply absurd to hand over the government to the city merchants. If there had to be a government, obviously it could not fail to be administered by the rural proprietors, who as everybody knew constituted the salt of the earth.

In short, the North saw the United States as a great world power, with strong, centralized government, great business, and rapid industrialization. The South feared these things. It wanted to keep the United States a nation of free landed proprietors as long as possible, understanding that the rapid growth of the great cities would produce a rootless proletariat and a herd mentality.

Besides that, the North was abolitionist and did not tolerate slavery; the South was slaveholding, adored slavery, and abominated any form of criticism of its way of life. It was an elegant way of life, sporting, chivalrous, generous, gentlemanly, similar in many respects to that of the sugar cane plantations in the center and north of Brazil at the time of the Empire.

As for the Negroes, whom the North wanted as laborers in its textile factories, the Southerner considered they were better employed as slaves on the South's plantations than as wage slaves in the factories of the North on starvation pay.

Between these two worlds—the North vociferating against slavery, the South wishing to propagate it in the new territories of the West where the empire of cotton was being extended—the pioneer who thought more of preserving his independence than of increasing his wealth, and feared all forms of centralization of power, was all in favor of Northerners and Southerners closing with each other and strangling themselves with each other's guts. While the South was Jeffersonian with deep reservations—for Jefferson, with his distrust of any kind of government and authority, and on account of his cult of independence of land-renters, was much more of a pioneer than aristocrat—the pioneer was Jeffersonian by conviction and with enthusiasm. Not only did it seem evident to him "that all men are created equal, that they are endowed by their Creator with certain unalienable Rights, that among these are Life, Liberty, and the Pursuit of Happiness," but he considered absolutely uncontestable the right of the people to reform or abolish any government that showed a tendency to destroy or reduce those rights.

In other words, the pioneer believed in the right to happiness. More than this, he believed in human perfectibility, for against the Puritan concept of an innately vicious human nature he set the doctrine of a human nature potentially susceptible to unlimited perfecting.

And here begin, too, his differences with Northerners, for while the North, the North of the Yankees—not that of the small country landowners, of course—fettered to the Calvinist concept of predestination and irredeemability of original sin, did not believe in the possibility of the rehabilitation of man through his own merits, the pioneer regarded the discriminatory God of the Calvinists, "a God of elections and reprobation, capable of condemning a whole race because the ancestors of that race had disobeyed a God of arbitrary will and discriminatory grace, as simply an immoral being, and said so frankly."[4]

But on this question of not accepting a discriminatory God, was not the pioneer moving away from Calvinism to return to the bosom of Catholicism, in which belief in the redeemability of original sin constitutes an article of faith? Not at all: the pioneer departed from the heresy of Calvin to fall into the heresy of Rousseau, which, by abolishing original sin and blame, transfers them to the societies in which man is compelled to live in full responsibility for the wrongs of the world and for the evils that afflict it. In other terms, the evils of the present are rather the consequence of faulty institutions than of the depravity of human nature, or of the capacity of man to do evil when he can do good.

With so great and fundamental an initial divergence, it may be understood perfectly that not always were the relations between pioneers and Yankees to be of the best. And yet, in accord with their motto of "live and let live," between North and South the pioneer gradually succeeded in holding himself equidistant in an unstable equilibrium. Let them leave him alone, free, independent, sufficient to himself and dreaming his American dream of an approaching perfect society, ideal, exempt from every flaw, without Negro slaves to call him "poor white"—that was all he asked of God. But either because he had not much faith in his prayers or because he addressed them to the wrathful, capricious God from whom he was beginning to alienate himself, and whom he had long distrusted, his vows and pleas went unheeded.

Now, as the North continued to vociferate against the South and the South grew more and more enraged against the North, stubbornly insisting on spreading slavery to the West, war between North and South became truly inevitable.

For some time it was still possible, thanks to the pioneer's neutrality, to maintain the status quo. From a certain point onwards, however, there was no compromise possible. And the war came, one of the most frightful wars in world history.

It was plain that in this struggle the side that attracted the pioneer would conquer in the end. The pioneer, despite his sympathies for the Southerner Jefferson, or perhaps because of those sympathies, ended by inclining to the North. The North won; it could not fail to win.

3

With the victory of the North over the South in the War of Secession, one might think that the already idealized image of the pioneer would be threatened no more. It would, rather, forever be incorporated into the popular imagination and into American culture, free of all graftings or impurities. Still, that was not exactly what happened. The immediate conqueror in the Civil War was, indeed, the pioneer. But the long-term victor would be the Yankee. With Abraham Lincoln assassinated on the morrow of victory, American national unification would proceed no longer under the generous aegis of the pioneer but in the tough fashion of the Yankee.

There begins the swift, vertiginous Yankeefication of the United States, a task for which the Yankee was to find strong allies in the human avalanches that were converging on America in quest of a better material life.

Just as the pioneer had superseded the Puritan, the Yankee was now to supersede the pioneer.

Thenceforth the Yankee is going to polish up everything, retouch everything, level everything, make everything neat. In spite of his prodigious capacity for taking over and assimilating others' creations, he will neither assimilate nor allow American culture to assimilate anything without first melting it down and remolding it after his own fashion. Religions, arts, philosophies, customs, symbols and images, political and family life, Bibles, dogmas and concepts—nothing more will enter America that he does not end by Yankeefying. For better or worse, but always Yankeefying.

The Yankee is going to remake everything, make everything like new. To make everything like new is the Yankee's passion, even if to that end he must polish with sacrilegious hand centuries-old bronzes covered with the patina of time. To change, plan, reconstruct, rectify, melt down, is at the very core of the Yankee mentality. But it is not a planning, a reconstructing and rectifying with eyes turned to the remote future. On the contrary: instead of making plans that are to last for millennia, the Yankee projects nothing—the house, the skyscraper, the automobile, social reforms—that cannot be carried out in the immediate future. His action is not influenced by the remote past or the distant future, but by the prospect of the immediate future, an extension of his own present, to the profit of himself and of those of his generation.

That is why the typically Yankee civilization is not a civilization with tendencies to base itself on stratified forms; it is, rather, a civilization that has an appointment with the near future and is always in a hurry. Yesterday it was hurry to win the war; today it is hurry to win the peace. Hurry to prove to the world that Thomas Paine, after all, was not so silly as he seemed in saying that he and his partisans had sufficient power to clean up all civilization: "We have it in our power to begin the world all over again."

Against this, it is true, those parts of the country—the Virginia of Richmond, or even the New England of Boston—most linked to the two English traditions of the nation, that of the South and that of the North prior to the Civil War, for a long time have been clamoring and rebelling in alarm. But that tendency to stratify traditional values has invariably been superseded by the impetuous agglomeration of the new migrations allied to the Yankees. No matter how literature, the movies, the museums, the universities, and a wisely organized propaganda may try to galvanize the past, to hasten to the assistance of the traditionalist part of the country that feels menaced in its Anglo-Saxon structure, tradition and the past are being superseded by the ideals that the Yankee has transmitted to the immigrant of recent generations about transforming America into the paradise of the common man, the man disburdened of the distant past and unworried about the remote future, the timeless man, the simple point of intersection of two eternities.

While the American traditionalist of the North and of the South takes up again the European motto, "What was good enough for my grandfather and my father is good enough for me," the motto that the imperial Yankee will teach the common man, the motto with which Yankees and common men will change the face of America and of the world will be a different one: "What is good enough for us must be good enough for everybody." If they, Yankees and common men, like skyscrapers, why should not others like them too? If they read, and like to read, the *Reader's Digest* and comic strips, why shouldn't others do the same? If they do not recognize hierarchies among the various kinds of labor, why should others discriminate? If they do so well with the "American way of life," why isn't that way of life adopted everywhere? If they are for free democracy, free enterprise, the American Constitution, why are North American economic and political institutions not adopted everywhere? What must be avoided and eliminated are differences, peculiarities. "Down with the different." And—awful fact!— differences, even peculiarities, are everywhere disappearing.

There is so much talk of the extreme cultural diversity of the United States, of a mentality of the North and a mentality of the South, of types in the East, the Midwest, and the West, all strongly marked by unmistakable characteristics, sometimes even antagonistic, that one might think such a leveling impossible. But the truth is that the miracle is being performed.

If it is true that one can still talk of a Northern mentality distinct from that of the South, of a Protestant mentality different from the Catholic, of liberalism in the Midwest and reaction in the South, of universalism in the East and isolationism in the Center, or of one American civilization of the Atlantic and another of the Pacific, as of social entities to which climate, geography, and form of production lend peculiarities that make them unmistakable, it is no less certain that, in general, one American is becoming less and less distinguishable from another American. The Yankee, subordinating men to things and not things to men, at the same time that he is extending his commercial chains, his trusts, his assembly lines, offering to all, from North to South, from East to West, the same clothing, the same foods, the same reading matter, the same radio and television programs, the same columnists, the same slogans, is slowly and gradually achieving, both on the international and on the national plane, what used to seem impossible. If it is true that in Europe and Latin America the job is barely started, since in both those areas the human, geographic, and social composition still varies from country to country, from city to city, and even from village to village, in the United States it may be said that the Yankee's work is on the eve of full consummation.

4

Incredible, the modifications undergone by the United States with the advent of capitalism and industrialism under the aegis of the Yankee![5]

For example, before the Civil War there was belief in the essential dignity of labor, but on the pioneer's terms: work as a means of winning and maintaining individual freedom, and not done or lent under conditions that might lead to servility or dependence. All tasks that suggested servility—work in factories, work as a waiter, as servant, as office boy— must be avoided. After the Civil War the concept that has been imposing itself is the Yankee's: work as an instrument of wealth if possible, as a matter of individual subsistence if necessary. In the moral code of the Yankee, work is justified by itself, whatever kind it may be, and is sanctified by the result. On this point the Yankee was to surpass the Puritan. While the Puritan, the historic proponent of the leveling of labor gradations, still had profound reservations about intellectual or artistic activity—poetry, music, sculpture, painting, literature, and particularly the plastic arts—having a horror, like most Americans even today, of being called "intellectual,"[6] the Yankee, direct heir of the Puritan tradition, as soon as he learned that literature, too, and also music, and also the theater, could lead to wealth (the era of the best sellers had already commenced), surrendered unconditionally to these new types of labor.

Before the Civil War the American was master of time. The pioneer having overcome the Puritan concept that it is necessary to work unremittingly, the South and West applauded minstrels, rhapsodists, poets, vagabonds, welcoming them everywhere. Storyteller bards, of the Mark Twain type, guitar slung over the back, saddlebags on shoulder, went from ranch to ranch, from farm to farm, from inn to inn, and, carrying the legends of the North to the South and bringing to the North the legends of the South, gave form to collective aspirations, sowed the country with dreams, with poetry and legend, and in short carried out a great work of integrating and spiritually unifying America.

Nor was it necessary to go far to the West to find them at the roadside. Walt Whitman, for instance, before his move to Washington, sang of America in Brooklyn, in New York, only a few steps away from the Yankee of Wall Street. And how the bard of Brooklyn sang!

Come, I will make the continent indissoluble,
I will make the most splendid race the sun ever shone upon,
I will make divine magnetic lands,
　　　With the love of comrades,
　　　With the life-long love of comrades.

I will plant companionship thick as trees along all the rivers of America,
　　and along the shores of the great lakes, and all over the prairies,
I will make inseparable cities with their arms about each other's necks;
　　　By the love of comrades,
　　　By the manly love of comrades.[7]

This man, evidently, the Yankee spirit would not dominate or subdue, and the ill-lighted factories of New England would not capture, because in him still predominated the pioneer spirit:

　　　Pioneers! O pioneers!

　　　Have the elder races halted?
Do they droop and end their lesson, wearied over there beyond the seas?

We take up the task eternal, and the burden and the lesson,
        Pioneers! O pioneers!

    All the past we leave behind,
We debouch upon a newer mightier world, varied world,
Fresh and strong the world we seize, world of labor and the march,
        Pioneers! O pioneers![8]

And how keen an ear the great bard had for the songs of America!

I hear America singing, the varied carols I hear,
Those of mechanics, each one singing his as it should be blithe and
    strong,
The carpenter singing his as he measures his plank or beam,
The mason singing his as he makes ready for work, or leaves off work,
The boatman singing what belongs to him in his boat, the deckhand
    singing on the steamboat deck,
The shoemaker singing as he sits on his bench, the hatter singing as he
    stands,
The wood-cutter's song, the ploughboy's on his way in the morning, or
    at noon intermission or at sundown,
The delicious singing of the mother, or of the young wife at work, or of
    the girl sewing or washing,
Each singing what belongs to him or her and to none else,
The day what belongs to the day—at night the party of young fellows,
    robust, friendly,
Singing with open mouths their strong melodious songs.[9]

He who thus sang and heard singing was the master of time and the
contemporary of all ages:

        It is not enough to have this globe or a certain time,
        I will have thousands of globes and all time.[10]

In the same period, in the West, another type of rhapsodist, years
before the Civil War, acme as he was of the first things that had
happened and "receptacle of things yet to happen, where the prophetic
tone of many others is announced," a certain Abraham Lincoln, the
future President Lincoln, after a long and silent apprenticeship to the
United States, first in Kentucky, then in Indiana, later in Louisiana, then
in Illinois—for he kept moving with the frontier—at the same time that
he was preparing himself emotionally to save the unity of the country,
was singing America in a rather different fashion: to the Southerners he
was transmitting the tales of the North and Midwest, and to the Northerners the magnificent folklore of the South. And how he could draw
effects from his anecdotes and his legends! He knew all kinds of tales,

light, fine, heavy, innocent, or scatological, and he had them ever ready for the taste of the most demanding and varied audiences. The pioneers, in the sheer delight of listening to him, with hours passing like minutes, minutes flowing like seconds, lost all notion of time. They were still masters of time.

5

How everything changed after the Civil War! The former masters of time, Yankeefied, gradually became the slaves of time. There are no longer so many bards on hand in the West. Running them out of the East, the Yankee takes upon himself the duty of banishing them also from the West and driving them out of the South. When it is a question of putting an end to the Bohemian class or to the pioneer images and concepts that clash with his own, the Yankee does not hesitate: he changes, modifies, imposes, demands, until he accommodates the idealized concepts and images to his own conceptions.

To take an example close to hand, see what he has done with the image of Lincoln! Ah, the contrasts between the Lincoln of pioneer reality and the Lincoln of the Yankee legends! If you believe the Yankee legends, Lincoln must have been an exemplary rail splitter all his life, the prototype of the laborer. Look further, and you will see Lincoln was none of that. He had been a woodcutter only because his father forced him to be, and he had a horror of farm work, for his great pleasure was reading, loafing, and talking. Furthermore, he himself said that his father had taught him to work, but had not taught him to like it. To believe the Yankee legends, Lincoln never went to school and his culture must have been produced by spontaneous combustion. Look more closely, and you find that Lincoln did go to schools and had teachers and excellent cultural training. To believe in the Yankee legends, from childhood Lincoln burned with impatience to abolish slavery. The fact is, he not only did not burn to abolish slavery, but was even profoundly irritated by the abolitionist societies of New England, for his great preoccupation, his dominant care, his obsession, was always to save the unity of the country, having abolished slavery only at the eleventh hour in order to hasten the end of the Civil War.

As far as that is concerned, Lincoln never made any mystery about his position in regard to the problem. "My paramount object in this struggle," he says in 1862 in an open letter to the editor of the *New York Tribune,* "is to save the Union, and is not either to save or to destroy slavery. If I could save the Union without freeing any slaves, I would do it; and if I could save it by freeing all the slaves, I would do it; and if I could save it by freeing some and leaving others alone, I would also do that."[11]

One cannot be plainer or more positive. Nevertheless, in spite of all this, the Yankees of the East and West, and even those of the South—because today Yankeeism, turned into a mental attitude, is independent of geography—have taken over Lincoln to present him in a new light. And not a day passes without some new myth appearing about Abraham Lincoln. And as there is no end to the buyers of myths, the Unifier is passing through the sieve of the strangest interpretations. Mr. X, supported by the legend that he himself helped to construct, feels authorized to pontificate, basing his words on Lincoln, about the uselessness of going to school. Why attend schools if Lincoln could get along without them? And so come forth long dissertations on the advantage of learning by correspondence. Mr. Y swears on the Bible that the best place to acquire culture is not in books and from teachers but in Nature, the environment of difficulties, that of pioneering and asceticism. The atmosphere propitious to a good education? The frontier, not the city; the country, not the university. The wild West, that is the natural habitat of genius. And all this based on Lincoln legends, legends of Yankee origin or inspiration.

New pedagogical theories preach that practical knowledge and pure action can dispense with theoretical knowledge and mental adaptability in all fields of knowledge, even in those related to contemplation; others, on the contrary, maintain that the theoretical knowledge acquired by correspondence after a few lessons is the only means of preparing a man adequately for action, by preserving his personality. And there is the name of Abraham Lincoln heading a string of examples.

And what of the new methods of pedagogy? Let parents send their prodigies to the new schools, with space sufficient for ten, twenty, a hundred or two hundred "vigorous American children," which is the way the advertisements read, and these schools, in a chaste and uncontaminated atmosphere of Puritanism, by initiating them into the druidic mysteries of outdoor life and intensive work in the shade of the trees, into the practice of agriculture and craftsmanship, will turn out after a certain time as many brand-new Lincolns in a corrected and enlarged edition to supply the country with new leaders.

Pedagogues or mere publicity agents, there are real geniuses for dis-

covering subtle relationships between school systems, medicinal nos-
trums, and the life of Abraham Lincoln.

Lincoln has been used for everything. There is no shift or strategem to
which the Yankee, the crypto-Yankee, or the Yankeefied American does
not have recourse in order to construct a Lincoln in his own image and
likeness. If it is necessary to alter his biography for that purpose, then
they do so. If it is necessary to modify the Lord's Prayer to that end,
they modify the Lord's Prayer.

6

As a matter of fact, the Lord's Prayer that is used today in the United
States is not the same that is used in other Christian countries. In Brazil,
for example, the most recommended prayer in Christendom speaks of
pardoning debts: "Forgive us our debts, as we forgive our debtors."
Now, the Lord's Prayer used in America, and certainly the one used in
England, does not speak expressly of debts but of trespasses—violation,
transgression, infraction, offense, sin, fault—as though to imply that
there is no thought of forgiving *money* debts, but only moral and juridical debts of another nature, when the truth is that, in the original Aramaic as well as in the Latin and Greek version of the Lord's Prayer, it is
money debts that are primarily emphasized. Indeed, the paternoster in
the form we use it, word for word, is in St. Matthew.[12] The Latin text
says: "Dimitte nobis debita nostra," which corresponds to the Brazilian
form of "Forgive us our debts."

The verb that has been translated as "forgive" has as its true meaning
"let go, release, free, liberate." The same sentence we find in Matthew
appears in classic authors with the sense of forgiving someone something,
some debt.

According to the best exegetes, the noun translated as "debts" properly
means in Greek the obligation that someone has to another. And the
verb derived from the same noun signifies, properly and primarily, to be
debtor to someone for something. Therefore it seems that both the Latin
and the Portuguese translations correspond perfectly to the Greek form.
But, it may be objected, St. Matthew did not write in Greek but in
Aramaic; so what certainty can there be that the Greek translation corresponds to the original Aramaic? The certainty is the nearest possible.

Historically, the Christians of the end of the first century, and much more those of the second, already knew the Greek translation, and in authors of that time we find innumerable quotations which correspond, letter for letter, to the text we possess today. Much more important, the codices of the fourth century and later present it as we read it. Consequently, historically it is certain that the text we have today corresponds to the text that the Christians of the late first century knew.

And granting that Matthew wrote his Gospel between 50 and 70 A.D., and granting also the love and veneration the first Christians had for the apostolic documents and teachings, historically and psychologically it may be accepted that in less than a century those documents had not been corrupted—and all the more because we find them identical in the most distant and different Christian communities. Thus we have the historical certainty that the text of Matthew we read today corresponds to the original Aramaic text of Matthew known by the early Christians and translated into the Greek.

Whence, then, the "Forgive us our trespasses"? Probably from St. Luke, who gives the Lord's Prayer in the following form (attempting to translate literally): "Father, hallowed be thy name. Thy kingdom come to us. Give us the supersubstantial daily bread and forgive us our sins, for we forgive every one who is indebted to us. And let us not fall into temptation."[13]

The original text of Luke is in Greek, and we have it just as the early Christians knew it. Comparing it with Matthew's, we find certain variants, for it omits certain petitions of Matthew and, above all, instead of saying, as Matthew does, "Forgive us our debts," it says, "Forgive us our sins."

After all this, what was the probable form used by Christ, that of Matthew or that of Luke?

The highest authorities[14] in modern Protestant exegesis think that Luke's form is the authentic one used by Christ, and give the following reason: The fact that the form given by Luke is shorter than Matthew's ought to lead us to think it the genuine one, for it would be inadmissible that the apostles and the early Christians would summarize or modify the Lord's Prayer; while it can more easily be accepted that with use, and by virtue of the fervor with which they used it, the apostles or the Christians might add petitions they thought would best complete some of those in the Prayer.

Nevertheless it is objected to these authorities that Matthew was the apostle of Christ, lived with Christ, listened to His preaching in his native tongue. Therefore he would have a more direct and immediate knowledge of His preaching. Luke, on the other hand, never heard Christ, nor was he ever in immediate contact with Him. He was a disciple of St. Paul, and wrote his Gospel, as he himself says in the prologue, through information he got from others who had been with Christ. Besides which, Christ probably spoke to the multitudes in Aramaic, since that was the common language in Palestine at that time. Now, philologists find frequent Aramaisms in Matthew, while Luke adapts the same expressions, which doubtless were originally Aramaic, for his readers who were of Greek culture, so that they might understand him better. (Which proves most directly that Matthew wrote among and for Jews, and Luke among those of Greek culture and for Greeks.) This is why Catholic authors consider that Matthew probably furnishes more literally the words of Christ.

The historically certain thing is that the Lord's Prayer, in the form in which it is prayed in Portuguese—"Forgive us our debts"—has been known and used by Christians since at least the end of the first century.

In regard to the form used by the Protestants and English and American Catholics—"Forgive us our trespasses"—how long can it have been in use? In point of fact, the oldest Bibles, both Catholic and Protestant, read "Forgive us our debts." The King James Version[15] and the Book of Common Prayer of the Anglicans and Presbyterians give it thus.

Since "debts" best translates the text of Matthew, giving broader meaning to the Greek term, why "trespasses," which limits the sense of the word merely to moral faults, to sins, to transgressions?

One other question remains. Who could have introduced the modification? The Englishman, the pioneer, the Yankee, the Puritan, the Catholic, the Quaker, the Lutheran Protestant? *Ecce probandum.* If it is true, as is asserted in criminology, that the best way to identify the author of an act is to find out who benefits from it, all indications in this case would seem to point to the Calvinist and the Yankee. To the Yankee, or to the Puritan, since Puritans and Yankees, or rather, Yankees and Puritans, are the ones who are least compromising in the matter of debts, especially when it is money debts.

The artifices, the care, the caution, the euphemisms they are capable of to safeguard the mystic value of money!

Forgiveness of debt? It does not exist in the Yankee conception of life. To give freely, or receive in exchange for nothing—simple alms—does not enter into play with Yankeeism, nor with Puritanism. Strictly speaking, one neither gives nor asks alms in the Yankee world. In the last extremity, instead of stretching out a hand to public charity, one sells pencils or apples in the streets, as the veterans of the 1914 war did during the Depression. To give frankly and freely, to forgive the debt, as Brazil forgave the debt of the Paraguayan war,[16] to work for nothing? All this is inconceivable in the world of the Yankee and the Puritan. Even the millionaires who lend their services to the State in time of war or emergency receive one dollar a year. They are the "dollar-a-year men." In that way the Puritan concept of the essential dignity of labor and of money is symbolically spared. And alms and the gratuity—not philanthropy—continue to be practically banished from American national life, where ideas are not transmitted but sold—to "sell" an idea—and where things, to be good, must smack of good investment—"a good marriage is a good investment"—while the supreme beauty is a million dollars—"looks like a million."

On the international plane the same artifices and euphemisms. In lend-lease, for example, what from the first was perfectly well understood to require no repayment was called a "loan." Or can anyone have presumed the Yankee was thinking seriously that some day he was to be fully indemnified for the buckets and incendiary bombs that, through lend-lease, he was to supply to his allies and good neighbors, when they were helping him to master the fire prepared purposely and at long distance to envelop and destroy his own house?

No, he was not. He *was* defending with lend-lease one of the features of the "American way of life" without striking at the foundations of the social and economic edifice that supports it. These foundations, by the very fact that they are fundamental for the evaluation of the capitalist world, have to be defended in every way against any corruption that may occur in the concept of the sanctity of debt. Except for Brazil, who paradoxically repaid the lend-lease loans, no one took those debts seriously.

The sanctity of debt and the dignity of labor are notions that neither the Puritan nor the Yankee nor the crypto-Yankee are disposed to let perish. Hence, in part, the effort they make to detach the idealized image of Lincoln from the real Lincoln, indolent and debt-ridden, whenever a Lincoln emerges from reality different from the moralizing, rail-splitting, hard-working Lincoln, the payer of debts and the Puritan emancipator of slaves, he of the Yankee legends.

Returning, however, to American symbolism, has the Yankee succeeded in completely imposing, with the new idealized image of Lincoln, his own conception of the pioneer? Up to the present, no. The real symbol of the pioneer was too deeply rooted in the American national consciousness for his image to be totally adulterated to suit the convenience of Yankeeism. In truth, the romanticized image of the pioneer is still triumphant everywhere and still gallantly resists the Calvinist modifications that the Yankee has been trying to impose upon it. If the real model is disappearing into the devouring abyss of the growing urbanization of the American way of life, the average American still finds inspiration in the symbol of the pioneer, and it is still his image that most fills American homes with legend, with poetry, and with dreams.

In summary: Until it was converted into a symbol, the image of the pioneer was always threatened. But ever since it became a symbol, it may be said to be more and more resistant to time and to the ages.

7

That is, in a way, what has been happening in Brazil with respect to the image of the *bandeirante*. Processes of purification very similar to those that modified the image of the pioneer have changed the image of the *bandeirante*. Indeed, substitute, in the process of canonization of images of Brazilian symbology, the *bandeirante* for the pioneer, the sugar planter for the Southern planter, and the Jesuit for the Yankee, and the simile, at least on the pure terrain of the conflict of images, will be perfect.

Very great were the difficulties created for the *bandeirante*, by the Jesuit deliberately and by the great sugar planter on account of the effect of the image that was on the point of being imposed on the national imagination, when the *bandeirante* picture was still far from being consolidated. For that matter, the struggle between the *bandeirante* and the Jesuit was inevitable, for while the latter incarnated the Counter Reformation and the desire to return to the spiritual unity of the Middle Ages under the aegis of the Papacy, the *bandeirante*, in his eagerness for wealth and power, consciously or unconsciously was already the instrument of modern capitalism, twin brother of the Reformation, born of the same bough and of the same dewdrop.

Of course, the Jesuits did not oppose the *bandeirante* for the sheer pleasure of antagonizing him, or to hinder the search for gold and other precious metals by official expeditions and by *bandeiras*, or to purposely interrupt the processes of transformation that were to convert the image of the *bandeirante* into a national symbol. Nothing of the sort. What they did oppose was the unbridling of greed, the predatory raids on the Indians, all that which, in short, would finally contribute to making capitalism possible. In this they were inflexible and did not allow themselves to be fooled by the euphemisms that served as pretexts for such expeditions. When it was truly a question of reconnaissance of the land and of seeking souls for the purpose of religious instruction, or searching for mines, the Jesuits themselves joined the *bandeiras*. But as soon as they divined that it was not just a case of searching for mines, but of hunting down Indians for slavery, they were the first to denounce the fraud. "These, Lord, are the true mines of this State, for the fame of gold and silver mines has always been a pretext with which they went out from here to seek the other mines."[17]

The Jesuit had a good and sufficient reason besides that of faith for opposing the *bandeirante*. This reason was that the backwoodsmen's raids constituted a double threat to the integrity of the empire that they were planning: first, because they deprived the littoral of the able-bodied men necessary for its defense against Calvinist attacks; second, because with their outrages the *bandeiras* were stirring up hatred in the natives, impelling them to side with the Huguenots against the Portuguese.

That it was not a matter of imaginary perils is proved not only by the French of Atlantic France but also by the twenty-five years of Dutch domination in Brazil. Were it not for the Jesuits, the heart of resistance in Rio de Janeiro, in Maranhão, and even in Pernambuco, Brazil, divided between Catholics and Calvinists, would not be what it is today. It is true that the *bandeirante* did conquer the backlands and extend the frontiers of the Empire, but the defense of the nation's boundaries and of its moral and spiritual structure was indisputably the work of the Jesuits.

Another achievement of theirs was the Portuguese laws for the protection of the Indians and for the encouragement of marriage between white men and Indian women. How they clamored against the scandal of chance unions or unions for pleasure in which colonial society was wallowing! And how they roared against the enslavement of Indian women!

8

It is obvious also that the Jesuit did not oppose legitimate union between whites and Indians on racial grounds. What he did oppose was lust and concubinage, the taking of the Indian woman as an instrument of pleasure outside of marriage. What he wanted was to encourage through Christian marriage the begetting of Christian progeny. He fought against the unions of white and Indian not because they were immoral in themselves, or, in modern language, anthropologically contraindicated, but only insofar as they degraded the whites and sacrificed the children.

Already at that time those worthy educators seemed to divine the effects that such unions were going to have upon the national character. It was as though they foresaw that, in view of the way it was going, it could not turn out well. And it did not.

What, indeed, could be expected of half-breeds conceived and reared outside of marriage, the issue of scandal and sin? Well-adjusted, integrated individuals, healthy in body and soul? Of course, that could happen only exceptionally. For three centuries the rule would have to be, as it was, emotional imbalance, inner discord, insecurity, instability, hearts hardened by resentment, marginalism, laziness, melancholy, vague desires of return to childhood in search of the father, an ideal father, "the father of the poor," revolt against the real father, maternal fixations, generalized social maladjustment, and all the peculiarities that, being common to neuroses and to pre-neurotic states in general, ethnologists and anthropologists of the Gobineau and Chamberlain type set down as hereditary attributes inherent in mulattoes and half-breeds.

Even in the illicit unions with Indian women the evil was not so grave. Although there was resistance to marriage, the colonists ended by marrying and legitimizing their offspring. "Most men here had had Indian women for a long time," relates the Jesuit Manuel da Nóbrega in 1551, "by whom they had had children, and marriage with whom they used to regard as great infamy. Now they are getting married and leading a respectable life."[18]

If from the random and irregular unions there issued the pallid, indolent, irresolute *mamelucos* that Agassiz encountered in Brazil in the nineteenth century, from the unions blessed by the Church came excellent human specimens, as was the case with the descendants of Diogo Álvares and Paraguassú, and as was the case with the posterity of innumerable Brazilian families, principally of the state of São Paulo, of Portuguese stock and *mameluco* branches.

In the unions of colonists with Negro women or slaves, normality and moral equilibrium would be more difficult. Because of the way in which they were contracted, those unions truly degraded all concerned: the white father, the Negro mother, and the mulatto son—above all the mulatto son.

It was degrading to the white father because the union, in principle, did not elevate him in his own eyes, arising as it did in most cases—let them say what they will about the natural preference of the Portuguese immigrant for Negro and half-breed women—from mere mechanical sexual compensation, resulting from the unavailability of women of the same color and culture as himself.

White women? The demand was immense and the lack so great that Father Manuel da Nóbrega wrote back to the Kingdom begging that women be sent, "even though they be wayward, for all would make a marriage."

Indeed, white women began to reach Brazil with some regularity only with the first governor-general in 1549. From this fact comes the observation of Capistrano de Abreu: "Beginning with the family, it is to be noted that the men of European origin came first and in greater number than the women of the same origin. Hence irregular relationships that further encouraged the custom prevailing among the natives of offering women to their guests. Irregular relationships, therefore, are characteristic of the early Brazilian family."[19]

In the fundamental triangle—Portuguese father, Negro mother, mulatto child—the one who perhaps inspires least pity is the Negro mother. Victim of injustice though she was, she was not always conscious of injustice, but like the Indian woman, took her serving as an instrument of pleasure to the white man rather as reward than as punishment. Furthermore, in all this, even in slavery in general, perhaps the Negro was less to be pitied than the white who enslaved him. For the white man—the Catholic white, naturally—was troubled by the injustice of what he was doing, while the Negro, with a thousand years of slaveholding cultural tradition behind him, was not always troubled by the consciousness of the injustice he was suffering.

As a matter of fact, the one who was destined to live out the great drama, the greatest drama, was the mulatto. A drama such as not even Aeschylus, nor Sophocles, nor Euripides ever imagined, nor any of the Greek tragedians. More dolorous than the tragedy of Oedipus, the Theban king condemned by the oracle to kill his own father and marry his own mother, was the tragedy of the mulatto condemned to do the same thing symbolically all his life.

And it will not be necessary to go to ethnography, or to anthropology, or to anthropometry, or to biotypology, to study the drama of the mulatto and to comprehend the near-impossibility of his being emotionally normal in the cultural panorama obtaining at the time of his emergence. For that, history's hint is sufficient.

Initially the mulatto came early to collective life, relegated by his environment to a subordinate plane, because the present-day absence of existing discrimination—in part his own achievement—did not obtain at that time. What did exist, on the contrary, was arbitrary legal discrimination according to color. First came the Portuguese of Europe, the legitimate Portuguese or son of the Kingdom; next, the Portuguese born in Brazil, of more or less distant Portuguese ancestry, the *mazombo*, the "Brazilian"; and then came the mulatto, the half-breed offspring of white and black, and the *mameluco*, the offspring of white and Indian.

No need to try to find out to what class each group belonged. Color was what determined that. High up, right at the top, the Portuguese of Portugal, son of the Kingdom. At the opposite extreme the *curiboca*, a mixture of Negro and mulatto, or the half-breed resulting from Negro and Indian, the extreme official degradation of the human being.

Between these extremes, the intermediate mixtures, with mutually hostile prejudices, some rising, others descending in the official scale according to their greater or less energy of will, and the moral and religious assistance they might be able to bring to bear.

The time and the environment, historical and social circumstances, institutions, class and caste conflicts—all conspired against the moral equilibrium of the mulatto.

And where were the domestic, educational, economic, or religious conditions capable of helping him check his conflicts with himself and his environment, halting or turning aside the development of his emotional difficulties? Such conditions simply did not exist in colonial Brazil.

Abandoned, forgotten, or denied by his father, reared at the breech-clout or skirt of his mother, in the Negro slave quarters, in the Indian long house, or in the slave shack in the forest, where his whole emotional life would be concentrated, the mulatto was destined to develop—with his revolt against the father and with his maternal fixations—the basis of future neuroses.

It may be asked, what of the mulattoes whom the *bandeirantes*, and later the feudal lords of the sugar plantations, or the equally feudal cattle or cotton barons, recognized legally, brought into the big house, and treated on a footing of equality with their legitimate children?

The case of these must have been still more painful than the others. Snatched from the arms of the black mother and handed over to foster mothers, the celebrated golden-hearted *madrinhas* of *bandeirante*, patriarchal, latifundian, and slaveholding Brazil, in those children neurosis would be established with even greater violence.

Ah, the horror of having to ask the blessing[20] of someone he hated with all the force of his hatred! Ah, the monstrousness of seeing his father all attention and tenderness to the intruder, the woman who had supplanted his own mother! And he unable to blast his father and destroy his foster mother, whom the social imperatives already incorporated into his subconscious mind force him to heed and respect!

Besides, there is his father's authority, absolute, unquestionable, irresistible, with power of life and death over the son, to force the mulatto ostensibly to accept the new situation: a father for whom he nourishes ambivalent sentiments of love and hate, and sometimes more hate than love; a mother not his own; and a home in which he lives on sufferance and in a subordinate position.

This mulatto's soul must, against his own will, be the battleground of terrible inner conflicts from which he will hardly emerge whole and normal. Nothing can help him: neither his father's kindness nor the kindness of his foster mother, nor the sincere friendship of his white half-brothers. The fact is that the nucleus of the neurosis will lie in the situation itself, independently of the quality of the persons involved.

With time he will realize the blamelessness of his foster mother for his rage, his anguish, and his terror. He will even feel a little tenderness for her. But it will be too late to dispel the diffuse resentment that he has nourished in his heart since childhood. He is by now a neurotic, a resentful man, indolent, melancholy, the authentic "neurasthenic mulatto of the littoral," as Euclides da Cunha has defined him. In him will be found, simultaneously or successively according to his emotive states, all the symptoms of the most varied emotional disturbances: indolence, inhibitions about work; sadness; indiscriminate woman-chasing, the reflection of his quest for the impossibly perfect woman of his childhood fixations, and of his urgent need to prove his virility to himself and to others; excessive sensitiveness; exhibitionism; social timidity when faced with genuine values; lack of continuity of effort; pretense of elegance or nobility as a defense against sensitivity; a masochistic pleasure in degrading himself and, at the same time, a morbid reaction to and excessive revolt against any form of criticism, censure, or advice; envy; the pleasure of self-adornment for the eyes of the world; weakness and debility confused with sentiment; passive instead of active kindness; love of privilege and lack of scruple in accepting the exception; persecution mania; morbid respect for the opinions of others, disguised under a mask of indifference; self-conceit as a psychological expression of narcissism, braggadocio, flashes of enthusiasm quickly turning into discouragement; disproportionate reactions to provocation or to aggression; constant melancholy yearnings complicated by a desire to return to the paradises of the past, to the "beloved childhood that the years will never more bring back"; the tendency to attribute to others and to external circumstances the responsibility for his own maladjustment; the habit of expecting everything from his foster parents and from governments; lack of initiative, and atrocious resentment for all who achieve or plan; boundless envy and admiration of the strong man, above good and evil, above the laws and principles of the Pantagruelian ideals of his childhood—all these are elements entering into the neuroses of Brazilian half-breeds, as into neuroses in general.

Even when the Indian or Negro half-breed is born of a perfectly regular union, within him is set up a conflict which, although it may stimulate him to acuity and personal vivacity, may also generate serious neuroses if unresolved in time. We refer to the conflict of the two cultures—the paternal and the maternal—which he, by force of circumstances, will have to solve either by leaning to the side of the maternal culture, or toward that of the father, as the *mameluco* of the *bandeira* did, or by mentally opting for the paternal only to remain sentimentally anchored in the maternal, in case he finds no way to reconcile the two.

If this conflict is sometimes violent in the son of parents of differing nationalities, why should it not be so in the half-breed, whose position, different from that of the father and from that of the mother, is apparent even in the color of his skin?

Now, the Jesuits, as though foreseeing all this, sought to encourage normal marriages, the foundation of normal upbringing. No one escaped their indoctrination. Even the powerful, and principally the powerful, were reached by the Jesuits so that they might set a good example.

"In this region there is one João Ramalho, the oldest man in this land," Manuel da Nóbrega informs us in a letter of 1553. "He has many children, with wide family connections in this whole backland. . . .

"This man, moreover, is a relative of Father Paiva, and here they became acquainted. When he came from the fatherland, which must be forty years and more ago, he left his wife back there, living, and has never heard of her again, but he thinks she must be dead, it has been so long ago. He wishes very much to marry the mother of these his children. He has already written back home and has never had any reply about this business of his."[21]

With Jerônimo de Albuquerque, however, the Jesuits could do nothing. There was no way to get him to marry the Indian woman who gave him innumerable half-breed children. He was later to marry a white woman.

Withal, in spite of the Jesuits' attempts to implant a little morality and respectability among the colonists, there was no restraining them. Excited by the Edenic vision of the new land, they gave themselves up to all sorts of excesses. Their motto and that of the time was that there was no sin in the tropics. Anyone who reads about this in the chronicles of the age, the *Tratado Descritivo do Brasil* (*Descriptive Treatise on Brazil*), by Gabriel Soares, for example, not to mention the reports of the Visitations of the Holy Office, is left with the impression that as regards sexual disorders and libertinage the world had never seen anything like it.

If the Jesuits could do little or nothing with the colonists, who else could restrain them? The Indians? But they actually looked with favor on the unions of their women with those privileged beings who seemed to possess the secrets of the gods. And the Portuguese government? The home government, with the aim of peopling the conquered land and of enlarging the Empire, at the same time that it encouraged the marriage of white with Indian, turned a deaf ear to the complaints and recommendations of the Jesuits and a blind eye to the intercourse that was going on counter to the most elementary principles and precepts of hygiene, dignity, and decency.

If it is incontestable, as one concludes from *The Lusiads*, that the discoveries were carried out under the aegis of the Faith and the Empire, or rather, to spread the Faith and the Empire, it is no less true that, as soon as the conquest was initiated, a tremendous struggle would begin between the Empire and the Faith, between the Counter Reformation and the Renaissance, between the Jesuit and the *bandeirante* on both the social and the economic planes. In the end, however, the *bandeirante* would triumph, aided by the maneuvers of the Court, always more interested in extending the Empire than in propagating the Faith.

At times, indeed, the Court gave the opposite impression. But this was only in moments of peril, when the fate of the Empire depended on the victory of Catholicism over Protestantism and paganism. As soon as the peril was averted, the decrees of the Court once more encouraged the *bandeirante*.

And it was not only against the Jesuit that this protection was extended. In the struggle between the two concepts and ways of life—those of the *bandeirante* and those of the sugar planter—here, too, it was the Crown that saved the situation by deciding in favor of the *bandeiras*.

9

There was a moment, however, when the ideal of the sugar planter seemed to condemn the ideal of the *bandeirante* to disappear. This was in the first century when, all hope of gold mines being lost to many, there were countless attempts to put an end to the ideal of quick riches, the ideal that was to end by nationalizing the conquistador, converting him into the *bandeirante*. Everything then seemed to conspire in favor of the sugar plantation against the *bandeira*. Already in 1551 the first governor-general himself, Tomé de Sousa, disillusioned by the ill-fated efforts in the quest for metals, advised the Court to stop the official expeditions into the hinterland: "I shall send some [expeditions], but it must be with much time allowed and little loss of men and goods . . . for I shall not speak further of gold unless Your Highness so orders."[22] In a letter from Bahia dated April 22, 1609, D. Diogo de Meneses, governor of the North, wrote to the King echoing those who sought to check the encouragement of these predatory incursions: "Your Majesty must believe that the real mines of Brazil are sugar and brazilwood from which Your Majesty has so much profit without costing your treasury a single penny."[23] In that epoch, according to Antonil's information, "being a sugar planter is a title to which many aspire, because it carries with it being served, obeyed, and respected by many."

At such a juncture it was still the Court in part that saved the *bandeira*. The King did not rest. He prohibited his faithful vassals from engaging in an endless number of useful kinds of work, reserving them for slaves, so that the whites should not form a taste for other tasks than seeking gold. With this he stimulated the *bandeirante*, against which neither warnings nor disillusionments prevailed. The *bandeirante* penetrated the jungle, scaled mountains, forded rivers choked with waterfalls, crossed peaks, fought against Indians, enslaved them or decimated them when he could not enslave them, and in short wrote upon the virgin soil of America the last chapter of *The Lusiads*.

And no gold. Signs of gold there were, but not gold in nuggets. This went on for a century, for two centuries. By what happened when there was still no positive trace of gold in quantity it is easy to imagine what took place when gold was finally discovered in the mountains of Minas Gerais at the end of the seventeenth century.

Gold! Gold! Now it was indeed gold. And that right on the Velhas River, on the surface of the ground, in a spot where for more than a century the *bandeiras* had crossed and recrossed.

Gold! The high point of the *bandeiras* had at last come.

"Nothing stops them, not the gorges and precipices nor thirst and hunger, nor the upheavals of Nature, nor fatigue of spirit, nor war, nor the pitfalls of unfamiliar terrain. In the period of the *resgate* [the opening up of the hinterland] these expeditions still had a terminal point, which was that of the first rivers navigated. In the period of gold, no limits were recognized; they dominated the desert for hundreds of leagues from the Tieté to Santa Cruz de la Sierra, from the ranges along the Atlantic to the place from which could be seen the profile of the Andean cordillera."[24]

And so the history of the Land of the Holy Cross at the end of the seventeenth century returns to the predatory and extractivist sign under which it had first begun, in order that the idealized image of the conquistador should live again, throughout the eighteenth century, in the image of the *bandeirante*.

This means that the ideal of the conquistador would have three centuries of continued triumphs in Brazil.

In the sixteenth century, the century of conquest, with the world barely emerging from the Middle Ages, it was inevitable that the image most fascinating to the popular imagination was that of the conquistador. In a day when the typical form of heroism was launching forth upon the seas to discover new worlds and return loaded with riches, those who turned the crusading impulse across the oceans toward the West would prevail over any other in the European's worship, especially the European who took ship for the New World.

It is true that in the seventeenth century, and particularly in the eighteenth, the excitement of the discoveries having passed, the afflux of precious metals producing in Europe the tremendous monetary inflation which was to put an end to feudalism, forcing the great lords to transfer their properties to the bourgeois, the dream of El Dorado having vanished, the world weary of the tremendous excitements of the Renaissance and tired of the gold fever, a new image, a new symbol, would take over the thought of the epoch. It was to be the farmer, that austere agriculturist that Hesiod, Horace, and Virgil, all reintroduced by the Renaissance, had transformed into the paradigm of all the virtues and an insuperable model of purity and virility. But it happens that the new ideal would only prevail where the ideal of conquest did not constitute a historic precedent, as was the case in the colonization of the United States, and not where the initial impulse of search for precious metals continued to be encouraged by the home government, as was the case in Brazil, where, since there was so much gold and silver in the Spanish possessions, no one could accept the thought that precious metals would not be found in the end in the lands conquered by the Portuguese.[25]

Now if, when there were no signs of gold in quantity, the custom of *bandeiras* was so persistent, it was inevitable that in the eighteenth century when gold and silver and diamonds were actually found, the *bandeirante* movement should reach its climax and the ideals of conquest and easy extraction of wealth should be stimulated and prevail over the ideals of constructive wealth, incarnate in the sugar baron or merchant of the littoral. The symbol of the *bandeirante* would triumph over the rest, contrary to what occurred in the United States, where the idealized image of the farmer as well as that of the merchant of the seventeenth century had never allowed themselves to be overwhelmed or conquered by the image of the conquistador.

If it is true that in the United States there were also colonists who broke away from the community in search of gold and wealth by predatory means, the fact remains that these never succeeded in altering the constructive sign under which the American civilization was founded.

It will be asked: Wasn't gold found in California? It was, but when this happened, in the nineteenth century, the *meaning*, the *rhythm* of

American history, with its cult of regular, constructive work, was already established and very firmly at that.

And it is not merely in this particular that the two civilizations are so different from each other. The United States discovered and exploited its gold for its own benefit, when the nation had already freed itself from England, while Brazilian gold, besides almost breaking up the country's incipient agricultural development, was hauled by the *arroba* and by the ton to Portugal.

In sum: Among us the *bandeirante* spirit ended by nearly always triumphing over the constructive, pioneer spirit, taking here—as is only right —the term "pioneer" in the sense of the tamer of the wilds, whose purpose is to create something enduring. Not that there is absolute incompatibility between the *bandeira* spirit and the spirit of the wagon trains, or that *bandeirante* and pioneer are definitely contradictory expressions between which there is no room for an intermediate type combining the qualities of both.[26] Not at all. Civilizations and cultures are nourished on both, since obviously the former does not permanently predominate over the latter, as still occurs to a certain extent in Brazil, where the rhythm of the *bandeirante* in that nation's history, opportunely predatory in the exploitation of brazilwood and perhaps in the first exploitations of the gold mines, remains still established despite and to the detriment of the pioneer spirit of constructive initiatives, and of the transitory triumphs of the constructive over the predatory.

10

No, not all was to the disadvantage of the spirit of the *bandeira*. As the evil of the exclusively male immigration into the lands of Santa Cruz was to redound to the benefit of the new social experience under the standard of racial tolerance and fraternity, the initial absence of a constructive pioneer spirit in favor of the *bandeirante* spirit, predatory and extractivist, was to produce in the long run the inestimable good of the expansion of national territory far beyond the limits designated for it by the Treaty of Tordesillas—and this, let us agree, is no small benefit. Had the early inhabitants devoted themselves only to farming, like the New England Puritans, or had they early discovered gold or silver deposits near the Atlantic as the Spaniards did, Brazil, with only the scanty population of the mother country to manage her immense colonial empire, would still be confined to the coastal zone. Because it was unquestionably the conjunction of these two historical circumstances —the failure to find such deposits immediately and the stubborn efforts to find them—that led the *bandeirantes* to explore and extend the national territory.

For that matter, in this question of opportunity for discovering gold deposits the Portuguese were not to get the worst of it historically. The worst would fall to the lot of the Spaniards, who, having discovered gold and silver on the very threshold of the conquest, had to suffer earlier and longer the weight of the direct and indirect consequences that the hallucinatory dream of quick riches brings everywhere, and among which perhaps it is not an exaggeration to include, along with *caudillismo*[27]— the "congenital disease of Spanish American republics"—the impossibility of molding the political and social unity of Hispanic America in the way that the Portuguese had molded the unity of the Lusitanian-Brazilian empire. While in two centuries of frustrated search for gold Brazil was expanding and becoming unified, the Spanish Empire, living on the exploitation of deposits of precious metals, was preparing its own partitioning according to the distribution of such deposits, a fact which was to condition in great measure the boundaries of the future Spanish-American states.

As can be seen, the Portuguese-Brazilians, though they had not yet had the luck to find gold at the most opportune moment—as happened with the Americans—were not at all ill-rewarded by historical chance. And it was perhaps thanks to this that, at the same time that they were confining to the frontiers of the South and the region of the mines some few sporadic outbursts of genuine *caudillismo*, they succeeded in extending the boundaries of their empire so far. "While the Spaniards in Paraguay had tamely stayed where Irala had put them," comments Southey, "while they cared nothing for the discoveries which the early conquistadors had made; while, indifferent, they watched the paths and roads opened by their predecessors grow over with new vegetation, and almost forgot the customs and the very language of Spain, the Brazilians kept on exploring the country for two centuries; months and years these stubborn adventurers would spend in the forest and the mountains hunting slaves or looking for gold and silver, following hints by the Indians."[28]

The result of such tenacity was that, going beyond the Tordesillas Line, they extended the frontiers of Brazil far beyond the narrow limits of the Papal bull, securing for themselves the greater portion of South America. "And finally they succeeded in securing for themselves and for the House of Bragança the richest mines, the greatest area of South America, the greater part of the habitable land, the most beautiful region."[29] Allowing for the subjective exaggeration of one who fell in love with Brazil from afar, this was in fact what actually happened.

11

As adventure, as epic, the history of the United States can show nothing comparable. A Fernão Dias Pais, an Antônio Rapôso Tavares, a Borba Gato only find their like among the giants of the conquests of Mexico and Peru, or among the French conquerors of Canada. "When one knows from his own experience," writes the sober Saint-Hilaire, "all the fatigue and hardship and peril that even today await the traveler who ventures into those distant regions, and when the details of the interminable wanderings of old Paulistas are considered, one is astonished, and led to believe that these men belonged to a race of giants."[30] And it was no less than the truth. Those portents of obstinate persistence "covered Brazil in all directions, they conquered the desert, penetrated into Paraguay, discovered the Piauí, the mines of Sabará and Paracatú, they went deep into the vast solitudes of Curitiba and Goiás, they explored Rio Grande do Sul; in the North of Brazil they reached the Maranhão and the Amazon and, having leaped the Peruvian cordillera, attacked the Spaniards in the very heart of their dominions."

It was inevitable: Some day, eventually, these monsters of energy would capture the collective imagination in a lasting way. And that was precisely what happened.

A singularly symptomatic fact is that the first Brazilian work really worthy to be called so, the poem O Uraguai by Basílio da Gama, the work that marks in the middle of the eighteenth century the first moment of Brazilian literary emancipation, as well as the first moment of the Mineira Conspiracy, is a book exalting the bandeirante and attacking the Jesuit.

Indeed, in this poem—in which is related the war of extermination waged in the name of Portugal and Spain by the bandeirantes against the Seven Towns of the Missions, because the natives, inspired by the Jesuits, would not submit to the Treaty of Madrid signed in 1750 by both countries—the hero is the bandeirante, the role of villain being reserved for the Jesuit.

After *O Uraguai* there were to emerge, with the great signs of "Brazil-ianity," new contributions to the process of promoting the image of the *bandeirante* to the status of symbol. Cláudio Manuel da Costa was writing his poem *Vila Rica*, and in 1781 Santa Rita Durão, a native of Mariana in the state of Minas Gerais, publishes the *Caramuru* in the style of Camoens, moved by "love of his fatherland," and because he deemed that the "successes of Brazil merited a poem no less than those of India." On pretext of reconstructing the shipwreck of Diogo Álvares and his gallant adventure with Paraguassú, the poem aims really at describing the land and the people of Brazil and the episode of the conquest.

With the sugar mill baron there was never anything of the kind. It is true that Antonil refers to the prestige enjoyed by such men; but cele-brating the lord of the sugar plantation never constituted the leitmotiv of Antonil's *Cultura e Opulência do Brasil*. Neither of that book nor the *Diálogos das Grandezas*, nor the *Tratado Descritivo* of Gabriel Soares. The glorification of the sugar planter was neither the objective nor the common trait of these works. Their common theme was the celebration of the riches of Brazil, economic propaganda in favor of the land.

Moreover, if proof were required—in matters in which it is not strictly proof that establishes conviction—to document the fact that the most idealized image was that of the *bandeirante* and not that of the sugar planter, there is no better testimony than that provided by the author of the *Tratado Descritivo do Brasil*,[31] who, unable to resist the mirage of great riches, after employing his sugar capital in the organization of a *bandeira* to the backlands of Bahia, lost his life there.

What happened to Gabriel Soares can have but one explanation: The rural and sedentary life of the sugar planter did not satisfy his dreams. He wanted wealth, yes, but quick, extractive wealth. And great adven-tures, besides. And probably the great majority of the sugar planters sided with Gabriel Soares, at least in the sixteenth and seventeenth centuries.

The fact is that during the first three centuries there was no taste for rural life in Brazil. The great fascination was exercised by the city, not the country.[32] Hence the prevalence of the European tendency toward urban concentration on the littoral, causing nearly all the rural land-holders of some wealth to maintain a dual residence—one in the country, another in the city—unaware that this living amid the pomp and diver-sions of urban society, one of the characteristics of colonial life, con-tributed nothing to the augmenting or preserving of their own fortunes; for, as Antonil has said: "The man who resolves to make his living from sugar must either retire from the city, abandoning the occupations of the republic that divert his attention, or keep two homes open, to the notable prejudice of the one in which he is not present in person, and with double expense."[33]

Between the country and the city the planters of the sixteenth, seventeenth, and eighteenth centuries did not hesitate. They chose the city, using their plantations in the manner indicated by Frei Vicente do Salvador, "not as owners but as men enjoying the usufruct, only to enjoy it and to leave it destroyed."[34]

Indeed, it is only in the second half of the eighteenth century, or rather in the early nineteenth, that, with the exhaustion of the mines and the vanishing of the El Dorado illusion, according to the deposition of the first viceroy, Conde da Cunha, the exodus from the city to the country is established. "With a mistaken policy, my predecessors introduced into this city luxuries and excessive expenses for improper amusements, as well as for useless carriages, to weaken and ruin noble and distinguished families, which they achieved with this disordered idea; with it all noble persons became financially hard-pressed and withdrew to their plantations and sugar mills, where they have been and are presently living without putting in an appearance, and without the means to do so.[35]

After the cycle of the *bandeiras* it is clear that many things are going to be changed in Brazil. It is clear that in the Center, the North, and the South there is going to be a consolidation of the patriarchal way of life of the sugar cane and coffee plantations, and the cattle ranches. Thenceforth the ruralization of the Brazilian population, obstructed by three centuries of *bandeirismo*, is going to be accelerated. The rising value placed upon the *fazenda*—the large plantation or ranch—on the farm tilled for major crops and the truck farm, is going to make country life necessary. Not only necessary but pleasant, and in a short while it will not be the profit motive alone that attracts men to the country but the beauties and sweetness of rural life as well as social prestige and dignity. "The Brazilian who can," Tavares Bastos will say, "becomes an agriculturist; he is going to practice the only truly *noble* profession in the land."[36] Thenceforth the cities are going to lose their population, the country gentlemen, "caryatids of the Empire and of the Republic," are going to become more and more powerful and courted. For all this, however, they will not entirely supplant the idealized images of the conquistador and the *bandeirante*. The ideal of conquest and swiftly acquired wealth, though subterranean and invisible, will be no less present in Brazilian life.

In truth, this presence was to persist down to our own day, shifting from the visible plane of history to the psychological plane in the recesses of individual conscience, making every Brazilian a battleground between the predatory impulses of the *bandeira* and the stable impulses of the patriarchate.

12

On this score, what took place in São Paulo is typical and can be summarized in a few words. As long as it was *bandeirante* and existed for *bandeiras*, that great state was one of the poorest and most backward in Brazil. Only later, much later, when the cycle of *bandeiras* was definitely ended, did São Paulo, with the advent of the coffee cycle and with immigration of the pioneer type—which at the close of the nineteenth century annually disembarked at the port of Santos more than 100,000 immigrants—move to the forefront of the Federation. All this was obviously the result of coffee and cultivation and immigration of the purely pioneer type, absolutely different from that of the period of the official expeditions into the backlands, for if there is a kind of progress linked to the pioneer spirit and not to the *bandeirante*, it is indubitably the progress of São Paulo.

In the case of São Paulo no one can be accurate without attributing its present progress to the colonist, that is, to the pioneer. To the pioneer and, *ça va sans dire*, to coffee.

What was strictly *bandeirante* in the progress of São Paulo—and this was also the case with the state of Rio de Janeiro—was the plantations that were abandoned after being swept by the green wave of exploitative farming practices into which the use of fertilizers, proper to stable farming, did not enter.

Well, in spite of all this, to judge by the misleading impression gained from the national literature about the *bandeirante*, one would think that modern São Paulo, the São Paulo of industry, the São Paulo of coffee, the São Paulo that is building the most superb industrial plant in South America, was the exclusive product of the *bandeirante* and of the *bandeira* spirit. For the resident of São Paulo, after four hundred years' history, is a perfect Yankee when it comes to attributing to the *bandeirante* qualities he never had. If, to enhance the symbol dear to him, it is necessary to attribute constructive qualities to the *bandeirante*, he will do it; if to glorify the type it is necessary to distort history, he will do that. Although borrowing from the pioneer to bestow on the *bandeirante* qualities, intentions, and motives he never possessed, it is still the idealized image of the *bandeirante* that, paradoxically, the most pioneer state in Brazil worships.

In the United States a thing, to be capable of arousing enthusiasm, must bear the label of pioneer; in Brazil, and especially in São Paulo, it must merit the epithet of *bandeirante*.

"This is extremely important," says Pierre Monbeig in his Sorbonne prize-winning thesis, "for a myth of the *bandeirante* has been created that has an absolute psychological efficacy. When one wishes to extol a rancher or a planter, the razer of forests, the founder of towns and cities, there is no more flattering title to bestow upon him than that of *bandeirante*. When one has said of a man that he is a real *bandeirante*, one has said everything. Let us allow for a very Latin overemphasis and not be astonished at seeing the *bandeirante* receive an indirect and post-humous promotion to colonizer."[37]

In fact, it no longer suffices that the *bandeirante* enlarged the boundaries of the nation, leaving to the pioneers the "concentric problem of populating it." Now they want him to have been a colonizer as well, a constructive worker with a precise political idea of what he was doing and what his actions would mean to the future.

To document the glorification of the *bandeirante*, there is no need to turn to Pedro Taques or to Frei Gaspar da Madre de Deus. Among the most austere and exigent interpreters and researchers into the history of the *bandeiras*—Afonso d'Escragnolle Taunay,[38] Alcântara Machado,[39] Cassiano Ricardo,[40] Júlio de Mesquita Filho,[41] or Alfredo Ellis Júnior[42] —we find reflections of the tendency to which Monbeig refers.

13

Why all this? For a very simple reason. An image was promoted to the status of a symbol, and that is highly important. Once an image is idealized and converted into a symbol, it is very difficult for it to be replaced or changed. Throughout the country sugar planters, patriarchs, ranchers, lawyers, men of letters, generals, priests, merchants, captains of industry, a regular variety of new social types, would present themselves as symbols to be substituted for the idealized image of the *bandeirante*.

Nevertheless, the latter continued to resist. Consciously or unconsciously, it is still perhaps the image most prized and worshiped by the Brazilian. Travel over Brazil, North, South, East, and West—Amazonia, the Northeast, Bahia, São Paulo, Minas Gerais, Rio Grande do Sul, the Federal District, all the islands, in short, of the Brazilian cultural archipelago—and everywhere, in one way or another, you will find the mark of the *bandeira*, with the ideals, the habits, the vices, the concepts, and the ways of life bequeathed by the *bandeirante*. When they are not ideals and concepts directly inherited from the *bandeira*, they are the ways of life deriving from the semi-constructive monocultures that, since the time of the *bandeiras*, have been serving as substitutes for the former gold mines. And when it is neither the one nor the other, it is the simple sentimental addiction, transmitted from generation to generation, to the idealized image of the *bandeirante*.

Still under this heading, we have a perhaps more suggestive example than that of São Paulo: the example of Rio Grande do Sul, in the colonial zone. In everything the development of the Azorian, German, and Italian—especially the German and Italian—colonial nuclei in Rio Grande do Sul resembles the formation and development of the pioneer nuclei in the United States. The analogy is almost perfect. The system of immigration by married couples and communities; the forming of villages and towns and cities with a sense of cooperation and mutual assistance; the unfolding of the resources of individual initiative; the wife tempering the patriarchal authority of the husband; craftsmanship, then industrial growth, small property, the religious and associative spirit. So pronounced is this transnational similarity at times that, on crossing certain sections of the North American Midwest, at sight of the divided, cultivated fields, the cities bristling with chimneys and smokestacks, the towers and steeples rising in the distance, one sometimes has the illusion that one is looking at a colonial region in the South of Brazil. The American landscapes go past the observer's eye like great extensions of the marginal landscapes of the valleys of the Jacuí and the Taquarí, in Rio Grande do Sul, and of the valley of the Itajaí in Santa Catarina. One's physical eye is looking at American scenery, but the mind's eye insists on seeing the Jacuí, the Taquarí, São Leopoldo, Santa Cruz, Blumenau, Joinville, Novo Hamburgo, Lajeado or Estrêla. On both sides, tilled fields and plantations. Everything divided up, everything cultivated. For kilometers and kilometers, not a patch of land abandoned. In the distance, down in the valleys, the smoke of potteries and the soot of factories.

Other similarities are the religious spirit, the political isolationism, the advance of pioneering families toward the West and North.

And so that nothing might be lacking in the comparison, in Rio

Grande do Sul are the coal mines of São Jerônimo, an excellent hydro-graphic system, absence of impassable mountains, a climate similar to the European, which facilitates the adaptation of the immigrant, and the coexistence of agriculture with craftsmanship, and later with indus-try. One final similarity is the division between Catholics and Protes-tants, the latter nearly always with a greater capacity to accumulate wealth than the former.

Indeed, to understand the successful development of the United States, there is nothing like the study of the development of the colonies of Rio Grande do Sul.

And yet in the midst of these resemblances there do exist some pro-found contrasts, perhaps the more important because of their psychologi-cal and cultural repercussions: the idealized image of the colonist, who in his way of life is nothing more than an undramatized pioneer, does not succeed in dislodging the image of the *bandeirante*, projected onto that of *caudillo*.

Why? Because, when the pioneer arrived, the image of the *bandeirante* converted into *caudillo* and later into rancher was already established in the popular imagination and had already conquered it.

In the United States the image of the pioneer came first, and was not dislodged by that of the rancher and the Yankee. In Rio Grande do Sul, Paraná, Santa Catarina, and very much more in São Paulo, there was psychological resistance to accepting it. Resistance and sometimes hatred. As long as Azorians, Germans, and Italians worked and frater-nized in pioneer forms of activity that complemented one another, it was the rancher who was dominant.

In the reciprocal influence of the way of life of the ranch and the colonies, up to now the ranch has always come off best. The colonist adopted many habits from the nomadism of the frontier: the horse, the *bombachas*,[43] maté, gambling. The ranch itself remains primitive. The rancher does not plant, he cultivates no gardens, he does not ornament the house, he eats no greens.

A still stranger fact is that the German-Brazilians, while taking pride in Germanic culture, do not attempt to trace back their ancestry to the first German immigrants who came to Brazil in 1824. There is no love of setting up family trees to establish a connection with the first colonists, in the fashion of the descendants of the *Mayflower* Pilgrims. On the contrary, they claim with greater satisfaction less modest ancestries, either through blood or through the culture of their ancestors.

In sum, in Rio Grande do Sul the pioneer never caught the popular imagination. On the contrary, emotionally the popular imagination has always resisted him, as it still does. And the most evident proof of this lies in the fact that during the last war the highly Brazilian symbol of the monument to the colonist, in the Praça Centenário of São Leopoldo, was destroyed by throwing it into the Rio dos Sinos. They destroyed and cast into the river, of all the things that Europe had bequeathed to Brazil, the most practical, the most constructive, and the best integrated with the land: the colonist.

14

If it is like that in Rio Grande do Sul and São Paulo, what must it be like in the rest of the country?

In Amazonia, to start with, there is almost no form of activity that is not *bandeirante*, predatory and extractivist. The rubber industry is predatory; the Brazil-nut industry is predatory; the guaraná industry is predatory. The arapaima and the tortoise industries are equally predatory. So true is this that the tortoise, the arapaima, the Brazil nut, and the rubber plants are on the way to extinction.

And there is no one more *bandeirante* than the rubber gatherer. In this case it might be said that the copy turned out more finished than the original. While the *bandeirante* still maintains a precarious form of society in his advance into the backlands, the rubber collector advances alone, armed against a Nature that concentrates itself to resist, rifle slung on his back and long knife at his belt, carrying his bucket and inside it the cups for affixing to the tree to catch the sap bleeding from the cut. About him only silence and solitude, a solitude filled with the roar of the jaguar and the heavy breathing of the jungle.

And what can be the force or inspiration that has brought him to Amazonia, which he can only think of leaving as quickly as possible? The *bandeirante* mirage of quick riches. It is the motive force behind everything in Amazonia. And returning is the general ambition.

Just as the colonial region of Rio Grande do Sul in many ways recalls the United States, Amazonia in many ways recalls *bandeirante* Brazil. From *bandeirante* Brazil emerged the term *brasileiro*, Brazilian, to designate the Portuguese who made his money in the colony and, back home again in his native village in Portugal, already fittingly Americanized, affronted his fellow countrymen with the pomp and show of his wealth. From Amazonia in the state of Pará came the term *paroara*, which designated not the man born in Pará but the Northeasterner who got rich in the rubber jungles and returned wealthy to his village in the Northeast.

In *bandeirante* Brazil there was the slogan, *Sub aequinoctialem non peccavit*. In Amazonia there is the legend of the island of Marapatá, according to which every newcomer who wishes to succeed must leave his conscience in the symbolical island, to pick it up again on his way back home. The legend comes, of course, from the time when Amazonia was swimming in wealth and was the point of convergence for outlanders greedy for quick riches, who, as soon as they had unscrupulously made their wealth in the flatlands, would go back to live in their lands of origin with some dignity, collecting their consciences, deposited in Marapatá, on their return trip.

Marapatá! What a magnificent example of the persistence of idealized images originating in the environment of the cultures to which they belong!

And to think that along this same line Amazonia has an even better one! We refer to the Syrian—the river trader—who carries on business there, up and down the rivers, sailing in the boat of the style called *regatão*, a kind reminiscent, although in a degenerate form, of the ancient Phoenician galley. Well, there is this impressive oddity about the Syrian river trader: He keeps absolutely faithful to the centuries-old ideals of his forebears. At once both sailor and merchant, as he was five thousand years ago, the new environment in a certain way imposes upon him no fundamental change at all in his way of life. The Phoenician of Amazonia is a repetition of the Phoenician of antiquity. Now as then, the same commercial procedures, the same economic metabolism.

In ancient times they built their ships of the cedars of Lebanon, ships with which they dominated the Mediterranean, the coasts of Great Britain, and nearly all the Baltic. Loaded with vases and statuettes in colored glass, like rare stones, with woolen, linen, cotton, or silk stuffs dyed purple, their trading was on the basis of barter. In exchange, Arabia furnished them gold; from India they got precious stones; copper came to them from Cyprus; silver, from the mines of Spain and Sardinia; tin, from the British Isles.

It is this same style of economic activity, which has become typical in the course of history, that the Syrian of Amazonia today carries on with his trading.

Supplied with every kind of merchandise, cloths and gewgaws as well as tools, beads, drinks, quinine, preserves, and grain, purchased in the markets of Belém or Manaus or Itaquatiara, there is no river, lake, or channel into which his boat does not penetrate.

He goes directly to the most distant point of his itinerary and only then does he begin, among the rubber gatherers, his barter trading. After two, three, or four months, he returns to the point of departure with his vessel's hold filled with great bundles of rubber, nuts, arapaima fish, manatee or tortoise, skins and furs, and all the rest that he has been able to collect during his risky rounds of furtive trading, unknown to the owners of nut and rubber trees.

Decidedly, there is nothing like Amazonia to permit us to form a judgment of the capacity for persistence of symbols in time and space.

15

And the Northeast? And Bahia? And the state of Rio de Janeiro? Have they perchance gradually worked out in their rural patriarchate any ideals of life capable of supplanting the ideals of the *bandeirante?* Examining the question superficially, one would say that in the entire North, except for Amazonia, the *bandeirante* and the system he represented has been supplanted by the sugar planter and by the latifundian, slaveholding regime of the sugar plantations, the basis of the whole economic and social structure of both royal Brazil and imperial Brazil. Four centuries of rural and urban patriarchate, of masters' homes and slave quarters, of mansions and huts, of stabilization and social hierarchization around the barons of the Empire, might be thought more than enough to dim the memory of the *bandeirante* and the *bandeiras* on acount of the great damage done by *bandeiras* and *entradas* to the sugar cane plantations in the period of the gold rush. They were not. In the North, too, the cycle of the *bandeiras* left its stamp on the psychology of collective ideals.

Once slavery was abolished, as soon as the old latifundian, slaveholding Brazil began to break up, a great part of the male population of the North went back the way it had come, imitating the early Portuguese colonists, later transformed into *bandeirantes* under the inspiration of the *bandeiras.* Or can the desires of men from Ceará, from Sergipe, Pará, Alagoas, Piauí, Maranhão, Pernambuco, and Rio Grande do Norte who emigrate to Amazonia in times of high rubber prices, leaving their families behind, be other than an ambition for quick wealth and the earliest possible return? Let there be no doubt on that point. The ambition is single and unique, identical to that of the Portuguese who immigrated into Brazil and to that of the *bandeirantes* who by thousands and tens of thousands advanced through the backlands in the gold cycle. In these exclusively masculine migrations, the general intention is purely predatory and extractivist.

Practical and constructive they are not, nor can they be, for it is one thing to emigrate—and this must be more and more underscored—with the intention of remaining permanently in the place of destination, and another, quite different thing to venture forth with one's mind ever fixed upon the point of departure. If, on the one hand, making the most generous assumption, it is possible to interpret the action of the man who emigrates alone and intending to return, as tending to spare his family the sacrifices of adaptation to the new environment, that action also admits the interpretation that the emigrant has doubts about his prospects and about the fate that awaits him. And these doubts, let us agree, are not the equivalent of the blind, constructive faith displayed by the man who emigrates with his family, his children, and his possessions, however blamable may be his imprudence and rashness from the sentimental point of view and from that of the safety of the group. The idealized image of him who emigrates to stay is the constructive image of the pioneer; the idealized image of him who emigrates only to be able to return to his starting point is the predatory image of the *bandeirante*.

The simple fact that the migrations of the patriarchal North, both the migration of its marginal types to Amazonia and that of its educated men to the South and Center, are still predominantly male, as internal migrations generally are in Brazil, is one more proof of the durability and persistence of the idealized image of the *bandeirante* in search of gold as compared with the other images and symbols that dispute with it the first place in the ideals of the Brazilians.

But it is not merely in this respect and in the North that the recurrence of the *bandeirante* is to be noted. The return is more complete and widespread. With the breakdown of patriarchal and imperial Brazil by virtue of the abolition of slavery—which, as Alberto Tôrres emphasizes, was "one of the few things with organizational aims" that Brazil has had, for, "socially and economically slavery for many years gave us all the effort and all the order that we then possessed, and founded the whole material production that we still have,"[44] giving to the country even a certain measure of order, good manners, sociability, politeness, respectability, food hygiene, and religiosity—in those areas into which the pioneer still could not penetrate the rule is the return to the ideals of the *bandeira*, lack of manners, lack of sociability, primitivism, bad taste, hope for the miracle of the mine—in a word, the way of life of the *bandeirante*.

16

Evidently, if the traces of the *bandeirante* and of the *bandeira* spirit are still so easily found even in São Paulo and Rio Grande do Sul and Paraná, where the presence of the pioneer and of new ideals make themselves most felt, it is unlikely that a cultural island entirely immune to the influence of the symbolic image of the discoverer could be found in the Brazilian cultural archipelago.

Can Rio de Janeiro be that privileged island? Only by a miracle could that happen, given the city's historical antecedents. And what historical antecedents! First came the Portuguese after gold. Then the French of Duguay-Trouin and Villegaignon demanding a heavy ransom for not setting fire to the city. Then, to confirm the model, came the turn of the thousands of Portuguese nobles and would-be nobles attached to the court of D. João VI. They took possession of the best houses, dislodged the dwellers therein, and took over the city. The model was definitely fixed.

From that time to this, except for slight intervals, Rio de Janeiro would never cease being what it is: a city of conquest and occupation, the ideal point of convergence and attraction for *bandeirantes* from the North, West, and South, who, having reached the frontier, fall back upon civilization, their eyes burning with greed, in their minds the notion, the old notion, that wealth has savor and is worth acquiring only when won by a bold stroke.

It will be said that the same thing occurs in Washington, capital of a land constructed by pioneers, and in all the capitals of the world; in Washington too there is the opportunist and the gangster. True. But there is a great difference to be pointed out. In Washington as in the United States generally, the gangster and the opportunist, the con man, the smuggler, the perjurer, when caught outside the law go to jail and are exposed to public execration, while in Rio de Janeiro as in Brazil generally—where for the unpunctual, the debt-ridden, the gamblers, those who manage to earn in coffee, rubber, sugar, or cotton, the sums needed to pay the interest, and interest on the interest, of debts resulting from pleasure trips to Europe, the expenses of administrative lawyers and of a standard of living that contrasts with the misery of the poor—there the benefits of economic readjustments are reserved, as it were for frauds, swindlers, and lawbreakers, the periodic reward of fiscal amnesties which both try the steadfastness of the good and encourage the shame-lessness of the adventurers. It is the latter who, courted, praised, and applauded, seem to testify that in life, except for a stroke of good fortune, there is no salvation.

17

Apparently, in one way or another, in Amazonia, the Northeast, São Paulo, Rio Grande do Sul, Rio de Janeiro, North and South and East and West, in all the islands of the Brazilian cultural archipelago, the mark of the *bandeira* is still, and always, to be found. The difficult thing, then, is not to point out the features that directly or indirectly derive from the unstable, predatory style of the *bandeira*, but to find in Brazil-ian culture aspects that do not fall into that sphere of influence. In ideas, in the expectations of rapid fortune, in the obsession with the stroke of luck, in absence of social organs for dealing with collective interests and not merely those of class and caste, in public life and in private life, there is no sector in which residues of the *bandeirante*'s way of life and the trade of the *bandeira* may not be found.

In the economic sector from North to South it is the survival of the preconceived notion that the good article to exploit is not the one that has possibilities in the internal market but the one that has some accept-ance in the foreign market: at first, gold, silver, brazilwood, sugar; later, coffee, sugar, rock crystal—everything, in short, to which can be given the euphemistic names of "black gold" or "white gold." Internally, noth-ing but emergency and subsistence crops, just as in the time of the *bandeiras*. With this difference, that in the time of the *bandeiras* there was immediate hunger, and today there is chronic hunger; and it is proper to distinguish between the two. The first, in loosening energies, constituted a stimulus to the *bandeirante* in his struggle against the wilderness, as it was a stimulus to the Parisian masses in the destruction of the Bastille. The second, by generating the discouragement, resigna-tion, and apathy of the weakened and undernourished populations of Brazil's hinterland, in whose eyes the last flickers of hope and vitality are fading, is like a camphor tree sentenced to long-term death. The former was the hunger that *bandeirantes* and *mamelucos* alleviated with wild fruits, fish, and the abundant, unmonopolized game of colonial Brazil;

the latter is the hunger of Jeca Tatú[45] and of the degenerate offspring of the *bandeirante*—marginal people undermined by syphilis, malaria, calcium deficiency, tuberculosis, running sores, and hookworm—all of whom hardly keep on their feet with their diet of fermented cassava meal, cassava meal with water and sugar, crude rum, and dried beef.[46]

In the agricultural sector, it is the indiscriminate devastation of the forests, supplying on the one hand the deficiencies of coal while on the other it extends the ravages of drought; the green waves of the coffee monoculture advancing and leaving in its wake both misery and desolation.

In industry, it is manipulation of the tariff, unbridled protectionism.

To such a point has the predatory style taken over Brazil's economic life that it would be an exaggeration to maintain that the search for and the exploitation of mineral wealth causes the greatest damage among Brazilians. Often its destructive effect is manifested within the supposedly constructive activities of the littoral, as for example in the case of the burning over of fields, which from North to South precedes the cultivation and planting of nearly all Brazil's agricultural products. This burning over, copied from the Indians by the conquistador and handed down to the colonizers who succeeded him, has caused more damage to the nation's arable lands than all the *bandeirante* devastations of mineral wealth. In the latter instance it is merely the deposit that is exhausted; in the former it is Nature. And there are the more and more frequent droughts of the Northeast to confirm it. While many of the former mining zones continue to be profitable for agriculture, the devastation produced from North to South in Brazil by the aboriginal process of cutting down some trees, burning them in a bonfire and setting fire to the adjacent vegetation that is to be replaced by the future cultivated field, is simply alarming. According to William Vogt, this, plus the use of cheap oxen-drawn plows that uproot the vegetable cover from the soil and open it up to the erosive action of tropical rains, creates "one of the most vampirish" economies existing anywhere in the world, and is directly responsible for the situation of penury in which the populations of various agricultural areas struggle today, not only in Brazil, but throughout Latin America, and even in the United States. With this difference, that the United States is spending nearly a billion dollars annually in the conservation of her natural resources, and all Latin America, with a much greater population and after hundreds of years of destruction, is spending less than 1 per cent of that amount.[47]

In the political field, the organization and dispersal of parties is carried on after the fashion of *bandeiras*. As long as there is an immediate prospect of booty, of jobs and portfolios to be distributed, there is great ardor and effort. Once the loot has been won, or not won, once the jobs are parceled out—less according to criteria of competence and ability than as a reward for the unconditional loyalty of talents long dehydrated of public spirit—there is disheartenment, apathy, and a wait for the new chief and the new *bandeira*.

18

Is there anything to be done about all this? Of course there is, and a great deal, too. For that, however, and to begin at the beginning, it is necessary not only to preserve the past and its tradition but also to react against tradition and the past, the false tradition and the false past; not merely to suffer history passively, as Brazilians have been doing until now, but to make history, deliberately, as up to now they have not done.

No, it is not a question of roundly rejecting or denying the past in order to transplant alien formulas, in the way that political regimes, codes, and constitutions have been transplanted. It is now a question of a great deal more. It is a question of reexamining the past and reinterpreting it in the light of the values and knowledge of the present day, not only to replace those ideal images that remain enthroned upon Brazilian altars long after their proper time has past, but also, and especially, by renewing them inwardly, to hasten the rectification of the master outlines that have presided over the building of the nation. For it is from those contours that, in the final analysis, the false symbols and the false myths that still inspire Brazilians have arisen, conditioning in a rhythm of arithmetical progression the march of a culture that could have been and perhaps ought to have been advancing for a long time— given its resources, even with the natural geographic limitations to which it is subject—in the rhythm of geometric progression.

Agrarian reform, economic reform, financial reform, constitutional reform? Certainly Brazil is in need of reforms and achievements of every kind—railways and highways, electric power, utilization of water-falls, immigration of the pioneer type, instead of the *bandeirante*—all this is being proclaimed daily. What remains to be proclaimed, however, is reform within the mind and spirit. Let us not be deluded. Without a reform of the spirit, without a reaction against the past, without a searching of the national conscience—a great collective self-examination that will make Brazilians realize within themselves, not only intellectually but emotionally, a radical change of ideals and attitudes toward life, their country, and the universe—despite all the prodigious material possibilities that have been knocking at the door so long, Brazil will continue to be what she is: a land that is making progress, but that is not ennobling itself; a land without a message for the world, a disorganized collectivity lacking in moral initiative and public spirit, a disarticulated society permanently hoping for more or less providential miracle-workers or *bandeira* leaders to come and solve problems that only those communities that are spiritually, morally, constructively integrated know how and are able to solve.

V

Faith and Empire

1

IF THE PERSISTENCE OF THE IDEAL IMAGES OF THE "BANDEIRANTE" AND THE pioneer in the evolution of the Brazilian and North American cultures is impressive, no less so is the phenomenon of the lastingness of the major outlines pursued in the sociological conditioning of the two histories.

Were the factors that determined a Brazilian development in the tempo of arithmetical progression the desire for rapid wealth, addiction to the past, racial tolerance, exacerbated individualism, prejudice against useful labor, victory of the material over the moral and spiritual in the triumphs of the Empire over the Faith? Despite four centuries of history, and despite the height to which Brazil has risen above the negative aspects of such tendencies, those same factors are the ones that still retard the march of Brazilian civilization in the present day.

The Bible, the break with the past, the spirit of community, racial discrimination, Puritanism (and later Puritanism tempered with a belief in the moral perfectibility of man), the cult of economic virtue and of the essential dignity of labor—were these the ingredients that played the greatest part in the early days of North America's development in geometric progression? In spite of three centuries of history we are still going to find in the Bible, in Puritanism, in racial discrimination, in the cult of the essential dignity of labor, and in the break with the past—principally in the break with the past—many of the determining points of the American civilization of our time.

2

The break with the past! Perhaps this remains the most characteristic trait of North American civilization in our day.

Indeed, everything in the United States is so new, so refashioned, so improvised, so recent, the various ways of American life present themselves as so uninvolved with the fixed forms of civilization consecrated by European tradition, that one sometimes has the strange sensation of being in the presence of a civilization suspended in time, in a land without past and without history. Very little exists in American cities that recalls or suggests the past convincingly. Neither venerable ruins nor crumbling Gothic towers, nor medieval castles rising on the distant horizon. Nothing, or nearly nothing, that resembles those old churches and belfries that give us our first impression of certain European villages, towns, and cities, as if we were confronted with old and loved acquaintances whose memory time had caused to grow dim in the distance but which had not vanished completely. What American cities have in common with other cities is only the universal landscape of smoking factories and the inevitable stage-set of sooty tenements along the railway tracks in the proximity of great urban centers. One would say, not a civilization that arose, but a civilization that happened.

Looking at things from that angle, there is more past in a humble alley of Ouro Prêto than in all of American civilization. And despite the colonial churches of Boston and the wonders of Williamsburg, the old colonial Virginia town recently restored to provide the United States with a past, we have the feeling that there is more historical density in a single quarter of Recife or Bahia than in all New York. Furthermore, none of the principal cities of Brazil's historical patrimony—Recife, Olinda, Salvador, Ouro Prêto, Mariana, Sabará—architectural reflections of the history of Brazil, the mere presence of which transmits to us through catalysis the physical sensation of the passage of centuries in receding time—finds its counterpart in American architecture.

American architecture, unstable, impermanent, in its eagerness to create the new, the useful and the practical, the bizarre and the unexpected, to adapt and make over styles sanctified by age, in proportion as it moves westward retains nothing or nearly nothing of its early purity, whether deriving from English architecture or Dutch or French or German. It is as if everything had been altered and transfigured for the express purpose of obliterating the past.

It is obvious that one cannot require a city like Chicago, barely a hundred years old, to preserve the history of the United States in the impressive language of stone. Chicago in this respect has done a great deal, indeed. It has altered the line of Michigan Avenue, one of the most beautiful in the country, at the risk of spoiling its perspective, in order to save the Water Tower, one of the rare architectural survivals of the conflagration that devoured the city. Nor is it right to make such demands of Miami, Detroit, Los Angeles, and innumerable other American cities that have burst from the ground overnight like fungi, to the wonder and confusion of the Americans themselves.

But what about the already old New York? New York, forgetful of herself in all the dominating impressiveness of her skyscrapers, the wearisome uniformity of her blocks of tenements or "luxury" apartment houses, the curious architectural eclecticism of her façades, is a city that has lost her memory. Where is her past? Where are the ancient monuments before which even the uninitiate can learn in a single instant of emotional contemplation the three centuries of American civilization that preceded modern New York?

Can that past be illustrated by the Cloisters, a monument of medieval style that the whim of an American millionaire caused to be taken from the castles of the Loire, stone by stone, pedestal by pedestal, paving stone by paving stone, title by tile, ghost by ghost, somber, entire, integral, so that there on the bank of the Hudson, upon the hill on which it was erected, there should never be any doubt about the genuineness of its origin?

There probably are, there must be, historic structures in New York, testifying to her Dutch, Anglo-Saxon, Irish, Italian, and German ancestry, but they are so overshadowed by the mass of the skyscrapers that they might be said to be lost or smothered by the whole.

For that matter, speaking of New York, and especially of the United States, a disconcerting land, like only unto itself, where the skyscraper is found two steps away from the old private house, the vulgar adjoining the sublime, the mediocre beside the inspired, wealth rubbing shoulders with misery, democracy and dictatorial groups, freedom and servitude, liberality and prejudice, boldness and aversion to the new, Puritanism and amoralism, materialistic worship of the real and an idealism of the purest abstractions—where contemporary civilization appears in all the forms that the arbitrary play of arrangements, combinations, and permutations can produce—it is not possible for the observer to contemplate the exception and the antithesis to the detriment of the principal and characteristic aspect. The urgent thing is to hit upon the tonic accent, on the phenomenon and not the anti-phenomenon, on the thesis and not the antithesis—in a word, to underline the determining and essential trait and not the accident. And in the case of architecture there is no pos-

sible doubt: The determining and essential trait of American civilization
is the break with the past.

It is true that New York is not the whole of American civilization. It
is probably a little more or a little less than its synthesis. A little more,
because it is an island internationalized up to a certain point, where
nearly all civilizations are to be found represented; a little less, because
it does not express the United States in all of its aspects.

And Washington? Planned and executed in Greek style, and urban-
ized in the image of Paris, instead of being an exception, Washington
is rather a confirmation. And, as confirmation, one of the most pictur-
esque chapters in American history.

So American architecture lacked a past? And a tradition? Well, tradition and past would be created. And in the American fashion, as was
fitting: speedily. What the Yankee and the pioneer, too, would not accept was that the civilization they loved should lack anything, whatever
it might be. After having looked about them and found that their world
was good, they, who had overcome all difficulties, who had expelled the
Frenchman and the Spaniard, who had put an end to the Indians, who
had freed themselves from England, who had linked the Atlantic with
the Pacific, who were beginning to impose new ways of life upon the
world, who were exporting, along with their products, from the Bible of
their religious beliefs down to the gospels of their political beliefs, were
they to be balked by so small a matter? Not the pioneer, and certainly
not the Yankee.

There was no past and there was no tradition. Very well. Strictly
speaking, the Yankee had never felt the need of that sort of thing, but
since he was getting to be an object of criticism such a state of things
could not go on. Everything had turned out right for him up to that
point. Why should it fail to now? No, it could not be.

Was there more of the past in Rome or in Greece? In Greece. Then
it was just a question of taking the great models of antiquity from
Greece. And damn the expense. There was the dollar, already strong,
already powerful, ready to stand up against everything.

The proper thing, then, was to build Washington in the purest Greek
style.

Along magnificent urban prospects rise veritable miracles of architecture: the Capitol, the Lincoln Memorial, the Supreme Court, the great
buildings of the Cabinet departments, and, more recently, the marvelous
National Gallery. In themselves, ignoring what they symbolize, each one
of these constructions is fully as beautiful and convincing, architectur-
ally, as is humanly possible. But regarded as a symbolical expression of
American civilization—excluding the White House, souvenir of a tradition superseded at the very moment when the latifundian, aristocratic,

slaveholding civilization of the Southern states seemed to be consolidating itself—no reserves of good will and desire to understand are adequate for the purpose. The spell of pure contemplation broken, the South American or the European will see in the external composition of these monuments only a typically American thing: the cost, or rather, indifference to cost. Because the Washington of the circles and diagonal avenues is precisely the opposite of the geometric style of squares and right angles of the majority of American cities. And it is not to be believed that the Americans themselves, who represent the two Anglo-Saxon traditions of the country—the Northern and the Southern—submit coolly to that strange symbolism within a stone's throw of the Coca-Cola advertisements.

If only it were a question of monuments in Roman style! With a little imagination it might not be difficult to find certain affinities between the Americans' sense of the grandiose and the Romans' taste for the monumental, between the baths of Caracalla and the undergrounds of the modern hotels of Chicago and New York, between the Coliseum and the sports arenas of Chicago, although those affinities may suggest other and less edifying ones—the mania for museums and collections, for example.

America is overflowing with museums and collections. This man has brought over India to furnish his palace. That one, back from a visit to China, has stuffed his New York apartment with so many statues of Buddha and Confucius, to the bedazzlement of his guests on receiving days, that it is surprising that there are any images left for the Chinese to worship.

Those collections and museums, nevertheless, lack what the pioneer and the American civilization in general lack: internal necessity and a historical sense of the past. We are confronted here by a civilization that, after three centuries of relative isolationism, still maintains its divorce from the past. And that is the first great impression we get of the United States.

3

The second great impression is the general worship of the essential dignity of labor. That is truly an impressive fact. If this cult differentiated Americans from one another, during the long predominance of

the Southern states, as soon as slavery was abolished it became more
and more marked.

With abolition and the migratory wave that succeeded it, all hierarchy
in the various lines of work tends to disappear, and with it, classes and
all forms of primacy of one profession over the rest. Just as St. Paul
envisions it in his Second Epistle to the Corinthians, and Calvin, evidently inspired by St. Paul.

That is to say, America, in its hunger for workers, by returning (only
to surpass it) to the Calvinistic concept of the dignity of all occupations,
was to end by leveling all. Since according to St. Paul,[1] the manifestation
of the Spirit is given to every man to profit withal, for to one is given
the word of wisdom, to another the word of knowledge, to another faith,
to another the gifts of healing, to another the working of miracles, to
another prophecy, to another discerning of spirits, to another divers
kinds of tongues, to another the interpretation of tongues—since this
is true, there is no reason to discriminate among these divine gifts.

"For the body is not one member, but many. If the foot shall say,
Because I am not the hand, I am not of the body; is it therefore not of
the body? And if the ear shall say, Because I am not the eye, I am not of
the body; is it therefore not of the body? If the whole body were an
eye, where were the hearing? If the whole were hearing, where were the
smelling? But now hath God set the members every one of them in the
body, as it hath pleased him. And if they were all one member, where
were the body? But now are they many members, yet but one body."[2]

Now therefore it will be no shame to work in this or that occupation;
what will be shameful will be failure to make use of the gift bestowed
by the Spirit. Shameful not to work, not to be socially useful. That is
the mystique that spread throughout the country and that, in the leveling
of professions and classes, is still being carried out to its ultimate
consequences.

Just one example to illustrate to what extremes North American culture goes in this leveling for the sake of the general exaltation of
occupations.

One morning in 1941 the forthcoming arrival of two persons connected with the Portuguese colony in San Francisco was announced. The
first was an illustrious Portuguese writer of international renown; the
other was the son of Portuguese parents, who had just won an important
boxing match in Chicago. Both, the champion and the writer, arrived on
the same day, at the same hour.

In Brazil, such a fact would raise a series of delicate problems. How
entertain the writer and how entertain the boxer? How give an ovation
to the fist without offending the brain? How pay homage to the brain
without humiliating the fist?

In the United States, in California, in San Francisco, and among Portuguese, there was no problem at all. It was promptly decided by the leaders of the colony to treat the two cases with absolute impartiality and entertain the writer and the boxer at the same banquet.

From what occurred with the Portuguese of California, anchored in the midst of the American civilization of the Pacific nearly three thousand miles from New England, cradle of Puritanism, it can be fairly estimated what must have happened to the millions of Irishmen, Germans, Italians, Poles, Russians, Frenchmen, Dutchmen, and Spaniards who, fleeing from Europe, weary of its wars, its castes, and its class privileges, flocked to hear the message of hope that the United States had been sending to them ever since her Independence.

The very least that must have happened is that all of them were completely de-Europeanized and gave themselves wholly, not only to the Puritan concept of labor, but to the other concepts of American culture. Also, until the newcomers absorb those values, until they assimilate the master outlines that define the American culture—Bible, Puritanism, break with the past, capitalistic orthodoxy, cult of labor—they understand very little of America and its institutions.

Nevertheless, that does not mean that the main lines of American culture are fixed and unsusceptible of modification. Not at all. To affirm that would mean to fall back on determinism and deny the splendid improvisational power of history, refusing man any capacity to change his own destiny. Now, that is absolutely not the case. If we find in American history, as in Brazilian, the persistence of the majority of its original master outlines, we also find great modifications of the early direction, insofar as what constitutes the American civilization of the present day is concerned.

4

Consider—not to go too far back—the violent contrast between the pessimism of the American civilization of early colonial times and the apparently definitive optimism of the present. The contrast between Calvinistic pessimism and the present belief in the possibility of perfecting man and humanity through his own initiative and diligence could not be greater. It is actually startling.

On this score, for those who insist on seeing the United States as merely the Carthaginian land of profit and the dollar, materialistic, imperialistic, closed and inaccessible to the nonutilitarian solicitations of life, American civilization holds the most violent surprises. And those who drag the world into war expose themselves to no small shocks when they exclude from their calculations the hypothesis that the American people, wrapped in material comforts, may be capable of generous acts or of fighting and dying in defense of nonutilitarian principles.

Take the North American apparently most impervious to the moral aspects of life, a Wall Street banker, or a rough captain of industry in the Midwest, a California real estate agent, or a New England financier who has accumulated millions—any one of those souls apparently composed only of figures and stock exchange quotations. Let a few humanitarian principles be thrown at those craggy cliffs, and inside them, hidden in some far garret of the soul, the missionary in them will be found, for generally speaking—save for the inevitable and irreducible exceptions, of course—every American, be he from the North, the South, the Center, the East, or the West, be he farmer, foreman, banker, teacher, laborer, clerk, or laboratory technician, is a potential missionary.

As long as it is a question of softening them up on a matter of business, and in terms of business, they are immovable and unapproachable, unscalable walls that feel no such embarrassment as do Brazilians in saying No. Direct and positive, without appreciation of the subtle art of cushioning the negative, they do not cultivate nor do they possess as Brazilians do the super-refined secret of the words "perhaps," "possibly," "when suitable," with which the latter, constrained, flee to indefinite postponements. "No" to the American is just "No." At most he concedes a "Sorry." But this "Sorry," which can be evasive in the average American, takes on a definitive force without his needing to resort to the "Definitely not" that in the United States marks the absolute negative.

But call Americans' attention to a humanitarian principle, and the rocklike crags, shaken, go spilling forth at long distance in Europe, in Asia, and even in Latin America and Africa, the cornucopia of their dollars.

On the home front, the same thing. In the world of business—"business is business"—rough and positive, they do not yield an inch. Yet when they die, those hard captains of industry, those impervious bankers, those autocrats for whom money seemed to be the sole concern, bequeath their whole fortune or a part of it to hospitals, to universities, to works of indisputable social utility.

Even discounting the extent to which the increasingly higher income tax has contributed to that social utility, plus raising the tax on inheritances and bequests made with selfish ends while exempting those made for social ends, even so, much credit must be accorded the Samaritan spirit of the nation.

True, not always does this aspect of American civilization appear clear, distinct, transparent. There are phases, even, in which it suffers serious collapses and is submerged in the mounting tide of equally strong and dynamic tendencies that oppose it in the world of business and competition, and among which looms large the unchecked cult of profit and success, together with the more recent acceptance of the Darwinian principle of the victory of the strongest. This cult and this acceptance, however, giving rise to the great contradiction of American civilization— on one hand the belief in the possibility of moral perfectibility and the consequent acceptance of the Christian principles of brotherhood, humility, and equality, and on the other the competitive, aggressive demands of earnings, profits, and material success—do not invalidate the fact of the predominance of the former over the latter, as the preservation *à outrance* of many North American traditions does not prevent, or at least has not yet prevented, the American's attitude toward the fundamental concepts of past, present, and future from inclining much more toward the present and the immediate future than toward the remote future and past.

Contradiction does not mean nullification or exclusion; it is rather a condition for evaluating the vitality of a tendency. If that is so, there is no denying preponderance, in the cultural evolution of the United States, to the belief in the natural goodness of man, in its already ancient conflict with belief in material success at any cost.

In thousands, in perhaps millions of American individuals, this fundamental contradiction of American culture probably has already been decided, once and many times, in favor of success, profit, and material triumph. In thousands, in millions of others, the two forces continue in unstable balance, swinging now one way, now the other, with substantial loss to both.

The whole of American civilization, however, in spite of the transitory triumphs of selfish tendencies over the altruistic, has been leaning (when the two forces do not fuse, and do not cancel each other out), has almost always leaned—above all since the nation's independence—toward the side of altruistic inclinations and to the belief in the moral perfectibility of the individual and the race.

A simple fact demonstrates this. Never up to the present, as Harold Laski has pointed out,[3] has a banker, a captain of industry, a businessman—a tycoon—attained the Presidency of the Republic, or been nominated as candidate for the Presidency. "No presidential candidate in the whole record has been a businessman." From George Washington to

Eisenhower, not one has attained power solely with his record of mercantile success. This means that, paradoxically, "in the civilization perhaps most dominated by businessmen, such men must renounce the hope of being kings."

Bankers, captains of industry, millionaires—certainly they still appeal to the popular imagination. But the homage rendered them is far from corresponding to the national cult of the humanitarian type. Those who triumph in the business world, without revealing somehow or other their belief in human perfectibility, without adding something to the American dream, are more or less voted into oblivion.

And which are the Presidents that most appeal to the popular imagination? Those endowed with practical sense? Polk acquired the state of Texas from Mexico, and yet not even that makes his a greatly reverenced name. And as for Jefferson, it is certainly not for having bought Louisiana from Napoleon that he is remembered, but for being the author of the Declaration of Independence. It is not the Presidents of the phase of great negotiations, then, whom America reveres and loves. Their great Presidents are those with moral messages—George Washington, Andrew Jackson, Abraham Lincoln, Woodrow Wilson, Franklin Delano Roosevelt. It is in them that America reveals herself.

For that matter, one can do no better than follow the behavior of the American people in relation to Wilson, especially the Wilson of the League of Nations, to understand that people's exact position as regards the natural goodness and perfectibility of humanity—a point on which one can never insist too much when it is a question of interpreting America. It is an example that not only clarifies the ideological position of the better part of the American people in regard to the belief in perfectibility, but also shows, through the resistance offered to Wilson, that the master outline of Calvinist pessimism has not yet been crossed and left behind.

In the terrible dispute over the League of Nations, in which the United States and Europe were summoned to declare themselves upon the problem of peace, Wilson was the anti-Machiavellian par excellence, the new man of America. He did not depart for the Peace Conference with words of resentment or hatred for the vanquished. On the contrary, he was all appeals for sincere understanding between men and nations. It was no time for retaliations or reparations, but for healing the wounds of war. Instead of covering the conquered with opprobrium, he was bent on a higher mission: to care for the widows and orphans, to protect the needy, to attend to the sick, and to establish security and peace among nations. His message was that the warring nations should forget the past and build everything anew on the foundation of his Fourteen Points, the famous Wilsonian principles. He had so much confidence in the persuasive force of those principles that, advised to have Republican senators accompany him, practical men of great experience in international affairs, a political measure that would assure him the support of the Old Guard, he summarily rejected the suggestion: "There are too many treaties made by practical men."

There was so much sincerity in Wilson that his proclamations actually succeeded in shaking old Europe. That was something new, something Europe had not heard of for a long time. And Wilson was received everywhere in triumph.

In Paris, however, there were watchful men—Clemenceau and Lloyd George—who did not let themselves be moved, and they spoke a different language, and they represented all that was Machiavellian and stratified in Europe.

For Clemenceau only one reality existed: France. The only reality for Lloyd George was the British Empire. Neither of the two believed in the regeneration of human nature. And neither of the two revealed any disposition to forget the lessons of the past. The old Tiger still bore too vivid in his memory the humiliation of the War of 1870, the defeat of France, Paris besieged, and the people starved, for his heart to be empty of hates and rancor. He had waited too long for revenge to lose it now. Now that it was within reach of his hand, was he going to consent to the coming of a vague son of a Protestant pastor from the other side of the Atlantic, from a country without tradition, without a past, without a history, trying to block his desire for revenge, the dearest longing of his life, with fourteen absurd, impossible principles? Preposterous! It was all very well to talk of general disarmament when one came from a country like the United States, isolated from aggressor countries by two oceans, and where space and opportunity were far from exhausted. But when one came from a land like France, twice invaded in the space of fifty years, and when one lived in Europe, where to be a neighbor is almost synonymous with being an enemy, it was necessary to think twice and not let oneself be carried away by the monetary enthusiasm of generous impulses. What France needed now was not principles or sermons. Principles? She had enough of them to export. What she needed was guarantees.

Lloyd George exudes neither hatred nor vengeance. He is too skeptical for that. He wants Great Britain's share in money. And if it is not possible to have it in cash, then he wants it in values that represent it—the colonies of the conquered, for example. This, on the score of immediate advantage. As for long-term advantage, according to the ancient tradition of his country, he wants the reestablishment of the European balance of power. His old-school politician's imagination could go no further. And none of that United States of Europe business. That dream had already cost Great Britain so dear that she could not consent to reviving it. What Great Britain still needed was a Europe divided, well divided, with England maintaining the balance and arbitrating all situations. A defeated Germany would cause no further worries. A victorious France, indeed, might yet become a danger at any moment. Therefore, caution with France's demands. But for all that, the principal thing was to check, as a preliminary, the salvationist impetus of the American visionary. And, especially, to discover in time the selfish intersts that Wilson's message concealed. Yes, because self-interest, however well concealed, was sure to appear sooner or later. Self-interest being the motive of all human actions—witness the Englishman Hobbes, and the no-less-English Locke, whose doctrine still inspired no small part of the American populace—Wilson's interest, when the right moment came, would rise to the surface. Nothing, then, must be done hastily.

On this last point Clemenceau and Lloyd George understood each other perfectly. To be sure, they had already heard vaguely of a country where a certain Abraham Lincoln had lived, and one Thomas Paine, and where visionaries could attain power overnight. But now it was a different matter. They were actually in the presence of one of those rare specimens of American fauna. And they could not believe what they saw, for such a man could not exist.

But the man did exist, and he was the President of the United States of America. But, in spite of all the evidence, after the first encounter with Wilson, Clemenceau still maintained, "Wilson is bluffing." And when he and Lloyd George finally saw that it was no bluff, but the sincere projection of profound convictions, they nearly yielded to despair.

Later, however, they recovered. Behold them now, astute, formidable political strategists, undermining Wilson's plan. Hence the slow, pertinacious, exhausting struggle in which Wilson, fighting on two fronts—on the one side against the Machiavellis of Europe and on the other against the isolationists and reactionaries of America—was not to come off best. Wilson's reserves of physical energy would end in exhaustion. The first collapse supervened. A first compromise, exacted of a sick man, was to lead to a second. And so from compromise to compromise, from capitulation to capitulation, it led to the Treaty of Versailles, in which not one stone of the majestic edifice of the Wilsonian principles was left upon another.

Afterwards came what is well known. Machiavelli triumphant, Rousseau routed, the United States turned back to its isolationism, going its own way once more in the cyclical alternations of a history in which the periods of predominance of a humanistic sense of life alternate with those in which the Darwinian principle of the victory of the strongest predominates, toward the competitive world of business, free enterprise, supply and demand, and success at any price.

Wilson's America yields place to the America of Coolidge. Now America is not particularly interested in those who plan to construct better worlds, but rather in those who announce the possibility of two cars in every garage, and other considerable comforts that the assembly lines have made possible. The symbol of America is no longer Uncle Sam. The symbol of America is Babbitt, a new type engendered by the Yankee to replace the symbol of the pioneer.

Have Americans desisted from preaching their messages of belief in the moral possibilities of humanity? Not yet. And the proof is the advent of the great Franklin D. Roosevelt, whose belief in the virtues of persuasion reached the point of deeming it possible to convert Stalin himself to his point of view. And the belief in perfectibility again came to be, at a given moment, America's belief.

Despite the fact that lynchings, racial discrimination, gangsters, struggles for economic and political power, and the imperialistic tendencies of certain financial groups seem to prove the contrary, the incontestable truth is that the belief in human perfectibility, stemming from the concept—at once Rousseauan and Jeffersonian—of the natural goodness of man, and in the unlimited possibility of the moral perfecting of humanity, passing from George Washington to Thomas Jefferson, from Jefferson to James Madison, from Madison to Andrew Jackson, from Jackson to Abraham Lincoln, from Lincoln to Woodrow Wilson, from Wilson to Franklin Delano Roosevelt, with all the collapses it has suffered, today constitutes one of the main features of the American people and its culture. In truth, beginning with Independence, the whole American civilization has been inspired by this belief and impelled by the dynamic forces that radiate from it. Furthermore, without it the whole social edifice of the United States—its democracy, its mystical theory of the majority with full consideration for minorities, its confidence in the virtues of persuasion, the respect of individual for individual, bank and commercial credit, fair play, the extensive use of advertising for the sale of ideas as well as for the sale of merchandise—would become absurd social phenomena devoid of all sense. And it is only with relation to the belief that man's tendencies are toward good, and that he is susceptible of being persuaded since it is possible for him to distinguish good from evil, that everything becomes clear, translucent, obvious, transparent.

5

The American's life, from birth to death, is conditioned on the one hand by his attitude toward the fundamental idea of the past, and on the other by his new attitude toward belief in human perfectibility. Hence his attitudes before the inevitable fatalities of the present, of life and death—suffering, anguish, sickness, love, and hate—the reflections of which can be found everywhere: in his manner of being, in his art, in his way of life, and even in his cemeteries.

The modern American cemetery! None of those imposing marbles, heartrending legends, or unfulfillable yearnings. Instead of the traditional, evocative, grave, depressing cemetery, a simple restful field distinguishable only with difficulty from a park or a golf course. With the euphemistic name of "Memorial Park," or "Maple Grove," or "Forest Lawn," in every way different from the old cemeteries, seeming rather to be places purposely made for lovers' meetings, they look like anything but burial grounds.

It is quite clear from this that the dead, like the past, do not impede the country's life, and that American society does not impose the obligation to show grief or weep for the past. On the contrary, it understands and respects the one who seeks to preserve it from profane eyes. To conceal grief is almost a social duty. For the American, the believer in moral perfectibility, timeless in relation to the past, worry, sickness, tragedy, and death—all that may combine to contaminate the atmosphere with melancholy must be avoided.

Just as there is no cult of death, there is no cult of tragedy. In grief complete composure is required, in joyousness all excesses are tolerated. Look at the modifications the American cinema has had to introduce into the concept of tragedy, look at the respect held for the drunken man, the tolerance of the comedian.

Why? Simple solidarity toward all that aims at making life more pleasant through laughter and gaiety. The American would rather be called crazy than emotional.

And his tolerance toward the drunk goes so far as to be moving. With evangelical patience he puts up with him, he who cannot console the unfortunate who displays his grief other than with that banal formula of courtesy, "Take it easy." As one might say, "Don't take the thing so seriously, don't despair, tomorrow'll be better."

That "Take it easy," besides being a natural antidote to American haste, is the saving formula for America in its most dramatic hours. And it serves for a thousand and one situations. Does that man scowl because his son has been called up? Take it easy. Is this man threatening heaven and earth over his income tax? Take it easy. Do the soldier's eyes glitter, are they almost glassy with desire as they rest on his girl's neck after five months of sea, of solitude, of jungle and bombardments, and now Martha's or Virginia's or Barbara's or Betty's neck is fragrant of honey and dew? Take it easy. Is the whiskey no longer what it used to be? Take it easy. Is there a drunk at the bar who spills his glassful of beer on the next man's suit? Take it easy.

In truth, the drunken American (not the psychopath, of course) behaves in such a way as to deserve the consideration of an amiable "Take it easy." Rarely does one encounter among them what the Americans call the "mean drunk," the kind that makes the most of a vague state of irresponsibility to say all the evil he thinks of himself and his fellow man, dredging up a subconscious load of repressions, frustrations, resentments, envies, and hates. And if the true nature of a people is revealed by the behavior of its common type of drunks, the American people's median nature must be excellent. Drunk, the American rarely gives cause for offense or affront. He tends rather toward noisy cordiality, to competition, to jovial expansiveness and laughter. Never to weeping.

To laugh is more important than to weep. As in the verses of Ella Wheeler Wilcox which figure among the items hung on the walls of a certain Washington restaurant, the haunt of inveterate brothers in Bacchus: "Laugh and the world laughs with you, weep and you weep alone."

It is evidently a people that, if not happy, makes no effort to appear unhappy. When he feels inundated with gaiety, the American is the first to proclaim it and want others to share in it. With what naturalness, even ingenuousness, he exposes to the sunlight the reasons for an occasion of joy! What he hides, what he does not try to share, are his motives for pain, his griefs, his worries, especially if those griefs and worries and hurts may contribute in some way or other to reducing, in the collectivity in which he lives, foreseen joys, enthusiasms, and pleasures anticipatedly savored for some time ahead.

And no talk of painful matters; no talk of sicknesses. That does not mean, obviously, that in the United States sickness is a forbidden subject. There is talk of illness, of course. Only not for the sake of sickness in itself, but to exalt the courage of those who rise above it. This is the case, for instance, of Helen Keller, who vanquished deafness and dumbness to become a genuine glory of America and of humanity. It is the case of Franklin Delano Roosevelt, who by his spirit conquered the handicap of infantile paralysis to become one of the dominant figures of our time, of all times. But otherwise, sickness, misfortune, adversity must only enter into the stories told to American audiences insofar as they are necessary for heightening a triumphant effort, and also, in the final case, to justify the failure of their heroes, as was the case of Roosevelt himself in his failures at Yalta on the eve of his death, or of Woodrow Wilson at Versailles, in the drama of the League of Nations.

6

Do you want to know the formula of the odysseys that delight the ordinary American? Read the novels of Horatio Alger. At certain moments *Sink or Swim, Try and Trust,* or *Strive and Succeed,* at the same time that they graft Yankee ideals on the image of the pioneer, seem to catch the secret of the purest and most elementary aspirations of the American soul so far as heroism is concerned.

To begin with, bringing up to date the celebrated Unitarian pastor's formula, you will present a boy of humble condition, the classic poor boy who always appears at the start of great careers: simple, pure in heart and body, generous, impatient, adventure-loving, rebellious, tenacious, persevering, and full of initiative, and, naturally, with a prodigious capacity for hard work. Among his general convictions must come, in first place, obviously, belief in God, an All-Powerful God, Creator of Heaven and Earth, who from the heights of His omniscience sees all and foretells all. Then, in sequences, as befits Puritan theology, will come belief in predestination, according to which God manifests His preferences by signing His elect with the mark of success in terms of money or power or triumph in competition. Now, as in the bottom of his heart the poor boy aspires to the Lord's unction, besides not envying millionaires and the powerful men already marked with the sign of divine preference, he is to do all in his power to attain, likewise, through wealth and success, the Lord's mark, and the Lord will permit him to sit at His right hand among the blessed on Judgment Day, in the compartment reserved for whites only, in the amiable company of George Washington, Abraham Lincoln, Henry Ford, Andrew Carnegie, John D. Rockefeller, and the other saints of his hagiology.

As firm and robust as his belief in God and predestination must be his

Puritan faith in the virtues of work, for outside of work there is no salvation. Beggars, monks, cenobites, anchorites, conventual and ascetic and vagabond people are all lost folk. On this point the poor boy will share the credo of Calvin, Lenin, and St. Paul: "He who does not work, shall not eat."

And do not scorn the result obtained by work. It is even fitting that this should be clearly expressed in terms of quantity and statistics. If, for example, you make a lawyer of the poor boy, and not an industrialist or businessman, cases in which it is easier to apply the statistical argument, you will have him, as a district or state attorney, win seventy-two out of seventy-three cases tried, without inquiring into the nature of these, their justice or injustice. In the face of seventy-two convictions the most recalcitrant hearer will surrender to the cult of the new hero, as already have yielded the most terrible adversaries of the poor boy, now headed straight for the governorship of the state, for the Senate, even for the Presidency.

You will now need to invent facts and action, many facts and much action, so that thanks to them the personality of the hero bound for triumph can be amply proved by strokes of private initiative, free enterprise. And it does not matter that since Alger's day a great deal of water has flowed down the Mississippi to the Gulf of Mexico, or that the trusts and cartels, in spite of the antitrust law, have tremendously reduced the opportunity for individual initiative in the play of free competition in the United States; it matters not that the poor boys of the last generation, the Fords, the Rockefellers, the Hearsts, the Morgans, have died, their skin parchment-like with age, awaiting impossible replacements. The myth of unlimited possibilities of the individual in the play of free competition must be maintained at all costs.

Because for the poor boy there must not be any impossibilities. Neither physical impossibilities nor metaphysical impossibilities. He must be in every way a modern edition of the Alger heroes, with fewer pretty speeches, more action, and less courtesy and circumlocution. Against him chicanery, revolver shots, knife thrusts, swindles, and cheats cannot prevail. Valiant, pious, nimble, hard-working, docile and gentle with the humble, friend and protector of animals—don't forget this aspect, for it is important—arrogant to the point of insolence with the powerful, he must lack no virtue.

But he must not die, and much less die of the disease of love. It is not a bad idea, on the other hand, it is even a good idea, for him to struggle, suffer, work, and conquer with his thoughts set on some lovely, no-less-perfect Martha who will accompany him along the roads of the world. No excesses, though. "Take it easy." Excesses are permissible only in work, because "hard work never killed anybody." No prolonged inner anguish, long and inconsolable sufferings, tearings of hair, swoons or heartrending jealousies. Leave that for the Latins. The ideal love is not that love "strong as death" of Tasso's Aminta, but sporting love, university love, on a basis of comradeship, without the absorption and intoxication of one personality by the other. Everything that oversteps this point will be mental torture, mental cruelty, accepted by American civil codes as grounds for divorce.

But enough of generalizations. Do not torment our hero with metaphysical afflictions and transcendental desires of solving the indefinite problems of to be or not to be. Leave that to the German students at the University of Heidelberg. Send our poor boy into the apprenticeship of life, to struggle, to work, and to his hobby, which is the most hygienic way of avoiding the idleness that generates disturbing thoughts and disruptive philosophies.

And in case of doubt about which paths to follow in the world of action? There will be no doubts. To combat them there will always be the Bible at hand in which to find an answer to anything. So common are these black-coated volumes, which the Society of the Gideons distributes free to all the hotels in America for the use and edification of travelers, that our poor boy will not have the slightest difficulty in learning the practical manner of handling them in hours of pressure, just as is indicated in the inside cover:

> If you are lonesome and discouraged, read *Psalms* 23 and 27.
> If you are in trouble, read *Psalm 34.*
> If you desire peaceful slumbers, read *Psalm 121.*
> If you desire peace, power, and plenty, read *John 14.*

All the tragic, dramatic, or simply complicated situations of life have been anticipated there, as also the manner of solving them. Thus our poor boy will have no problems of an ethical or metaphysical nature to solve. Indeed, even if the immediate solution of his problem is not in the Bible, there will be no lack of worthy institutions to help him, for a moderate remuneration, to get out of any impasse, by solving for him any problem of a vocational, ethical, or sentimental nature. The essential thing is for the poor boy not to waste time on personal problems, for all the time he can devote to work—preferably the kind of work that requires physical effort—will be little enough.

And in the end? Well, in the end it will be necessary for him to have a smashing, indubitable success. Because without ultimate success, an immense, absolute, smashing, unquestionable final success, there is really no story in the Yankee sense.

With this kind of story the same thing happens in the United States that happened at the close of the Middle Ages with the romances of chivalry. Just as at the close of the Middle Ages and the beginning of the Renaissance the great vogue was fictional chivalry, so in the United States, once the epoch of pioneer heroes was at an end, the Alger type of novel came to help the average American maintain the myths that are dear to him, far beyond their time and life cycle.

And what happens when reality does not permit the myth of the happy ending? In that case the story breaks off, the disagreeable chapter is cut out. It is, for that matter, what Henry Ford's apologists do with the Amazonian chapter of that great man's life.

Why this silence? Where there is no triumph, there is no story in the Yankee sense. The watchword is, maintain the myth of the infinite possibilities of the individual along with the sacred mystique of the happy ending.

7

What to conclude from all this? There is only one conclusion, and that is that the American belief in the possibilities of success, if it has not replaced Puritan pessimism, is still far from exhausted. On this score, modern American culture does not merely confirm the original attitude but goes beyond it, since the modern American, in many respects, in his belief in success and in human perfectibility is the opposite of the *Mayflower* Puritan. If, on one hand, the early colonist, with his gesture of embarking for the New World, turning his back on the past, and taking with him his wife, children, and possessions, unconsciously demonstrated a great confidence in the future and in a better life, on the other, as a Calvinist, exposed to tremendous hardships and bound fast to the doctrine of the irreparability of original sin, naturally he had to be limited in his belief in the essential goodness of man. The same is no longer true of the American of our times, since in him the fundamental pessimism of Calvin about the irredeemability of original sin has been tempered by the influence of the other branches of Christianity, as well as by the predisposition to optimism that prosperity and the increasing mastery of Nature have brought to him. Add to this the circumstance, not to be scorned, that Quakers, Unitarians, Baptists, Methodists, Christian Scientists, evangelical Protestants, Lutheran Protestants—to cite only a few branches of the 140 sects of Protestantism—place the tonic accent of their precepts not on the winning of wealth, like the Puritan, but on the spirit of evangelical brotherhood, so that merit can not be evaluated solely in terms of wealth but also in terms of social service, and one will have in part, at least, the explanation for the cyclical rise of optimistic doctrines over the pessimistic in the totality of American civilization.

As can be seen, there has been a significant change for the better in the evolution of the main lines of American culture.

8

And in Brazil? Can as much change have occurred in the fundamental outlines of Brazilian civilization? Certainly many things have been transformed for the better—and woe to the people of Brazil if this had not happened!—after the impact of the first moments of Brazilian history, when all was desire for quick riches, addiction to the past, dreams of returning to Europe, exacerbated individualism, unconcern with the moral aspects of life, prejudice against useful labor. But not so much that the main lines of Brazil's development can be regarded as dimmed or nonexistent. On the contrary, the desire to return to Europe, the addiction to the European and Portuguese past, the lack of faith in human perfectibility, and the lack of respect for the essential dignity of labor have left deep scars on her social body, and they are still so prominent among her social attributes that it is impossible to ignore them. For good or ill, many of these outlines of her development still continue in full sway.

Let us consider, to start with, the case of the Brazilian's addiction to his Portuguese and European past. While not comparable to the French Canadian's fidelity to his traditions of pre-Revolutionary, Catholic France, even so, when compared to the attitude of Americans toward England, it is actually touching.

A hundred years having passed since the arrival of the *Mayflower* in the New World, during the armed conflict in 1754 between French and English for possession of the Mississippi valley, Americans saw in the war nothing but a struggle between England and France for the conquest of an empire. It was as though that struggle had nothing to do with them. Indeed, the colonies as a whole furnished little aid, and that in a most unsystematic way, and the attempt to inspire in the colonists a sentiment of duty to the King found not the slightest echo. It did not trouble them that the British government was forced to send numerous regular troops to fight colonial battles, nor did they lament the fact that it was English soldiers and not the provincial forces that won the war. On the other hand, they saw no reason whatever to renounce their right to trade with the enemy.[4] It is clear from this that the attitude of their ancestors in turning their backs on Europe was thus early producing results.

Consider now the reactions of the Brazilians in the struggles between the Portuguese and the French or between the Portuguese and the Dutch.

A hundred years after the arrival of the first governor-general in Brazil, which was when the more or less systematic settlement of the colony began, the Dutch had utterly beaten the Portuguese in Recife and Olinda, and had taken possession of the whole Northeast. So great was the superiority of the Dutch, on both land and sea, that the Portuguese ended by entirely abandoning the Northeast to the dominion of the conquerors. Well, during the twenty-five years of Dutch domination, the Brazilians never ceased fighting for the restoration of the Northeast to the Crown of Portugal. And in the end it was not only the Portuguese who reconquered the lost territories but also the Brazilians—*mazombos*, Negroes, Indians, and mestizos—who never wavered in their fidelity to Portuguese culture.

Indeed, to illustrate the fidelity of the Brazilians to the Portuguese past, there is a still more expressive and more recent example. We refer to the episode of their political emancipation. While the United States broke away from England in a violent fashion, severing with fire and sword all bonds with George III, in Brazil it was actually the son of D. João VI, Prince Dom Pedro, who was proclaimed her first Emperor. And as if this were not enough, when that same Dom Pedro renounced the Crown of Brazil, the Brazilian Empire, of European origin, patiently waited for the majority of Dom Pedro II—son and grandson of monarchs who, after all, preferred a tiny European kingdom to the vast South American empire—in order to hand over the government of the country to him.

As an example of fealty to the Portuguese past one can ask no more and no better.

Also, this addiction to Europe and European traditions brings about a further illuminating feature, the emotional resistance of Brazilians of the past generation to the new facts of American civilization.[5]

Indeed, in the same proportion as the new generations let themselves be fascinated by the United States, accepting almost at once the new facts of American culture, the past generation, when in direct contact with that culture, seeks to reject them.

Ah, the incomprehension of Brazilians of the past generation in judging, on their very arrival, the facts of the North American civilization! What a difference between those judgments and the ones they pronounce on arriving in Spain, in Portugal, in Italy, in France—especially in France, where their surrender to the local charms and wonders is immediate, instantaneous! They enter Paris and they have no feeling of coming to a strange city. The sensation is rather that of a sudden awakening in one's own home after a Platonic slumber. They wander through the Champs Élysées with the triumphal gaiety of a *rentrée chez soi*. Here they recognize the Seine, the river of great literary yearnings; beyond, the Arc de Triomphe, the Eiffel Tower; then the Tuileries, Notre Dame, the Café de la Paix. Later, Versailles, Fontainebleau. And as those places and monuments are the reflection of a culture with which they are impregnated, as all their mental categories are already prepared for those images which have long been dear to them, they give themselves up to a long, voluptuous idyll with the rediscovered civilization, as if they had been temporarily lost, or had strayed away from it.

Those same Brazilians of European background react, nevertheless, in a different way when confronted with the United States. In the presence of the new, the never-before seen, the strange, the not yet definitively consecrated, in their shock they temporarily lay aside their best faculties of receptivity toward American civilization and its values. And they become incapable, in a great number of cases, of the immediate sympathy required for understanding. Instead of communicating, they resist. Instead of yielding, they react. Whether it is lack of initiation into American culture or the incapacity or intolerance of men trained in a certain way for forms of culture different from that to which they are accustomed, the fact is that they react and resist.

How they resist! How they inveigh against the United States and American civilization! They tear down everything, from top to bottom, without finding a single thing satisfactory.

The Statue of Liberty? A mess. Coney Island? A place to sweat en masse. New York? An enlarged Novo Hamburgo, a monstrous enlargement of Novo Hamburgo. Broadway, with all its succession of theaters, dance halls, night clubs, movies, and penny arcades—a servile copy of the *Kerbs* of the German colonial region in the South of Brazil where the colonists, with the same nonchalance and less noise, devote themselves to the vulgar pleasures of the dance, the shooting gallery, the slot machines, shouting, drinking, and group singing.

The English spoken in America? A language of barbarians that, to earn the title "civilized," to be able to express abstractions and generalizations, has had to borrow from the Latin languages more than 50 per cent of its vocabulary. And which, to maintain the illusion that this vocabulary has always belonged to it, has altered and Anglicized the pronunciation of words, forcing *them*, the Latins, to learn them twice over.

Luckily, it is not possible to inveigh and react like this for long. As days and weeks and months pass, the denial and irony will begin to ring false and find no inward echo. In the presence of the mass of impressive realities with which American civilization will go on pressing in upon them and convincing them, in the face of the evidence of its comfort, its idealism, and its high level of living—buildings that house populations as great as those of cities; railways and highways crisscrossing each other in all directions; chimneys smoking everywhere in the distance; sports-loving people everywhere, all apparently gay, healthy, and cordial; everywhere the joy of living or the appearance of it, physical health, moral health or its semblance; well-being and joviality; an almost total absence of envy, wretchedness, and slander; the majestic projection of skyscrapers upon the scarlet background of the horizons; trains on top of the ground and trains underground and under rivers; bridges, ships, planes, miles of docks, enormous warehouses stuffed with goods; parks, country houses, and idyllic nooks; streamlined vehicles gliding by like meteorites without the eye's having time to follow their going; the spontaneity of gaiety, the absence of revolt—in the face of all this, no longer will denial be possible, nor even neutrality. All this renewed day in and day out, week after week, month after month, year after year, makes that inveighing, in which at first there was some conviction, no longer practiced even for the sake of panache. Then the critics gradually give way to the sympathizers, the sympathizers to the panegyrists, provided they have not entirely lost, in the implacable practice of criticism and demolition, the salutary capacity for recognizing, sympathizing, and applauding. They no longer criticize, they applaud. And if they do not applaud, they explain and accept. They accept the way of American life, the hurry, the cafeteria, the drugstore, the absence of dragoons, the emancipation of women, the skyscrapers, the loud-colored taxis, Coney Island, streets with numbers instead of historic names, the Statue of Liberty, the slogans, and even Coca-Cola. Moreover, Coca-Cola served in the American style, half the glass lined with crushed ice, now tastes to them on sultry days like the nectar of the gods; the drugstore, with its long counters behind which veritable prestidigitators cause culinary curiosities, sherbets, and alluring cool drinks to spring forth, with its polished apparatus from which flow milk and cream, the coffee that fortifies and the syrups that comfort, suddenly seems to them the last word in civilization and convenience; the party becomes the highest and simplest of the ways to bring people together socially.

At this stage of events they will have to reef their sails against their enjoyment and enthusiasm in order not to wind up, due to the action of the imponderables, the slogans and advertisements, espousing Wall Street, Christian Science, isolationism, racism, chewing gum, and the horror of those loud ties that delight the average American male.

In any case, however, this reaction has been timely and necessary. By restoring their inner equilibrium, it broadens the orbits of their comprehension and their sympathy for the examination of things without petty restrictions. Perceiving now that they are in the presence of something new and immense, something that needs to be faced without preconceived notions, studied receptively, and interpreted without prejudice, they will understand that that "something new" can only be understood through the North American's position in relation to the fundamental concept of the past. And also in respect to the other main outlines that presided over his development: the Bible, the exaltation of labor, and the belief in the possibility of moral perfectibility.

9

If for the American, profoundly Jeffersonian, man is generally good— bad only when he does not find conditions that permit him to be good— to the Brazilian, as well as to the European, culturally Machiavellian, or at least more Machiavellian than Rousseauan, man is generally evil unless he proves the contrary. With eyes ever turned toward the past, as if the thousands of years of wars, revolutions, and cataclysms in which Europe has foundered belonged as much to his own experience as to that of the Europeans, the Brazilian gravitates about other realities than those of Rousseauan optimism. Believing that man is susceptible of material progress, nevertheless he feels that as far as the moral aspects of life are concerned, there is no way to extirpate doubts and distrusts that his own experience or his own past do not justify.

The consequences are, in the United States, optimism, a general state of sympathetic receptivity, of understanding and good will toward men; in Brazil, the "foot behind" (as they call it), reserve, vigilance, a diffuse ill will that polished words and emphatic declamations cannot manage to disguise; in the United States, stimulus, good reception to initiative; in Brazil, distrust, discouragement, suspicion of hidden selfish interest in the highest purposes; in the United States, life understood as integration in a duty or a dream; in Brazil, life viewed as pursuit of wealth and pleasure, as a "wearisome trade," something quite irremediably prosaic; in the United States, where the climate permits greater expenditures of energy, life facilitated and smoothed; in Brazil, where the climate requires conservation of strength, true odysseys of marches and countermarches to obstruct and impede the simplest operations of a civil, commercial, and administrative nature; in the United States, a progressive capitalism, more and more conscious of its social responsibilities; in Brazil, a capitalism of the European type, which still believes in trusts and cartels, in small production and high prices, and which in its relations with its workers still battens on the feudal, paternalistic concepts of the eighteenth century; in the United States, the good side of human nature being able to develop itself in plenitude; in Brazil, backbiting, suspicion, fear of ridicule—that stupid Brazilian fear of ridicule— discouraging the positive qualities to the benefit of the negative; in the United States, belief that goodness will win out over evil in the end, and health over sickness; in Brazil, doubts and mental reservations of every kind.

There is no end to the differences between Brazilians and Americans in facing the essential problems of life and death, of joy and grief, of sickness and health. The insouciance with which Americans proclaim their states of gaiety and the shamefaced way in which Brazilians conceal their fleeting states of happiness! They hide them as if they constituted scandalous monstrosities, real provocation to the gods. Scarcely does someone perceive their intimate joys when they shrink into themselves, grow serious, taken aback, like a criminal caught red-handed. When they ought to laugh out loud, they barely smile. That broad guffaw that Homer passed down to Rabelais, the healthful belly laugh of the apogee of the Middle Ages and the Renaissance, is scarcely to be found among Brazilians. Their smile is rather the smile that Machado de Assis admittedly received from Lucian of Samosata, a smile that comes more from others' mistakes and ridiculous actions than from the euphoria of one's own joys.

But in presenting their grounds for grief, their reasons for disquiet, damage done by their waywardness, how loquacious, how prolix Brazilians are! Their susceptibilities, their idiosyncrasies, their moral and physical allergies, their sufferings—these they have not the slightest constraint in exhibiting, turning them over and over, discussing them, dissecting them in broad daylight. It is their weak point. They display those things in their talk, in their constant sighing, in the eruptions of their prudery. Because the pearl is the oyster's disease, not to be sick of some real or imaginary disease is among Brazilians almost proof of poverty of spirit, a lack of self-respect, so much so that being sick is the general rule among them.

Exaggeration? Caricature?

Let Brazilians honestly recall mentally their private tables, and the tables of their hotels, tables loaded with bottles of remedies; let them call to mind their appointments, their meetings bristling with susceptibilities. What is the most persistent subject? Politics, literature, business, theater, movies, football? No. These are quickly exhausted as topics of interest. But there is one subject that is never exhausted, that never fails —disease, sickness.

Is the conversation forced, does it fail to take shape, is it necessary to enliven it at any cost? Why, you need only mention sickness. Then it becomes delirious. And the flame of the mind, which was flickering, and the conversation, which was dragging, take on new life, and the gathering becomes lively, fuses together new personal attractions, is prolonged until late into the night, and does not end before the last guest has exhausted, with luxuriant detail, his latest sufferings or his latest convalescence.

And not even by frequent repetition do these stories fail to provoke general interest. From the time the inevitable patient appears, lying in bed, hovering between life and death, his success is assured. The more doctors he has consulted, the more laboratory tests and examinations he has submitted to, the more candles he has lighted to St. Anthony and the other saints of the calendar, the more promises he has made for his relatives and friends to pay for, the more spiritualistic passes he has got his favorite spiritualist or medium to make, the better. The important thing is that at a given moment our patient has been completely disillusioned or that his enemies have well-founded hopes that he will not be spared. At that point, the providential physician or witch doctor must turn up. He examines the patient, palpates him, cites or does not cite similar cases, and decides on an operation. Because it is indispensable to the effect of complete dramatization that there be an operation. The operation is carried out, the patient hovers between life and death, the natural resistances of the organism react, and the patient is saved to reenter the prosaic routine of daily life.

Let this framework of the story be filled with details, deepen the colors of the dramatic passages, heighten the anguish of family and friends in the proper places, let the most prolonged conjecturings about analogous diseases and their specifics be made in the style of those instruction leaflets that accompany patent medicines, exaggerate the doctor's learning and his personal devotion (don't forget this point about personal attentions; it is particularly important, more important sometimes than his knowledge of his specialty), and you will have an oral novelette as certainly successful among Brazilians as the stories of poor boys in which all turns out well are among Americans.

For that matter, the happy ending is the great if not the only point of contact between this kind of story and the sort preferred by Brazilians.

Otherwise, between Brazilians and Americans, aside from those common denominators that constitute the patrimony of all America—Western tradition, hybridization, the sentiment of liberty—the rule is opposition and contrast. And when it is not strictly a matter of striking contrasts, like those that stand out from the reactions of both peoples toward the fundamental concept of the past and the idea of moral perfectibility, where there are only differences of degree and not of substance, the balance of constructive reactions leans almost invariably toward the Americans.

10

That is what happens, for example, as far as the Bible is concerned, or rather, in questions of religion generally. While the Americans, religious almost by definition, continue to read the Bible, still the greatest best seller in America, the Brazilians, more and more irreligious, still live dependent on the past triumphs of the Empire over the Faith, uncompromisingly faithful to one more of the main outlines of their cultural development. It will be said, Is not Brazil the greatest Catholic country in the world? To judge by the census statistics, it is indeed: In a population of fifty million, nearly 95 per cent are avowed Catholics. But these include real Catholics, anticlerical Catholics, spiritualist Catholics and non-practicing Catholics. In point of fact, in these four centuries of royal prerogative, in which the State always prevailed over the Church until the Church was separated from the State, the religious spirit has deteriorated.

Were they all really Catholic, it would be incomprehensible that the Brazilian clergy numbers scarcely six thousand priests, of whom more than half are foreigners, while in the United States, a Protestant country, for a Catholic population of thirty million there are about thirty thousand priests, that is, one for every thousand persons.

It may be objected that this does not prove that Brazil is not a deeply Catholic country, but only that the Brazilian has no vocation for the priesthood.

Let us not have any illusions. Lack of vocation means merely absence of the ambience and cultural atmosphere for the emergence of vocation. And how can there be such a propitious atmosphere if the whole history of Brazil reflects the triumph of the Empire over the Faith? During the whole colonial period there is not a single time when the Church registers a consistent triumph over public power. During the Empire the same thing is true. As the Mexican Antônio Gómez Robledo notes, the royalist policy of oppression of the Church, always at least latent, and aggravated in the closing years of the Colony, was further exacerbated in imperial Brazil.[6] In 1854 there were only twelve dioceses in the vast area of Brazil, and not another one was created until the time of the Republic, while a country with a Catholic minority like the United States could count, around 1889, eighty-four bishoprics.

"There was, in reality, no religious consciousness in Brazil, if we except a few concrete cases. In the majority there only existed the religious institution without an adequate religious conception."[7]

Were there a real religious spirit, vocation for the priesthood would spring up, and Brazil would not have to borrow priests from the United States to supply—in this field, too!—her needs. For that matter, no other interpretation is given by the cardinals, archbishops, bishops, and prelates resident in Brazil, in their pastoral letter of 1952: "But how can ecclesiastical and religious vocations arise in the environment of worldly, selfish, pleasure-loving families, which unhappily are to be seen abounding in our time? Only by miracles do lilies spring up in swamplands."[8] However deeply religious the medieval forerunners of Brazilian civilization might have been, it is clear that vocations for the priesthood could not withstand the triumphs of the Empire.

Nevertheless, to say that the Brazilian has no vocation for the priesthood is sociologically worth as much as to declare, solely on the basis of statistics and results, that the Brazilian has no natural vocation for work.

11

And here we come to the last of the fundamental outlines of Brazilian culture—the dislike of useful work and all that is connected with it: initiative, organization, cooperation, and the technical and scientific spirit.

After those four centuries of *bandeirismo* and patriarchalism, can it be that the Brazilian attitude concerning the creation of a propitious atmosphere for the emergence of technical vocations for useful work, has been substantially and definitively altered? Even here, however much things may have changed, and certainly they have changed a great deal and continue to change, how Brazilians still cling to the prejudices of the past, and how slow their evolution has been!

Incredible as it may seem, not even the abolition of slavery had the magical virtue of effecting definite, radical transformations for the better in the realm where everyone was hoping that miracles were going to take place. In many ways, at certain moments abolition actually served to aggravate the situation.

It was inevitable. On May 13, 1888, it was only legally and in very limited aspects that slavery was abolished in Brazil. While the United States enjoys all the economic consequences of abolition in the labor market, continuing nevertheless to maintain in the South the same racial prejudices of the preceding period, Brazil, enjoying all the con-sequences of abolition on the plane of equality of the races, forgetting that the equalization could only be consolidated on the plane of the elevation of the dignity of labor, continues to nourish the absurd preju-dices inherited from patriarchs and *bandeirantes* against work in many of its forms. Once slavery was abolished, it was not every form of activity that Brazilians came to appreciate. On the contrary, in keeping with old prejudices, innumerable forms of work, instead of dignifying the indi-vidual, were held to lower and debase him. As in the Brazilian concept of social dignity labor was compatible only with a small number of occupations and activities, it was clear that in the scale of activities all types of work formerly entrusted to slaves and artisans, as well as the subordinate functions that were historically reserved to them in trade and industry, were of course excluded, all of which incapacitated the other segments of society through lack of experience, cultural atmos-phere, social discipline, apprenticeship, and vocation, to enter without reservation into the industrialism of the nineteenth century, which was to make the greatness of the United States.

Within this picture, the former masters and their descendants, in-stead of setting an example by working, wanted to keep on conceiving of life in the patriarchal fashion, in the guise of true patricians awaiting (and expecting) new privileges, while freedmen and descendants of freedmen, lacking better examples and better images, tried to conceal their origins by cultivating the same reservations as their former masters against labor, craftsmanship, trade, specialization, mechanization, in-dustry, and science with constructive, not merely ornamental, ends. No compromise with the subordinate forms of labor necessary to industry, commerce, and farming. Such activities, everything outside the function of the *bandeirante* or of the patriarch, and the functions for which the *bandeirante* and the patriarch had some consideration—soldier, physician, lawyer, bureaucrat, priest, writer—if it was not becoming to people of high society with many centuries of real or supposed nobility in their veins, it was not becoming to the ex-slave.

The result is that in a country at that time essentially agricultural, slave labor, the basis of Brazil's patriarchal economy, was abolished, without promoting the necessary appreciation of free labor, which ought to have been an integral factor in the situation. Instead of mechanics, engineers, chemists, agronomists, artisans, qualified skilled labor and specialists, thousands of law graduates with a ring on the finger to prove at a glance that they do not work with their hands; thousands of literary men filling public offices with stale air; thousands of candidates for the sinecure and the coveted title of *malandro* (translatable as "sponger," "cadger," or *"fainéant"*).

Instead of devotion to duty, lack of conformity of individuals toward the tasks, functions, and occupations committed to their care; poorly done service, ill-finished work, inefficiency, deterioration, unpunctuality, procrastination; work regarded as a dishonoring stain. And as the atmosphere is not propitious to the effects of unconscious moral saturation in the belief in perfectibility, since skepticism and defeatism is the rule, nobody is satisfied with what he has, few put their hearts into what they do, all feel more or less robbed in what they have lost or in what they have not won through the action of the social transformations with which they would not or could not keep up.

Other consequences of these patrician and *bandeirante* restrictions on useful work are, on the economic plane, mere subsistence wages, as if the wage-earner were no more than the substitute for the slave; on the moral plane, a swelling finickiness toward the jobs linked with the shame of former slavery, vanity carried to sickly extremes, pedantry, self-sufficiency, the national cult of Malasarte—the hero who solves all situations without effort and without work, by craftiness, intrigue, calculation, astuteness.

12

Do you want to know the type capable of personifying the legion of good-for-nothing spongers the Empire bequeathed to the Republic? There is a stupendous example, whose equal there never has and prob-

ably never will be found. It is the hanger-on José Dias, in the novel
Dom Casmurro, by Machado de Assis. In Machado de Assis' prodigious
creation we are going to find embodied, even in the days of the Empire,
on the eve of abolition, the first complete historical symbol of the
national *malandro*. Only that? No, much more, because to tell the truth,
José Dias is also the only integral, irrefutable, finished symbol of
Brazilian culture. Caricatural and Rabelaisian symbol, if you will, but a
symbol at all events.

To start with, he has the desire for quick riches and, naturally, a
distaste for every kind of useful work. It may not be a desire for wealth
as devouring as that in the two preceding centuries, the "sacred hunger"
of the *bandeirantes*, but it is still the desire one way or another to find a
mine, or at least, in the absence of a mine, to make a lucky strike that
will allow him to do nothing. José Dias, when he first appears in
Itaguaí, a place through which men passed in former days in quest of
gold, is evidently wandering in search of adventure. A fever epidemic is
laying waste the region. José Dias, who has with him a manual and a
case of medicines, passing himself off for a homeopathic doctor, cures
the overseer of a plantation and a slave woman, and will take no pay.
This is a happy stroke. The grateful patriarch proposes that he stay
there, with a small salary.

"José Dias refused, saying that it was only right to bring health to the
thatched hut of the poor.

" 'Who's stopping you from going anywhere? Go wherever you want,
but fix your residence with us.'

" 'I'll be back in three months.'

"He was back in two weeks, accepted food and lodging with no other
pay except what they might want to give him as feast-day presents."[9]

Soon José Dias has found his treasure. It is not much. But, lacking a
mine—and mines have been scarce for a long time—it serves. At least he
no longer needs to bother with a job, but only to defend his position in
the house without working.

Everything goes just right for José Dias. When the patriarch, a slave-
holder, perhaps foreseeing abolition, is elected to Congress and goes to
Rio de Janeiro with his family, leaving the plantation to the care of
the overseer (always the return of wealth to Europe or to the coast),
José Dias has his room at the rear of the country estate. One day, when
another fever epidemic is raging in Itaguaí, the patriarch tells him to go
to the plantation to look after the slaves. José Dias stands silent, sighs,
and finally confesses he is no doctor.

"He had taken that title to help in publicizing a new school, and
hadn't done so without a great deal of study, but his conscience would
not permit him to accept any more patients.

" 'But you've cured some before.'

" 'I believe I did; but a more accurate statement would be that it was the remedies prescribed in the books. They're the ones, yes, they—by the Grace of God. I was a charlatan. . . . Don't deny it; the motives for my action might be, and were, worthy; homeopathy is truth, and to serve the truth I lied; but it is time to set it right.' "[10]

He was not dismissed. The patriarch could no longer get along without him. The dependent had the gift of making himself agreeable and necessary. "His absence was felt as keenly as that of a member of the family."

José Dias had won his game, and had his "mine" all staked out and secure. So secure that when the patriarch died, the widow, Dona Glória, very grateful for the grief that afflicts José Dias, will not let him give up his room. She insisted on his continuing as a family dependent.

" 'Stay, José Dias.'

" 'I obey, *senhora*.' "[11]

We have here, therefore, very vividly, the two prime outlines of Brazil's development—the search for rapid wealth and the dislike for useful work—to which the natural complements would plainly not be lacking, that is, the absence of professional preparation and a purely ornamental show of learning. "He was widely read, though only in a superficial way, enough to be amusing of an evening or in an after-dinner chat, or to explain some phenomenon, to talk of the effects of heat and cold, of the poles, and of Robespierre."[12] As for his style, the dependent loved superlatives. "It was one way of giving a monumental aspect to his ideas; if there were no ideas, it served to prolong the sentences."[13] An unpleasant duty he immediately promoted to "a *most* unpleasant duty." "In serious, grave situations, *most* grave."[14] Our José Dias clever? Extremely clever. According to Pádua, he was "a man of capacity and could speak like a deputy in the halls of Congress."[15]

And as for religion, morality, and a belief in the moral perfectibility of humanity? José Dias positively did not have the soul of a crusader. Nor was he the man to burn with a passion for justice. He always acted exactly as he walked. He walked slowly, "not the dragging slowness of the lazy, but a calculated, deliberate slowness, a complete syllogism, the premise before the consequence, the consequence before the conclusion."[16] If in passing before a church he had seen thieves making off with the Virgin's diadem, he would never attack the thieves to prevent the sacrilege. He certainly would go to complain to the police, though. He was what may be called a practical idealist.

For instance, in the case of the love between Capitú and Bentinho, the future Dom Casmurro, José Dias does not intervene directly when he catches them whispering in corners. The straight line was not for him.

His ruling passion was the capricious curve, the maneuver, the intrigue, the denunciation.

" 'Dona Glória, are you going on with your idea of putting our Bentinho in the seminary? It's high time, and there may be some difficulty about it even now.'

" 'What difficulty?'

" 'A great difficulty.' "[17]

Dona Glória, naturally, wanted to know what it was.

"José Dias [the narrator, Bentinho himself, relates], after a few moments of concentration, came to the door to see whether there was anybody in the hall; he did not notice me, went back and, lowering his voice, said that the difficulty was in the neighboring house, the Páduas'.

" 'The Páduas'?'

" 'I've been on the verge of saying this for some time, but didn't quite dare to. It doesn't look right to me for our Bentinho to be always in a corner with old "Turtle's" daughter, and that is the difficulty, because if they start lovemaking you'll have a time trying to separate them.'

" 'I don't think so. Always in a corner?'

" 'In a manner of speaking. Whispering little secrets, always together. Bentinho almost never leaves there. The little girl's a scatterbrain; the father pretends he doesn't see them; he'd be tickled for things to go so far that—— I understand your expression. You don't believe in such calculating schemings, you think everybody has a frank, open heart. . . .' "[18]

José Dias was all sheer malice and did not believe in anyone's frank, open heart—except, of course, that of his protectors.

" 'There now!' he told Bentinho confidentially. 'Never has anybody heard me say a thing about people like that. Why? Because they are noble and virtuous. Your mother is a saint, your uncle a perfect gentleman. I have known distinguished families; none is ahead of yours in nobility of sentiments. The talent your uncle finds in me I confess I have, but it's only a single one—it's the talent for knowing what is good and worthy of admiration and appreciation.' "[19]

In the matter of virtues the only one he really cultivated was gratitude —a virtue always highly esteemed by patriarchs and bandeira leaders. On the occasion of the patriarch's death, José Dias was remembered.

"He received a small bequest in the will, a bond and a few words of praise. He copied the words, framed them and hung them in his room, over his bed. 'This is the best bond,' he often said. . . . In short, he was a friend, I shall not say the best friend, but then not everything is best in this world. And don't see in him a servile soul; the bowing and scraping he did came rather from calculation than from his nature."[20]

The very denunciation made by José Dias had been pure calculation.

He was making himself out a pious fellow to Dona Glória, reminding
her of the promise to make Bentinho a priest and prevent the family
fortune from winding up in the hands of Capitú, daughter of old
"Turtle," whom he did not like, a situation that in the future might
unsettle his position as dependent.

José Dias' new stroke hit the mark once more. Dona Glória ended by
deciding to put Bentinho in the seminary.

" 'Well, since you haven't lost the notion of making him a priest,
that's the main thing. Bentinho's bound to follow his mother's wishes.
And then, too, the Brazilian Church has high destinies. Let us not forget
that a bishop presided over the Constitutional Assembly, and that Padre
Feijó governed the Empire. . . .'

" 'Governed like the ass he was!' Uncle Cosme interrupted, yielding to
old political grudges."[21]

And with regard to the past and to Europe, how did our hero behave?
Ah! José Dias was terribly attached to the past.

"He was one of the last to wear white starched trousers strapped
under the shoes in Rio de Janeiro, and perhaps in the world."[22]

As for Europe, that was his great soft spot.

"He often told about a trip he had taken to Europe, and he confessed
that if it had not been for us, he would have already gone back there; he
had friends in Lisbon, but our family, he said, under God, was everything to him.

" 'Under or above?' asked Uncle Cosme one day.

" 'Under,' repeated José Dias, full of reverence.

"And my mother, who was religious, liked to see that he was putting
God in the right place, and smiled in approval."[23]

Was José Dias cured of the Old World? Had his first enjoyment of
Europe caused satiety in him? Not yet. At fifty-five, "lean and drawn,
with the beginnings of a bald spot," a "black satin cravat, with a steel
ring inside" holding his neck stiff, and a "printed cotton gown, light
indoor costume," "which looked like a full-dress coat on him"[24] José Dias
was still dreaming of Europe. Most fervent of *mazombos*, all his maneuvers, as soon as he sensed that Bentinho was avoiding the seminary,
turned toward liberating him from the cassock and carrying him off to
Europe and staying there while Bentinho studied law.

" 'Since you cannot be a priest and prefer the law. . . . Laws are beautiful, without disparagement of theology, which is better than anything,
as the ecclesiastical life is the most holy. Why shouldn't you go abroad
to study law? Better go to some university, and, at the same time that
you study, travel. We can go together; we shall see foreign lands, hear
English, French, Italian, Spanish, Russian, and even Swedish. Dona
Glória will probably not be able to go with you; even if she can and

does, she will not want to handle the business affairs, papers, applications, and see to lodgings and go here and there with you. . . . Oh, the law is extremely beautiful!'

" 'Is it agreed, you'll ask Mama not to put me in the seminary?'

" 'As to that, I'll ask, but asking's not getting. My angel boy, if will to serve were power to command, we'd be aboard ship as easily as we are here right now. Ah, you can't imagine what Europe is! Ah, Europe!'

"He lifted one leg and did a pirouette. One of his ambitions was to return to Europe; he spoke of it often, without succeeding in tempting my mother or Uncle Cosme, however much he praised its climate and its beauties. . . . He did not count on the possibility of going with me, and staying there during the eternity of my studies.

" 'We're as good as aboard ship, Bentinho, as good as aboard!' "[25]

Can more be needed to understand the exact position of José Dias as far as the concepts of the past, religion, moral perfectibility, and labor are concerned? All that is lacking now is to learn what the family dependent's reaction is toward the problem of racial crossing. Unhappily, this point in the life of José Dias is obscure. The circumspect, the exceedingly circumspect Machado de Assis, perhaps because of the very circumstance that he himself was mulatto, furnishes us no information. So nothing is known of our hero's sexual life. And yet, judging by the quantity of lively, dark-skinned reminders of José Dias one encounters at every step in the street, in public offices (which today are substituting for the old patriarchal family in sheltering, clothing, feeding, fattening, and encouraging and giving importance to the vocation of dependent), the presumption that his life was not impeccable on this score must not be ignored, even though not the slightest trace of his activities of this nature is left—even in this, José Dias was the complete good-for-nothing.

13

Great José Dias! For the iconography of a culture wedded to the past, unconcerned with the moral aspects of life and unburdened with the cult of the essential dignity of labor, there is none like him.

Spain has Don Quixote and Sancho Panza; England has a whole Shakespearian gallery of rascally symbols; France has Tartarin de Tarascon and Cyrano de Bergerac; Portugal has the Counselor Acácio;

the United States has Babbitt and Donald Duck; but Brazil has José
Dias. He is the best. As the symbol of a culture one cannot ask for
more.

Since José Dias and with the coming of the Republic, it is true,
legions of idlers have appeared whose supreme ideal in life is likewise to
do nothing, and in whose opinion he whom God helps is better off than
he who helps himself, who takes care not to get in bad with the boss because he who has a patron won't die a pagan, and he who can, commands, and he who must, obeys. For that matter, if they did not exist
in such great numbers, Walt Disney would not have found so quickly
the model for his extraordinary José Carioca.

Many of them, masked or not, have a quality that José Dias never
possessed—a sense of humor, that is, the capacity to see clearly, under
the realities of ostentation and under the surface, the essential realities,
and to laugh at them all. But not the great majority. They lack José
Dias' breeding, the fine breeding of the second Kingdom, the class and
gentle manners of the old-time family dependents.

With the republican regime it is possible that public education has
much improved in Brazil, but as far as bringing up children is concerned it has been disastrous. So long as there were statesmen of the
Empire, nothing was yet amiss. The worst was to come later, when the
bandeira spirit, long checked on the frontiers, rolled back upon civilization in the train of the caudillos. Then it came indeed! The noble line of
fainéants began to rot. And instead of the José Dias of the great days,
with steady nerves, there emerged the neurotic spongers and idlers of
the last generation who, caught up with no sinecure into the vortex of
the economic and social transformations of our time, would end by
pontificating on spiritualism or communism, or by converting into insolence toward their fellow man their maladaptation to the chaotic social
order rising out of the ruins of slavery in Brazil.

Socially injurious persons, these good-for-nothings? Not at all. Merely
socially and emotionally maladjusted.

Restless, unstable, fed on myths and mirages long since superseded,
the ills from which they suffer, like those of the mazombos and half-
breeds, are not congenital. They are the fruits of Brazil's historical past,
of her economic misfortunes, of errors of interpretation of her essential
characters, of the precariousness of her teaching and rearing of the
young, and, above all, of the lack of political, moral, and spiritual guides.
Easy prey to every form of demagogy, they are the victims of a lack of
real leaders.

Poor leaders! They do not know how to preach either by word or
precept. The most capable of them do not go beyond economic solutions: they indifferently raise minimum wages and build housing for

workers. And when the raised wages have only contributed to reducing the working days of the idler and the housing has not enhanced the joy of living or improved the habits of living, the leaders flounder in despair. They do not understand that they are not facing an exclusively economic phenomenon, but an emotional, deeply emotional one, and therefore simultaneously an economic, moral, and spiritual one. They do not perceive that when the *fainéant* in his moral and emotional immaturity prefers the hut to the house, he is not succumbing to ingratitude but only surrendering to his desire to return to the period of his childhood, rebelling, by transference, against the social environment that is the projection of the father who has abandoned him, or whom he has never seen. And they perceive even less that the absence of any taste for useful work in the idler is only the reflection of the example that comes from above and of the very culture with which he is unconsciously impregnated.

The *malandros* of today are sick men, more sick in soul than in body, Miguel Pereira one day uttered his famous outcry, "Brazil is one vast hospital." It is probably as much a hospital of neurotic, immature, and maladjusted individuals as it is of physically sick ones. What they need more than anything else is emotional orientation, guides that will aid them to shake off the neuroses that the national history has imposed on them, and not wooers of multitudes and sybarites enamored of the prestige of high position. Their problem is not merely one of houses instead of huts. What they need is insecticides, sulfa, penicillin, and truth in massive doses.

Above all, truth. Not the criticizing truth of detractors and demolishers, but the constructive truth of builders who, as they point out the disease, also indicate the specific for the cure, who have a message to give, something to say and the courage to say it. In a word, what they need, what all Brazilians need and have needed for four hundred years, is genuine leaders, taking here the word "leader" in the Mosaic sense of spiritual and moral head, inspirer and leader of the people through the virtues of persuasion and example.

In truth, leaders in this sense and in the sense of molders of cohesive nations have been very few in Brazil, if she has ever had any. Indeed, theoretically it is logical that it should be so. Nothing else should be expected sociologically of a culture founded and developed on the *bandeiras*, upon the basis of conquest, authority and force. When it is a question of extending the Empire or of defending it, there is no lack of great men. But when it is a question of giving a structure to the nation, of telling the world and themselves what they are aiming at, the picture is not very edifying. The rise of genuine civil leaders like the American ones—Jefferson, John Adams, Abraham Lincoln, Wilson,

Roosevelt—occurred in Brazil only by exception. What is most probable is that the heroes of her culture, like those of the Hispano-American cultures, nourished on the idea of conquest and the defense of mineral deposits, would be of the military type required by the discipline of the camp. In Brazil, Caxias, Osório, Deodoro, Floriano. In the Hispano-American republics, Bolívar, San Martín. Soldiers, or at least *caudillos*. They would rarely be strictly civilian. In Brazil, except for the military chieftains and the *bandeirantes*, who have been really the first and only molders of the nation—for it is around them and their concept of heroism and their work of conquest that Brazilian ideals still gravitate—it is futile to look for heroes or civil leaders with a permanent, enduring appeal to the popular conscience.[26] They simply do not exist. And they do not exist because the main lines of Brazilian culture have never been propitious to them.

Really, if there have been, in these four centuries of Brazilian history, conflicting cultural outlines, blocking the rise of inwardly harmonious men, those outlines have indubitably been those of the Latin civilization transplanted to America. The contradictions have been tremendous. First arose the fundamental contradiction between Catholicism and capitalism. However much some Catholic thinkers outdo themselves in arguments to demonstrate that the contradiction does not exist, the facts testifying to the contrary are indestructible. And it is not only a question of opposing concepts between which there may be room for the golden mean. It is a matter here of something more: it is a question of concepts and conceptions of life contradictory among themselves, for between the concept of the legitimacy of the victory of the strongest and fittest—which is the predominant law of the world of capitalistic mercantilism—and the law of Christian cooperation, there is no room for a mid-course. Any compromise between the two is bound to be precarious.

After this first incompatibility others no less profound would occur: the insoluble contradiction between Protestant liberalism and Catholic liberalism; between Thomism and the subproducts of Protestantism; between the concept of natural goodness and the Catholic concept of original sin; between determinism and free will.

The consequences would be those now known—a stupefying mental anarchy and terribly contradictory representative types scarcely at peace with themselves and with the world, and a marked prevalence of the Dionysian type over the Apollonian in that restless succession of *caudillos* that constitutes the history of the Latin American peoples.

But if it has been more or less this way until now, how will it be from here on into the future? Will the men of Latin America continue to be irremediably restless, troubled, groping in darkness for a course of salva-ion, and those of Anglo-Saxon America perfectly at ease and comfortable within the main lines of their culture? In other terms, will capitalism and Protestantism go on from victory to victory, stigmatizing the reluctant rhythm of the civilization of the Catholic countries? Will Economics continue to prevail over Ethics, and Empire over Faith? What will the signs of the times be?

VI

Signs of the Times

1

No, NOT ALL IS DISSIMILARITY AND CONTRAST BETWEEN BRAZIL AND THE United States. In the midst of the diversities that accentuate the differences between the two cultures, Brazilians and North Americans currently have between them one great trait in common: immaturity—taking here, of course, the term in its psychological sense, or rather, in its psychoanalytic meaning of emotional maladjustment or lack of adequate adaptation to life and reality.

Brazilians maladjusted? Of course it was not to be expected, granted the very abnormal circumstances of their development, that they should have entirely purged the errors of the past and freed themselves from the terrors that their nature inspires in them. Unhappily, their nature has not yet been tamed, and the errors of the past are yet to be redeemed.

And what of Brazilian cordiality? Isn't cordiality a symptom of maturity? Strictly speaking, that cordiality does not exist to the extent it is proclaimed. What does exist is a general acceptance as cordiality of what is no more than courtesy, that same courtesy that Count Hermann von Keyserling—evidently inspired by the fundamental principle of anthropogeography that man is a product of the earth's surface—saw with certainty as one of the most marked traits of Brazilian character. Discounting the exaggerations resulting from oversimplification, the author of *South American Meditations* saw everything plain, seeing in the Brazilian not properly the cordial man but the man Nature predestined to courtesy.[1]

Blocked by the mountains of the littoral, obliged to confront the insidious forest where dangers constantly lie in wait, on land, on water,

222

and in the air, having to adjust himself to a climate for which the white man has never served an apprenticeship, it was practically impossible for him to conquer the tropics as the Anglo-Saxon conquered the temperate zones of the earth. He would, indeed, have to develop faculties and qualities adequate to the new environment, and among these, sensibility and a delicate courtesy.

While the Anglo-Saxon found in the New World natural conditions that were more or less similar to those of Europe, and problems long known to him and which he had long ago learned how to confront, the Portuguese in Brazil faced a world completely strange to him, with very few similarities to his original habitat. For him the cold was probably no novelty, but the tropical heat with a high degree of humidity was unknown to him. The type of virgin forests of North America would not be something new, not absolutely new, in the experience of the European. But the tropical forest of Brazil, the jungle that advances to the very edge of rivers like a veritable well of verdure, certainly would not inspire in him any pantheistic ardors of immediate mastery. On the contrary, his dominant sentiment would be terror, the cosmic terror that persists in the Brazilian even in our day.

In Brazil man would have to conquer Nature by feeling his way, temporizing, detouring, distrusting, wriggling, tricking, biding his time, waiting for opportunities, developing subtleties that, in the end, by mimetism, he would communicate to the social guest in the form of a delicate courtesy. Hence the *jeito*, the famous Brazilian "way" (means, order, twist, skill, propensity, and so forth) of doing things—"Let's find a *jeito*," or "We have to find the *jeito*," the best way of getting something done—which the foreigner never quite succeeds in comprehending, a sign that the word *jeito*, with no exactly corresponding term in the principal Western tongues, fills a necessity of expression peculiar only to Brazilians and not to other peoples. Hence also, in part, their social manner, their politeness, their hesitations, their *jeito*, their *delicadeza* or courtesy, which is perhaps one of the characterological traits most peculiarly Brazilian. So much so that the Brazilian's courteous delicacy is not uniform from North to South or from East to West. On the contrary, arising from the soil, it varies according to the greater or less dominion of man over Nature and is theoretically in direct ratio to the cosmic terror Nature inspires in him. In the states of Amazonas and Pará, where man's mastery of Nature is slight and where cosmic terror is the dominant sentiment, we are going to find the most "delicate" people in Brazil, the most courteous, that is, and without doubt the people most delightful to deal with.

No longer can the same be said of the man of Rio Grande do Sul, in whom cosmic terror really does not exist. Neither can it be said that *delicadeza* or *jeito* is the distinctive trait of São Paulo's psychology. It is, rather, a quality of the man of Minas Gerais, courtesy tempered with distrust—the courtesy on account of the mountains and dangers he has had to face every time he decided to cross the bounds of his municipality, and distrust because of the type of economic activity he practiced and in which lack of discretion often meant robbery, assault, and murder. "Every terror," says Keyserling, "demands a defense. Hence, in man's relationships, the primacy of metaphor over the direct order, of etiquette over simple communication, of courtesy over frankness."[2]

Jeito or *delicadeza*, however, do not signify cordiality, and much less do they mean maturity. At times, actually, the contrary is true. Courtesy may be merely a means of defense for restraining aggressive impulses. There are neurotics who are terribly good at the *jeito*. They are courteous almost by definition.

No confusing courtesy with cordiality, then. Cordiality is something else. And the Amazon will still have to spill a great deal of water into the Atlantic before Brazilians have attained fullness of cordiality and fullness of maturity. Furthermore, if there is a phenomenon visible even to the eyes of the blind and audible even to the ears of the deaf, it is, unhappily, that of their psychic instability. From the most clear-cut cases of megalomania on the verge of schizophrenia to the more benign cases of correctible maladjustments, everything in that people still betrays and confirms, under the transports and declamations of a superficial cordiality, emotional immaturity from which stem, in the last analysis—and not to the contrary as many claim—all other immaturities, political and economic, if not also psychological, social, spiritual, and cultural ones.

The time has passed when, deluded by hasty interpretations of certain facts of their historical development—the abolition of slavery without bloodshed, for example—Brazilians piously believed in the vaunted basis of their emotional equilibrium. Today, after the general revision of values that modern historiography, aided by modern psychology, is carrying on in all sectors of the social sciences—say what they will of the bloodless way the abolition of slavery was effected in Brazil, or the proclamation of the Republic, or the founding of the New State (episodes in which the symptoms of immaturity are confused with the symptoms and evidences of common sense and cordial spirit)—the same errors can no longer be nourished.

No illusions, then. Emotional maturity, or even simple emotional subnormality, is perhaps not yet the rule but the exception. At least that is what can be concluded from the scanty and limited scientific or statistical data that turn up here and there connected with psychotechnical examinations of some professional segments of the Brazilian populace. Limited and scanty as these data are, they leave no doubt about the state of the collective emotions of Brazilians, and they are as much a cause for alarm as the concrete and positive data on American maladjustment.

2

Americans maladjusted? So, that nation—which is not addicted to the past, which believes in the pursuit of happiness and in the perfectibility of men and things, which works as if it is having a good time, which does not cultivate grief, which does not prize tragedy; which neither encourages nor amplifies susceptibilities, romantic without hysteria, religious without mysticism, rather philanthropic than charitable, idealistic without metaphysics, sober in love and in the pleasures of the table; which finds in its sense of humor an inexhaustible source of sociability and gaiety—so that nation also suffers from the emotional ills that afflict Brazilians? Does it, too, suffer from the maladjustments to the point where already one may talk about them as an American national problem?

However strange it may seem, that is indeed the situation. At least, it is what not only European psychiatrists, neurologists, psychoanalysts, and anthropologists state, but also and especially what the North American anthropologists, neurologists, psychiatrists, and psychoanalysts themselves tell us on the basis of their experience, giving facts and statistics.

The assertion, indeed, has another proof, and that is the demand and consumption enjoyed in the United States by books that deal with the problems of emotional maladjustment.

This consumption is simply phenomenal. A book that treats of the problem of the individual's emotional relationships with reality, whether it is called *Peace of Mind*,[3] *Peace of Soul*,[4] or *The Mature Mind*,[5] is a book that has as many possibilities of becoming a best seller in the United States as clandestine books of a scatological nature have among Brazilians.

Visible in the showcases of all bookshops, where they are specially displayed, with entrée into the palace of the rich and the tenement of the poor, leafed through on airplanes, trains, streetcars, buses, subways, shining on the banker's desk and on the worker's modest corner shelf, in the scientist's library and on the bookkeeper's shelves, in the housewife's sewing basket and on the doctor's worktable, what mysterious, strange messages can these books transmit, that so many hearts give them free entry and so many minds open up to them in excitement? Can it be a question of the discovery of the philosopher's stone? Of a new philosophy or a new religion capable of dissolving in the vast estuary of common aspirations and universal brotherhood the diversities of origin, language, and tendencies that divide and separate individuals, peoples, and nations? Nothing of the sort. Their secret—up to a certain point this is also the secret of the *Reader's Digest*—is in the formulas for salvation and the messages of hope they contain for those sick at heart. What the American reader seeks in them, apart from his natural curiosity about the new fact and the new science, is the message of hope that may relieve him or help to relieve him of the tension in which he lives because of his own maladjustments.

3

Why is this? What are the causes or motives of this phenomenon?

Here is a paradoxical fact: The motives or causes of the phenomenon —to use here once again, for lack of a better term, the word "cause" analogically to express vital facts—are the same master outlines that presided over the development of the two cultures. In Brazil it will be racial tolerance, desire for quick riches, addiction to the past, victory of the material over the spiritual, exacerbated individualism, prejudice against useful work, unconcern with the moral aspects of life, scorn for the economic virtues; in the United States, the break with the past, racial discrimination, Puritanism, the belief in the natural goodness of man and in his perfectibility, the pursuit of success at any price, a reverential regard for the economic virtues.

The fact is really paradoxical, and paradoxical because there seems to be a certain contradiction in that both love and dislike of work, both addiction to and break with the past, both relief and disbelief in human goodness, both the cult of and the scorn for the economic virtues, end by leading to the same result. Indeed, in terms of logic, the contradiction is transparent and inescapable. It happens, however, that here, once more, we are not in the presence of natural phenomena, in which events are repeated in logical order, but in the presence of facts impregnated with life, instinct, intelligence, and passion, with which common logic has nothing to do. And where there is life there must always be contradiction, without there necessarily being incompatibility or (to use a term from philosophy) incompossibility. Furthermore, the Greeks knew that. And it is because they knew it that without contradiction they erected temples to Apollo and to Dionysus—one symbolizing humanity in quest of spirituality, light, and beauty; the other symbolizing humanity chained to the base pleasures of lust, wine, and the table—side by side, and they did not enter the temple of the one without also entering the temple of the other.

In life, contradiction comes from the circumstance of our thinking of vital phenomena impregnated with passion, in the mechanistic language of cause and effect, and in terms of the logic of nature, instead of in terms of vital or historical linking, which is what, without blindly determining them, conditions the lives of individuals and cultures. Therefore it is necessary to make it quite clear that clinging to the past or breaking with it, love of or distaste for useful labor, skepticism or optimism, do not function, in the case of Brazilian and American immaturity, as mechanical causes but rather as concauses or historical causes.

Beyond that, maturity or immaturity, moral health or neurosis, being phenomena impregnated with life, have no causes in the common sense of the word; they have, rather, a past and motives, just as occurs with historical phenomena. Besides, even as a background or motive for immaturity or neurosis, addiction to or separation from the past, love of or distaste for work, belief or disbelief in human goodness, worship of or scorn for economic virtues, never function isolatedly in their original form. They act two by two, three by three, already twisted and distorted by human passions in the hallucinating play of arrangements, combinations, and permutations of values that *life* bears in its train.

On the other side, not all Brazilian and American neuroses originate in subjective magnifications of the importance of those master outlines. There are neuroses that have nothing to do with them. Still, that does not prevent, in general, the fundamental outlines of the two cultures, combined and geared to one another, from ending by conditioning the nuclei from which radiate the emotional conflicts of the individual with himself and with the environment in which he lives. As Karen Horney observes: "The fact that in general the majority of individuals in a culture have to face the same problems suggests the conclusion that these problems have been created by the specific life conditions existing in that culture. That they do not represent problems common to 'human nature' seems to be warranted by the fact that the motivating forces and conflicts in other cultures are different from ours."[6]

4

In the case of Brazilian neuroses, for example, are exceptional gifts of intuition needed to perceive that they arise, above all, from the way that racial tolerance developed in Brazil?

The startling thing, knowing the conditions, the terrible moral conditions of racial crossing in Brazil, is not that there are so many immature, neurotic *mazombos* and half-breeds; the startling thing is that well-adjusted half-breeds occur and continue to occur in greater and greater numbers. After all, it is only a little over sixty years since slavery was abolished and the feudalism and *bandeirismo* of Brazilian customs began to be nullified. And it is not in two or three generations, or even in ten, that the consequences of social diseases like slavery and promiscuity will be eliminated.

Decidedly, the Jesuits of the sixteenth and seventeenth centuries knew what they were doing when they forgave the sinner while waging unremitting war on the sin. The sinner would disappear; not so the sorry consequences of his moral infractions. The latter would have repercussions down through the ages, like those of original sin.

Other consequences that were not to disappear were those arising from greed and the pursuit of quick riches, together with scorn for the economic virtues.

Just as in the past, on the economic plane, the antagonism between greed and Catholic morality generated the most abject of all capitalisms, the capitalism which, with all the gold it gave to the churches, never succeeded in soothing its guilt complexes or in making the businessman's occupation quite respectable, even when carried on honestly—that same antagonism would give place in our time not only to the merchants who discourage their sons from the career they themselves have adopted, but also to the troubled merchants who, utterly lost by their own inner standards, permit themselves everything, knowing that there is something intrinsically unhealthy in the pursuit of gain, usury, and extraordinary profit to which they devote themselves counter to the canonical virtues. And this, let us agree, is not exactly a sign of maturity.

And here we come to the third source of Brazilian maladjustments: the relegating of religion to a subordinate plane, a thing which, according to Jung, one of the most renowned psychiatrists of our time, has never contributed to the emotional improvement of anyone. On the contrary (still according to Jung), the parting from one's original religion is at the root of all neuroses, as the return to religiosity is the beginning of the cure. "During the last thirty years," he says, "I have been consulted by people from all the civilized countries of the world. I have treated many hundreds of patients, the greatest number being Protestants, a smaller number of Jews, and not more than five or six practicing Catholics. Among all my patients in the second half of life—that is, above thirty-five years of age—there has not been a single problem, in the final instance, that was not one of finding a religious opening for life. It can be stated with assurance that they all fell sick because they had lost the thing that the living religions of all the ages transmit to their adepts, and none of them really achieved a cure without having reacquired the religious sense."[7]

And the maladjustments resulting from the exaggerated clinging to the past? The one who best defines them is Joaquim Nabuco, when he says that we, Brazilians and Americans in general, through belonging to America only through the superficial layers of our spirit and to Europe through our stratified layers, are condemned to terrible instability, and that this will last until within us "the memory of our common European origin" is extinguished.[8]

This, plainly, is a masterly definition of the general phenomenon of the *mazombo* psychology. And it would be quite perfect if Nabuco had not included in it, on a footing of equality with the South Americans, the Americans of the North, whose maladjustments and instabilities originate in their violent rejection of the past rather than from their clinging to it, although cases of *mazombismo* like that of Henry James and Henry Adams are not exactly uncommon. As for Brazilians and Latin Americans of purely European origin, however, the definition fits beautifully, seeing that living physically on the new continent with the mind turned toward the Old World constitutes one of the oldest obstacles to the full, desired advent of Brazilian maturity.

But if *mazombismo* is the oldest, it is not the gravest source of the Brazilian's maladjustments. The gravest, and the one that most frequently generates immaturity and neuroses, is the absence of a taste for useful work, because it is intimately bound to the other main outlines of Brazilian culture, especially to the expectancy or hope of rapid fortune and to the absence of a spirit of cooperation. It is perhaps in the latter that the deepest roots of his maladjustments are fixed, among which must be conceded a place apart, naturally, to the extremely Brazilian habit of leaving until tomorrow what can be done today, a habit that, at the slightest pressure to get things done immediately, there being no objective reason for not doing them, can instantaneously let loose veritable states of panic and irritability.

Or can it be that the so-called Brazilian laziness has a biological and racial background? Can it be as biological and racial as the so-called Brazilian melancholy? Much, evidently, is due to the tropical climate, because it is not right to expect that man in hot climates can continuously produce as much as in temperate or cold climates, or that he can maintain the same level of vitality as when he lives in pleasanter latitudes. Equal responsibility should be given to the state of chronic substandard alimentation in which the Brazilian lives, some through absolute lack of nourishment, others simply through not knowing how to eat properly.

But the great responsibility for Brazilian laziness, perhaps the greatest, lies at the door of the emotional prejudice against certain forms of activity.

The proof? Observe the half-breeds and *mazombos* not yet reconciled to work in the most varied functions: at the counter, in the workshop, in the office. After some time we are going to see that all of them leave plenty to be desired in the matter of turning out work, and employers, above all foreign employers, will naturally conclude that there is nothing to be done about it, that laziness is congenital and racial in them.

Now let us take those same mulattoes and those same *mazombos* and put them on a football team. We shall then witness great transfigurations. *Mazombos* and mulattoes who had no energy for work, whose indolence was taken as congenital, whose energy seemed nil, run for ninety minutes on the field, struggle together like wild men, do not spare themselves, and do not weaken for a second. Why the contrast? Because football is something they learned to love in childhood and in school—if they had any schooling—while useful labor has always been demeaned in their eyes. Because they have never been given heroes of constructive work to idolize, while the heroes of their football fields, together with the symbol of Malasarte, have filled their childhood dreams and reveries.

With them the same thing happens that historically took place with the mestizos. Setting aside the occupations that corresponded, one way or another, to those they worshiped as children in the Indian long house, they were useless, turbulent fellows. Hardly adaptable to useful forms of labor, they ended by degenerating into the human castoff described by Agassiz. And yet in the occupation of woodland guide, of the *bandeirante*, of the boatman, of the guerrilla fighter, of the tamer of deserts, no one could excel them.

Can anything further be necessary before we recognize the significance of the dislike of work that *mazombos* and half-breeds develop in childhood as the initial nucleus of their future maladjustments and of the neurotic indolence which serves them as a culture broth? Being emotional on the basis of their prejudices against constructive labor, through the nonexistence or lack of a suitable idealization of the symbols that dignify it, their reactions in this case had to end by being emotional and neurotic, as a great number of reactions which up to now have been attributed to racial indolence are neurotic and emotional in their origin. Add to the distaste for work the other ingredients of their training— excessive love of the past, search for quick wealth, irreligiosity, and unconcern with the moral aspects of life—without forgetting, of course, the geophysical and economic factors, and we shall have torn away a little more, in one way or another, the veil that covers the mysteries of the neuroses afflicting the Brazilians.

5

In the United States, on another plane, things happen the same way. Paradoxically, those same outlines of America's development—racial discrimination, the break with the past, Puritanism, and, to be sure, the belief in the essential goodness of man and humanity, and finally the extreme glorification of labor as a means and as an end—are the main things responsible for her neuroses. And all this without contradiction, just as there is no contradiction in the fact that in Nature there are simultaneously both struggle and cooperation.

Touching on racial discrimination, for example, it is hardly necessary to bring up here, in their sharpest forms, the horrors committed by the Nazis against the Jews before and during the last war, or the lynchings of Negroes committed in the South of the United States, or the heartrending conflicts that take place in the bosom of Jewish families when one of the members takes a notion to marry outside his people, to know what the individual is capable of when saturated with preconceived ideas of ethnic superiority. It will suffice to recall the consequences of the intercourse between the white man of the southern United States with Indian, Negro, or half-breed women. As these relationships could never be openly displayed, what a state of anguish, unpropitious to their emotional equilibrium, must have governed those encounters! Hence the dissimulation, the consciousness of guilt, the sadism in relation to the social group of the community, the fanaticism, the cruelty, the lack of courage and virtue to redeem through marriage the crime of abandoning their half-breed children, the rationalizations of every kind about the

Negro's inferiority as a defense mechanism, the anti-Negroism, the separation of the races in tight compartments and with it the retarding of the solution of the North American racial problem.[9]

Having mentioned these examples to illustrate the various kinds of emotional disturbance that racial prejudice usually produces, we can pass on to the master outline relating to the break with the past.

Here, too, it will be easy to see that this break, excellent as it was for American civilization in an almost infinite number of ways, has not always come about to the benefit of the moral and emotional balance of the American man.

Among the millions who emigrated in order to better their living conditions, breaking forever with the past, how many must have overestimated their own strength of mind only to succumb to the inner heartbreak of the separation? When it is said that only the strong emigrate—a theory, for that matter, very debatable indeed—it is because we recognize the violence that the individual does to himslf in uprooting himself from his land, his people, his original culture, and all the values that are dear to him, to begin a new life in a world in which he will have to mold a new adaptation. And here again no great gifts of imagination are needed to conceive of the moral traumas that these displacements of strong men or of mere escapists must have generated in the course of American history.[10]

Therefore we have still another main outline of American culture with sufficient potential to unleash neurotic or pre-neurotic states.

Let us pass on now to Puritanism.

Are we not in the presence of another source for generating and conditioning neuroses? Has not Puritanism, like Protestantism in general, deprived its adepts of the only really efficacious means of cure or relief by abolishing those two great instruments of emotional control—confession and complaint—on the pretext of improving and elevating the norm of social community life?

It is possible that the Catholic, with his complaints, outbursts, and imprecations, does not contribute, when maladjusted, to the good appearance of the emotional state of the society in which he lives, but psychologically, by confessing or complaining, he is reducing by catharsis his aggressiveness and the pressure of inner torments. In any case, in difficult moments, in the face of crises like the one undergone by the United States in 1929, he will have much less recourse to suicide or to acts of desperation than the Protestant, and his need of treatment in hospitals and asylums will be far less than the latter's.

Consequently, if in regard to the United States it is not possible to fail to think in terms of Puritanism when it is a matter of the emergence of practical capitalism, it is also not possible when it is a question of the emotional maladjustments of its people.

And the belief in the natural goodness of man—can it, too, be a generator or a conditioner of neuroses? It is. With all its apparent innocuousness, even this romantic belief, which on no soil, not even the soil of its origin in France, has triumphed as it has in America, has not been able, with all the benefits it has brought to American civilization, to avoid causing or conditioning a great number of maladjustments in it. Furthermore, can there be anything more perilous to the emotional balance of the individual than to burst forth into life believing in the goodness of human nature, only to end by facing situations in which this natural goodness is converted into myth, mockery, and lie in the conflicts of the ideal with reality?

Plainly, such a belief, when carried to extremes—and in the United States that is what rather frequently happens—offers as much possibility of developing neurotic immaturity as does the blackest pessimism.

We come now, finally, to the last of the great master outlines of American culture, the cult of work. The same thing is true of this one as of the other ingredients of American culture: it has both obverse and reverse. By itself, conditioned to the rule of each one's doing what he can without requiring of himself and of others more than what is possible, in America, as in all parts of the earth, it brings only benefits. Conditioned, however, as it is in the United States in all cases, to the rules of accomplishment, and accomplishment to the rules of time prescription, its effects can be disastrous. To that end it suffices to transfer the rules of accomplishment from the world of the assembly line to the world of creation or intellectual, philosophical, or even scientific research. Then the consequences are anxiety, troubles, futile bustling about, the panic of the deadline, insecurity, cold sweats, if not ulcers, cancers, and the neurotic states that devastate the heart of American civilization.

To conclude: Just as in Brazil the blind love of the past, racial tolerance, irreligiosity, scorn of the economic virtues to the point of hating useful labor, and unconcern with the moral aspects of life to the point of the very deterioration of religiosity, constitute almost invariably the historical ingredients of Brazilian maladjustment, in the United States it is in the break with the past, in the belief in the natural goodness of man, in Puritanism, and in the exaggerated cult of work that the really obligatory and inevitable components of American neuroses are to be found.

6

Still, there is a difference, a great difference, to point out between what is taking place of late in Brazil and in the United States as far as maladjustments are concerned. The number of American cases increased tremendously after World War I, and have not yet given any sign of cessation or decline, while the Brazilian cases—and the same can perhaps be said of the Latin American—have been gradually yielding, generation by generation, and everything indicates that they may be, if not completely liquidated, considerably reduced within this very century.

And it is perfectly comprehensible that this may be so. Beginning with the first World War, the two great motive forces of American civilization—capitalism and Protestantism, which, in harmony and perfect consonance with the other master outlines of his internal development, formerly assured the American man a relative ethical and emotional balance—have been far from providing the strong inspiration that governs stable social attitudes and individual reactions. To be sure, both still assure him the shelter of a relatively solid social edifice capable of protecting him against immediate external menaces. But they no longer shield him against the assaults of doubt about the validity and force of values that are still dear to him. The truth is that capitalism and Protestantism are in crisis. Shaken in their framework, more and more empty of substance, both Protestanism and capitalism, institutions that seemed destined to perpetuity and whose possibilities seemed inexhaustible, are surviving more by the force of inertia than by the imperial power of expansion that characterized them in the three preceding centuries.

Strictly speaking, no longer does anyone conform to the reigning capitalistic order, nor does anyone believe in the sacrosanctity of its laws. And if there is a firm tendency in our time, it is decidedly not to keep economics and ethics separated in watertight compartments, but increasingly to subject wealth, property, profit, production, interest—in short, all the divinities of capitalism—to the dictates of social justice. From the Russian Revolution to the New Deal, not one of the great social transformations of our day—communism, fascism, national socialism, anarcho-socialism, justicialism, or new statism—whatever its content of truth and error, has failed to demonstrate this tendency toward the prevalence of ethics over economics. Consciously or unconsciously, the great common denominator of our time is this and no other: the desire to return to a social order in which ethics once more controls economics, for no one any longer trusts that the result of the free play of economic forces and of the full expansion of capitalism under the exclusive aegis of the law of supply and demand will turn out to be the general good, as the physiocrats of the last two centuries used to proclaim. On this score the signs of the times are unmistakable.[11]

Another sign of the times is the decline of the Protestant movement and the more and more accentuated tendency toward a solution Catholic in nature. "Protestantism as a church for the masses," says Paul Tillich, "can continue to exist only if it succeeds in undergoing a fundamental change."[12] To continue to exist, however, it will have to "reformulate its appeal so that it will provide a message that a disintegrated world seeking integration will accept. It has to remold its forms of life, its constitution, its rites, and its individual and social ethics. But the precondition for any readjustment is that the Protestant leaders become aware of the seriousness of their situation."[13]

Definitely, the crisis of Protestantism and the crisis of capitalism are the two great crises of our time.

Should we add a third to these two, the crisis of Catholicism? There are not lacking, of course, those who do so. But in general they are Protestant thinkers whose capacity for projecting their own afflictions upon the world hardly disguises the old habit of taking the part for the whole. These not only declare that Catholicism is in crisis, but they also affirm that we are facing a real and irremediable decadence of the entire West.

But are we justified in speaking of the decadence of the West simply because capitalism and Protestantism are threatened? Is it honest to speak of the crisis of the Church and proclaim the end of Catholicism with the same nonchalance and lightness with which the systematists of the past century did, at the very moment when Catholicism is undergoing a vigorous resurgence in England and the United States, and precisely when the social order preached in the Middle Ages by the Scholastics and in modern times by Leo XIII and his successors is only just emerging from the three-century crisis that the Reformation caused in it?

This is clearly not the position of Paul Tillich. Although he may not have utterly despaired of the possibilities of Protestantism, he recognizes that the present times are rapidly ripening for Catholicism. "Protestantism," he says, "is still in a position where it can appeal to the needs of the present-day world, but perhaps the world will soon cease waiting and go over to some type of catholicism . . . [that has] more power of mass integration than Protestantism has."[14]

Another who does not allow himself to be deceived by appearances, nor confuse the part with the whole, is F. S. C. Northrop, Professor of

Philosophy at Yale.[15] Northrop feels that what is taking place is something different from what the prophets of despair are preaching. In his opinion the modern crisis is much more the crisis of capitalism, of liberalism, of nationalism, and of Protestantism than properly the crisis of Catholicism. So profound is his conviction in the matter that he does not hesitate to warn that the new synthesis capable of conciliating the various conflicts going on in the West and in the world—among which that of the traditional democracies against communism, and that of the medieval Catholic concept of moral and social values based upon natural and divine laws against the modern Protestant concept, at once democratic and pragmatic, the concept that the authority of ecclesiastic and civil laws proceeds only from humanistic conventions dictated by the majority—will arise, if it arises in the West, not in the countries situated in the Protestant orbit but in some one of the countries of Latin origin and tradition, most probably in Mexico, Brazil, or French Canada.

Nevertheless, one should not ignore the possibility that the new message may arise in the midst of the North American Catholic minorities—where the drama of Catholicism is being more sharply felt —the normal thing, even, if logic prevailed outside of nature, is that it should appear precisely where there are the most conditions of internal harmony capable of being projected over the external blunders.

Now as the Catholic countries are beginning to offer more probabilities and possibilities to that end than the Protestant ones, the decline of emotional maladjustments in the Catholic countries and the increase of the same maladjustments in the Protestant lands is easy to foresee.

However that may be, one thing can be proved immediately. While the American people are fleeing from normality, the Brazilian people are heading slowly in the direction of it. And if it is true that American immaturity has worsened after the last two wars, or rather, since the Civil War, it is no less true that Brazilian immaturity has, in a general way, been declining. This is due to the fact that the times are ripening not only in favor of the ecumenical solutions of Catholicism, but also in favor of the other main outlines of Brazilian culture, a thing that is no longer occurring either with Protestantism or with the other main outlines of American culture, the stability of which, after attaining its apogee in the early days of this century, has been suffering the hardest knocks. While nearly all the master outlines of American culture—the break with the past, isolationism, Protestantism, capitalism, racial discrimination, nationalism—are being impugned and derogated, the lines of Brazilian culture formerly most combated, such as racial tolerance, are being more and more sanctioned by universal consent.

Let us consider once more, as an example, the case of racial mixture,

which until recently provided the scandalous note to Brazilian civilization. If it is true that miscegenation is still the principal factor responsible for the emotional maladjustments of the Brazilian populace—
not, obviously, to the point of psychological hybridism—it is no less true
that those maladjustments are more and more changing into maturity
and social integration. To start with, physiological hybridism almost in-
evitably used to degenerate into psychological hybridism. Later, however,
was to come the half-breed's individual and collective struggle for self-
assertion and dignity, a struggle that came to graft upon the tired organism of a transplanted culture the great and powerful traits of Brazilian
originality. And as soon as the campaign for the rehabilitation of the
Negro matures in Brazil, as the campaign for the rehabilitation of the
caboclo has matured, as soon as the time is come when Brazilian mulattoes, instead of falsely claiming to be *caboclos*, lying and aggravating
with the lie their inner anguish and anxieties, can speak serenely, without
shame and without subterfuges, of their Negro ancestors, as the *caboclos*
speak of their Indian ancestors, there will no longer be a racial problem
in Brazil.

In this conflict the weak and the mediocre are annihilated, but those
who survive, like Aleijadinho in sculpture, Padre João Maurício in music,
Machado de Assis in the novel, Cruz e Sousa in poetry, Rebouças and
Patrocínio and a host of others who, under the Empire and under the
Republic, have left the mark of their passing on several fields of activity
—law, medicine, engineering, plastic arts, craftsmanship—fusing into a
single strong and original culture the two or three cultures that used to
keep them spiritually divided within themselves, stand as an indication
not only that the rehabilitation of the mulatto is possible, but also that
the end of his *via crucis* is not far distant.

7

Moreover, that is what is also happening with the immaturity resulting
from the addiction to the past, in the social phenomenon of *mazombismo*, the decline of which, ever since the Minas Gerais revolutionary
plot, has been accentuated daily, becoming positively vertiginous at the
commencement of the Modernist movement.

In a general way, since the *Conjuração Mineira* and even before that, social conflicts have not been lacking over the Brazilian's identification with and integration into the environment in which he lives. None of those movements, however, has probably contributed as intentionally and directly to the extinction of the *mazombo* and the raising of the status of the Brazilian as the cultural revolution that has been under way in Brazil from the time of the first Great War—more precisely, beginning with the Modernist movement.

More than thirty years having passed since the inception of this so-called Modernist movement, we now have sufficient perspective to know that, with it, for the first time a genuinely autochthonous revolution of ideas came about in Brazil. It was not something brought over from Europe ten, twenty, or even thirty years behind the times, as has been the case with the other cultural, social, and political agitations that have occurred in Brazil—Romanticism, Indianism, *Condoreirismo*, Naturalism, Parnassianism, Realism—which were never more than simple reflections of European cultural movements.

With the *Semana de Arte Moderna*—the Modern Art Week—of São Paulo, the point of reference of the Modernist movement, and the politico-social revolutions stemming from it or concomitant with it, above all with the Revolution of 1930, something quite different happened. There was, indeed, a first capturing of a consciousness of the national reality, a collective desire to seek out the unknown quantities of Brazilian destiny. The participants then entered upon a typically Socratic phase of self-searching, a phase in which, groping, twisting and turning, denying and experimenting, being seldom right and often wrong, now veering to the right, now to the left, now advancing toward a constructive and responsible type of state organization, now retrogressing toward one of a dictatorial nature unconsciously modeled on the *bandeira*, they still find themselves today, and will probably remain until the perfect resultant of their parallelogram of forces appears.

Nevertheless, it cannot be said that before the Modernist movement there had been no seeking for Brazil. There was, no doubt of it. José Bonifácio, Tavares Bastos, Rui Barbosa, Euclides da Cunha, Oliveira Lima, the Baron do Rio Branco, Capistrano de Abreu, Alberto Tôrres, Graça Aranha, Monteiro Lobato, to mention only the most famous, did just that. It happens, however, that this seeking led to results very different from those of the Modernist movement. Why? Because there was no acceptance of Brazilian reality, nor sufficient detachment to accept it just as it was in fact. Some rationalized, concealing the painful aspects of the country, to present the reality they desired, that is, a Brazil for the consumption of chauvinists. Others, face to face with Brazil, grew despairing, regarding all as lost. Of acceptance of Brazilian reality, just as it really was, there was very little.

Rui, the great Rui, for example, spent his whole life, under the Empire as under the Republic, quarreling with Brazil, because Brazil under the Empire, having English institutions, was not like England; and under the Republic, having a constitution inspired by the American constitution, was not like the United States.

Rio Brancao the great Baron do Rio Branco, after living twenty years without visiting Brazil, would not permit Negroes or mulattoes in Itamaratí[16] because it was essential that foreigners should not deem Brazil a land of half-breeds.

At bottom they all thought like the lawyer Paulo Maciel, in Graça Aranha's novel *Canaan*. His greatest wish is to leave Brazil and exile himself and his family in some corner of Europe.

"My desire is to drop all this, become an expatriate, abandon the country and go with my family to live quietly in some nook of Europe. . . . Europe. . . . Europe!"[17]

To sum up, in their encounters with reality these Brazilians all ended by either rationalizing in defense of Brazil or despising her for being the Brazil she was.

Now, with the Modernist movement, something changed. Brazilian intellectuals passed from chauvinistic self-exaltation and from critical self-flagellation to the Socratic period of self-analysis. Now they accept themselves just as they are—which is something, for, as Jung emphasizes, we cannot change what we do not accept. "Condemnation does not liberate, it oppresses. I am the oppressor of him whom I condemn, not his friend or his companion in suffering. I do not mean by this, at all, that we ought never to judge those whom we wish to aid and improve. But if the doctor wishes to help the human being, he must be capable of accepting him as he is. And in reality he could only do so when he sees himself and accepts himself under the same conditions."[18]

Transposing the concept to the plane of culture, how assist Brazil to extricate herself from the dramas in which she is struggling, if we do not accept her as she is? And how cure her of her psychological hybridism and her transcendental mulattoism, if her racial hybridism is reprobated *in limine?*

A century ago the learned Carlos Fredericko von Hart, as though foreseeing the situation and the problem arising from it, counseled the future historian of Brazil not to pass over this point in silence but to confront it decisively. "Never, therefore, must the historian of the Land of the Holy Cross lose sight of the fact that his task embraces the most grandiose elements; for it is his charge to describe the development not only of a single people, circumscribed within narrow limits, but of a nation whose present crisis and color fusion belong to world history, for it is still in the midst of its higher development. He may not recognize some unfavorable event in so singular a conjunction of different elements, but he can recognize the conjuncture that is most felicitous and important as far as the purest philanthropy is concerned. In its principal points the history of Brazil will always be the history of one branch of the Portuguese; but if it aspires to completeness and to merit the adjective pragmatic, it will never exclude the Negro and Indian races."[19]

That is exactly the orientation that has been followed not only by historians but also by the artists, thinkers, and sociologists who have had most influence on Brazilian culture since the Modernist movement.

If it is true, as Hegel said, that America, both North and South, would only have a history, and therefore an existence of its own, when it became capable of denying "dialectically" its past, of assimilating it fully and feeling it not as something alien but as something intrinsic and natural to themselves, for until America achieved such an assimilation it would continue to be a "continent without history," a reflection, a dependent of European history—if that is true, then, there is no reason for us to be concerned about the historicity of Brazil. If there is in the Americas today a culture that is accelerating its integral assimilation of the past, that culture is the Brazilian. On this score no other on the continent surpasses it. Neither the North American, nor the Mexican, nor the Argentine, nor the Peruvian, the Colombian, the Chilean, the Uruguayan, or the Cuban.

As for the North Americans, we already know how much the rejection of Europe has been hindering them in fully assimilating their Western past. If this, on one hand, makes them strong and gives them that air of ease that European and Latin Americans succeed only with difficulty in imitating, by freeing them from the profound conflicts between the ancient and the modern values that torment Latin Americans, it weakens them, on the other hand, as Northrop remarks, since it incapacitates them for the just evaluation of the conflicts between the different political, social, aesthetic, moral, and religious ideals that constitute the essence of Western culture.[20]

The Mexicans, now, at the same time that they attempt to assimilate their pre-Cortés past—which is entirely laudable—demagogically persist in denying their Spanish past—which is utterly deplorable.

As for the Peruvians and Colombians, precisely the contrary is the case. Having completely assimilated the Hispanic past, they are still resisting, through their elites, accepting and giving free course to their pre-Columbian heritages.

That is what, in a certain sense, is taking place in Argentina as well—aggravated by the fact that while the Peruvian and Colombian elites already accept themselves as Americans, the Argentines are reluctant to admit any form of Americanism, for they want Argentina to be simply a bit of Europe set down in the New World.

Happily, none of this occurs in Brazil. The Brazilian, at the same time that he has incorporated his Portuguese past, has been assimilating his indigenous and African past—and even the elements hostile to his tradition—precisely in the fashion that Hegel indicates: fully, feeling his several pasts not as something alien but as something native to him, natural and inseparable from his destiny. While in the city of Mexico there is not a single monument to Cortés, in the bay of Rio de Janeiro there is even an island that bears the name of the French Calvinist Villegaignon. This, not to mention the liking inspired in all Brazil by the name of another great Calvinist conqueror, Prince Maurice of Nassau.

The historians of the Conquest list as the great advantage of the Spaniards over the Portuguese the finding of indigenous cultures in an advanced stage of civilization in Mexico and Peru, as in all Central America, a circumstance that permitted them from the start to recruit excellent labor among nonmigratory, industrious Amerindians, for agricultural work as well as for the construction of the superb churches and cathedrals with which Spain transported to the New World the dying fires of the Middle Ages. From the point of view of technique, there is no doubt that it was a decided advantage. But from the point of view of national integration, the advantage fell to the lot of the Portuguese, for in the long run the Spaniards' advantage was to turn into a disadvantage—that of the psychological resistance of Aztecs, Zapotecs, Incas, and Mayas to giving up their original culture and being incorporated into the national culture of Mexico and Peru, as the indigenes of Brazil were into the Brazilian. While even in the first generation we find the Indian half-breeds of the *bandeiras* cooperating with the *bandeirante* in the work of conquering and extending the Empire, wholly given over to the ideal of their own Westernization, ferocious enemies of their ancestors on the maternal side—a line that did not count among the Amerindians of Brazil—Aztecs, Zapotecs, Mayas, Incas, and their descendants, nostalgic for their pyramids and works of art that the implacable conquistador destroyed, have prolonged their resistance to Western culture down to our day.

It is a singular fact in the process of dialectical assimilation of the Brazilian past that until, by mentally fleeing from Brazil, they accepted themselves as they were, Brazilians had not the slightest international importance. And yet as soon as they began to accept Brazilian reality, the terrible and mysterious Brazilian reality, they commenced projecting themselves outward with a vigor never before attained. On the basis of Brazilian motifs we have, in music, the worldwide projection of Villa-Lobos; in painting, that of Cândido Portinari; in architecture, that of Niemeyer; in sociology, that of Gilberto Freyre; in the novel, that of Erico Veríssimo, José Lins do Rêgo, and Jorge Amado.

How Brazil has changed, with this new attitude!

Formerly Brazilians turned their eyes toward Europe and their backs toward Brazil. Today, without repulsing Europe and without denying their European cultural past, and likewise their Indian and Negro past, they are spiritually and geographically turning toward their own inwardness.

Formerly they simply did not know what the national reality was. Today they see the Brazilian reality taking shape; not a reality made only of noble metals that, fused together, did not become bronze, but reality made bronze as Nietzsche desired it, and that must be like the alloy achieved by Benvenuto Cellini when he added to the precious metals that did not acquire the proper consistency the detritus and impurities he had been reluctant to use.

Formerly the Brazilian reality of the sugar mills of the North was the Maçangama of Joaquim Nabuco's *Minha Formação*; today the Brazilian reality of the sugar plantations is also that of the *Menino de Engenho* of José Lins do Rêgo; formerly, the Brazilian reality of Ceará was "the wild green seas of my native land" of José de Alencar; today it is the drought and *O Quinze* of Raquel de Queirós; formerly the sun was the "royal astral body," the "king-star," and the moon was "the Ophelian watch-tower of lost wayfarers"; now the sun is the sun and the moon is the moon. Formerly it was the facile turn of poetry, and if on one hand there was some rare poet integrated into Brazilian reality and capable of accepting and loving it to the full and submitting, in the Goethian manner, the fantasies of subjectivism to the discipline of objectivity, on the other hand the *mazombos*, the immature, the maladjusted, the plaintive, the whining and despairing were still legion despite the fact that fifty years had passed over the ruins of Brazil's romanticism. And the virile poetry, the great poetry of acceptance of reality and of life, in which the good and the bad are present, the beautiful and the ugly, the high and the low, all combining, through the effect of contrasts, to the harmony of the whole—the poetry of a Camoens or of a Walt Whitman or of a Manuel Bandeira—was scarcely to be found in the nation. On the contrary, in the anemic and tearful poetry of those who delighted in pitying themselves, in the poetry of those who made an effort to be unhappy, in the poetry of those who sighed for "the aurora of my life which the years will bring back no more," it was as though all the subterranean currents of the national soul were melted. For that matter, were there no accord and correspondence between the popular soul and the morbidity of such yearnings, certainly that poetry and those poets would not have attained the popularity they enjoyed.

That does not mean that Brazil has not had great poetic talents. She has, but immaturity was so prevalent in her poets that nearly all, perhaps for lack of will to live, died before they were twenty-five. Castro Alves died at twenty-four; Junqueira Freire, at twenty-three; Casimiro de Abreu, at twenty-three also; Álvares de Azevedo, at twenty; the one who went furthest, Fagundes Varela, reached thirty-four. Gonçalves Dias attained the exceptional age of forty-one, and Bernardo Guimarães, who nearly reached his sixties, was a regular Methuselah. And all or nearly all were, not excluding the Indianists, "Europeanizing, almost classic Lusitanian" poets.[21]

Poetry of maturity, of adjustment or of the eve of adjustment, save for one or two exceptions in the past, only begins to crop up after the Modernist movement. Indeed, from this movement dates the appearance of something fresher, healthier, and more integrated into reality and closer to maturity. It is in the Modernist phase that poetry ceases to be simple cosmic terror or amplification of lamentations, yearnings, and displeasures, to become something more: interpretation of the Universe, triumph over grief, conscious struggle against the assaults of despair and maladjustment. It is from that time and only from that time as a point of departure, with Manuel Bandeira, Carlos Drummond de Andrade, Mário de Andrade, and Cassiano Ricardo, to cite only a few among many, that a new element, nonexistent in Brazilian poetry of earlier periods, emerges —humor, perhaps the great dividing line in the definitive emancipation of Brazilian from Portuguese and European poetry.

Humor, it is true, is still not in its full maturity; it is only on the eve of maturity. That does not matter. As a sign of the times, it is valid as a pre-announcement that in poetry, too, and in poetry as in everything else, full maturity is plainly upon us.

8

And in the case of maladjustment originating in dislike of work, what are the signs of the times? Even here, they are unequivocally in Brazil's favor. In this sector also, in spite of everything, Brazil is beginning to take seven-league strides, and that is due, naturally—in great part, in its best part—to the pioneer type of colonizers that have been flowing into Brazil since the first part of the nineteenth century. In fact, since the coming to Rio Grande do Sul of the first German immigrants in 1824— which may fairly be said to mark the first great moment of the new migratory policy—there has never ceased to spread, from south to north in Brazil, a new concept of work, in contradistinction to the *bandeirante* and patriarchal concept that "idleness is better than busyness."

Nor would it be possible to make the progress that has been going on of late in São Paulo, Rio Grande do Sul, Paraná, Santa Catarina, Goiás, the Federal District, and a large part of Brazil, without a great deal of effort and a new conception of the exact position of work in the scale of fundamental values.

Another consequence of the coming of the German colonists to Rio Grande do Sul, discounting the episode of the Muckers' fanaticism[22]—a chapter of American Mormonism transplanted to South America—is the strengthening of the religious spirit and its being cleansed of the superstitions and ridiculous beliefs of *bandeirante* and patriarchal Brazil. Indeed, in proportion as the spiritualized Gothic of the new churches of the colonial region emerges, along with the baroque churches and chapels, and the Jesuits and other religious orders recover their importance as educators, never has the Brazilian's religious spirit ceased to cleanse itself, currently finding high and vigorous expression in the Catholic fervor of Alceu Amoroso Lima and Gustavo Corção.

One last consequence of the coming of the German, Italian, and Portuguese colonists in couples, in families, in communities, is the change in Brazilian mentality as far as the development of the associative spirit and of the economic virtues is concerned. Really, in the old struggle between the deep-rooted men and the adventurers, the number of those who make a fortune in Brazil through continuity of well-directed effort has been increasing. And with them the number of recreational and civic societies is increasing also.

Still, even here it behooves us not to lay much stress on the improvement, because in the play of reciprocal influences, not only have the worshipers of practical and economic virtues infected the worshipers of the stroke of luck and of the *bandeirante* virtues, but the contrary has also occurred, and very frequently. And this, unfortunately, has been the rule with the colonists who leave their families and their fields to catch in the city the contagion of the *bandeirante* barracks virtues. After a time they no longer want to return to the country and they stay in the bordellos and saloons of the city to prove their inwardly questioned virility by the quantity of women they may eventually possess, and to dream of sinecures and strokes of luck, like the other specimens of the great Brazilian frustration who, through the *bicho* game,[23] rum, and syphilis, complete their integration into the traditional forms of Brazilian culture.

Or can the mania for sex and quick riches be already extirpated from Brazilian culture, or at least confined to the elite?

Would that that were true! The truth is that the cult of rapid wealth, the El Dorado dream, the pleasure of the big party or the "little party at home," at the slightest acquisition of money and precisely where the minimum and the essential is lacking, persists in all sectors of the national life.

In his Munich letter von Hart called the attention of the future historian of Brazil to the fact that had most stirred him. "I speak of the numerous stories and legends about the underground wealth of the country that are the sole element of romanticism in the land, and they take the place, for many Brazilians, of the innumerable fabulous stories of knights and ghosts that furnish European peoples with an inexhaustible and ever new source of popular poetry. It seemed to me that the superstition of the people was, so to speak, concentrated in those tales."[24]

But what von Hart, in 1845 never saw is that this desire for quick wealth, completely separated from the economic virtues recommended by Calvin and by the Jesuits—thrift, work, utilization of time—would have a more curious and still graver counterpart, the almost absolute disbelief that wealth can be acquired or attained by anything other than luck or a stroke of fortune.

Indeed, hardly had the German colonists of Rio Grande do Sul commenced to prosper and grow rich through useful work and practice of the economic virtues that the region of the Jacuí valley, crisscrossed with rivers, made possible and profitable—and the same must have occurred in the Italian colony years later—when legends and myths began to circulate about the origin of those small fortunes. Of this man, for instance, it was said that he had found the treasure of the Jesuits; of that one, that he had found a basin of gold in his back yard; of the other, that he had got rich by passing counterfeit money.

That anyone could grow rich by steady work, and not through mineral deposits or luck, was something the direct descendant of the old *bandeirantes* could not comprehend.

And to think that this kind of myth and legend is common to the whole country! Is someone rich and yet has found no gold mine, nor come into money by inheritance, nor won a prize in the lottery or the *bicho* game? Then he stole it or else he is mixed up in some shady deals. When it is not such legends that beguile the popular imagination, it is those expressing terror: the legend of the headless mule and that of the *saci*, the little one-legged Negro who chases travelers on the roads, both common to all Brazil; that of the *boiúna*, the great snake, and that of the enchanted dolphin, in Amazonia.

Von Hart thought that in Amazonia the effects of terror stood out above those that arose from the desire for quick riches. Here, however, the most likely thing is that von Hart was deceived, for even in Amazonia the preconceived notion that it is impossible to get rich from useful labor (the man who works has no time to make money) was to prevail finally over cosmic terror.

One illustration for this assertion is the fact that when Henry Ford moved to Fordlândia, there was no convincing the mestizo that the American millionaire's purpose was to start great plantations of rubber trees. However great might be the rubber hunger of the Ford Motor Company and of all American industry, then still dependent on the English planters in the Far East, the mestizo was convinced that Ford knew of the existence of gold deposits in Belterra and the rubber plantations were a mere pretext to gain possession of the mines.

And the Brazilian's imaginative capacity for connecting any form of activity with the search for gold, diamonds, and precious stones did not stop there. Six years after Ford's withdrawal, in the countryside and throughout all the national territory there are still many people convinced that his withdrawal was not motivated by the failure of the plantations but by the working out and exhaustion of vast platinum deposits in the region, the value of which must have been enough to repay many times over the millions of dollars invested by Ford in Fordlândia and Belterra.

And now? Well, now at least the conclusion is obvious. At the root of Brazilian immaturity lies, on the one hand, cosmic terror, and on the other, the distortion of all values in view of the desire for quick riches.[25]

Brazil is faced, then, with two problems: one, that of overcoming terror by conquering Nature; the other, that of overcoming maladjustments by reorienting Brazilian life toward more useful and respectable values than those cultivated to date. The former is a problem of education and technique; the latter, a problem of revising Brazil's history with the specific aim of freeing her people from the errors and prejudices inherited from their elders.

The problem of technique, upon which their scanty capacity for attention has been more concentrated recently, is gradually being more or less solved. And there are Volta Redonda, Paulo Alfonso, the São Francisco valley, and the industrial plants of São Paulo, Rio de Janeiro, and Rio Grande do Sul to prove it. But it still remains for Brazilians to solve the problem of ethical and spiritual reorientation, which will only be possible through the revision of their history with the express object of purging, with their own mistakes, the errors of their culture, without sacrifice of facts, just as Goethe wished it, for whom the writing of history was one form of self-liberation from the oppression of the past. No, it is absolutely not a question of altering the pure facts of Brazil's history as guarantee of a specific ideal and alien to the facts themselves. It is, rather, a question of utilizing the cathartic possibilities of history, for if it is true, as Trevelyan points out, that individuals will never entirely comprehend "their own emotional opinions, prejudices, and reactions" unless they have a knowledge of the history of their own country,[26] it is no less true, as Schlesinger emphasizes, that in times of crisis and confusion "a whole people may find light and orientation in an intelligent examination of the past."[27] A typical example of this kind of orientation was the one that the American people found in the fireside chats of President Roosevelt, in one of the most difficult moments of their history.[28]

Despite the fact that there is no dearth of historians to support the point of view that history does not require special interpretation, but that the facts speak for themselves (Seignobos, Ranke, Fustel de Coulange), the truth is that not only do the facts not speak for themselves but in order to make sense they perforce have to be interpreted. Indeed, purely narrative history does not exist. In the proper ordering and exposition of the facts of history the dialectic of interpretative thinking is implicit. That is why every generation and every epoch makes its own interpretation of history, without this procedure's implying any alteration of the facts. It is, rather, a seeking of new revelations and meanings in the ever-open mystery of the past, in the light of new criteria and points of view. To the ingenuous realism of those who think that knowledge of history is gained by piling up documents upon documents in the belief that they speak for themselves, Croce replies that "one thing grows out of another, but not thought," that the mind is history and uses documents and narrations to modernize "the vital inner evocation" in the process of which those "things" are resolved. In this sense, "true history is contemporary history," as much as "life is a perpetual present tense," and only "interest in present life can move us to investigate a past fact."[29]

This same thought we are going to find in one form or another in Troeltsch and Burckhardt and Dilthey. If to Troeltsch the function of history is understanding the present, according to Burckhardt only the knowledge of the past can free a people from the symbols that chain it to its customs.[30] And if to Dilthey reflection upon life makes us profound, and reflection upon history makes us free, according to Croce we ought to confront the past, reduce it to a mental problem, and solve it in a proposition of truth that is an ideal premise of our life. "It is what we do daily when, instead of being cast down by adverse incidents and being ashamed of errors committed, we examine what has happened, we inquire into its origins, we have recourse to its history, and with a well-informed consciousness, following intimate inspiration, we determine what is fitting and what it is up to us to do, dedicating ourselves to doing it."[31] Under these conditions, in the view of José Honório Rodrigues, "the supreme task of historiography would be analogous to that of tragedy, which, according to Aristotle, effects a purgation (*katharsis*) through the sentiments of pity and fear. After contemplating it, a state of purified spirit is produced in the spectator, because he has comprehended the profound reason of things."[32]

But it is not only the historiographers currently in highest repute who have seen the cathartic possibilities of history. Karen Horney, one of the most respected disciples of Freud, was already persuaded, contrary to the master, that for the psychoanalyst to comprehend the drama of the patient and to help him out of the ills that afflict him, he would have to familiarize himself with the historical process of his patient's upbringing, a process almost invariably coincident with that of the formation of the culture to which he is connected. "When we focus our attention on the actual neurotic difficulties we recognize that neuroses are generated not only by incidental individual experiences but also by the specific cultural conditions under which we live. In fact the cultural conditions not only lend weight and color to the individual experiences but in the last analysis determine their particular form."[33]

There is no reason, then, to hesitate. What we are most in need of is to utilize "the function of catharsis that historiography fills, by shaking off submission to the fact and to the past."

9

In point of fact, that is also the need—and quite urgent need—of Americans, among whom the immaturity stemming from the master outlines of their culture, beginning with the results of the break with the past, becomes aggravated instead of diminishing.

Indeed, beginning with the first World War—even with the War for Independence and the Civil War—with the arrival in the United States of the great human avalanches that came to double, triple, and further multiply her population in the last eighty years (thirty million immigrants entered the United States between 1848 and 1940), the phenomena of the maladjustment, immaturity, and social instability of American civilization—divorce, gangsterism, juvenile delinquency—begin to stand out.

Why is this? It is no more than a consequence of the immigrant's violent break with the past. That break, which in the epoch of the early settlers took time to accomplish itself and was not, in any case, brought about with the sacrifice of the immigrant's original culture, became traumatic as soon as the United States started increasing in international importance.

It could not be otherwise. In the early days of settlement the immigrants carried their original culture with them; they came really to colonize. Their customs did not change except insofar as the change was imposed by local factors. For the rest, they continued to speak the same language, to pray from the same Bible, to enjoy the same rights and laws as in their country of origin.

With the advent of Independence and the Civil War, principally with the Civil War, all that was changed.

The immigrant no longer came essentially to settle down or to struggle with the unknown; he came, principally, to benefit from the privilege of becoming American. It was not as a prospective pioneer that he came; he was, he might be, a *bandeirante*, ready to endure anything to get rich and to find his "mine."

Already by that time the United States, with its economic power, its railways, looms, factories, and inventions, its powerful merchant marine, its plenty, its coal mines, its universities, its Constitution serving as a model and inspiration for a great number of Western constitutions, its messages of hope for the world, had become too important for the immediate benefit of American nationality to be relegated to a secondary plane. That anyone might come to the New World with the purpose of preserving his own culture and nationality was something that neither the immigrant from Europe nor the American who received him could understand. Furthermore, even today nothing shocks the American more, both the native and the naturalized, than the resistance of those who, being able to become naturalized, do not do so. Preoccupation with the earliest naturalization possible has become obsessive, increasing as the prestige of the new fatherland increases.

It is up to the immigrant, then, to submit both self and family to the most drastic processes of rejection of the old culture and incorporation into the new.

Now, this rejection of home and country could not be tranquil; it had to be traumatic, even when the immigrant was fleeing the discriminatory laws, the humiliations, military service, hunger, or the authoritarian limitations of Europe. However prepared he was to renounce all the past and everything connected with the past, the break could not be made serenely. And as Geoffrey Gorer stresses in *The American People*, one of the most important books for the understanding of the phenomenon of the American of most recent extraction, unless the immigrant had come as a child, or was endowed with exceptional psychological plasticity, that self-transformation was impossible to consummate integrally: "Culture is strong and pervasive, and the national character which is the embodiment of a local culture is acquired above all in the earlier years of life; will power alone is not enough to modify those motives and ways of viewing the universe which spring from unrecognized and unconscious sources; the majority of mankind cannot remold themselves by taking thought. Consequently the greater number of immigrants, though they had rejected as much of Europe as they could, were still incomplete Americans; their own persons, their characters, their ways of thought, usually their accent, carried the stigmata of the Europe they had rejected."[34]

All of them, some more, some less, would relive in one form or another the drama of Joseph Conrad. Polish by birth and culture, Conrad became, at the age of about thirty, a British subject, ending by mastering English so completely that he became one of the most renowned writers in the English language. Had he entirely forgotten Poland? No. The fact of having abandoned his land was his lifelong guilt complex, his private drama. He traveled, he wrote novels of every kind in various latitudes of the earth: *Typhoon, An Outcast of the Islands, Lord Jim,* in an incessant flight from himself and his doppelgänger. And yet his drama, his sense of tragedy, his guilt, the ever-present guilt in the pathetic lives of his heroes, is one thing only: the guilt of the renegade, of the outcast.

In the United States not all would be turned into Conrads, but all, some more and others less, would end by rationalizing their flight and their guilt. How? In two ways: one, by giving Europe up for lost, as being plunged into an irreparable decadence; the other, by magnifying America, now the best of all possible and imaginable worlds.

It may be objected that these consequences are going to end with the first-generation immigrants. Quite wrong. Because then a problem of the utmost gravity arises, as it is indeed now arising and becoming aggravated, the problem of the second generation, that springs from the insistence of the still culturally foreign parents that their children enjoy the rights of the new nationality in their fullness and as soon as possible. Since the parents cannot transform themselves, their children must be transformed. They, the self-subordinating immigrants, earn their living somehow, and their children, without the direct and permanent paternal care that was the forte of patriarchal America in pioneer days, are turned over to the moral and civic guidance of the public school, experiencing their most important period of development not under the masculine guidance of the father and the male teachers who guided the development of the George Washingtons and the Lincolns before the women public school teachers of New England spread throughout the country in the service of its accelerated Yankeefication, but under two exclusively feminine influences: that of the teacher and that of the mother, since the latter, "whatever her cultural ways, retains emotional importance as the source of love, food, and care that she is.

"And when this transmutation had taken place," concludes Gorer, "the parents themselves would be rejected as old-fashioned, ignorant, and in significant ways alien. The more successful the immigrant father was in turning his children into Americans, so that they had no other allegiances or values, the more his foreignness became a source of shame and opprobrium, the less important did he become as a model and guide and exemplar. Whatever her language and ways, the mother retained emotional importance as a source of love and food and succor; but to grow up to be like the father, to do no better than he had done, to be the same sort of person he was, would be failure indeed and would be so regarded by the father as much as by the son."[35]

And at this stage of things who is going to substitute for the idealized image of the father whom every son is instinctively led to imitate? The normal thing would be for the choice to fall upon the heroes and symbols of American history, for they exist in abundance and for all purposes, but one must not exclude the possibility that the son, thrust toward maternal fixations, may end by narcissistically carving out his symbol in his own image and admiring himself in everything that differs from his father. Is his father European and he American? Then Europe must be all vice, evil, decadence, and America all virtue, honesty, decency, justice. Is the European all skepticism and pessimism? He will be belief and optimism. Is there a European way of life? In opposition there must be an American way of life, which naturally has to be the best, in accord, for that matter, with what has been established by his (female) teacher ever since his first theme, the title of which, "Why the American Way of Life Is the Best," has never left any room for alternatives.

As if the excellences of American civilization were not obvious, he will feel an urgent need to proclaim them at every step, apropos of everything and of nothing at all. "This is a free country" and "I am an American citizen," or perhaps better, "I am a taxpayer," are expressions that he will use at every moment. And the more recent, the more immature, the more maladjusted he is, the more he will repeat them.

Another expression he will never tire of using is, "You can't push me around," which is equivalent to the Brazilian, "The one who commands me is myself."

The fact is that he resents nothing so much as authority. Everything that recalls or suggests national power, respectability, orderly behavior, tradition, gravity, culture, authority, learning, is suspect to him. In his opinion even more than in the pioneer's, authority is something fundamentally unhealthy and should be accepted only as an inevitable evil.

Therefore, for the politicians who would win his support it is imperative to display in their persons an absence of authority, or any desire for authority. "They [the politicians] must be conspicuously plain citizens, with the interests and the mannerisms of their fellows; whatever their private termperament they must act as 'one of the boys,' glad-handed, extravert, mindful of first names, seeing their subordinates in their shirt sleeves and with their feet on the desk, democratically obscene in their language, with private interests, if any, simple and within the reach of all."[36]

And it will do the politician no harm electorally to lend himself just a little to ridicule, for nothing pleases the maladjusted American of the last generation so much as the humorous situation resulting from the device of treating serious things lightly and light things seriously, as Mark Twain did in his A Connecticut Yankee in King Arthur's Court.

"In the face of people or situations which might evoke such feelings [i.e., of respect and awe of personified authority] every effort is made by the use of levity, incongruousness, or elaboration to reduce them to a status where such feelings will no longer be appropriate."[37]

What is back of all this is an immense psychic instability, an enormous guilt complex transferring itself from the guilty to the real victim of the guilt—the father—and from the latter to all that is identified with his image: tradition, Europe, authority, respectability, proper behavior. Thence also the narcissistic necessity to think all that is American invariably right, virtuous, decent, good, and everything foreign and European decadent, vicious, evil. This is so much the case that the contempt for respectability and tradition that results from distortions of sensibility is not entirely sincere; the same man who behaves unsuitably and disrespectfully toward the venerable, loses no opportunity to mention to his acquaintances, with exaggerations, the personal connections he may have with important personages. In this he is more snobbish than anyone.

In truth, his great desire, as it was the desire of the late George F. Babbitt of nostalgic memory, is to inaugurate a new type of heroism. To realize this ideal of life, the American will submit to everything. He reads How to Win Friends and Influence People, by Dale Carnegie, and he learns how to behave at table according to the formulas of Emily Post; he marries noble titles in Europe, or, if more modest or less rich, he joins all the orders and associations that confer striking titles upon themselves: the Knights of Columbus, the International Association of Lions Clubs, the Benevolent and Protective Order of Elks.

10

Of course, the descendants of the *Mayflower* company, and of Poca-
hontas, the aristocrats of Virginia, Philadelphia, Boston, Westchester
County, those along the Hudson, in New York, or even those of Forest
Hills and Garden City on Long Island—Americans of fifty, a hundred,
two hundred, or three hundred years' descent, do not look kindly on this.
They react by turning toward the past. Through a process of regression,
and of tardy *mazombismo*, they become slaves of the European tradition.
In a reaction very similar to that which led the Confederates to Brazil,
they go to live in Europe, they buy castles on the Riviera, they form their
societies closed to the *nouveaux riches* and to café society; and naturally
they wear only clothes tailored in the English style.

But to the *Mayflower* descendants the American of the last generation,
in shirt sleeves, feet on top of his desk, thumbs stuck in his suspenders,
an immense cigar clamped in his jaws, mentally inventorying his possessions—"You can't shove me around"—reacts like Cicero in the Roman
Senate: "You are nobles, your nobility is going to end with you; I am a
plebeian, my nobility is going to begin with me."

And it really is beginning, if it is not already in full swing. As he is the
acquisitive man par excellence, the great example of maternal fixation,
the man who goes shopping to commemorate Mother's Day, everything
is done to please him—politics, advertisements, shirt styles, designs on
ties, the latest automobile models with their little novelties. On his account and for him the Department of State extends its services abroad;
it is so that he may be able to buy everything at once—house, car, radio,
refrigerator, television—that this thing, excellent to be sure, called install-
ment buying has been instituted. And it is for him that the magic word
NOW has been refurbished. Hardly a newspaper is opened, an advertise-
ment displayed in which the word—that word which widens the infant's
eyes and which American civilization has especially refurbished since the
Civil War for the use and enjoyment of the last-generation immigrant's
son—does not stand out, once, or many times. The pioneer was the man
of the present. The son of the immigrant, like a baby, is the man of *now*.

Are you thinking of buying a refrigerator? Do it *now*. Are you thinking
of trading in your television set? Do it *now*. Are you thinking of buying
a house. Not a minute to lose. Babbitt and Babbitt, specialists in selling
things that no one needs, is right there for "the pleasure of serving you."
But do it *now*. Tomorrow will be too late. *Now, now, now.*

The advertising agencies are quite right in saying that advertising is not just an art, but a science. Because truly the greatest scientists, the greatest psychologists, the greatest interpreters of America are not her teachers; they are her inventors of advertisements, celebrating in the newspapers, on the radio, and on television the symphony of the present, the vertiginous moment that is passing.

Meanwhile, in a challenge to Boston and Richmond, chewing gum or with a cigar in his teeth, the most pampered and adulated man of the century, His Royal Highness the Common Man, elicits uproarious guffaws from Babbitt with his new type of humor:

> Remember Grant,
> Remember Lee—
> The hell with them,
> Remember me!

It is to this break of continuity between the more recent immigrants and their children, and between both generations and immigrants of the preceding generations, that psychiatrists and anthropologists—with Geoffrey Gorer at their head, for his precision and clarity[38]—attribute, and apparently quite rightly, the larger share of responsibility for the conditioning of the modern American character, and the enormous tribulation that afflicts it.

Since the rejection of the father—in this case being rejected is on a par with rejecting—has never exactly contributed to bettering the moral and emotional balance of anyone, whether half-breeds or Anglo-Saxons, the consequences, some serious, some benign, nearly all of them startling, will not take long to manifest themselves.

Some benign effects: faces without a history and more and more devoid of psychological density; loud ties; infantilism; sports shirts with colored patterns and designs to make a child's eyes pop; perfectionism; the "our boys" of the last two wars instead of the "our men" of the wars in the English tradition and of the wars of Independence and Secession; "Mother's Day"; the success of comic strips and animated cartoons; the increasingly cultivated feminine symbols; Uncle Sam, as Keyserling has already noted, relegated to a secondary plane, summoned merely to represent on posters, with pointing finger—"I Want You"—the disagreeable chores connected with the purchase of government bonds or military enlistment; the maternal symbols of Liberty and Fortune, the former with her torch burning and the latter with her cornucopia spilling out dollars over the nation, more and more loved. And what of the 1,825,000 men rejected for military service in the last war on account of psychic disorders? And the 600,000 dismissed after the first screening? And the half million who tried to desert?[39]

Now the serious consequences: sexual crimes, the high percentage of criminality among immigrants of the first and second generations. The most famous criminals of America—Al Capone, Dillinger, and the like— are almost all products of father-rejection combined with poor assimilation of American values in the process of hasty nationalization, because in truth those great criminals and most of the ones who jam the prisons of Sing Sing and the like, immature worshipers of the ideal of the superman in terms of success at any price, which is what first insinuates itself wherever there is no father to respect and no time to assimilate and refine the mental categories of America, are nothing more, in principle, than maternally fixated individuals, childish idealizers of American myths. Finally, "last but not least" (to use here one of the most conspicuous turns of phrase of George F. Babbitt in his after-dinner toasts), it is essential not to forget the repercussion that this conflict of generations and these infantile fixations are having, not only as regards the social ascent of the American woman but also as regards her progressive "Amazonization." Even if one does not take literally the violent attacks of Philip Wylie in *Generation of Vipers* with respect to this, we are here in the presence of fractures too exposed not to be mentioned.

If today, in the United States, the most beautiful women in the world are to be found, whether they are judged by Latin standards or Nordic, it is also easy to note that one of the consequences of the "Momism" to which Strecker refers could not fail to be, in the United States, the increasing Amazonization of the formerly frail sex.

11

And have not similar or identical transformations taken place in Brazil? Is the Brazilian woman not becoming Amazonized, too? Happily, not yet. Certainly the Brazilian woman is no longer viewed and desired as that angelic, serene figure that the framers of the Constitution of 1891 wished to preserve from the hurly-burly of the marketplace by taking away her right to vote. To be sure, she is no longer the professional martyr of *bandeirante* and patriarchal Brazil who was not allowed to learn to read so she could not exchange notes with lovers. But from that to concluding that she is becoming Amazonized would be to exaggerate matters.

The Brazilian woman was too accustomed to seeing in man the hunter, the predator, and afterwards the master and lord, to have lost, with her womanliness, her air of a frightened doe, the delicacy that characterizes her. And then there never has been, in Brazil, what could rightly be called a violent break with the past. Nor an insistence on effecting nationalization at top speed. Brazil not having until very recently the importance of the immigrants' countries of origin—Germany, Italy, Portugal, and, most recently, Japan—and the Brazilians continuing, on the other hand, to maintain an attitude of almost colonial reverence toward European culture, and to exercise not the slightest pressure, save in time of war and exacerbated passions, upon the immigrant to become naturalized—when he was not left entirely to himself, or a whole series of limitations on and obstacles to his acculturation and naturalization were not created—it is easily comprehensible that the various consequences of the break with the past that have occurred in the United Stats, including the Amazonization of women have not occurred among Brazilians.

As the Portuguese father—and the same can be said, up to a certain point, of Germans and Italians, if not also of other nationalities immigrating into Brazil—has never bothered to subordinate himself, since instead of modestly wanting to become naturalized or culturally acclimated in new patriotic fervor, the European in Brazil at times assumes an air at once important and impertinent, as of one who is actually coming to colonize and civilize, the cases identical or similar to the American ones cannot be cited as the rule or as a social phenomenon peculiar to Brazil. They are merely the exceptions.

With the *mazombo*, in any case, the guilt complex was probably not fixed upon rejected Europe but on Brazil. It was doubtless the sense of guilt arising from his not giving himself sufficiently to the environment in which he lived. And this guilt he would seek to assuage by rationalizing against the country in the same way that the second generation American rationalizes against Europe. By rationalizing and transferring. The rationalization can be summed up in the phrase "Brazil, a lost country"; the transference, in the moral retaliations that some practice on others under the general rubric of "lack of patriotism." The less the *mazombo* gives to Brazil, the more lost the country is. In the centers where one really works and builds, there is none of that. In the nuclei of parasitism is where Brazil, since King João VI, has been living at the edge of the abyss.

Besides, the *mazombo* does not resent either the weight or the glorification of authority. On the contrary, at the same time that he himself seeks to invest himself with authority—"Do you realize to whom you are speaking?"—he never gives any sign of the esteem and respect he may have for the public man by calling him by his first name or nickname, however intimate he may be with him. On the contrary, when he calls him by his first name he is, as a rule, showing contempt. It is by prefixing honorific titles—doctor, colonel, general, counselor, minister, ambassador —that he demonstrates respect, awe, and liking.

If the immaturities of the last-generation Americans have anything in common with those of the Brazilians, it can hardly be with those of the *mazombos*. It will be, rather, with those of the mulattoes. There, indeed, the neurotic or pre-neurotic drama of the mulatto—his xenophobia, his displaying affection through use of the first name or nickname, his narcissistic need of self-adornment and of over-estimating himself, appreciating all that is Brazilian and depreciating all that is foreign—has much in common with the immaturities of the immigrant's son in the United States.

The simile is imperfect only in regard to the other ingredients of the two cultures, for, while to soften the insolence and arrogance of the mulatto, and to reduce the Amazonization of the women, there is in Brazil only the fear of force and of the sanction of authority, to soften the aggressiveness of the last-generation American and hasten the rise of women in the social scale in the United States there is Jeffersonian liberalism, the belief in the goodness of human nature as regards the formal and structural modifications of society, a belief that fits like a glove the inner need of the maladjusted last-generation men and women not to feel guilty of anything and to attribute their maladjustments and frustrations to the social contracts to which they are bound, transferring the blame for everything either to the environment in which they live or to the firm in which they work (labor contract), or to the social contract that, emotionally immature as they are, they do not know how to maintain.

12

Can these be merely the consequences of Rousseauan liberalism and of the belief that man is naturally good, everything depending on the social contract to which he may be bound? No.

In the same way that, correctly interpreted, liberal doctrine leads to the edifying aspects of American civilization, which are neither few nor small, if interpreted literally and carried to extremes, besides the divorces

that it occasions it may have, and has had, equally alarming consequences: infantilism, ingenuousness, mental debility, that same mental
debility that Theodore Dreiser so well studies in the person of the salvationist pastor in *An American Tragedy*. And next on the canvas is the
figure of Pluto in Walt Disney's cartoon comedies, indubitably a caricature taken from real life, as though confirming the possibility of Dreiser's
personage.

Pluto! There you have the ideal example. There is no one like him for
believing in the moral aspects of life. He honors the hound his father and
the stray mongrel his mother, he does not kill, he does not steal, he does
not covet his neighbor's bitch, he does not sin against chastity, he bears
no false witness, he covets nothing belonging to others. He takes so
seriously his love of his fellow creature, in whose goodness he piously
believes, that on seeing a nest of baby chicks that have lost their mother
he feels maternal impulses and goes to take care of them like a real hen.
He looks after the chicks like the best of nursemaids. In reward he only
receives the ill-treatment of the urchin gang and of the housewife. At
times he feels impelled to punish the meddlers. But a gesture from the
housewife is enough to set him back on the straight and narrow path,
from which, indeed, not even in thought has he ever completely departed. To him what counts in life above all is human goodness and
moral duty.

And yet no one takes him seriously. Why? Because no one fears him.
Pluto is the spirit of conciliation and friendship. Tender, friendly, he
constantly dreams of peace among brothers, deep in a vague humanitarian dream that by his preaching an ocean of brotherhood will one
day inundate the earth, joining all beings in one broad embrace. His
good faith, as far as the possibility of world brotherhood is concerned,
knows no limits. Also, he believes everything he is told. Since it has never
crossed his mind that the word also serves to conceal thought, he has
never learned the subtle art of seeing through words. Hence his incredible artless candor, his ingenuousness, which is his strength but also
his weakness, and, at times, his despair.

Now, within these moral and spiritual characteristics, what is it that
Pluto could be in contemporary life? It was written that he had to be
the immature and frustrated creature that he is.

Nevertheless, physically he does not differ from other dogs. Organically
he is the same. Structurally there is nothing wrong with him. He even
has the most noble of origins, an origin that probably falls not a whit
below that of the dogs that came over on the *Mayflower*. His most
noble ancestor may be the faithful dog of Phaedrus, that faithful canine
who, when the thief tempts him with a piece of meat so that he will not
bark in defense of his master's property, promptly roars: *"Multam
falleris, namque ista subita me jubet benignitas vigilare, facias ne mea*

culpa lucrum," or as it might be phrased, "That's the last straw: you want to make a profit out of my guilt," or, reduced to small change in popular coin, "*Comigo não, ladrão* [With me, no, you thief]."

What is it, then, that happened to Pluto? Physically, nothing. But he went off by himself to read the Bible without the aid of interpreters, and the *Social Contract,* and this is how he turned out. What made him different, let there be no doubt about it, was his free interpretation of the doctrines of Rousseau and Jefferson, excellent in themselves. If, instead of his having picked up the *Social Contract,* or the *Cuore* (*Cuore, An Italian Schoolboy's Journal*) of Edmondo de Amicis, or the *Life of George Washington* by Parson Weems, or the *Life of Abraham Lincoln* in the sanctimonious style of Lamond, they had given him Machiavelli's *Prince* to read, or Nietzsche's *Thus Spake Zarathustra;* if, instead of teaching Pluto to love his fellow creature as himself, they had taught him to despise his fellow, to consider him as a competitor and by definition a scoundrel; if they had showed him that the ugly thing is not stealing but being caught at it; if they had warned him that what is harmful in life is the little lie, while the big lie, the superlie, the all-embracing lie, the overpowering lie, is a formidable instrument of success; if, instead of putting a passion for truth into his head, a passion as strong as that of Epaminondas, they had instilled in him beautiful theories to clothe the most ignoble intentions with a cloak of honesty, Pluto's career would have been very different. A snarl of his would suffice to make the earth tremble and Russia bow her head.

Since he misread Rousseau and enlisted in the Salvation Army, he was ruined.

And that is the sort of result that may come about from the liberalism born of the American Revolution, with the ideas of human goodness and the possibility of the moral perfecting of humanity, when not tempered with the Christian doctrine of the struggle between good and evil.

It may be argued that Pluto does not exist; he is a fictional personage. So is Donald Duck. But for all that they do not fail to be representative of certain types of American reality. For that matter, if they were not symbolical characters drawn from reality, possible and probable in their plausibility, just as much as Henry Ford and Woodrow Wilson were real in their salvationism, they would not enjoy all the popularity they have. It is not in themselves alone that they have value, but as symbolical personages of a humanity that likes to see itself interpreted in the language of symbols. In this language, if Pluto is the typical representative of the frustrations of a limited number of idealists exiled in time, incapable of understanding the meaning of the period in which they live, Donald stereotypes the other side of America: the America of frustration resulting from a belief in competition, free enterprise, publicity, and success.

13

And what of Mickey Mouse? Mickey Mouse is not American and is not original. He has too many historical antecedents for that. Behind all his actions always lies an old-fashioned heroism. Musician, sculptor, explorer, swordsman, and adventurer, there is always a Helen or a Roxane in his destiny. It is for her that he fights, labors, and conquers.

He reminds us of the Greek Ulysses, or El Cid, the Spanish national hero. Pluto and Donald, no; they are absolutely original, and in literature have no citable antecedents, at least antecedents with any title to symbol; they are original products of American civilization. It is in Donald and Pluto, not in Mickey Mouse, that Americans see themselves. They are to each other exactly what Don Quixote is to Sancho Panza in the Spanish soul, and for the iconography of the straight salvationists of America there is nobody like Pluto, as there is nobody like Donald for the daguerreotype of the aggressive, irrepressible, and competitive side of the American civilization of our time.

Pluto misread the *Social Contract,* as well as the episode of the cherry tree in the life of George Washington, that episode which has addled so many brains in the country; Donald, now, misread Horatio Alger and the biographies of the tycoons who win out through audacity and tenacity, by hard work, independently of circumstances of time and place, and went out into the world in quest of bustle and success, which in American catechisms is the inevitable reward of those who persevere.

With this difference, that the tycoons found frontiers to conquer, worlds to discover, infinite possibilities ahead. Donald finds none of this. Starting out in life believing in success, free enterprise, individual initiative, free competition, the power of the will, and the virtues immanent in work, he keeps on forcing his way, competing, elbowing, quacking angrily, and always getting it in the neck.

Does he quit trying to win at any price? Never. The happiness of the "average guy," the workman, the common man of America, does not attract him. Not being meek and humble of heart like Pluto, he wants triumph, success, applause, at any price. He goes at everything with that obsession. Wherever he may be, he seeks to be admired, he never refuses an opportunity. He passes a boxing ring, for example, where fights are going on. Shortly Donald has his gloves on and is getting thoroughly beaten up. Poor fellow, he hasn't the athlete's build! For that matter, only one thing exists in him that is compatible with his urgent drive—limited intelligence. And it is clear that he was not born to shine in sports. But Donald refuses to resign himself. He is incredibly tenacious in the face of ridicule. He quacks, he shrieks insults, he loses his temper —and then he is ready for another. He wants to fight at all costs, stubbornly. He angers the bystanders. He waves his fists, he fights, and he ends as he always does, getting it in the neck.

But right after that, when one thinks Donald is going to quiet down, there he is wanting to triumph as a tenor. He quacks away; the audience, though tolerant, bursts out laughing, and the guffaws drown out his voice. Since he believes that quacking and singing are the same thing, he will not admit defeat. Anyone else would bow his head and retire discomfited, humiliated. Not he. He will make them like his voice if he has to beat it into them. He wants to force everything—tastes, preferences, convictions, admiration. A perfect Yankee. And probably a Republican.

These antecedents being known, is Donald to be admired, neurasthenic though he is? Obviously not. What is admirable is that he is not yet completely crazy and shut up in an insane asylum, as happens to thousands of Americans in quest of success when they lose touch with the times in which they are living.

But what is it that is wrong with Donald? Since he is a real American, hard-working, active, clean-cut, dynamic, energetic, resourceful—to cite once again our friend Babbitt—why does he fail so often? The fault is not with Donald, as it is not with Pluto. The fault is in the integrated whole of American culture, with its distortion of all values subordinated to the exaltation of work, of activism, and of accomplishment, with the consequent banishing of repose, of confession, of self-analysis, of reflection and contemplation from the pioneer habits of America. The American no longer contemplates; the American no longer reflects; the American no longer knows how to rest. If Donald could rest and reflect and contemplate—matters in which his good friend José Carioca could be very useful to him—he would perceive that in the United States there is no longer any possibility of fortunes turning up overnight, that the frontier has ended, that free enterprise and the myth of the infinite possibilities of the individual in the world of free competition have ceased to be operational; that with the frontier conquered, the Pacific reached, there is no more room for the plenitude of economic liberalism, or for free enterprise, in the sense that obtained prior to the last two wars; that both are only possible in Brazil, where there are frontiers and space to be conquered; that the State, whether the Republicans will or no, is going to have to intervene more and more in the economic world. As Donald—and with him millions of Americans—has a horror of reflection, he keeps on getting beaten up and suffering, like millions of others who become irritated, accuse themselves, swing toward com-

munism swept along by frustration because they are unable to excel the
feats of their fathers and of previous generations, or discern the causes
of their failures and defeats.

And why doesn't he contemplate, why doesn't he reflect?

For the same motives that *mazombos* and half-breeds dislike useful
work and action: because they have not been taught to respect contemplation and reflection. On the contrary, they have been taught to
love movement, work, action, to consider repose as a vice, and to see in
idleness the most terrible of all sins.

Vacation? It is a thing he has never really had, nor ever really learned
to enjoy, for the thing given the name of vacation in the United States
is no more than a change of activity, and the doctrine that "hard work
never killed anybody" is what prevails. Moreover, "time is money," and
there is no time to waste on unproductive practices.

14

All very true. On the score of comfort, social order, and production of
material goods, no one can wish for more or better. It is an admirable
world for those who are satisfied with comfort alone. But it remains to
be seen whether the rules and methods for the production of comfort
and material goods function with the same result on the spiritual and
cultural plane, or to what point the conquest of learning can be submitted to the same time-prescription that governs the accomplishments
of the assembly line. That the United States has grown in power and
wealth there is no doubt. Has it grown in wisdom in the same
proportion?

There is, there must be, something wrong in that business of submitting by simple analogy the intellectual, the professor, the artist, and
even the inventor and the scientific researcher—in a word, the creator—
to the discipline that holds for the producer of consumer goods. While
the latter works on the plane of the measurable, his work being measurable, in terms of time and result, the raw materials of the other
are the imponderables, mystery and the infinite, where the flashes
of intuition are not submitted to clocks or calendars. That the intellectual and the boxer should be entertained at the same luncheon,
as was done by the Portuguese of California, is understandable and

even attractive. But that the essential differences in the methods of getting the maximum from the boxer and the maximum from the professor are not recognized, goes beyond the limits of reason and is equivalent to wanting the causal laws governing the physical phenomena of the Universe, in which facts repeat themselves, to be the same that govern world history, where facts succeed one another.

And don't the Americans perceive what is happening? Of course they do. They continually tell each other at every moment, "Relax. Take it easy. Stop worrying." There are even campaigns for a change of goals and even an appreciable literature on the subject. But what does not exist, really, is any sincere intention of changing. The narcissism of the common man has taken over American civilization. For that matter, contributing to the same result, it is not only the common man who is stirring. No, the three forces supposedly in conflict—the immigrant, the last-generation American, and the traditionalist American of three hundred years' standing—have for a long time been converging toward the same goal. The immigrant wants to change nothing, because he is tired of forcing himself to make new adaptations; the three-centuries-old American wants to change nothing, because he is a conservative by definition; and the American of the last generation wants to change nothing, because to change is to think, and to him thinking is a task in which he feels in imminent danger of unseating his brain. So the three together, each in his own sector, end by persuading the whole country that the American way of life is the right one, in its whole and in its parts, and that the United States, in its whole or in each of its parts, is the best of all possible worlds imaginable. Thence the resistance to any change in the master outlines of its culture.

It is obvious that the Negroes who live in the South of the United States and can neither worship in the white man's churches, nor attend his schools, nor, in many states, vote, will not always agree with this. Nor the other racial minorities of America who because of their race have no access to the so-called "exclusive" places.

It is obvious, too, that that smiling optimism, that obsession with viewing American reality through rose-colored glasses, has provoked its reactions and its refusals to conform in the hearts of thinking men, and that along with the America of Horatio Alger there emerges the America of Theodore Dreiser, of Melville, of O'Neill, of John Steinbeck, and of that extraordinary Arthur Miller, who in *Death of a Salesman* has composed an authentic Greek tragedy with the simple ingredients of American life.

The American writers—those who really count—live, save for very few exceptions, in a state of protest. Since the Civil War, nonconformity with and satire and protest against the "American way of life" have never ceased. In truth, all such writers are satirists of and nonconformists to American culture in some or all its master outlines.

Thoreau protests against work subjected to time and to the rules of material productivity by going to live alone, like Robinson Crusoe on his island, in the middle of New England; Henry James, long undecided between Europe and America, winds up permanently settled in England, no longer recognizing as his land the America invaded by the Philistines. T. S. Eliot goes further. He becomes an English subject like Conrad. Sinclair Lewis protests against the Babbitt, against racial discrimination, and against the lie of American innocence. Theodore Dreiser—there is the great nonconformist. Faulkner forgets the bitterness of Yankeeism by reconstructing the Southern past. Steinbeck sympathizes with the bums in *Tortilla Flat*. Thomas Merton retires to a Trappist monastery. John dos Passos protests. The more moderate, like John Marquand, gently mock the snobs of New England. Mencken, instead of letting himself get irritated by the "American way of life," irritates his fellow countrymen by guffawing loudly at the expense of what they revere as sacred and untouchable. And when, overcome by indignation, the patriots ask him why he doesn't move out of the United States, why he doesn't go away, Mencken good-humoredly gives this reply, which is as good as a judgment: "I can't; this country is very comfortable."

Let no one be deluded, however, as to the importance of Mencken's laughter and of the protests of other writers in the whole of American life. Their social and cultural influence is small, and they know it. Smothered by the false rumors of advertisers, far from attaining the importance attributed to them outside the country, they hardly manage to make a ripple in the waters of that immense estuary of optimism that is America.

Essentially, America is still the America of Horatio Alger. Of Horatio Alger, of the break with the past, of the immoderate belief in human perfectibility, of activism, and, of course, of the "happy ending."

Of what compromises, of what adaptations, of what heresies is the American cinema not capable in order to achieve that result! Provided that this objective be attained, the mutilating of novels, the altering of history, the reworking of biographies have not the slightest importance. The essential thing is that the sacred myth be maintained, with the aid of which the American, at the same time that he defends himself against the prophets of discouragement and despair, continues entertaining, in the midst of his setbacks, the illusion of the survival of values dear to him, far beyond the time and the vital cycle that originated them.

15

As may be clearly seen, it is narcissism at its height. What is more, of the perilous narcissistic induration of the American culture of these recent times nothing speaks louder than the two great experiences of the Roosevelt administration, the New Deal and the entry of the United States into the last war. In vain did thinking men—economists, sociologists, essayists—denounce the doctrine and practice of producing for the sake of producing, always producing without ever stopping; in vain did they warn that free enterprise would lead the country into a terrible crisis; in vain did they beg and plead for a change of course. No one paid any attention to them. Not only were they not listened to, but they were actually execrated by the community as harmful to business. It was necessary for the 1929 crash to come and the house threaten to fall in, for the people to surrender, panic-stricken—a neurotic panic, perfectly geared to the magnification of economic virtues, which led many to suicide—to the psychoanalytic treatment of Roosevelt, who in his speeches, at the same time that he interpreted the disease, indicated the remedy: "We have nothing to fear but fear itself."

Did they yield themselves to their healer fully and willingly after that? Not at all! They gave themselves up to him grumbling, gnashing their teeth, and there were even some who preferred Germany's victory to seeing any attack on the causes of the neuroses which had held them in thrall all their lives, since infancy.

Heavens, how they inveighed against Roosevelt!

Later came the business of the United States' entry into the war. In vain did Roosevelt plead for abandonment of the isolationist policy, which he called suicide. In vain did he put his whole heart into arguments, inviting the country to reflect, showing that since George Washington and Monroe the world had not stood still, and that in the face of the Hitler phenomenon it was high time for Americans to review their foreign policy. Collective narcissism was too advanced for the therapy of persuasion to yield results. And it did not. Pearl Harbor, shock therapy, was needed for the country to wake up.

Did Roosevelt by any chance win absolute confidence this time? He did not. The power of isolationist narcissism was such that, with the United States in the midst of war, with American soldiers dying on all fronts, isolationists and pacifists held their conventions clamoring for immediate peace with Japan. It was not Japan that had attacked the

United States. It was Roosevelt who had forced Japanese militarism into doing so, with his absurd demands in the Orient.

And the sun did not burst, and the George Washington Bridge in New York and the Golden Gate Bridge in San Francisco did not collapse in ruins, and everything went on as if nothing had happened.

And is the country not changing? It is, of course, but it is being transformed from the outside, by external events, and not from the inside as it was before the Civil War. Before the Civil War the United States sent messages out to the world; now the United States sends out manufactured products and defends itself, as if there were nothing more positive to do amid the shipwreck of capitalism than to preach to the starving peoples of the world and to the underdeveloped countries the advantages of the "American way of life."

With these antecedents, obviously, it was not to be expected that the results of the protests and campaigns for rectification of the main outlines of American culture should be more than mediocre. And they are not. It suffices to say that where American immaturity has most diminished is in the sector of racial discrimination. If it is true that the improvements achieved on that score are not as significant as they should be, it is no less true that, after the barbarous lynchings of Negroes in Detroit in 1943 through excess of zeal in the matter of the economic virtues, or, more specifically, to avoid the competition of Negro labor emigrating from the South to the North, the situation of Negroes and mulattoes under Roosevelt, Truman, and Eisenhower, tireless champions of civil rights against the discrimination that state and local autonomies try to maintain, has been improving, and tending to improve still more. As to the rest, however, it is an impasse, or impasse and deterioration. With regard to the excesses of the worship of work and production, for example, except for certain enterprises and universities which are already giving contracts to scientists without assigning specific functions to them, leaving the research, the schedules, everything, to the discretion of the scientists themselves, nothing else can be cited as evidence of a change of course.

The time to rest and think having come, or the time to modify the American way of life, resistance is general. "Thinking takes time," explains an American industrialist, "and isn't always pleasant. To shut the office door, put your feet up, and look out the window seems somehow to be letting the stockholders down. We easily convince ourselves that we are making great efforts when we measure ourselves by the number of engagements we keep, people we see, and reports we read, but, actually, the thing business needs most today is an occasional quiet hour for the boss."[40]

Before the Civil War, even in the strongest redoubts of Calvinism, there was still the Protestant Sunday, consecrated to prayer, to contemplation, with the banishment of all and every type of activity. Today not even this remains. Today, the Sunday, the Sunday rest, is integrated into the activism of the weekend, which is when the American, after driving a hundred and fifty miles or so in his car, moves about most and devotes himself most to his hobby, in accord with his habits of making maximum use of the time available. This they call "constructive use of leisure time." Not even the rashest prophets of Calvinism could have foreseen that their teachings about work, about idleness and the necessity to keep busy in order to stave off vice, would yield such results.

And yet those results are there, almost unbelievable, almost indescribable, converting the idle American into an abstraction already difficult to conceive.

16

How the American detests resting or being still! To meditate, to ponder, can be more important than acting, but the American is happier doing than reflecting. To tell the truth, he feels happy only when acting, accomplishing. Life to him is accomplishment. And when there is no longer any accomplishment possible, he is sadness itself, suffering at retiring from the arena, the end so sadly symbolized in the suicide of James Forrestal, the American of the last generation who, after making his life a series of successes—in sport, in business, in public life—ends by throwing himself to death from the window of the hospital where he had gone to rest. His penultimate act was to copy, in a translation from Sophocles, the passage in which Ajax, on the threshold of eternity, thinks of the mother who at the close of the day, with heart desolate and hair whitened over her temples, will have to hear the story, murmured in the air, of the son who has passed on: "Worn by the waste of time, comfortless, nameless, hopeless save in the dark prospect of the yawning grave. . . ."[41]

There is more than a simple individual tragedy in the drama of that son of a Scottish immigrant who spent his life competing and winning and who jotted down notes in a diary in order later, when he could rest and contemplate, to utilize them in a book of meditation and synthesis that he had long planned and never came to write. There is in this a national drama, the pathetic drama of a country that, having the best schools of music, does not produce a great musician; or, having the best professors of philosophy, produces no great philosopher; or, having the best teachers of plastic arts, produces no truly great painter or sculptor; a country that, having the most widely read writers in the world, does not get a single one among them to agree with the current narcissistic hardening of its culture; that, having attained to leadership of nations, has no liking for it, nor ever quite know what to do with that leadership; and, having two political parties originating with Jefferson and Hamilton—really great men—no longer produces a great man for all its hunger after heroism, except when a defect in the heel (Wilson) or infantile paralysis (Roosevelt) forces her potentially great men to immobility and to "the silent orgies of meditation."

As long as the United States was fulfilling only a national and isolationist destiny, all was very well, because it was a question of nothing but an American problem. Now, though, it is a matter of more, much more. It is Christian culture that is at stake, and the world, evidently, cannot remain waiting for a heel deformity or infantile paralysis to bring about the miracle of furnishing the United States with great men, after the fashion of those in whom American civilization was fertile in pioneer times, to bring the nation out of the crisis it is experiencing and out of the chaos in which it is writhing.

17

And what to do until the new leaders appear?

Miguel de Unamuno,[42] who understood symbols and knew better than anyone the cathartic possibilities of historical interpretation, one day had this inspiration: He proposed to Spaniards that they undertake a great journey in quest of the tomb of Don Quixote. Disappointed at the prosaic quality of Europe and Spain in his time, of our time, Unamuno's hope was that, having found Don Quixote's grave, the Spaniards, and with them the Europeans, newly inspired by the uncontaminated idealism of the Manchegan knight, might once more perform great deeds.

We, Americans and Brazilians, can perhaps do better. Instead of sallying forth in search of the tombs of our fictional personages, we ought to undertake a journey through the histories of Brazil and the United States and see whether on those broad highways that guard the secret of our development we can find symbols that, having lived through and endured our problems in body and soul, will be capable of inspiring us in reforming the main outlines of our respective cultures.

Epilogue

1

Every day, winter and summer, spring and fall, in sun, snow, or rain, whether the cherry trees are in bloom or not, there is a constant pilgrimage in Washington. The object of the pilgrimage is the Lincoln Memorial, the monument to the proto-martyr of the unification of the country. But it is not only in Washington that these civic pilgrimages take place. Indeed, they extend, on a lesser scale, to other points. Wherever there is a spot, a site, a souvenir, a historical relic evoking the image of the Unifier, there will always be Americans there seeking to fathom their secret and their meaning. And there is no end to these pilgrimages. In Washington, besides the Lincoln Memorial, they include the theater in which Lincoln was assassinated and the house in which he died; in the state of Illinois they lead to New Salem, the little community in which Lincoln spent the great years of his formative period and which is being rebuilt house by house, cabin by cabin, just as in pioneer days, so that Americans may steep themselves in the ambience in which their hero passed the most decisive years of his development; in Springfield, the pilgrims are attracted by the tomb in which lie the mortal remains of the Patriarch. The number of pilgrims who, in Washington, in Springfield, New Salem, or Gettysburg sally forth annually in quest of the monuments which celebrate the image and the legend of the Unifier, reaches the hundreds of thousands, perhaps the millions.

In Brazil, keeping due proportions, the proportions it is necessary to bear always in mind when features of Brazilian civilization are compared with features of the American, a somewhat similar phenomenon is taking place. Winter or summer, spring or autumn, in sun or in rain, whether the jacarandas are in flower or not, in Ouro Prêto, Mariana, Tiradentes, Sabará, Congonhas do Campo, São João d'El-Rei, rarely is there no observer to be found standing in rapt contemplation of the works that Aleijadinho sowed throughout Minas Gerais in the second half of the eighteenth century.

In Ouro Prêto he is detained by the doorway of the church of São Francisco and the lateral altars of the churches of São João and Nossa Senhora da Piedade; in Sabará, by the façade, the pulpit, the balustrade, and the Atlantids flanking the nave of the Carmo Church; in Congonhas do Campo, by the sixty-four figures of the Stages of the Last Supper, the Garden, the Prison, the Scourging, the Road to Calvary, and the Crucifixion, and by the São Jorge do Consistório da Matriz do Pilar and the twelve prophets of the Santuário.

And to think that for a long time, for more than a century, outside of Minas Gerais no one took any interest in those statues, and only a small number of the curious, foreigners most of them, knew of their existence!

Not now. Now the work of Aleijadinho is being studied. Now people come from all parts of the country to contemplate it, and the number of these pilgrims—*sursum corda!*—swells from year to year.

Can those pilgrimages of Americans to Washington, New Salem, or Springfield, and of Brazilians to Ouro Prêto, Mariana, Sabará, São João d'El-Rei, or Congonhas do Campo, have any deeper meaning, or do they merely express the artistic curiosity for art monuments that are in themselves worth taking the trouble to see?

The Lincoln Memorial, of course, all in marble in the middle of a Greek wood, with its Doric columns framing the superb statue of the Unifier, is of a beauty that justifies not one but many trips to Washington. And New Salem, reconstructed in the manner that Williamsburg has been, holds a moving interest for a civilization still nostalgic for the pioneer. The monument in Springfield is not entirely devoid of interest.

As for the intrinsic value of Aleijadinho's works, that is well known. However much one travels over Brazil, and not only Brazil but the two Americas, including even Peru and Mexico, in whose churches are to be found prodigies of the baroque—however far one travels in search of works of art for purposes of contemplation, comparison, and contrast of artistic values, nothing will be found in the field of sculpture comparable to the work done by Aleijadinho. To discover anything like the totality of monuments that the carver of Vila Rica has bequeathed to posterity in the form of statues of saints, façades of churches, lavabos, volutes, high-reliefs, pulpits, and altars, executed here in stone and there in wood, it is necessary to take oneself a little farther back in space and time. In space, it may be necessary to extend the investigation to the Old World; in time, to go back to the Renaissance, because perhaps only in the Old World and during the Renaissance, nowhere else and in no other epoch, shall we be able to identify works equivalent or similar.

So even if these pilgrimages were nothing more than mere movements of artistic curiosity, they would be fully justified.

Nevertheless, it would be a pity if their meaning were only that and no more. What a pity if their significance went no further than the limits of simple curiosity! Why? Because, with all the intrinsic value of the works of art to which the names of Lincoln and Aleijadinho are connected, Aleijadinho and Lincoln have much more to tell us and much more to give of themselves to the American and Brazilian cultures than the works that evoke their memory.

In the atmosphere of the cultures to which they belong, as examples, as norms, as inspirations, both Lincoln and Aleijadinho seem to have caught the secret of everything that is lacking in those cultures.

2

Does American civilization lack a taste for contemplative life? Lincoln had it as few men have.

Does American civilization lack real conviction of the civil equality of all races? Lincoln was a great teacher of equality.

Does American civilization lack the feeling for world unity? Lincoln had it to a high degree.

Does American civilization not know how to relax, not know what to do with mental receptivity? Lincoln was the master of a kind of wise relaxation.

And yet Lincoln cannot be understood without American civilization, as the latter cannot be understood without Lincoln, the two are so interlocked.

To start with, Lincoln was born, like millions of Americans, in a pioneer's cabin. When he came into the world on February 12, 1809, in Hardin County, Kentucky, although two centuries had passed since John Smith arrived at Jamestown, in Virginia, and a hundred and eighty-nine years since the *Mayflower* had made port at Plymouth, in New England, conditions in Kentucky, as for that matter those along the whole movable frontier of the American West, if they were not contemporary with the *Mayflower* and John Smith, were still quite primitive.

Within a short time the great change in his life was to be a typically American pioneer adventure: the move farther west, to the territory of Indiana, toward which the frontier was advancing. Lincoln's father, a pioneer of some standing in Kentucky because, besides being a farmer, he was a carpenter and the holder of a small official post—a circumstance that invalidates the moving descriptions made in United States public schools about the extreme poverty of the Lincolns—not wishing, on the one hand, to be called "poor white" by the Negroes from the Southern plantations who were beginning to invade Kentucky, and tempted, on the other hand, by the new frontier and by the news of the fertility of the great valleys of the West recently opened up, sets out in a hired wagon with his whole family for Indiana, where they make camp on the banks of Little Pigeon Creek. They were days of great excitement for young Abe, then at the age of eight. To reach the site, covered with ancient forest, still damp from the days of Creation, to find himself suddenly beside his father, ax in hand, cutting down the trees of the virgin woods, trimming off their branches, to sleep in the open and to see the clearing grow, and in the middle of the clearing the new cabin, struck by the sun's rays filtered through the tops of the forest trees, and inside the cabin the living room with earthen floor beaten smooth, and the fireplace, was probably more than he had asked of God in his prayers.

Suddenly, an unexpected blow in the midst of his felicity—his mother died. In that first winter a terrible plague had spread through Indiana, the most terrible in memory since the territory had begun to be inhabited. On that occasion not only did Lincoln's mother die but several of his relatives on the maternal side who had also moved to Indiana. This was to be the most painful blow of Lincoln's life. Others would come later, but from this one, perhaps for being the first, perhaps for being unexpected, and because he was only nine when it befell him, he would never completely recover. And it all happened swiftly. His mother, knowing that she was going to die, called her two children to her bedside. She was very weak, and the children had to bend over her while she gave them her last messages. Laying pale hand on Abraham's head, she told him to be good to his father and his sister; and she told both to be good to each other, expressing the wish that they should live as she had taught them, loving their fellow man and worshiping God.

And then the end. Lincoln's father himself—note this circumstance well, psychoanalysts!—is the one who makes his wife's coffin; it is he who lays her body in it, he it is who lowers the coffin into the earth.

Lincoln was then barely nine years old.

And hardly does he enter upon his convalescence from fate's first blow, beside his sister and his father, to whom he transfers all his filial love as his mother had recommended in the shelter of the cabin, where all slept side by side in winter to keep warm—note this well, psychoanalysts!—when a new blow is reserved for him. Barely a year having passed, his father leaves him and his sister to the care of relatives and departs on a trip to Kentucky, whence he returns married to a widow who had been his sweetheart before he married Abe's mother.

The human being has a limit for work, for fatigue, for pleasure, and

also for understanding and suffering. That nine-year-old's limit of understanding and of capacity for enduring, when he had lost only a year
earlier the one he had loved most in the world, was to experience a
severe shock. To see his father now, to whom he had transferred all his
affection and tenderness, coming into his house, the house that had been
his mother's, married to another woman, and this other woman invading
his house with three more children, was more than he was able to bear.

From that moment he could never again get along well with his
father. He obeys him because he is obliged to, he follows his instructions
because he is obliged to, but love for that father he will only feel mixed
with resentment, a resentment that he never entirely overcame.

Thus in Lincoln was established the primordial nucleus of a future
neurosis. Whether the neurotic picture was to be completed was going
to depend, now, on the situation he might have to face and on the
degree of emotional comprehension he might achieve about the origins
of his drama.

"As he shot up, he seemed to change in appearance and action,"
testifies a contemporary. "Although quick-witted and ready with an
answer, he began to exhibit deep thoughtfulness, and was so often lost
in studied reflection we could not help noticing the strange turn in his
actions. He disclosed rare timidity and sensitiveness, especially in the
presence of men and women, and although cheerful enough in the
presence of the boys, he did not appear to seek our company as earnestly
as before."[1]

3

Lincoln neurotic? Not yet, perhaps. The parasite would take time to
germinate. For the time being it is merely a question of a boy who
suddenly changes his habits. And it is true that he no longer wants to be
like his father. Formerly he liked to hunt with the rifle; now, nobody
sees him with gun in hand. He used to like playing and working alongside his father, and did not like to study; now he works only reluctantly,
his only pleasure is study and reading. Already adolescent and gawky, he
lives stretched out on the floor, reading. He reads, he devours everything that falls into his hands, "even the torn bits of paper in the

streets," as Cervantes would say. Hardly does he hear of a book in a distant cabin, for leagues around, than Lincoln sets out on the road soliloquizing and stopping to chat along the way until he gets the coveted book.

And his resentment against his father? Ah, there was no way to dissolve it. Subjectively Lincoln ingratiates himself with everybody. Even his stepmother—in spite of the old and sometimes unfounded tradition that there is no good stepmother, a tradition that has prevented man from inventing a symbol capable of counterbalancing the dramatic symbol of Cinderella—Lincoln ends by loving very much indeed. After she is widowed for the second time, not before, she is the first person he goes to visit after his election as President; with his stepmother he is all affectionate vigilance, care and attention—a real son. With his father, however, there was no way to reconcile himself.

When old Thomas Lincoln is dying, and the news is carried to his son, the latter does not go to be with him in the last moments. He asks the messenger to take this elucidative message to his father: "Say to him that if we could meet now it is doubtful whether it would not be more painful than pleasant; but that if it be his lot to go now he will soon have a joyous meeting with the many loved ones gone before, and where the rest of us, through the help of God, hope ere long to join them."[2]

There was a diffuse resentment in him hard to understand. Almost on the threshold of his majority, shortly before his trip on a raft to New Orleans, where he had occasion to observe a slave auction, Lincoln's reactions already were bearing the mark of the resentful man. For example: Not being invited to a wedding attended by the whole community, he wrote and distributed a satire relating the marriage in his own way and exposing the bride and groom to ridicule. And the satire he composed in a letter to a friend, on the girl who refused his first proposal of marriage! Being rejected, or considering himself rejected, was a situation Lincoln still did not know how to endure.

Long before those explosions of resentment at any kind of rejection, another thing had occurred, tremendously important from the psychological point of view for the understanding of the Lincoln phenomenon.

Lincoln was talking with his sister and his stepmother's little girls under a tree, when his stepbrother John came up with a land terrapin in his hand, and, on impulse, hurled the creature with all his might against a tree, smashing the shell.

Lincoln's reaction is disconcerting. He heaps furious recrimination on John's act; and shortly afterward, invoking a passage from the Bible, he delivers a vehement dissertation on cruelty and makes the girls cry.[3]

What happened to make Lincoln act that way? At that time, of course, no one could hit upon the explanation. Today, when the mechanism of the subconscious and the phenomenon of emotional projection are better understood, the explanation would be easier. Lincoln, at the moment when the terrapin's shell was crushed, saw in the exposed, unprotected terrapin the projection of himself and his own drama. Ever since his home had been split in two by the death of his mother and the second marriage of his father, he had never ceased to think in terms of preserving unity, the constant maxim of his life. "A house divided against itself cannot stand," he says in 1861, against the insistent advice of all his friends.

4

The whole obsession of his life would be to preserve unity, to preserve the Union.

Not losing sight of the identification that takes place from early years in the recesses of every child's sensibility between the maternal image and that of the land from which his food comes, and, by extension, between the home and the domestic horizons, and later between the domestic horizons and the native land, the fatherland, it can be understood how much Lincoln identified the Union with the maternal image.

Has the Union not been destroyed, is it unthreatened? Lincoln is then a lazy man, a talker, a teller of tales, a picaresque fellow, an Indian style and catch-as-catch-can wrestler, the best, most carefree of companions.

At the slightest sign of threat to the Union, however, Lincoln is no longer the same. He is immediately transfigured. He turns serious, apprehensive, mysterious. Are there disorders in Mississippi and St. Louis and may the Union be broken up? Lincoln hastens to make a speech about the dangers to the unity of the country resulting from the lynchings and disorders.[4]

Unity, union: there is the leitmotiv of his cogitations.

Is the Union threatened? No one thenceforth will see him laugh or tell picaresque anecdotes. During the whole Civil War no one saw him smile other than sadly.

That is why his life is what it was: periods of calm and integration alternating with terrible periods of depression.

The neurosis in him is cyclic. He goes through some periods carefree; but a little incident, a nothing, really, suffices to bring out the hidden man. The prospect of marriage, how it makes him suffer! He writes of this to the most intimate of his friends. "I am the most miserable of mortals. If what I feel were equally distributed to every human family, there would not be a single happy face on earth. Whether I am ever to improve, I do not know; my horrible prophecy is that I shall not. To go on as I am is impossible; I must die or improve. . . ."[5]

Previously, in New Salem on the occasion of the death of Ann Rutledge, with whom he was not even in love but to whom he was only a good friend, he becomes completely disoriented. He is seen on the public roads, indifferent to work and to passersby, in a sorrow too hastily interpreted as love for Ann Rutledge, when everything indicates that he was mourning less for his friend than, all over again, the death of his mother.

Wherever his own drama is projected, wherever the prospect of separating mother and son appears—his pathetic group—there will Lincoln be. Once, already a famous lawyer, he learns that a former boon companion of his back in New Salem, in whose house he had visited many times, was going to be tried for a capital crime in another city. Lincoln immediately writes to the young man's mother offering to defend him. It is a moving one, that letter of his. But this is nothing compared to the defense he offered, in which the stirring note, the note which none of those present—Puritans and Protestants little given to tears—could resist, was the reference to the separation of mother and son and to the gratitude he owed to the lady whose son was going to be tried. When Lincoln had no home, she had given him home and shelter, being like a second mother to him. As for the young man's father, also a great friend of Lincoln's, not a word about him. The father, symbolically, was to him always a suspect figure.

Lincoln invariably magnifies the maternal, not the paternal, symbols.

Herndon, who was his office companion and wrote the most valuable and exact biography, and who is to Lincoln as Eckermann is to Goethe, says that Lincoln, ever receptive and approachable on any subject, avoided talk of his childhood. "If he happened to mention the topic, it was always with great reluctance and significant reserve." As candidate for President, it was very hard to get out of him, for campaign purposes, the notes they called "autobiography."

Herndon obviously does not see the truth. He thinks that the poverty surrounding Lincoln's infancy had left its mark on him; and hence the subsequent insistence of all biographers on darkening a poverty that was the same for millions of other Americans born like Lincoln in pioneer cabins, under conditions exactly the same as his, or worse.

Nevertheless, Herndon does mention this fact: Once—one single time—Lincoln did discuss his childhood. This was in 1850, on a buggy trip to the court in Menard County, Illinois, where they were going to deal with a case in which they would have to argue the problem of hereditary traits. While his companion drove the horse, Lincoln talked of his mother, mentioning the qualities he had inherited from her.

From her had come to him his "power of analysis, his logic, his mental activity, his ambition, and all the qualities that distinguished him."

Farther on, after discussing individuals of his mother's side of the family, Lincoln ends with "God bless my mother. . . . All that I am or ever hope to be I owe to her."[6]

And he fell into profound silence. In the autobiography, stating that his days of schooling did not amount, all told, to a year, Lincoln is not lying; he is merely presenting the truth in his own fashion. Saying that on the score of heredity he owed everything to his mother, Lincoln is not lying; he is only committing an enormous error of judgment—an error of judgment, for that matter, very common in those who analyze themselves without the aid of someone with sufficient authority to correct errors of interpretation. Because in fact there is nothing more illusory and far from historical truth than the mental backwardness of the paternal side, which Lincoln suggests by implication.

Among the Lincolns—not on the maternal side—is where pastors, teachers, people of some intellectual tradition can be found.

Another thing. Lincoln in his autobiography says that his father hardly knew how to write. That is not true. It is enough to examine, in Carl Sandburg's biography of Lincoln, an autograph of old Thomas Lincoln to prove that it is no signature of a semiliterate man.[7]

Why, then, does Lincoln state untruths—he, the accurate, truthful man par excellence? Because where his father and mother were concerned he never had any impartiality and detachment in his judgments. On that subject he never ceased to be immature and neurotic.

Or can there be any other explanation for that mysterious mask of sadness to which all his biographers allude without being able to penetrate? They all seek the diagnosis; the physical, biological, and causalist explanations that have arisen for Lincoln's sadness are countless. Yet, if there is a diagnosis that Lincoln's whole life confirms, it is that of neurosis.

His life in this regard is a constant dance on the edge of the abyss. In the most unexpected moments the neurosis, and through the neurosis, sadness, may suddenly assail him.

On the day, for instance, when in Springfield, on the platform of the train that will carry him to Washington and the White House, Lincoln suddenly lapses into sadness, that contagious melancholy which only he could transmit.

The melancholy that radiates from his brief farewell address!

My Friends:

No one, not in my situation, can appreciate my feeling of sadness at this parting. To this place, and the kindness of these people, I owe everything. Here I have lived a quarter of a century, and have passed from a young to an old man. Here my children have been born, and one is buried. I now leave, not knowing when or whether ever I may return, with a task before me greater than that which rested upon Washington. Without the assistance of that Divine Being who ever attended him, I cannot succeed. With that assistance, I cannot fail. Trusting in Him who can go with me, and remain with you, and be everywhere for good, let us confidently hope that all will be well. To His care commending you, as I hope in your prayers you will commend me, I bid you an affectionate farewell.[8]

5

Ah, Lincoln's periods of depression, when he cannot work and shuts himself up in his study, indifferent to everything and everyone for days on end! Ah, Lincoln's walks at night, talking with his ghosts!

And how did Lincoln manage to cure himself? This question is countered by another: Did Lincoln ever cure himself? No, it appears that he never recovered completely. After the crisis of his marriage he takes a notion to apply for the post of chargé d'affairs in Bogotá.[9] His inner suffering he thought to resolve at the time by escaping his environment and his own destiny, as if the environment, not his complex, were what was responsible for his unhappiness.

In fact he was never entirely cured. Even on the eve of assassination he had those horrible nightmares mentioned in all the biographies. Not even when taken as presentiments do those nightmares fail to offer clear symptoms of neurotic background.

No, Lincoln was never completely cured. What he did succeed in—and in this lies his greatness—was to attain a balance with the aid of the Bible.

What Lincoln owes to the Bible is truly impressive. To start with, he owes his style to it. Lincoln's style! That ductile, flexible style which at once has the resonance of bronze, the righteous wrath of the Old

Testament prophets, and the sweetness of the Sermon on the Mount, only the Bible itself could give him.

Could Lincoln have also owed to the Bible, to the New as well as to the Old Testament, the periods of peace of mind he enjoyed? It is more than probable. An assiduous reader of the sacred book, the teachings it contains on the subject of the recuperation of those sick at heart, sick at soul, of all who are sick, could not have escaped him. In this the Bible gives much more positive satisfaction than all the books of Doctor Freud plus those of his disciples. Indeed! Isn't Freud's doctrine the doctrine of the Gospels turned into scientific jargon?

Or can there be a single psychoanalytic interpretation of the congenital human afflictions that does not find a simpler counterpart in the Gospels with at least two thousand years' priority?

For example: For Freud the origin of our ills, of our immaturities, of our neuroses, is the complex of revolt against the earthly father. It is from this revolt that the guilt complex comes. The Bible goes further. It says that the origin of our ills is original sin. There, in the first days of Creation, is where the guilt of all humanity, of all individuals, originated.

Who is right? Apparently, the Bible. Why? For a very simple reason. There are indigenous tribes in which the Oedipus complex is not to be found, but in none has the guilt complex failed to be encountered, or rather, minus the scientific jargon, the guilt, the old guilt of original sin which has tormented man from the earliest days of Creation. At bottom it is from this, and not from the Oedipus complex of revolt, that all seek to free themselves, individuals, nations, cultures. Hence the universal clamor of reciprocal accusations. No one wants to be guilty, because all people know or evaluate the price of guilt. In the present crisis, to the United States the guilty one is Russia, and for Russia the guilt falls on the United States; for England the guilt is divided between the United States and Russia, therefore she, England, in the present crisis as in all crises, washes her hands of it, because she is innocent. *Mea culpa, mea culpa, mea maxima culpa*, is what no one says any more. Hence the impasse in today's world.

Another example: For psychoanalysis the origin of the neurosis, the complement of the revolt against the father, is the maternal fixation; and all one need do to cure the individual is to free him from incestuous fixations.

But this is Christ's first message to the world! The thing which psychoanalysts make such a hullabaloo over having discovered, a twelve-year-old boy was already proclaiming two millennia ago in the Temple, among the doctors. When his mother found him, he, annoyed, informed her and his earthly father, "How is it that ye sought me? wist ye not that I must be about my Father's business?"[10]

As the Gospel does not transmit words without meaning, this first message is definitive. Whosoever will go about his Father's business, has first to emancipate himself from the maternal lap and the maternal fixation.

After that, and after the lesson taught by Abel's murder, to proclaim the maternal fixation as something new is the same as to break down doors that are already wide open, and come forth like Taine's personage roaring at high noon that the sun has just been born.

On the subject of cure what else does psychoanalysis say? It says that there are only three processes of cure—shock, analysis, and self-analysis —and that of these the most efficacious are, first, shock; second, analysis; and in last place, the most precarious of the three, self-analysis.[11]

What does Christian, or rather, Catholic doctrine say? That there are only three roads to redemption from sin—grace, confession, and penitence, that is, the examination of conscience accompanied by the intention of amendment.

The psychoanalysts will say that psychoanalysis does not demand penitence, nor does it determine the orientation. That results from the free choice of the patient. Strictly speaking, they ought to say that in its earliest phase it *used* not to determine the orientation. A few years after Freud's death one of the most highly reputed psychoanalysts of our time, Karen Horney, reversing Freud—and all the American school is with her—says, no, it is not possible to cure if, at a certain stage of treatment, the doctor does not begin influencing the patient toward a change of course.[12]

What does psychoanalysis say about the cure? It says that the cure comes only when the feeling of guilt is wiped out.

Two thousand years ago, according to the New Testament, Gospel of St. Luke, chapter 5, verse 20, which corresponds to St. Matthew, chapter 9, verse 2, and to St. Mark, chapter 2, verse 5, a certain rabbi of Galilee told the paralytic, "Man, thy sins are forgiven thee." He means that the palsied man's disease was not paralysis but guilt. Note well. The Master does not say to the paralytic, "Arise, for thou art cured." He does say, "Arise, thy sins are forgiven thee." And He even adds, when the scribes and Pharisees start censuring Him, "Whether it is easier, to say, Thy sins be forgiven thee; or to say, Rise up and walk?" (Luke 5:23). One single time does Jesus say to the sick man, "Rise, take up thy bed, and walk" (John 5:8). But later, finding him in the temple, He adds, "Behold, thou art made whole: sin no more, lest a worse thing come unto thee" (John 5:14). Which is equivalent to saying that the palsied man's disease was not properly paralysis but guilt, sin.

Again, in the matter of treatment, psychoanalysis points out a number of requisites of the good psychoanalyst: respectability, calm bearing, spotless reputation, detachment, superiority to passions.

Apparently they are the qualities, all of them, that the Roman Apostolic Catholic Church demands of her priests. With this difference, that the confessor, the priest, must be a bachelor and maintain chastity, things not required of the psychoanalyst. Now, however decent he may be, however austere and spotless, he will never be able to compete on this point with the chaste confessor. Why? Because the latter can demand or suggest greater detachment from worldly things and from the material values for the purposes of the cure; he has authority for this. With what authority, on the other hand, can it be done by the psychoanalyst who is married and has children, and charges, in the United States as in Brazil, inordinately high fees per hour of treatment?

One day a rich young man approached Jesus and asked Him what he should do to gain eternal life. Jesus then, after reminding him of the Ten Commandments, told the rich young man to sell all that he possessed and give it to the poor, and to follow Him. "And he was sad at that saying, and went away grieved: for he had great possessions" (Mark 10:22).

That sad youth would never make a good confessor. Nothing, however, would prevent his becoming a good psychoanalyst.

Ought psychoanalysis to be abolished? By no means. Even though Jung recognized the superiority of religious confession over the psychic, he did not cease to practice his noble profession of psychoanalyst. Besides, in the state in which the world of today is living, covered with sin, who but the psychoanalyst can peel away, little by little, the crust from the souls that have lost their faith, before they can come to understand the utility of the priest, from whom they flee as the Devil from the Cross?

There are souls whose crust of sin does not yield even to psychoanalysis, nor to confession, nor to shock, souls that prefer adoring themselves to adoring God. For these and other cases, more or less grave, evidently it is good, it is necessary, that besides the confessionals the doors of hospitals and psychotherapeutic clinics be ever open, for without hospitals and psychotherapy what would they do who have broken with Catholicism because of confession?[13] Although psychoanalysis is not exactly the austere confession of the Catholics, in which the patient has to bend the knee, thus breaking his narcissism at the very start of his treatment, but only the confession of those who lie down on the couch with their backs to the doctor—as they might, with even greater advantage, lie immersed in a tub of warm water, in the fetal position, the more comfortably and conveniently to remember their first sins—it is in any case confession and the beginning of humility. And this is quite a good beginning.

It is this road, or anyway the road to self-analysis, that of the examination of conscience, which, being the most perilous and the most precarious (above all when based on the Bible or on the treatises of Doctor Freud), was the one taken by Lincoln.

Why precarious? Why perilous? Isn't it the procedure of writers and artists? Was it not the procedure of the Greeks, and were not the Greeks the models of equilibrium?

The Greek sense of balance is a joke, a rumor invented by the French to link with the Greeks the love which they, the French, have for clarity and balance. In fact there never was any Greek sense of balance in the degree to which it has been proclaimed. No matter how much the Greeks followed the Socratic methods of *gnothi seauton*, no matter how they sought to reconcile pleasure with spirituality, worshiping Apollo and Dionysus at the same time, they never attained perfect equilibrium. Indeed, it was the Greeks who first recounted the dramatic situations of life and were the real inventors and creators of tragedies loaded with incest.

Tragedies loaded with incest? But can there be tragedy in which there is no incest? Or where incest is not implied? Tragedy without incest is drama. Drama with incest is tragedy. No one speaks of the tragedy of Calvary, but of the drama of Calvary. Tragedies are the dramas of Shakespeare, of Aeschylus, Sophocles, Ibsen, O'Neill.

And why is self-analysis dangerous? Because there is always the possibility of the wrong interpretation of one's own emotions. If men of the stature of a Lincoln or a Rousseau, or even of a St. Augustine, are provedly subject to errors of emotional judgment, what cannot happen to the ordinary mortal? Add to this possibility the no lesser one of misreading the books that guide in examinations of conscience—the Bible, Freud's treatises—and the danger is quite visible. The neurosis, aided by free and hasty interpretation of Freud, may end in the most unrestrained existentialism, as, aided by the free interpretation of the Bible, it may end, indeed has often ended, in a new religious sect, like those which from time to time have appeared ever since the thirteenth century to aggravate the spiritual imbalance of the West, and to break the social peace, the political peace, the economic peace which the world enjoyed in the so-called ten-century-long night of the Middle Ages.

Happily, this was not the case with Lincoln. Certainly he experienced terrible crises of negation. Also it is true that, of Quaker origins, no sect of Protestantism ever fitted his way of looking at the world and life; in him, however, never did revolt against the father turn into revolt against God and against his fellow man.

Lincoln differs in this from the average of humanity. He does not transfer his guilt. Wounded in his love-world, he does not wish to split heads wide open, nor does he harden himself with reason, like Robespierre or Karl Marx, nor does he close his heart to love and affectionate contact with men. In relation to his own stepmother he finally comes to have sentiments very close to filial, a thing which the Brazilian Machado de Assis—who has thrown people off the track with his epilepsy, when his real drama is neurosis, and who attains in *Memorial de Aires* his full maturity and full acceptance of life, apparently conquering all complexes —never did achieve.

Lincoln was all affection and loving care for his stepmother, whom he actually defended against the excesses of her own son John, his stepbrother. Moreover, perhaps it was his stepmother, through her patience with and affection for Lincoln, and through the love she devoted to him, who was the only person to have any intuition of the Lincolnian tragedy, a tragedy stamped upon all his portraits, on all his statues, on the whole vast iconography of Lincoln.

Indeed, perhaps that tragedy is the only thing that Lincoln has in common with the American civilization of our time. Otherwise, all is contrast.

While the American civilization of our time is hurried, making years fly by like months, months like weeks, weeks like days, days like minutes, Lincoln is slow and reposeful, as if he had a secret pact with eternity; while American civilization worships work for work's sake, by preference manual and material work, Lincoln works materially with reluctance because his pleasure is meditation and intellectual labor; while American civilization distrusts solitude, Lincoln is a contemplative man; while American civilization is Protestant and all for philanthropy, Lincoln is all for charity; while American civilization is the slave of the economic virtues, Lincoln loses no sleep over money, nor does he grow impatient looking for work, though he walks leagues and leagues in quest of a book; while American civilization places property rights above all, Lincoln, after offering indemnification to the planters of the South for the loss of their slaves, with a stroke of the pen annuls property rights over four million slaves; while American civilization in its books, in its advertisements, speeches, sermons, is prolix because it has not time to be brief, Lincoln is all synthesis in his Gettysburg Address, one of the most beautiful and significant bits of prose in world history; while American civilization is one of moralism without mysticism, Lincoln is a mystic in permanent communication with God; while American civilization takes delight in isolationist practices, Lincoln thinks in terms of universality and of one world; while American civilization reinforces in its American way of life the enormity of "my country, right or wrong," Lincoln as a Congressman votes against war on

Mexico for the purpose of conquering Texas, throwing his political career out of the window because he thinks his country's position deserves condemnation; while the modern American does not believe in the past, Lincoln does not cease to think of Shakespeare and Plutarch in the peace of the starry nights; while American civilization reads the Bible after the fashion of the Gideons, Lincoln reads it profoundly, like the mystics of the Middle Ages; while American civilization has no time for conversation, for *causerie* or soliloquy, Lincoln loves talk, and on his long walks is seen to soliloquize or carry on a dialogue with his phantoms; while Americans believe that material inventions are everything and all the rest almost nothing, Lincoln, in the presence of a lightning rod intended to protect the house of a rich man, remarks that the new invention will not sufficiently protect the rich man against the lightning bolts of his own conscience.

Any doubt or hesitation is impossible: it is in Lincoln and no one else that American civilization must seek inspiration for the reformation of the main outlines of its culture, if it wishes to emerge reinvigorated from the crisis of our time. He it is who holds the secret of the things it lacks.

6

And Brazilian civilization? It has Aleijadinho. Do Brazilians lack sufficient love of work? He has it and to spare; he spends his life working from sun to sun, to the extreme limits of his powers. Do Brazilians lack the associative spirit and the capacity for teamwork? Aleijadinho has both in generous plenty, to the point of making collaborators of his slaves and his pupils. Do Brazilians lack belief in wealth earned by useful work and in a sense of the social function of money? He has it by the handful. Never was money more usefully and painfully earned than Aleijadinho's; and the money he earns he distributes among the poor in the churchyards of the temples in which he works. Do Brazilians lack the spirit of "Brazilianity" and of initiative? He has it beyond all others; he is the first to make use of Brazilian materials in his statues. Do Brazilians lack the faith that moves mountains and builds empires? He has it, profound, unshakable.

Is the idealized image of Brazilians' preference the *bandeirante*, the lucky object of fortune's sudden smiles? Aleijadinho's image is Saint Francis of Assisi. Do Brazilians not work on account of the climate or their liver? Aleijadinho achieved his work while losing pieces of himself, moaning with pain. Do Brazilians not practice religion because they do not believe in confession? Aleijadinho never failed to confess and go to Mass every Sunday and holy day.

What privileged being is this whose gifts and virtues remove him so far from his fellow countrymen's defects and at whose command the devils of covetousness, of the flesh, of gluttony, lust, sloth, and temptation fall back?

No, he was not born to privilege. In this Aleijadinho is not like the men of the Renaissance. For the execution of their works the geniuses of the Renaissance had in their favor fullness of strength and physical health, while Antônio Francisco Lisboa, overcome by syringomyelia, or Lazarus' disease—leprosy, perhaps, or scrofula, for in their retrospective diagnosis of Aleijadinho's malady the doctors are not in agreement— had to rise above the piercing pains that scourged him and triumph over physical deformation and the tremendous limitations imposed on him by the implacable disease, in order to transmit to the world his moving messages of beauty. Still more, while the men of the Renaissance found in their environment and in the epoch in which they lived ideal conditions for the harmonious development of their propensities, in Aleijadinho's case the environment, the epoch, the historical and social circumstances, the institutions, the prejudices of race and class and nationality, almost everything, was adverse to him.

To begin with, he was born a slave, the natural son of a Portuguese carpenter and an African slave woman, the black Isabel, like millions of other mulattoes. It was probably not the fact of his father's having declared him free on the occasion of his baptism, as is recorded in the church of Our Lady of the Conception in Vila Rica on August 29, 1730,[14] that was to immunize him entirely against the memory and influence of the fatal sign under which he had been born. On the contrary, the irritability and social instability that manifest themselves in him later on seem to indicate that the violence of the then ruling passions of freed mulattoes against whites and of the latter against blacks and mulattoes, as intense as the rivalry already growing between Brazilians and Portuguese, left deep marks on Aleijadinho's impulsive temperament. Native to the land, a bastard and a mulatto, his position in the struggles that preceded the *Inconfidência*—that eighteenth-century movement of patriots to free Brazil from the colonial regime—was marked out for him in advance. He was to be a part of that immense legion of the oppressed to whom everything was denied and who could gain a place in the sun only at great cost. But if the conditions of his birth were not propitious, were those of his infancy and adolescence propitious?

Of Aleijadinho's childhood it is known only that he passed nearly the whole of it not with his slave mother but with his father and foster mother, in Vila Rica, where he learned his first letters and possibly his bit of Latin.[15] What other kind of education could the Vila Rica of those days offer him? The Ouro Prêto of today, at that time merely a huddle of wood and adobe buildings and rough chapels tucked away in the deep forest, during the first half of the eighteenth century knew no other occupation than gold-hunting. It had abandoned agriculture, quit cattle-raising, and even dismantled a start at industry to devote itself exclusively to the winning of rapid fortune. And there was no room for other thoughts. Nor did the adventurers who converged in avalanches on the region have time to waste on problems of education, nor was Portugal particularly interested in improving the cultural level of the colony where gold, after two centuries of futile and desperate search, had just been discovered.

And yet, if Aleijadinho lacked adequate secondary instruction, it cannot be said that he lacked opportunities to gain an excellent technical education.[16] The period of greatest splendor in the exploitation of the mines having ended around 1750, in Vila Rica, as in all the towns and villages of the province, the great cycle of urbanization begins. Everywhere, in a prodigious outpouring of colonial art, rise the most beautiful religious monuments. No longer are hunters of precious stones and metals all that flow into Minas Gerais. They include also the master carvers of saints' images from Portugal and Bahia and Recife, architects, sculptors, medalists, engravers, back from or too late for the *bandeiras*, in whose company, through direct apprenticeship as well as through the effect of unconscious psychological saturation, Aleijadinho would serve his most fecund apprenticeship. He who had learned the elements of design in his father's workshop and who as a child had continually climbed about the scaffolding of works under construction, watching, like the urchins of the time, of all times, the movements of the workmen and artisans, and who made little crude carvings of wood, would not be long in assimilating the secrets of specialties that were to lead him to glory.

7

But how far we are still from the creator of the almost speaking figures of the minor prophets in the main church in Congonhas do Campo! In that period Antônio Francisco Lisboa is rather a dilettante than an artist. Knowledgeable in designing the base of a church or of an altar, at carving in stone and wood, sometimes architect, sometimes sculptor, so far no marked and definite vocation can be noted in him—in which fact he is quite mulatto and quite Brazilian. The chief memories his contemporaries have of him in that phase of his health, which probably extends to the age of forty-five or perhaps forty-seven (for no one really knows precisely), are of a mulatto full of life and energy who amuses himself and has a good time.[17] Short, dark-brown, stout, with thick neck and an average, though somewhat sharp-tipped, nose, kinky hair, strong voice, and ready speech, Master Antônio, violent, sensual, and licentious, is fond of gay meals and uproarious parties, and never misses a dance.[18] All he earns is spent on joyous night-long sprees, orgies, and great dinners. Greed, lust, and gluttony. As for the artist, he had not yet appeared. A genius he may have been by that time, but a wasteful, extravagant genius in deep hibernation, smothered by greed, lust, and gluttony.

Suddenly, that irrepressible, exuberent, disorderly, selfish, promiscuous man, who seems to radiate health through every pore, enters upon a physical decline. His fingers and toes swell up, his body arches, his face takes on a leonine look, a progressive deformity takes possession of him, never more to let him go. Nervous leprosy—everything leads to this belief, and probably it was the popular diagnosis—was Aleijadinho's malady.

Here commences one of the most painful and edifying lives of all time. Master Antônio, the pleasure-lover, the Bohemian, the dissolute man, disappears from the scene to yield to "the Cripple"—the Aleija-dinho—the artist, the creator to whose infirm and twisted hands it might be said the disease had instantaneously transmitted the magical and divine power of communicating form, life, intensity and beauty to the immobility of stone.

The disease progresses and never lets up. He suffers horrible pains in his fingers, his joints, his whole body.[19] But the artist refuses to die, and in proportion as his body disintegrates, his spirit grows ever stronger.

Can he still entertain worldly ambitions and hopes of cure? Neither the one nor the other. He now divides among the poor all the money he earns, just like St. Francis of Assisi, the saint of his devotion.[20] Thenceforth he will have but one passion: to create, to work. He works always, he never stops, in his fever of creativity.

He is slowly dying, and still he works.

At or before dawn the slaves who are at once his assistants and his pupils carry him in a closed litter out to the blocks of stone to which he is going to give form and life. And there Aleijadinho remains, now in the recesses of the churches under construction, now in the shade of the vaulted archwork, now in the open air of the atriums, now hidden by a tent that protects him from the gaze of the curious, until there is no more light by which to continue.[21] When he finds himself with chisel and stone-hammer in his fists before the soapstone brought from the mountains of Itacolomí, soft under the sculptor's tools but resistant to the impact of time, he forgets his sickness, his pain, his hatred, and his weakness, and delivers himself over to the joy of creation.

The day's work over, he finds himself restored to the harsh reality of his situation. He passes night after night moaning, without anyone's being able to bring him consolation or relief.

His only solace was reading or meditation on the Bible, of which, if we are to believe the legend, he possessed Gothic and Byzantine copies that inspired him in his work.

Next morning there he goes again on his way to work, in his litter, on horseback, on the backs of his slaves. Wherever he may be, the nearer his end may come, in Vila Rica, in Mariana, in Sabará, in Congonhas do Campo, the rhythm of his life does not change. And the disease goes on corroding him inside and out, without destroying him, forcing him to drag himself along on leather kneepads and to use a contraption that the slaves fastened onto the stumps of his arms—in order that he could still handle his chisel and his hammer.[22]

Does Vila Rica amuse herself, does Vila Rica conspire, does Vila Rica grumble, does Vila Rica bedeck herself and steep herself in the perfume of the flowers from her new gardens, does Vila Rica organize processions and jousts and tourneys? Aleijadinho labors on. Does Vila Rica cry out on the corners, on the streets, in the inns, against the six hundred dragoons posted along the royal highway and beside the mines to prevent gold smuggling? Aleijadinho completes the façade of the Carmo Church. Does the Viscount of Barbacena in 1789 assume the captaincy of Minas Gerais and decree the collection of delinquent taxes? Aleijadinho carves in stone, above the heads of angels, among garlands of flowers of the pulpit of the Church of St. Francis, the panels of Jonah and the whale, of St. John the Evangelist with his symbolical eagle, in such a manner that the whole seems worked not in stone but in bronze. Does Tiradentes, like a flame on the march, preach revolution everywhere? Aleijadinho finishes the frontal medallion on which St. Francis appears receiving the stigmata. Does the Viscount of Barbacena discover the *Inconfidência* plot and order the arrest of the conspirators? Aleijadinho, his heart gripped by pain, begins the figures of the Stations of the Cross for the church of the Good Jesus of Matosinhas, in Congonhas. Is Tiradentes hanged in 1792 in Rio de Janeiro, and his body drawn and quartered, and his head dispatched to Vila Rica to be exposed on the end of a pole in the main square as a warning to others? Aleijadinho continues his work on the figures of the Passion.

8

What did that man still want of the world and of life, to carry on his struggle nearly thirty-five or forty years? Of the world, clearly he wanted nothing more, but he indubitably had an appointment with posterity and could not stop. From the world he wanted only one thing now: not to be seen, not to be watched. Aleijadinho's pact was not with the present; it was with the future. To the future, and to the future only, did he seem to direct the message of his work and the still more important message of his life and his example.

It is a singular fact that very little is known of Aleijadinho's life, but of the little that is known from bringing together and comparing the statements of his last contemporaries with the documents of the churches and the receipts and subcontracts for the works executed by him, there is no episode that is not the equivalent of a great pedagogical message. The difficulty in this case is not in discovering episodes that lend themselves to edifying interpretations of his life. The difficulty is to discover in his life anything that is not pregnant with a lesson or message for Brazilians. Everything in him is a lesson, everything in him is a message. And messages fully congruent with the master outlines of Brazilian culture.

Indeed, nothing positive is yet known about Aleijadinho's life, and yet he, with his use of soapstone instead of marble in his statues and bas-reliefs, in a complete harmony with Brazilian reality, is giving us a lesson in initiative and technique. No marble in Vila Rica? For anyone else that fact would have sufficed to paralyze a vocation. With him it was different. In his wanderings about the region he was to discover in the Itacolomí range an abundance of a stone from which he had already made basins. Immediately he perceived that here was a material to experiment with in sculpture. The stone of Itacolomí—wonder of wonders! —at once soft and resistant, with its rose tones, was the best he could wish for, lacking marble, for his plans. Right! Everything was solved. And the resistance factor? Well, if basins of soapstone withstood the winds and rains in the hands of the *bandeirantes*, why should not soapstone statues do likewise?

There we have, therefore, Aleijadinho's first lesson, a lesson in initiative and technique. And how Brazilians need lessons like that in order to master their fear of the land! It is not in the quest for quick riches and with merely humanistic culture, or by transplanting to Brazil the scientific knowledge of Europe without adapting it to local reality—as in the golden age of rubber the Customs building, prefabricated in England, was transplanted to Manaus—or by transplanting to the Amazon the methods of planting rubber trees effective in Ceylon, or by importing tractors to operate on granite slopes, or by planting turnips in land more suitable for oaks, or by working with the sun straight overhead instead of taking advantage of the early morning or sunset hours, or by nourishing themselves on *feijoada* in the deep tropics, that Brazilians are going to solve the problems of cold and heat, of production and distribution. For that they need a little more than simple humanistic, ornamental culture. They need technical knowledge, they need more respect for science and scientists, above all when they are of the type of Pascal, who never entered his workroom without offering up this prayer: "Forgive me, Father, if, a mere earthworm, I dare lift the edge of the veil that covers Thy mysteries!"

Another lesson from Aleijadinho is teamwork. It is a lesson that will not escape those who, after the impact of the overall impression, examine more closely the statues of the minor prophets of Congonhas. The fact is that not all have the same finish. Those of the prophets Isaiah, Hosea, and Daniel—where Aleijadinho's art reaches its maximum splendor— were evidently executed by the sculptor, while in all the rest, in which can be seen a lack of finish and the indecisive hand of apprentices, only the plan and general guidance can be his own, the greater part being owed to the collaboration of his pupils.

If Aleijadinho had not done so, had he not taught the trade to his slaves and disciples, instilling into them the constructive habit of working together, could he, an invalid, have bequeathed to posterity the marvelous group at Congonhas do Campo?

But it was not in the field of technique and through his work that Aleijadinho left us his best examples. The greatest, the definitive ones, come from his own life. In that, no one surpasses him, no one equals him, in the history of Brazil.

To begin with, a second lesson of initiative and technique and adaptation to reality, as though he understood that this was the lesson Brazilians most needed.

With the disease his toes drop off; at times the pain is such that he himself, in desperation, lops them off. Later comes the fingers' turn. Does he give up? Does he yield himself up to public charity? He is not capable of it. True precursor of the international movement for the recovery and rehabilitation of cripples into social activity, and precursor also of prosthetic devices, he himself invents the instruments that complement his crippled hands, and the kneepads that make it possible for him to move from one place to another. What a lesson in energy for the country where the least indisposition serves as pretext to avoid work and where through lack of initiative thousands of handicapped men are leading a vegetative, embittered life, when through the processes of rehabilitation and readaptation of the handicapped they could be turned into elements useful to the family and society!

After this magnificent lesson in technique and initiative come his admirable lessons against three great fallacies: the fallacy of the ethnic inferiority of the mulatto and of the impossibility of ransoming him for maturity; the fallacy of virility associated with Don Juanism; the fallacy that only ambition for money and only self-interest are capable of realizing progress and building the greatness of civilizations.

The fallacy of virility associated with libertinism and with Bohemia! On this point, as for that matter on all the others, to prove that it is not in libertinism, in indiscriminate chasing of the female, that man gives the best of himself, but rather in the periods of putting forth effort, the periods of chastity and decency, when talent and character live in harmony, Aleijadinho does not preach with words—he preaches by his example. As long as he was a libertine, as long as he was promiscuous, except for the natural children that he (in all probability) went about distributing among the various places through which he passed—sure candidates for revolt against the father and for future neuroses like his own—he would have left no important signs of his passage upon earth. Afterwards, and only after the visitation of God's grace in the shape of a deforming disease—psychoanalysts would give to *grace* the name of *shock* —had freed him from obsession with sex and Don Juanism, was he to produce his great work. While a dandified, exhibitionistic mulatto, he would have no access to the future. But when he seeks to subdue himself, when he tries to hide from everything and everybody, when he slips stealthily through the streets in the shadow of dusk, when he wants not to be noticed, when he covers himself with a cloak and broad-brimmed hat in order not to be seen and recognized by anyone, that is when he leaves everywhere the true marks of his passing.

As far as the winning of rapid wealth is concerned, the lesson is analogous. When a slave to greed, a bondsman to the flesh and to sin, avid for money in order to buy with it the pleasures of the table in the sumptuous banquets he gave, very little or nothing does he contribute to elevating the environment in which he lives and the civilization to which he belongs; but when he sees in money, rather than the instrument of sin, the symbol of labor and the instrument of social destiny, his works attain full maturity.

Did the Aleijadinho of the second phase scorn the economic virtues? No, he did not. Few can have taken so seriously the question of the way to earn money and the use to make of it. An incident that happened to him well illustrates his position in the matter. His contemporaries relate that one day he was robbed of the gold he had received in payment for his work. His wrath knew no bounds. He vociferated in rage, he who had become meek and humble of heart. At first sight one does not well understand the reason for such wrath. But later everything becomes clear.

What enraged him was not the harm done to him, to Aleijadinho, but the diversion of the money he had reserved for the poor into the hands of thieves and robbers, of whom there was an abundance in Minas Gerais. Could this anger be canonically sinful? No theologian would answer in the affirmative.

In matters of money, as in other matters, Aleijadinho kept for himself only what he strictly needed, distributing the rest among the poor, for there was an abundance of them, too, in Vila Rica as throughout the province—when the hunters of rapid fortune, once the gold of the sluices was exhausted, were returning to the littoral.

9

Another lesson from Aleijadinho, to cap and confirm the foregoing ones: that of choice of the image idealized, of the symbol to imitate. In the first phase of his life the symbol he pursues is, from all indications, the symbol of the *bandeirante* and of Malasarte. The cult of Malasarte is present in the resentful man who revenges himself for the offense of the Minas governor-general's secretary by making him ridiculous in a caricature of St. George that Aleijadinho prepared for the Corpus Christi procession. In this example the freedman's resentment was more powerful than his artistic vocation or the respect due to the saint. The cult of the *bandeirante* lies in his avidity for money and, as soon as it is obtained, in the worship of the good life.

In the second phase of his life Aleijadinho's symbol is St. Francis of Assisi. It is no longer by imitating the *bandeirante* or Malasarte that he attempts to overcome his limitations and afflictions. Now that his afflictions and limitations have redoubled with his disease, he seeks to conquer them in his imitation of the humblest of mortals. And—paradoxical fact —it is only through that imitation that he, an immature man, attains to full maturity. At first he created caricature—monsters, deformed things, so reminiscent of the impressionists of today. Now he makes Daniel, and Isaiah. It is no longer the baroque of St. George, nor the rococo of the Atlantids; now he is the classicist of the prophets of the Santuário.

The prophets of Congonhas! How those statues breathe health! No one would believe them the work of a mutilated artist. Majestic, serene, tranquil, an air of immortality seems to incorporate them into the landscape which surrounds them.

No, there is no doubt that the creator of those marvels was a Renaissance man born out of time, lost in the eighteenth century. More than that, he was a genius touched with a halo of saintliness.

What rule can this new and edifying lesson from Aleijadinho contain? It contains a rule two thousand years old, and this rule is that the road to full maturity is the quest and imitation of saintliness.

How so? Is, then, normality a synonym of sanctity? And what of Carlyle's heroes, and the persons who surround us, so good, so pleasant, so cordial? The fact is, they are not normal. At best they are subnormal. Only the saint is normal.

What is "normal"? Psychiatrists and psychoanalysts struggle to define it. And yet they have no doubt at all about what is abnormal. Abnormal, immature, according to them, are the maladjusted, the inhibited, the egoist, the miser, he who gives nothing of himself and only receives. That is, the less one gives of oneself to the society in which he lives, and the more one demands of it—hospitals, clinics, police, insurance— through mental weakness, or through madness or inhibition or avarice, that is to be immature and abnormal.

Now, if that is the immature, abnormal man, normality and maturity must be, can only be, the contrary. That is to say, the man who gives most of himself and demands least of the society in which he lives, that man who with the motto, "Every man according to his possibilities, to each according to his needs," gives most of himself and receives least for himself—that man is the normal, that is the mature man. But that one is

not necessarily the tycoon or the commissar; that one is the saint, there
is no getting away from it. And when this saint's name is St. Francis of
Assisi, then it is full maturity, full normality, and not the subnormality
that psychoanalysis keeps confusing with maturity.

10

Returning, however, to the Americans who make pilgrimages to Washington, New Salem, Springfield, and Gettysburg, and the Brazilians who
journey to Ouro Prêto, São Joao d'El-Rei, Mariana, Sabará, and Congonhas do Campo, have they, perchance, a sense of apprenticeship to and
identification with the soul of Lincoln and the soul of Aleijadinho,
as if they had a greater and greater sense of quest and recognition of
saintliness in the kind of heroism achieved by each of the two, and
were impregnated with the subconscious conviction that outside of
sanctity there is no genuine greatness?

Judging by the present state of the world, the most probable thing is
that they do not yet have it, because, on the day they do and the two
great lessons have been nationally assimilated, we Americans and Brazilians—and with us the Europeans, Spanish Americans, Asiatics, and
Africans—with the main outlines of our respective cultures corrected,
shall all be once again believing, if not in the possibility of the Kingdom
of God on the face of the earth, at least in that millennial dream that
Prometheus explained to Ahasuerus in Machado de Assis' story: "The
times will be set aright. Evil will come to an end; the winds will no
more scatter either the germs of death or the clamor of the oppressed, but
only the song of perennial love and the blessing of universal justice."[23]

Bibliography

List of works mentioned in footnotes, with details of publication.

Abreu, J. Capistrano de. *Capítulos de História Colonial.* Rio de Janeiro: Sociedade Capistrano de Abreu, 1928.

——. *Caminhos Antigos e Povoamento do Brasil.* Rio de Janeiro: Sociedade Capistrano de Abreu, 1930.

——. *O Descobrimento do Brasil.* Rio de Janeiro: Sociedade Capistrano de Abreu, 1929.

Adair, E. R. "Economics," in F. J. C. Hearnshaw (ed.), *Mediaeval Contributions to Modern Civilization.* New York: Barnes & Noble, 1949.

Adams, Henry. *The Education of Henry Adams.* New York: Modern Library, 1931.

Adams, James Truslow. *The Epic of America.* Boston: Little, Brown and Company, 1947.

Alcântara Machado, José de. *Vida e Morte do Bandeirante.* São Paulo: Livraria Martins Editôra, 1943.

Antonil. *Cultura e Opulência do Brasil.* São Paulo: Cia. Edit. Nacional, 1933.

Aquinas, Saint Thomas. *Philosophical Texts.* London: Oxford University Press, 1951.

Aranha, Graça. *Canaã.* Rio de Janeiro: Garnier, n.d.

Azevedo, J. Lúcio de. *Épocas de Portugal Econômico.* Lisbon: Livraria Clássica Editôra, 1947.

Bagú, Sergio. *Economía de la sociedad colonial.* Buenos Aires: Libr. El Ateneo Editorial, 1949.

Barroso, Gustavo. *Judaísmo, Maçonaria e Comunismo.* Rio de Janiero: Civilização Brasileira, 1937.

——. *Brasil, Colônia de Banqueiro.* Rio de Janeiro: Civilização Brasileira, 1937.

Basso, Hamilton. *Mainstream.* New York: Reynal & Hitchcock, 1943.

Belloc, Hilaire. *How the Reformation Happened.* London: Jonathan Cape, 1950.

Bowen, Catherine Drinker. *John Adams and the American Revolution.* Boston: Little, Brown and Company, 1950.

Brandão, Ambrósio Fernandes. *Diálogos das Grandezas do Brasil.* Rio de Janeiro: Dois Mundos Ltda., n.d.

Brannon, Peter A. "Southern Emigration to Brazil," *Alabama Historical Quarterly,* Vol. I (1930), Nos. 2-4.

Buarque de Holanda, Sérgio. Prefácio às *Memórias de um Colono no Brasil*, of Thomas Devatz. São Paulo: Livraria Martins, Editôra, 1941.

Burnham, James. *The Managerial Revolution*. New York: The John Day Co., 1941.

Calvin, John. *Calvin's Calvinism*. Translated by Henry Col. Grand Rapids, Mich.: W. B. Eerdans Publishing Co., 1950.

Camoens, Luis de. *The Lusiads*. Translated by Leonard Bacon. New York: The Hispanic Society of America, 1950.

Castro, Josué de. *La alimentación en los trópicos*. México: Fondo de Cultura Económica, 1946. (Spanish translation.)

Cortesão, Jaime. *A Carta de Pero Vaz de Caminha*. Rio de Janeiro: Ed. Livros de Portugal, 1943.

Cox, Earnest Sevier. *Teutonic Unity*. Richmond, Va.: privately printed, 1951.

Crèvecoeur, Hector St. John. "Letters from an American Farmer, 1782," in Commager, Henry Steele; and Nevins, Allan (eds.), *The Heritage of America*. Boston: Little, Brown and Company, 1951.

Croce, Benedetto. *Teoría e historia de la historiografía*. Buenos Aires: Eds. Imán, n.d. (Spanish translation.)

Cunha, Euclides da. *À Margem da História*. Pôrto: Livr. Lello & Irmão, 1946.

Douglas, Marjorie Stoneman. *The Everglades: River of Grass*. (Rivers of America.) New York: Rinehart, 1947.

Dunn, Ballard. *Brazil, the Home for Southerners*. New York: G. B. Richardson, 1866.

Eça de Queiroz. *Correspondência*. Pôrto: Livr. Lello & Irmão, 1926.

———. *A Ilustre Casa de Ramires*. Pôrto: Livr. Lello & Irmão, n.d.

Edmonds, James E. "They've Gone—Back Home!" *The Saturday Evening Post* (January 4, 1941).

Ellis Júnior, Alfredo. *Raça de Gigantes*. São Paulo: Edit. Ellis—Novíssima Editôra, 1926.

Fanfani, A. *Cattolicisimo e Protestantismo nella Formazione Storica del Capitalismo*. Milano: 1934.

Fenn, William Wallace. "The Revolt Against the Standing Order," in *Religious History of New England*. Cambridge, Mass.: Harvard University Press, 1917.

Ferreira Brêtas, Rodrigo José, "Traços Biográficos Relativos ao Finado Antônio Francisco Lisboa," in *Antônio Francisco Lisboa—O Aleijadinho*. Rio de Janeiro: Publiçacões da Diretoria de Patrimonio Historico e Artístico Nacional [in press].

Forrestal, James. *The Forrestal Diaries*, Ed. by Walter Millis with the collaboration of E. S. Duffield. New York: The Viking Press, 1951.

Franklin, Benjamin. *Autobiography.* New York: Random House, 1944.

Freyre, Gilberto. *Casa-Grande e Senzala.* Rio de Janeiro: Schmidt *Editor,* 1936. (In English translation: *The Masters and the Slaves.* Translated by Samuel Putnam. New York: A. A. Knopf, 1946.)

——. *Brazil, an Interpretation.* New York: Knopf, 1951.

Gobineau, Comte de. *Essai sur l'Inégalité des Races Humaines.* Paris: Firmin-Didot, Imprimeurs-Editeurs, 1854.

Gómez Robledo, Antonio. *La filosofía en Brasil.* México: Imprenta Universitaria, 1946.

Gorer, Geoffrey. *The American People.* New York: W. W. Norton, 1952.

Griffin, Charles C. "Unidad y variedad en la historia americana," in *Ensayos sobre la historia del Nuevo Mundo.* México: Instituto Panamericano de Geografía e História, 1951.

Hart, Carlos Fredericko von. "Como escrever a história do Brasil," *Revista de Imigração e Colonização, ano.* IV (June, 1943, Rio de Janeiro).

Herndon, W. H. *Herndon's Life of Lincoln.* Cleveland: World Publishing Co., 1949.

Hill, Lawrence F. "Confederate Exiles to Brazil," *Hispanic American Historical Review,* VII (1927).

Hobson, J. A. *God and Mammon.* London: Watts, 1931.

Horney, Karen. *The Neurotic Personality of Our Time.* New York: W. W. Norton, 1937.

——. *New Ways in Psychoanalysis.* New York: W. W. Norton, 1939.

——. *Self-Analysis.* New York: W. W. Norton, 1942.

Huxley, Julian S., and Haddon, A. C. *Los problemas raciales.* Buenos Aires: Edit. Sudamericana, 1951. (Spanish translation. The translator of *Bandierantes* has been unable to identify the English original in order to quote directly from it.)

Jones, M. "The Southern Confederacy in South America," *United Daughters of the Confederacy Magazine,* 1948.

Jung, C. G. *Modern Man in Search of a Soul.* London: Routledge and Kegan Paul, 1949.

Keyserling, Herman, Count. *South American Meditations.* London: Jonathan Cape, 1932.

Klineberg, Otto. *Raza y psicología.* Paris: UNESCO, 1952.

Krogman, Wilton M. "The Races of Mankind," in *The New Information Please Almanac, 1949.* Ed. by John Kieran. New York: Farrar, Straus and Company, 1949.

Kropff, Oscar von. "Imigração Norte-Americana para o Brasil," *Revista de Imigração e Colonização,* IV (1943, Rio de Janeiro).

Laski, Harold. *El liberalismo europeo.* México: Fondo de Cultura Económica, 1953.

————. *The American Presidency, an Interpretation.* New York: Harper & Brothers, 1940.

Leite, Serafim, S.J. *Novas Cartas Jesuíticas (de Nóbrega a Vieira).* São Paulo: Cia. Editôra Nacional, 1940.

Liebman, Joshua. *Peace of Mind.* New York: Simon & Schuster, 1946.

Lincoln, Abraham. *The Life and Writings of Abraham Lincoln.* Ed. by Philip van Doren Stern. New York: Modern Library, 1940.

The Lincoln Reader. Ed., with an introduction, by Paul M. Angle. New Brunswick, N.J.: Rutgers University Press, 1947.

Macedo Soares, José Carlos de. *Fronteiras do Brasil no Regime Colonial.* Rio de Janeiro: Livr. José Olympio, 1939.

Machado de Assis. *Dom Casmurro.* Rio de Janeiro: Garnier, n.d.

————. *Várias Histórias.* Rio de Janeiro: W. M. Jackson Inc., 1952.

Magalhães, Basílio de. *Expansão Geográfica do Brasil Colonial.* São Paulo, Cia. Ediôra Nacional, 1935.

Mello, Franco, Afonso Arinos de. *O Índio Brasileiro e a Revolução Francesa.* Rio de Janeiro: Livr. José Olympio, 1937.

Mesquita Filho, Júlio de. *Problemas Sul-Americanas.* São Paulo: Livraria Martins Editôra, 1946.

Monbeig, Pierre. *Pionniers et Planteurs de São Paulo.* Paris: Librairie Armand Colin, 1952.

Monjas, Padre Manuel. *La confesión.* Madrid: Eds. Fax, 1948.

Murtinho, Joaquim. *Relatório do Ministério da Indústria.* Rio de Janeiro: 1897.

Myrdal, Gunnar. *An American Dilemma: The Negro Problem and Modern Democracy.* New York: Harper and Brothers, 1944.

Nabuco, Joaquim. *Minha Formação.* Rio de Janeiro: Garnier, 1900.

Nash, Roy. *The Conquest of Brazil.* New York: Harcourt, Brace, 1926.

Newman, Louis Israel. *Jewish Influence on Christian Reform Movements.* New York: Columbia University Press, 1925.

Nóbrega, Padre Manuel. *Cartas do Brasil, 1549-1560.* Rio de Janeiro: Publicações da Academia Brasileira, 1931.

Northrop, F. S. C. *The Meeting of East and West.* New York: The Macmillan Co., 1946.

Oliveira Viana, J. F. *Populações Meridionais do Brasil.* São Paulo: Cia. Editôra Nacional, 1933.

Overstreet, A. H. *The Mature Mind.* New York: W. W. Norton, 1949.

Paine, Thomas. *The Life and Works of Thomas Paine.* New Rochelle, N.Y.: 1925. Vol. VI, pp. 20-21.

Parrington, Vernon L. *Main Currents in American Thought.* Vol. I. New York: Harcourt, Brace, 1930.

Pirenne, Henri. *Historia económica y social de la Edad Media.* México: Fondo de Cultura Económica, 1952. (Spanish translation.)

Pires do Rio, J. *O Combustível na Economia Universal*. Rio de Janeiro: Livr. José Olympio, 1942.

Prado Júnior, Caio. *Evolução Política do Brasil*. São Paulo: Editôra Brasiliense, Ltda., 1947.

Prado, Paulo. *Retrato do Brasil*. São Paulo: Editôra Brasiliense, Ltda., 1944.

Queiroz, *see* Eça de Queiroz.

Quental, Antero de. "Causas da Decadência dos Povos Peninsulares nos Últimos Três Séculos," in *Prosas Escolhidas*. Rio de Janeiro: Edições Livros de Portugal, 1942.

Randall, Clarence B. *A Creed for Free Enterprise*. Boston: Little, Brown and Co., 1952.

Ribeiro, João. *Crítica*. Vols. I & IX. Organização, prefácio e notas de Múcio Leão. Rio de Janeiro: Academia Brasileira de Letras, 1952.

————. *História do Brasil*. Rio de Janeiro: Livr. Francisco Alves, 1935.

Ricardo, Cassiano. *Marcha para Oeste*. 2 vols. Rio de Janeiro: Livr. José Olympio, 1940.

Rios, José Artur. "A Imigração de Confederados Norte-Americanos no Brasil," *Revista de Imigração e Colonização* (September, 1948, and December-January, 1949).

Robertson, H. M. *Aspects of the Rise of Economic Individualism*. New York, Augustus M. Kelley, 1933.

Rodrigues, José Honório. *Notícia de Vária História*. Rio de Janeiro: Livr. São José, 1951.

————. *Teoria da História do Brasil*. São Paulo, Instituto Progresso Editorial, S.A., 1949.

Rodrigues, Nina. *Os Africanos no Brasil*. São Paulo: Cia. Editôra Nacional, 1935.

Roosevelt, F. D. *My Friends: Twenty-eight History-Making Speeches*. Ed. by E. H. Kavinsky and Julian Park. Buffalo: Foster & Stewart Publishing Corp., 1945.

Salvador, Frei Vicente do. *História do Brasil*. Rev. By Capistrano de Abreu and Rudolfo Garcia. São Paulo: Weiszflog Irmãos, 1918.

Sandburg, Carl, *Abraham Lincoln*. Vol. I: *The Prairie Years*. New York: Harcourt, Brace, 1926.

Schlesinger, Arthur M. *The American as Reformer*. Cambridge, Mass.: Harvard University Press, 1951.

Schupp, Padre Ambrósio, S.J. *Os Muckers*. Translated into Portuguese by Alfredo Clemente Pinto. Pôrto Alegre: Selbach & Mayer, n.d.

Sée, Henri, *Origen y evolución del capitalismo moderno*. México: Fondo de Cultura Económica, 1952. (Spanish translation.)

Semple, Ellen Churchill. *Influences of Geographic Environment*. New York: Henry Holland Company, 1947.

Sheen, Fulton J. *Peace of Soul*. Garden City, N. Y.; Country Life Press, 1948.

Siegfried, André. *L'Âme des Peuples*. Paris: Hachette, 1950.

Simonsen, Roberto, *História Econômica do Brasil*. Vol. I. São Paulo: Cia. Editôra Nacional, 1937.

Soares de Sousa, Gabriel, *Tratado Descritivo do Brasil em 1587*. Comentários de Adolfo Varnhagen. São Paulo: Cia. Editôra Nacional, 1938.

Sombart, Werner. *The Jews and Modern Capitalism*. Translated from the German. Glencoe, Ill.: The Free Press, 1951.

Sorokin, Pitirin. *The Crisis of Our Age*. New York: E. P. Dutton, 1941.

Strecker, Edward A. *Their Mothers' Sons*. Philadelphia: J. B. Lippincott Co., 1951.

Taunay, Afonso d'Escragnolle. *História Geral das Bandeiras Paulistas*. Vol. I. São Paulo: Tipografia Ideal, 1924-1936.

Tavares Bastos, A. C. *Cartas do Solitário*. São Paulo: Cia. Editôra Nacional, 1938.

Tawney, R. H. *Religion and the Rise of Capitalism*. New York: Harcourt, Brace, 1937.

Tillich, Paul. *The Protestant Era*. Translated by James Luther Adams. Chicago: University of Chicago Press, 1951.

Tocqueville, Alexis de. *De la Démocratie en Amérique*. Paris: Librairie des Médicis, 1951.

Tôrres, Alberto. *O Problem Nacional Brasileiro*. São Paulo: Cia. Editôra Nacional, 1938.

Tôrres, João Camilo de Oliveira. *O Positivismo no Brasil*. Rio de Janeiro: Edição Vozes de Petrópolis, Ltda., 1943.

Trevelyan, G. M. *An Autobiography and Other Essays*. London: Longmans, 1949.

Troeltsch, Ernst. *The Social Teaching of the Christian Churches*. London: Allen & Unwin, 1949.

Tucker, H. D. "Confederates in Brazil," *United Daughters of the Confederacy Magazine* (July, 1951).

Unamuno, Miguel de. *Vida de don Quijote y Sancho*. Buenos Aires: Espasa-Calpe Argentina, S.A., 1948. (The English translation omits the introductory section pertinent to this book.)

Vasconcellos, Simão de. *Vida do Venerável Padre José de Anchieta*. Rio de Janeiro: Imprensa Nacional, 1943.

Vega, Lope de. *El Nuevo Mundo de Cristóbal Colón*, in *Tesoro del teatro español* de Don Eugenio de Ochoa. Paris: Livr. Europea de Bandry, 1838.

Veríssimo, Érico, *A Volta do Gato Prêto*. Pôrto Alegre: Livr. do Globo, 1946.

Viana—*see* Oliveira Viana, J. F.

Vieira, Antônio. *Cartas* (in Basílio de Magalhães, *q.v. supra*).

Vogt, William. *Road to Survival.* New York: William Sloane Associates, 1948.

Weaver, Blanche H. C. "Confederate Immigrants and Evangelical Churches in Brazil," *Journal of Southern History*, Vol. 18, No. 4 (November, 1952).

Weber, Max. *The Protestant Ethic and the Spirit of Capitalism.* New York: Scribner, 1950.

Whitman, Walt. *The Poetry and Prose of Walt Whitman.* New York: Simon & Schuster, 1944.

Williams, Eric. *Capitalism and Slavery.* Chapel Hill, N. C.: University of North Carolina Press, 1944.

Notes

Chapter I Race and Geography

[1] Comte de Gobineau, *Essai sur l'Inégalité des Races Humaines;* H. S. Chamberlain, *Foundations of the Nineteenth Century.*

[2] A. de Tocqueville, *De la Démocratie en Amérique.*

[3] J. Pires do Rio, *O Combustível na Economia Universal,* p. 33.

[4] Oliviera Viana, *Populações Meridionais do Brasil,* pp. 146-150.

[5] No page references are offered, for reasons explained below. [Translator's note.]

[6] On May 17, 1954, in a historic decision, the Supreme Court of the United States proscribed racial segregation in all public schools, putting an end once and for all to the "separate but equal" doctrine.

[7] J. Capistrano de Abreu, *Caminhos Antigos e Povoamento do Brasil,* p. 64.

[8] Simão de Vasconcelos, *Vida do Venerável P. José de Anchieta,* I, 67.

[9] Earnest Sevier Cox, *Teutonic Unity.*

[10] Jaime Cortesão, *A Carta de Pero Vaz de Caminha,* p. 240.

[11] *Ibid.,* p. 201.

[12] *Ibid.,* p. 204.

[13] *Ibid.,* p. 212.

[14] *Ibid.,* p. 210.

[15] The *feijoada* is a dish composed of a variety of black bean, cooked with jerked beef when meat is available (the poor never get much of it) and with various condiments—a staple diet among the poorer Brazilians. There is a more elaborate *feijoada,* with extra meats, etc. added, but this is enjoyed only by families in better economic conditions. *Cachaça* is a kind of rum. [Translator's note.]

[16] William Vogt, *Road to Survival,* pp. 152 *et seq.*

[17] Huxley and Haddon, *Los problemas raciales,* pp. 246-247. [The Spanish translation is the one cited and here retranslated. Translator's note.]

[18] *Ibid.,* pp. 38-39.

[19] Ballard Dunn, *Brazil, the Home for Southerners,* New York, G. B. Richardson, 1866; Lawrence F. Hill, "Confederate Exiles to Brazil," *Hispanic American Historical Review,* VII (1927), 192-210; Peter A. Brannon, "Southern Emigration to Brazil," *Alabama Historical Quarterly,* Vol. I (1930), No. 2, 74-95, No. 3, 280-305, and No. 4, 467-488; M. Jones, "The Southern Confederacy in South America," *U. D. C. Magazine,* 1948, pp. 28-32; H. D. Tucker, "Confederates in Brazil," *U. D. C. Magazine,* July, 1951, pp. 10-22; Blanche H. C. Weaver, "Confederate Immigrants and Evangelical Churches in Brazil," *Journal of Southern History,* Vol. XVIII, No. 4 (November, 1952), 446-468.

[20] James E. Edmonds, "They've Gone—Back Home!" *Saturday Evening Post,* January 4, 1941, pp. 30-46.

[21] *Ibid.,* p. 33.

[22] Sérgio Buarque de Holanda, preface to the *Memórias de um Colono no Brasil,* by Thomas Devatz (Livraria Martins, São Paulo, 1941), p. 25.

[23] In *Revista de Imigração e Colonização,* X (1949), 19.

[24] *Ibid.,* p. 20.

[25] Some people attribute to the founders of Vila Americana the introduction of the sewing machine into Brazil.

[26] José Artur Rios, "A Imigração de Confederados Norte-Americanos no Brasil," p. 17.

[27] Euclides da Cunha, *À Margem da História,* pp. 108-109.

[28] Ratzel's anthropogeography is set forth in English in Ellen Churchill Semple's book *Influences of Geographic Environment,* New York, 1911 (New edition, 1947).

[29] Afonso d'E. Taunay, *História Geral das Bandeiras Paulistas,* I, 56.

[30] W. M. Krogman, "The Races of Mankind," in *The New Information Please Almanac, 1949*, p. 740.

[31] Huxley and Haddon, *op. cit.*, p. 29.

[32] Otto Klineberg, *Raza y psicología* (UNESCO, Paris, 1952), p. 41.

Chapter II Ethics and Economics

[1] José Honório Rodrigues, *Teoria da História do Brasil*, p. 42.

[2] See J. Pires do Rio, *O Combustível na Economia Universal*.

[3] Ernst Troeltsch, *The Social Teaching of the Christian Churches*, II, 1002.

[4] Max Weber, *The Protestant Ethic and the Spirit of Capitalism*.

[5] R. H. Tawney, *Religion and the Rise of Capitalism*, p. 32.

[6] In Tawney, *loc. cit.*

[7] E. R. Adair, "Economics," in *Mediaeval Contributions to Modern Civilization*, p. 245.

[8] See Pitirim A. Sorokin, *The Crisis of Our Age*.

[9] *Ibid.*, pp. 18 *et seq.*

[10] Tawney, *op. cit.*, p. 32.

[11] *Ibid.*, pp. 32 *et seq.*

[12] *Ibid.*, p. 35.

[13] *Ibid.*, p. 36.

[14] In Adair, *op. cit.*, pp. 246-247.

[15] St. Thomas Aquinas, *Philosophical Texts*, p. 347.

[16] *Ibid.*

[17] Innocent IV, "De Usuris," in Tawney, *op. cit.*, p. 44.

[18] On this theme see José Honório Rodrigues, *op. cit.*, p. 36.

[19] One of the few exceptions is Gobineau himself. But, as Chamberlain says, Gobineau was not really a Catholic: he was a pagan.

[20] Despite the fact that this thesis seems to us irrefutable, there is no lack of authors, both Protestant and Catholic, who contest it. For greater clarification of this debate, fundamental nowadays, see (besides the works of Weber, Tawney, and Troeltsch already mentioned) H. M. Robertson, *Aspects of the Rise of Economic Individualism* (New York, 1933); A. Fanfani, *Cattolicismo e Protestantismo nella Formazione Storica del Capitalismo* (Milano, 1934); José Honório Rodrigues, *Notícia de Vária História* (Rio, 1951); J. A. Hobson, *God and Mammon* (London, 1931); Henri Sée, *Origen y evolución del capitalismo moderno* (México, 1952); Henri Pirenne, *Historia económica y social de la Edad Media* (México, 1952).

[21] Yes, it is true that Spaniards and Portuguese enslaved and exploited the Indians. But, as James Truslow Adams observes, "If the white man robbed the Indians of their independence and wealth, they also felt that they had a gift of priceless value to bestow in return—the gift of the Christian religion, as they understood it, and of eternal salvation. With all their cruelty, it never occurred to the Spaniards but that the Indian was a human soul to be saved, as well as exploited. In the new empire that Cortés built up, the Indian might be socially and economically subordinate, but he had his rights as an integral part of the common society, and Spanish civilization, as transplanted to Mexico, was a civilization in which the Indian was included and in which he survived, mixing his blood in marriage with the whites. That fact was of prime importance for the savage and the white man." (*The Epic of America*, p. 19.)

[22] See Tawney, *op. cit.*, p. 115 (Chapter II, iii: "Calvin").

[23] John Calvin, "The Eternal Predestination of God," in *Calvin's Calvinism*, p. 31.

[24] Paul Tillich, *The Protestant Era*, p. 231.

[25] Tillich, *op. cit.*, p. xxv.

[26] See Gilberto Freyre, *Casa-Grande e Senzala* (*The Masters and the Slaves* in English translation, University of Chicago Press); and also his *Brazil, an Interpretation*, p. 204.

[27] See Afonso Arinos de Mello Franco, *O Indio Brasileiro e a Revolução Francesca* —"As Origens Brasileiras da Teoria da Bondade Natural."

[28] Capistrano de Abreu, *Capítulos de História Colonial, 1500-1800,* 4a. ed., revista, anotada e prefaciada por José Honório Rodrigues (Sociedade Capistrano de Abreu, Livraria Briguet, Rio de Janeiro, 1954).

[29] In her book *The Everglades: River of Grass,* Mrs. Douglas endorses the hypothesis that John Smith may have got his inspiration from the story of Juan Ortiz, as the latter told it to the Knight of Elvas, who published it in Portugal in 1557. This story, translated into English, might have been adopted by Smith in his second version of A *True Relation of the History of Virginia.* We believe, however, that the hypothesis of John Smith's having been inspired by the Caramurú Paraguassú episode ought not to be excluded.

[30] B. Franklin, *Autobiography,* p. 137. [The passage cited resulted from Franklin's experience at Carlisle, where the Indians were given rum after concluding a treaty. Their self-abandonment to intoxication and excess led their chief orator to say that if the Great Spirit made all things for a purpose, then rum was created for the Indians to get drunk. The full comment, with the irony so characteristic of Franklin is: "And indeed if it be the design of Providence to extirpate these savages, in order to make room for the cultivators of the earth, it seems not impossible that rum may be the appointed means." Translator's note.]

[31] See Nina Rodrigues, *Os Africanos no Brasil.*

[32] Luis de Camoens, *The Lusiads* (The Hispanic Society of America, New York, 1950), IV, 102. Translated by Leonard Bacon. By permission of the Hispanic Society of America.

[33] "In this land," declares Father Manuel da Nóbrega in 1550, "all or the majority of men have a heavy conscience on account of the slaves that they possess, against all reason." (*Cartas Jesuíticas—Cartas do Brasil, 1549-1560,* publications of the Academia Brasileira, Rio de Janeiro, 1931.)

[34] *lundu:* originally a rustic, Afro-Brazilian dance with song; *fado:* a plaintive, melancholy, fatalistic song, or the music and dance for such a song. [Translator's note.]

[35] Paulo Prado, *Retrato do Brasil,* p. 106.

[36] The examples of the great Fray Bartolemé de las Casas and of the Jesuit Pedro Correia, who, touched by remorse, were transformed from ferocious oppressors and exploiters of Indians into their ardent defenders, demonstrate the contrary.

[37] Antera de Quental, "Causas da Decadência dos Povos Peninsulares nos Ultimos Três Séculos," in *Prosas Escolhidas,* pp. 95-142.

[38] Werner Sombart, *The Jews and Modern Capitalism,* pp. 11-15.

[39] Tawney, *op. cit.,* p. 80.

[40] On this, see *Primeira Visitação do Santo Ofício às Partes do Brasil, Denunciações de Pernambuco, 1591-1593,* São Paulo, 1925. It is well also to consult the *bandeirantes'* last wills and testaments, wherein abound cases of conscience.

[41] Tawney, *op. cit.,* p. 72.

[42] See in José Honório Rodrigues, *Notícia de Vária História,* p. 54.

[43] Calvin defended usury for the first time in a letter to his friend Oecolampadius. This letter marks his break with canonical doctrine on the sterility of money.

[44] Hilaire Belloc, *How the Reformation Happened,* p. 123.

[45] Harold Laski, *El liberalismo europeo* (Spanish translation), p. 97.

Chapter III   Conquest and Colonization

[1] *The Lusiads,* IV, 97 (The Hispanic Society of America, New York, 1950). Translated by Leonard Bacon. By permission of the Hispanic Society of America.

[2] Lope de Vega, *El Nuevo Mundo de Cristóbal Colón,* Act I, sc. 2 (in Ochoa, *Tesoro del teatro español,* p. 594).

[3] In Jaime Cortesão, A *Carta de Pero Vaz de Caminha,* p. 207.

[4] *Ibid.,* p. 220.

[5] *Ibid.*, pp. 213-214.

[6] Roberto Simonsen, *História Econômica do Brasil,* I, 51.

[7] Capistrano de Abreu, *Caminhos Antigos e Povoamento do Brasil,* p. 65.

[8] This circumstance is probably of much greater importance than the *quality* of the immigrants. The countries colonized by the immigration of convicted criminals who have every intention of rehabilitating themselves (as was the case with the early settlers of Australia) derive more benefit from such immigration than those others settled by immigration of *hidalgos* of the purest lineage intent only on "making America."

[9] That is how John Adams can say of the American Revolution that it was effected before the war actually began: "The Revolution was in the minds and hearts of the People." (See Catherine Drinker Bowen, *John Adams and the American Revolution.*)

[10] Charles C. Griffin, "Unidad y variedad en la historia americana," in *Ensayos sobre la historia del Nuevo Mundo,* p. 108.

[11] James Truslow Adams, *The Epic of America,* p. 30.

[12] *Exod.* 22:25.

[13] *Deut.* 23:19-20.

[14] *Deut.* 28:12.

[15] See Louis Israel Newman, *Jewish Influence on Christian Reform Movements.*

[16] Werner Sombart, *The Jews and Modern Capitalism,* p. 249.

[17] James Burnham, *The Managerial Revolution,* pp. 204-205.

[18] Sergio Bagú, *Economía de la sociedad colonial,* p. 127.

[19] *Ibid.,* p. 137. See also Eric Williams, *Capitalism and Slavery.*

[20] Bagú, *op. cit.,* p. 131.

[21] André Siegfried, *L'Âme des Peuples,* p. 166.

[22] In the Hispanic world the Spaniard who grew rich in the Western Indies was called an *indiano.* [Note: this does not mean "Indian," which is *indio.*]

[23] "As today the Portuguese who has lived in this land, on returning to his own land gains the name of 'Brazilian,' perhaps then the *mazombo,* having gone to the metropolis, returns with the rights of a true Portuguese, or *reinol* [native of the Kingdom itself], as he was then called, and this was one more incentive for the voyage." (Capistrano de Abreu, *Introdução aos Diálogos das Grandezas do Brasil,* pp. 30-31.)

[24] Sombart, *op. cit.,* pp. 27 ff.

[25] This was the term designating the earliest administrative divisions of Brazil; from these *capitanias* came the provinces, now called states. [Translator's note.]

[26] Hector St. John Crèvecoeur, "Letters from an American Farmer, 1782," in *The Heritage of America,* edited by Henry Steele Commager and Allan Nevins, p. 354.

[27] The *sabiá* is a songbird of the thrush (Turdidae) family, revered in Brazil much as the nightingale is in Europe. The poem was written in Portugal. [Translator's note.]

[28] The *Inconfidência* ("lack of loyalty") was a patriotic movement at the close of the eighteenth century, with the aim of freeing Brazil from her status as a colony of Portugal. Betrayed to the authorities, the uprising failed and its leader, Tiradentes, was hanged and quartered. Nevertheless, the failure was a glorious failure, and Tiradentes' name (really a nickname) is honored in Brazil as one of the great names in that country's struggle for independence. [Translator's note.]

[29] João Ribeiro, *Crítica,* IX, *Os Modernos,* 22.

[30] Eça de Queiroz, *Correspondência,* p. 17.

[31] Caio Prado Júnior, *Evolução Política do Brasil,* p. 70.

[32] The closest translation of "gadget" in Portuguese, in our opinion, is *engenhoca,* offered by Érico Veríssimo in *A Volta do Gato Prêto,* p. 270.

[33] A personage of Brazilian folklore analogous to Till Eulenspiegel, the personification of cleverness in rascally pranks and adventures. [Translator's note.]

[34] J. Lúcio de Azevedo, *Épocas de Portugal Económico,* pp. 18-19.

[35] As the nutritionist Josué de Castro well emphasizes, ". . . the Portuguese colonists, through their ambition of quick enrichment, of making themselves masters of the land, of its gold and its treasures, instead of continuing in the colony the tradi-

tion of cultivating food plants that would furnish them with resources for a complete diet, launched themselves furiously into the cultivation of sugar, 'white gold,' the exportation of which would yield them fabulous profits; or else they devoted themselves directly to the search for gold hidden in the veins of the earth. Occupied in these mercantile trades, they completely abandoned their traditions of agriculture, and thus impoverished their standard of nourishment." (*La alimentación en los trópicos*, p. 128.)

[36] In Roy Nash, *The Conquest of Brazil*, p. 153. [Translator's note: The words in brackets are from the Brazilian translation of the work named, but are not in the original edition in English.]

[37] In Paulo Prado, *Retrato do Brasil*, p. 14.

[38] In Oliveira Viana, *Populaçoes Meridionais do Brasil*, p. 84.

[39] In Capistrano de Abreu, *Capítulos de História Colonial*, p. 55.

[40] Nash, *op. cit.*, p. 105.

[41] Simão de Vasconcelos, *Vida do Venerável P. José de Anchieta*, I, 32.

[42] Simão de Vasconcelos, in Gilberto Freyre, *Casa-Grande e Senzala*, pp. 112-113.

[43] Cáio Prado Júnior, *op. cit.*, p. 35.

[44] Alberto Tôrres, *O Problema Nacional Brasileiro*, p. 38.

[45] Perhaps the best interpreter of the American's position with regard to the past is Thomas Paine: "Every age and generation must be as free to act for itself, *in all cases*, as the ages and generations which preceded it. The vanity and presumption of governing beyond the grave, is the most ridiculous and insolent of all tyrannies. . . . It is the living, and not the dead, that are to be accommodated." *The Life and Works of Thomas Paine* VI, 20-21.

[46] King Sebastian, religious to the point of mania, crusaded against the infidel and invaded Morocco only to be killed (and his army routed) in the battle of Alcazarquivir in 1578, thanks to poor generalship on his part. There is an ancient legend that Portugal will regain her former greatness when D. Sebastian comes back from those sandy wastes. [Translator's note.]

[47] Sixteenth-century Portuguese writers. Barros was a humanist, historian, author of a grammar of the Portuguese language; Ribeiro was a poet and novelist whose works reflect sentimental sorrow over his unhappy love for a cousin of his. [Translator's note.]

[48] The old convent of São Bento, secularized and remodeled, has been occupied by both houses of Parliament since 1834. [Translator's note.]

[49] Hamilton Basso, *Mainstream*, p. 124.

[50] The *bacalhoada* is a meal prepared with the fish called *bacalhau*, generally dried salt cod. *Feijoada* has been described above (note 15, p. 302); naturally, the *feijoada* of the well-to-do class is considerably more elaborate and savory. [Translator's note.]

[51] *Vatapá*: a dish made of cassava flour or meal mixed with fish or meat and cooked in palm oil. *Carurú*: boiled greens with shrimp or fish, the whole also cooked in palm oil. Both dishes are heavily peppered. [Translator's note.]

Chapter IV   Image and Symbol

[1] Vernon L. Parrington, *Main Currents in American Thought*, I, 4.

[2] James Truslow Adams, *The Epic of America*, p. 35.

[3] Parrington, *op. cit.*, p. v.

[4] William Wallace Fenn, "The Revolt Against the Standing Order," in *Religious History of New England*, pp. 77-123.

[5] In this business of thinking that the formulas adopted by the United States ought to be universalized, making his own rules victorious, the Yankee would find only one serious competitor: the Soviet commissar.

[6] This antipathy to any form of speculation or activity from which immediate economic results cannot be obtained led, in the nineteenth century and the early years of the present century, many of the finest minds, philosophical and artistic, of New

England—to emigrate to Europe for lack of a hospitable cultural milieu in their native land.

[7] Walt Whitman, *Leaves of Grass*, "For You, O Democracy."

[8] Whitman, *op. cit.*, "Pioneers! O Pioneers!"

[9] Whitman, *op. cit.*, "I Hear America Singing."

[10] Whitman, *op. cit.*, "A Song of Joys."

[11] *The Lincoln Reader*, ed. by Paul M. Angle, p. 403.

[12] Matt. 6:9-14.

[13] Cf. the King James Version: "Our Father which art in heaven, Hallowed be thy name. Thy kingdom come. Thy will be done, as in heaven, so in earth. Give us day by day our daily bread. And forgive us our sins; for we also forgive every one that is indebted to us. And lead us not into temptation; but deliver us from evil" (Luke 11:2-4). [Translator's note.]

[14] Among these should be included Holzhamer.

[15] Matt 6:12. "Trespasses" is used in Matt. 6:14-15, though not in the Prayer itself, in the King James Version. [Translator's note.]

[16] Reference to what we call the War of the Triple Alliance, 1865–70, in which Paraguay fought Brazil, Uruguay, and Argentina, acknowledging defeat after half her population had been killed, including her dictator, Francisco Solano López. [Translator's note.]

[17] Antônio Vieira, *Cartas*, I, 68, in Basílio de Magalhães, *Expansão Geográfica do Brasil Colonial*, p. 37.

[18] Manuel da Nóbrega, *Cartas do Brasil*, p. 119.

[19] Capistrano de Abreu: *O Descobrimento do Brasil*, p. 130.

[20] It was long the custom for a son, on any occasion when he took leave of his father, to ask the latter's blessing, however temporary the separation. [Translator's note.]

[21] In Serafim Leite, S.J., *Novas Cartas Jesuíticas (de Nóbrega a Vieira)*, p. 52.

[22] In Paulo Prado, *Retrato do Brasil*, p. 61.

[23] *Anais da Biblioteca Nacional*, LVII, 54.

[24] João Ribeiro, *História do Brasil*, p. 227.

[25] In Brandão's *Diálogos das Grandezas do Brasil*, p. 42, occurs this resentful comment: "It must be that gold, silver, and precious stones are only for the Castilians, and that God reserved these for them; because, although we Portuguese inhabit the same land that they inhabit, we being more eastern (the part in which by all rights there ought to be more mines), we have not been able to discover any in all the time that our Brazil has been peopled, yet they discover many every day."

[26] One must not forget that there have also been *bandeiras* for purposes of settlement. Nor have they contributed less to Brazil's geographic expansion merely because they are less typical.

[27] *Caudillismo*, from *caudillo*, a leader, a chieftain, or "boss," whether military or political, generally self-imposed, a man whose strength of character and personality are such that he is recognized by the rank and file as a natural leader and is blindly followed by them. Examples throughout Latin American history are so numerous that they constitute almost a system, permeating society from top to bottom on all levels. From the *caudillos* generally emerge the dictators. [Translator's note.]

[28] In Afonso d'E. Taunay, *História Geral das Bandeiras Paulistas*, I, 3.

[29] *Ibid.*, p. 4.

[30] *Ibid.*, p. 3.

[31] Gabriel Soares de Sousa, *Tratado Descritivo do Brasil em 1587*.

[32] See in Oliveira Viana, *Populações Meridionais do Brasil*, the chapter "Formação do Tipo Rural."

[33] Antonil, *Cultura e Opulência do Brasil*.

[34] Frei Vicente do Salvador, *História do Brasil*, 3rd ed. revised by Capistrano de Abreu and Rodolfo Garcia, p. 42.

[35] Felisbelo Freire, *Os Portuguêses no Brasil*, in Oliveira Viana, *op. cit.*, p. 228.

[36] A. C. Tavares Bastos, *Cartas do Solitário*, p. 268.

[37] Pierre Monbeig, *Pionniers et Planteurs de São Paulo*, pp. 107-108.

[38] Afonso d'E. Taunay, for example, says in his great work on the *bandeiras* that "the *bandeirante* is the pioneer of Brazil."

[39] José de Alcântara Machado, *Vida e Morte do Bandeirante*.

[40] Cassiano Ricardo, *Marcha para Oeste*.

[41] Júlio de Mesquita Filho, *Problemas Sul-Americanas*.

[42] Alfredo Ellis Júnior, *Raça de Gigantes*.

[43] *Bombachas:* the very full, baggy trousers, gathered at the ankle or tied below the knee, worn by the Argentine and southern Brazilian cowboy, who is known as the *gaúcho* in Portuguese and the *gaucho* in Spanish. [Translator's note.]

[44] Alberto Tôrres, *O Problema Nacional Brasileiro*, p. 72.

[45] Jeca Tatú is the name that in Brazilian speech represents the *caboclo*, the half-breed of the interior of Brazil. [Translator's note.]

[46] "Attempting to ascertain the fundamental causes of this defective diet, which has had so much weight in the socioeconomic evolution of our people, it is to be noted that they are due more to sociocultural factors than to factors of a geographic nature" (Josué de Castro, *La alimentacíon en los trópicos*, p. 12).

[47] See William Vogt, *Road to Survival*, p. 137.

Chapter V   Faith and Empire

[1] I Cor. 12:7–10.

[2] I Cor. 12:14–20.

[3] Harold Laski, *The American Presidency*, p. 48.

[4] *An Outline of American History*, prepared for the United States Information Service, pp. 30-31. [Edition in English. Original quotation is from the edition in Portuguese.]

[5] The resistance of certain Brazilian grammarians and philologists to the incorporation of foreign words is another proof of fidelity to the Portuguese past.

[6] Antonio Gómez Robledo, *La filosofía en Brasil*, pp. 46-47.

[7] João Camilo de Oliveira Tôrres, *O Positivismo no Brasil*, p. 328.

[8] In *A Igreja ante os Problemas Atuais*, p. 7.

[9] Machado de Assis, *Dom Casmurro*, p. 14.

[10] *Ibid.*, p.14.

[11] *Ibid.*, p. 15.

[12] *Ibid.*, p. 15.

[13] *Ibid.*, p. 11.

[14] *Ibid.*, p. 13.

[15] *Ibid.*, p. 74.

[16] *Ibid.*, pp. 11-12.

[17] *Ibid.*, p. 7.

[18] *Ibid.*, pp. 7-8.

[19] *Ibid.*, p. 76.

[20] *Ibid.*, p. 15.

[21] *Ibid.*, p. 9.

[22] *Ibid.*, p. 11.

[23] *Ibid.*, pp. 15-16.

[24] *Ibid.*, p. 11.

[25] *Ibid.*, pp. 79-80.

[26] If the Baron do Rio Branco had not consolidated the work of the *bandeirante*, it is quite probable that, as far as national fame is concerned, his name would have had the same fate as that of Mauá, whose heroism the country has never comprehended. [Baron de Mauá, nineteenth-century industrialist born in Rio Grande do Sul, organized the Bank of Brazil, built the first railway, headed the largest shipyard in South America, formed a company for gas lighting, and another for navigation of the Amazon. He was also a Congressman.]

Chapter VI Signs of the Times

[1] See Keyserling, *South American Meditations*, pp. 39 ff. and 207 ff.

[2] *Ibid.*

[3] Joshua Liebman, *Peace of Mind*.

[4] Fulton J. Sheen, *Peace of Soul*.

[5] A. H. Overstreet, *The Mature Mind*.

[6] Karen Horney, *The Neurotic Personality of Our Time*, p. 34.

[7] C. G. Jung, *Modern Man in Search of a Soul*, p. 264.

[8] Joaquim Nabuco, *Minha Formação*, pp. 40-41.

[9] See Gunnar Myrdal, *An American Dilemma*.

[10] It behooves us not to forget that America, to use the felicitous expression of the Argentine historian José Luis Romero, "has been the theater of the most gigantic experiment of transculturation that has ever been performed." See Committee for Cultural Action (Organization of American States), *Bases para el desarrollo de programas de geografía e historia de América*, p. 20.

[11] See James Burnham, *The Managerial Revolution*, the chapter on "The Theory of the Permanence of Capitalism," pp. 29-37.

[12] Paul Tillich, *The Protestant Era*, p. 229.

[13] *Ibid.*

[14] *Ibid.*

[15] F. S. C. Northrop, *The Meeting of East and West*.

[16] The Itamaratí Palace is used by the Ministry of Foreign Affairs. The Baron do Rio Branco held that cabinet post for ten years, after long service abroad as a diplomat. [Translator's note.]

[17] Graça Aranha, *Canaã*, p. 327.

[18] Jung, *op. cit.*, p. 271.

[19] C. F. von Hart, "Como escrever a história do Brasil," in *Revista de Imigração e Colonização*, ano IV, Vol. II, June 1943.

[20] Northrop, *op. cit.*, p. 30.

[21] João Ribeiro, *Crítica*, I, *Clássicos e Românticos*, 95 and 131.

[22] See Padre Ambrósio Schupp, S.J., *Os Muckers*.

[23] The *bicho* (animal, "varmint") game is the Brazilian equivalent of the numbers game in the United States. See footnote 25, below. [Translators note.]

[24] Van Hart, op. cit., p. 228.

[25] We wonder whether the peculiarly Brazilian *bicho* game is not an authentic expression of subconscious terror as well as of the extremely typical Brazilian aspiration for quick riches. Even lacking a scientific interpretation of all that material of dreams and nightmares peopled with lions and tigers, snakes and elephants, monkeys, cats, and dogs, which the banking lists cabalistically reduce to numbers—an interpretation that would certainly delight the psychoanalysts insistent on advancing the study of the relations between dream symbols and the thoughts of daily life—it is easy to draw conclusions in the affirmative.

[26] G. M. Trevelyan, *An Autobiography and Other Essays*.

[27] Arthur M. Schlesinger, *The American as Reformer*, p. ix.

[28] F. D. Roosevelt, *My Friends: Twenty-eight History-Making Speeches*.

[29] Benedetto Croce, *Teoría e historia de la historiografía*, p. 12 (Spanish Translation).

[30] In J. H. Rodrigues, *Teoria da História do Brasil*, p. 19.

[31] *Ibid.*, p. 20.

[32] *Ibid.*, p. 19.

[33] Horney, *op. cit.*, p. viii.

[34] Geoffrey Gorer, *The American People*, pp. 25-26.

[35] Gorer, *op. cit.*, p. 26.

[36] Gorer, *op. cit.*, pp. 40 ff.

[37] *Ibid.*, pp. 41-42.

[38] Gorer, *op. cit.*, p. 26.

[39] See Edward A. Strecker, *Their Mothers' Sons*, p. 6.
[40] Clarence B. Randall, *A Creed for Free Enterprise*, pp. 6-7.
[41] *The Forrestal Diaries*, p. 555.
[42] Miguel de Unamuno, *Vida de don Quijote y Sancho*, pp. 11-22.

Epilogue

[1] W. H. Herndon, *Herndon's Life of Lincoln*, p. 25.
[2] *Ibid.*, p. 13.
[3] *The Lincoln Reader*, p. 26.
[4] *Abraham Lincoln, His Speeches and Writings*, pp. 76-85.
[5] *Ibid.*, "Letter to John T. Stuart," p. 115.
[6] Herndon, *op. cit.*, pp. 2-4.
[7] Carl Sandburg, *Abraham Lincoln, I, The Prairie Years*, p. 24.
[8] Abraham Lincoln, "Farewell Address at Springfield, Illinois."
[9] *Abraham Lincoln—His Speeches and Writings*, p. 114.
[10] Luke 2:49.
[11] Karen Horney, *Self-Analysis*, Chapter I, pp. 13-36.
[12] Horney, *New Ways in Psychoanalysis*, pp. 276-305.
[13] "Many sinners," Tertullian wrote, seventeen centuries before Freud, "more concerned with their shame than with their cure, try to avoid or postpone the confession of their sins to the priest. They are sick men who, not daring to reveal their secret spiritual infirmities to the physician, perish rather than consent to blush for a few moments. . . ." ". . . Why do ye disdain this one means of salvation; this one medicine that can cure you? Why does the sinner refuse the confession instituted by Jesus Christ for the purpose of restoring his soul's health to him?" (*De penitentia*, Ch. 9, in Padre Manuel Monjas, *La confesión* [Ediciones Pax, Madrid, 1948], p. 88.)
[14] Rodrigo José Ferreira Brêtas, "Traços Biográficos Relativos ao Finado Antônio Francisco Lisboa," in *Antônio Francisco Lisboa—O Aleijadinho*, p. 23.
[15] *Ibid.*
[16] *Ibid.*
[17] *Ibid.*, p. 24.
[18] *Ibid.*, p. 23.
[19] *Ibid.*, p. 24.
[20] *Ibid.*, p. 33.
[21] *Ibid.*, p. 26.
[22] *Ibid.*, p. 25.
[23] Machado de Assis, *Várias Histórias*, p. 254.

Index

Abreu, Casimiro de, 243
Abreu, J. Capistrano de, 95, 158, 238, 305*n*
Abreu, Manuel de, 137
Adair, E. R., 54
Adams, Henry, 229
Adams, James Truslow, 140, 303*n*
Adams, John, 219, 305*n*
Aeschylus, 158
Afonso IV, King of Portugal, 119
Agassiz, Louis, 157, 230
Alberdi, Juan Bautista, 12
Albuquerque, Jerônimo de, 73, 161
Aleijadinho (Antônio Francisco Lisboa), 270–71, 284–93
Alencar, José Martiniano de, 242
Alger, Horatio, 260, 263, 264
Alvares, Diogo (Caramuru), 69–72, 105, 157, 168
Amado, Gilberto, 13
Amado, Jorge, 241
Amicis, Edmondo de, 259
Anchieta, José de, 105
Andrade, Carlos Drummond de, 243
Andrade, Mario de, 243
Antonil, 163, 168
Antoninus, St., 54, 86
Aquinas, St. Thomas, 55–56, 58, 66
Aranha, José Pereira de Graça, 238–239
Arguedes, Alcides, 12
Aristotle, 57, 247–48
Assis, Macado de, 207, 237, 294; "José Dias" of, 213–18
Azevedo, J. Lúcio de, 119
Azevedo, Manuel Antônio Álvares de, 243

"Babbitt, George F.," 252–55, 261, 264
Bacon, Francis, 135
Bagú, Sergio, 101
Bandeira, Manuel, 242, 243
Bandeirante: in Amazonia, 174–76; his influence today, 179–82; image of, 155–56, 162–74; moral code of, 111–17; in North, 176–77; in Rio de Janeiro, 178–79
Barbacena, Viscount of, 288, 289
Barbosa, Rui, 238–39
Barros, João de, 94, 125
Bastos, Tavares, 238
Bates, Henry Walter, 28
Bell, Alexander Graham, 117
Belloc, Hilaire, 85
Bolivar, Simón, 106, 220
Bonifácio, José, 106, 121, 238
Brasil, Vital, 137
Brazil: attitude toward work in, 118–22, 134–37, 210–17, 243–46; cordiality in, 222–25; eating habits of, 129–30; economics in, 50–53, 179–80; emotional maladjustment in, 222–31, 236; geography and climate of, 17–25, 32–33; "Mazombism" in, 107–10, 111, 113, 229; melancholy in, 76–80; Modernist movement in, 237–43; pessimism in, 206–9; politics in, 180–81; race in, 11–17, 33–47; race and marriage in, 67–75, 99, 156–64, 236–37; religious spirit in, 209–10; republican leaders of, 218–20; settlement of, 92–95, 102–6; tradition in, 123–28, 202–206, 241–42; U.S. Southerners in, 36–42; women in, 67–75, 255–57; *see also* Aleijadinho; *Bandeirante*
Burckhardt, Jacob, 339
Burnham, James, 100

Caldas, João Pereira, 41
Calvinism, 57, 60, 62–65, 84–87, 132, 188, 199
Caminha, Pero Vaz de, 24, 25, 32, 67, 93, 94
Camoens, Luís Vaz de, 68, 77–79, 93, 168, 242
Capone, Al, 255
"Caramuru," *see* Alvares, Diogo
Cardim, Fernão, 18
"Carioca, José," 261
Carlos I, King of Spain, 82

311

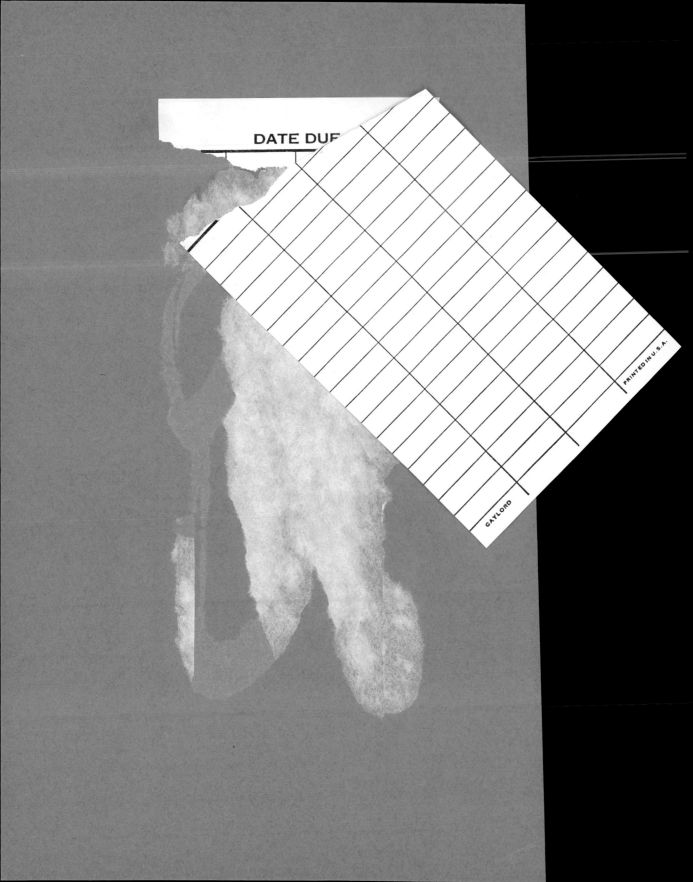